Human-Computer Interaction: Emerging Technologies and Applications

Human-Computer Interaction: Emerging Technologies and Applications

Edited by Samuel Wallace

CLANRYE
INTERNATIONAL
www.clanryeinternational.com

Clanrye International,
750 Third Avenue, 9th Floor,
New York, NY 10017, USA

ISBN: 978-1-63240-918-8

Cataloging-in-Publication Data

Human-computer interaction : emerging technologies and applications / edited by Samuel Wallace.
    p. cm.
Includes bibliographical references and index.
ISBN 978-1-63240-918-8
1. Human-computer interaction. 2. Human computation. 3. User interfaces (Computer systems).
4. User-centered system design. I. Wallace, Samuel.
QA76.9.H85 H85 2020
004.019--dc23

For information on all Clanrye International publications
visit our website at www.clanryeinternational.com

Contents

Preface

Human-computer interaction (HCI) refers to the usage and designing of computer technology for communication between the computer and the user. As a field of research, HCI studies the way humans interact with computers and design technologies that facilitate this interaction. An interface between humans and computers is essential to this interaction. Internet browsers, desktop applications, computer kiosks and handheld computers use graphical user interfaces. Voice user interfaces are required for speech synthesizing and speech recognition systems. Research in this domain is focused on designing new computer interfaces, implementing interfaces, studying human computer use and sociocultural implications, etc. The ever-growing need of advanced technology is the reason that has fueled the research in the field of human-computer interaction in recent times. The aim of this book is to present researches that have transformed this discipline and aided its advancement. As this field is emerging at a rapid pace, the contents of this book will help the readers understand the modern concepts and applications of the subject.

The information shared in this book is based on empirical researches made by veterans in this field of study. The elaborative information provided in this book will help the readers further their scope of knowledge leading to advancements in this field.

Finally, I would like to thank my fellow researchers who gave constructive feedback and my family members who supported me at every step of my research.

Editor

Recognition of Symbolic Gestures using Depth Information

Hasan Mahmud ⓘ,[1] **Md. Kamrul Hasan,**[1] **Abdullah-Al-Tariq,**[1]
Md. Hasanul Kabir,[2] **and M. A. Mottalib**[3]

[1] *Systems and Software Lab (SSL), Department of Computer Science and Engineering, Islamic University of Technology (IUT), Dhaka, Bangladesh*
[2] *Department of Computer Science and Engineering, Islamic University of Technology (IUT), Dhaka, Bangladesh*
[3] *Department of Computer Science and Engineering, BRAC University, Dhaka, Bangladesh*

Correspondence should be addressed to Hasan Mahmud; hasan@iut-dhaka.edu

Academic Editor: Marco Porta

Symbolic gestures are the hand postures with some conventionalized meanings. They are static gestures that one can perform in a very complex environment containing variations in rotation and scale without using voice. The gestures may be produced in different illumination conditions or occluding background scenarios. Any hand gesture recognition system should find enough discriminative features, such as hand-finger contextual information. However, in existing approaches, depth information of hand fingers that represents finger shapes is utilized in limited capacity to extract discriminative features of fingers. Nevertheless, if we consider finger bending information (i.e., a finger that overlaps palm), extracted from depth map, and use them as local features, static gestures varying ever so slightly can become distinguishable. Our work here corroborated this idea and we have generated depth silhouettes with variation in contrast to achieve more discriminative keypoints. This approach, in turn, improved the recognition accuracy up to 96.84%. We have applied Scale-Invariant Feature Transform (SIFT) algorithm which takes the generated depth silhouettes as input and produces robust feature descriptors as output. These features (after converting into unified dimensional feature vectors) are fed into a multiclass Support Vector Machine (SVM) classifier to measure the accuracy. We have tested our results with a standard dataset containing 10 symbolic gesture representing 10 numeric symbols (0-9). After that we have verified and compared our results among depth images, binary images, and images consisting of the hand-finger edge information generated from the same dataset. Our results show higher accuracy while applying SIFT features on depth images. Recognizing numeric symbols accurately performed through hand gestures has a huge impact on different Human-Computer Interaction (HCI) applications including augmented reality, virtual reality, and other fields.

1. Introduction

Gesture-based interaction has been introduced in many HCI applications which allow users to interact intuitively through computer interfaces in a natural way. Rather than using traditional unimodal inputs, blending alternative style of interactions, such as hand gestures along with mouse and keyboard, introduces more degree of freedom (DoF) to the computer users. Nowadays, hand gesture-based interaction is a prominent area of research which has a huge impact in the design and development of many HCI applications like controlling robots through hand gestures, manipulating virtual objects in an augmented reality environment, playing virtual reality games through different hand movements, communicating through sign languages, etc. We need these types of interaction to achieve interaction design goals like effectiveness, efficiency, affordance, and feedback.

Hand gesture can be defined as the movement of hands and fingers in a particular orientation to convey some meaningful information [1] like pointing to some object through index fingers, expressing victory sign or OK sign, waving hands, grasping an object, etc. Symbolic hand gestures represent some specific symbols like 'OK' sign or gesture that represents numeric symbol '1' (raising the index finger and bending all other fingers). In most of the cases, these gestural movements conveys single meaning in each culture having very specific and prescribed interpretations. More importantly, symbolic gestures are alternative to verbal discourse structure, different from everyday body movement which is consciously perceived. These gestures are observed in the spatial domain and are called static hand gestures characterized by the position of fingers (finger joint angle, orientation, and finger bending information). Unlike static hand gestures, dynamic gestures are considered in the temporal domain, presenting gesture as a sequence of hand shapes which includes starting through ending hand pose (e.g., hand waving, boxing).

There are different approaches to capture and recognize these gestures. Computer vision-based approach imposes restrictions on the gesturing environment, such as special lighting conditions, simple and uncluttered background, and occlusions (the gesturing hand is occluded by other parts of the body) [1]. Due to these restrictions segmentation of hand may cause the reduction in hand gesture recognition accuracy. Hand poses, generated in the process of gesticulation, can also be detected by means of wearable sensor like datagloves. The data-gloves are embedded with the accelerometer, gyroscope, bend sensor, proximity sensor, and other forms of inertial sensors [2]. These sensors collect hand-finger motion information as multiparametric values. However, the sensor-based gesture recognition approaches have limitations in terms of naturalness, cost, user comfort, portability, and data preprocessing.

The recent advancements in stereo vision camera that utilizes depth perception from smaller to larger distances have opened a huge scope for the researchers to work with depth information [3]. Traditional web cameras do not provide the depth values (the distance of the gesturing hand from the camera). Depth information can help eliminating occlusion problems easily and can quicken the segmentation process with less error. In an occluded background, using depth information it is possible to extract the gesturing hand movement information including other important features (e.g., finger bending information) which can be effectively utilized in feature representations. Moreover, static gesture can be performed by the users with varying hand size, changes in hand position (orientation, rotation), and different illumination conditions. Scale-Invariant Feature Transform (SIFT) [4] is an algorithm that works better for these types of variation. The algorithm generates key points from images and provides 128-dimensional feature vectors.

In this research work, we try to recognize symbolic hand gestures representing 10 numeric symbols from 0 to 9. These are very close gestures, differing only in slight variations (e.g., the difference between numeric symbol 2 and numeric symbol 3 is due to the presence/absence of one finger only) of finger positions. With the help of depth data stream, after a quick and robust segmentation process, we have calculated depth threshold based on which the contrast varying depth images are generated according to the depth map of the individual gesture. This process was applied to 100 image instances per gesture. In each image for the same gesture, we got the different number of SIFT keypoints. By combining the keypoints, we have generated bag-of-feature (BoF) vector with the help of the k-means clustering technique to generate uniform dimensional feature vectors and classified using a multiclass SVM.

The main contributions of this paper are as follows:

(i) Generating contrast varying grey-scale depth images according to the depth map to utilize local shape information of hand fingers which has contributed to the improvement of recognition accuracy.

(ii) Applying SIFT over depth images to achieve image invariant properties (translation, scaling, rotation, illumination, and local geometric distortion).

The remainder of the paper is described as follows. Section 2 elaborates the related research. Section 3 describes the proposed approach. Section 4 presents the experimental results. The last Section 5 describes the conclusion and the future scope of the work.

2. Related Works

Human hand is a highly articulated model, prominent in making deft poses. To recognize those hand poses many research works have utilized RGB cameras and applied either template-based approaches or model-based approaches on RGB images. Conventional RGB image-based gesture recognition techniques need to consider many research challenges, such as light sensitivity, cluttered background, and occlusions. However, the recent emergence of depth sensors has given an opportunity for the researchers to utilize the depth information in order to overcome those challenges. The depth data stream provided by the depth sensors (e.g., Microsoft Kinect, Intel Real Sense, Asus Xtion Pro) corresponding to the hand gesture images has given new dimensions to conduct research in hand segmentation process, finger identification techniques, finger joint detection, and finger tracking. Depth value indicates the distance of the gesturing hand from the RGB-Depth (RGB-D) camera in millimeters appropriate to make the segmentation process faster. Among the depth sensors, we have used Microsoft Kinect depth sensor that captures depth image in 640×480 resolution in a frame rate of 30 fps and 11-bit depth under the environment consisting of any ambient light. Depth information helps to extract additional features which can significantly improve the recognition results. Many researchers have developed depth sensor-based applications like interactive displays through Kinect [5], a system for therapeutic interventions [6], robot navigation through gestures [7–9], Kinect-based American Sign Language (ASL) recognition [10], etc. Other different applications of Kinect depth sensor includes categorizations of indoor environments by mobile robots equipped with Kinect [11], measuring canopy structure for vegetation [12], just to name a few.

From the depth sensors, the most common features used in hand posture recognitions [13] are skeleton joint positions, hand geometry, hand-finger shape, area, distance features, depth pixel values, etc. Generally, these features can be categorized as local features or global features. The major challenges of these feature descriptors are variations of gesturing hands while articulating an emblem or symbolic gesture. A gesture may slightly differ in terms of hand shape and size, variations in translation, or rotation of the fingers for the same gesture. A robust hand gesture recognition system should be invariant to the scale, speed, and the orientation of the gesture performed.

The approaches that are followed by static gesture recognition system from binary images in [14] and time-series curves in [15] do not facilitate the possibility of extracting local finger context information. The authors in [14] have captured RGB images from webcam and converted them to binary images and applied SIFT algorithm to determine the recognition accuracy. In binary images, the finger context information, shape, orientation, bending fingers, and occlusion, cannot be preserved, a limitation that can be overcome by utilizing depth map information of the gesturing hand. SIFT keypoints are important feature points which are well distributed and contain information about not only thumb and baby fingers but also finger bending information of index, middle, and ring fingers. Figure 1 shows the differences of SIFT keypoints in gesture 8 mapped into the binary image (7 keypoints) (Figure 1(b)) and into depth image (56 keypoints) (Figure 1(d)). This information is not present in the case of binary image or time-series curve. SIFT works on local oriented features rather than topological shapes of opening fingers which are considered as the global features. In [15], global features are used to generate time-series curves (Figure 1(f)) after the segmentation process as shown in Figure 1(e) from the hand shape represented in binary image. The edit-distances are calculated to apply distance-based matching algorithm, such as Finger-Earth Mover's Distance (FEMD). Edit-distance-based matching algorithms are not completely rotation, orientation invariant because they are measured by comparing time-series trajectories based on the proximity distance and not based on the local shape information. Moreover, the temporal information is better for dynamic gesture recognition rather than static gesture recognition [16].

Local features measure the characteristics of a particularly important region of the object, superior in discriminating fine details. In [17], shape descriptor-based algorithm and weak learning-based strong classifier were applied to recognize three symbolic gestures (palm, fist, six). Their goal was to get orientation invariant property of those gestures. They have used SIFT features as local features in weak classifier for hand detection and trained each classifier independently. The accuracy, in this case, depends on the large set of training images which they have not considered. They have used a varying number of training images for individual gestures. They have not considered the fact that SIFT features extracted from the different gesturing image can form a natural group of clusters having feature vectors of the unified dimensions appropriate to feed into a classifier that can recognize more than two classes. We have achieved this by clustering feature descriptors and generating BoF features. In [18, 19], the researchers have considered Haar-like features, applying learning-based techniques to recognize hand gestures. They required a huge number of images for training and testing with high computational power and they have not considered the scale-invariant property for object detection.

Global features measure the characteristics of the whole image and face difficulties in capturing fine details. An example would be the contour representation of a hand gesture image (e.g., the hand contour image of Figure 1(e)) which gives hand-finger shape information from the whole image. The limitations of contour-based recognition methods are that they are not robust on local distortion, occlusion, and clutter [20]. To extract the complete hand posture information while a finger and a palm are overlapped, such as bending fingers, as shown in Figure 1(d), the consideration of hand contour as the global feature representations is not enough. The similar problems are also mentioned in the recognition approaches like skeleton-based recognition methods [21], shape contexts based methods [22], and inner-distance methods [23]. A solution to these problems was proposed using a novel distance-based measurement technique called Finger-Earth Mover's Distance (FEMD) [15]. They represented the shape of hand fingers as a global feature (the finger cluster) by analyzing time-series curve. In the curve, the Euclidean distance between each contour point and the center point is considered in one dimension and the angle of these contour points made with the initial point relative to the center point is considered as another dimension. Figure 1(f) shows the time-series curve of the topological hand shape considered as finger parts and matches those fingers only, not the whole hand shape. Features only from opening finger parts may not give good recognition results. Rather features including bending finger parts as local features will play a significant role to improve the recognition accuracy. We have considered those features in our proposed approach. Moreover, for gesture recognition, they [15] have applied template matching with minimum dissimilarity distance which may not give improved recognition accuracy on both changes in orientation and rotation of a particular pose. We propose to overcome this problem using local features found as SIFT keypoints. Edit-distance-based time-series matching approaches are more applicable for dynamic gesture recognition due to their spatiotemporal features, rather than static symbolic gesture recognition. Template-based approaches are good to recognize the shape as a whole but lack in terms of invariance. SIFT algorithm is known to be robust for its distinctiveness and invariance to rotation, scale, and translation in object recognition. Depth image acquired using Kinect depth sensor suffers from low grey level contrast that can cause an unstable set of keypoints. Recently in [24], the researchers used Kinect-based depth map information to discard the SIFT keypoints that are located at the boundaries of an object. They applied Canny's edge detection algorithm [25] on depth images and generated an object model to store depth values and distance to the nearest depth edge for the remaining SIFT keypoints. They have used Euclidean distance-based nearest neighbor algorithm to rank the keypoints matches and performed RANSAC-based homograph estimation for object pose estimation. Their aim was to identify predefined objects in the surrounding environment for the visually impaired. To extract a stable set of SIFT keypoints different techniques were proposed by the researchers. Preprocessing on the medical image (retina image) was done to reduce the number of SIFT keypoints in [26].

In [27], the researchers have extracted the SIFT keypoints from both the color and the depth image and tried to find

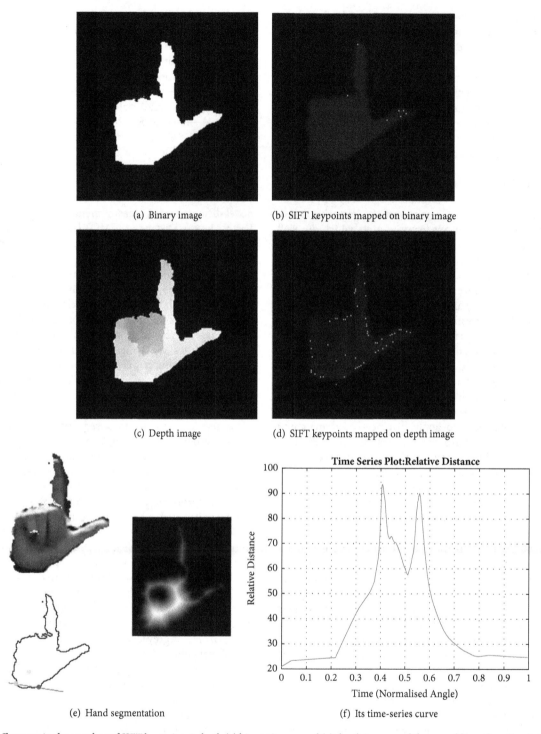

(a) Binary image   (b) SIFT keypoints mapped on binary image

(c) Depth image   (d) SIFT keypoints mapped on depth image

(e) Hand segmentation   (f) Its time-series curve

FIGURE 1: Differences in the number of SIFT keypoints in both (a) binary image and (c) depth image and the use of finger bending information.

out the correspondence of SIFT keypoints between those two images. They have combined SIFT descriptor with Harris corner detector to compute SIFT features at predefined spatial scales. They enhanced the depth image contrast by applying histogram equalization without utilizing the depth values explicitly of the gesturing hand to generate contrast varying depth images. However, we have considered the depth map

information to determine the contrast level and generate depth silhouettes accordingly.

SIFT algorithm along with its different variants like PCA-SIFT [28], SURF [29], and GLOH [30] has been applied in various applications such as image stitching, object recognition, and image retrieval. SIFT and SURF algorithm were also applied in simultaneous localization and mapping (SLAM)

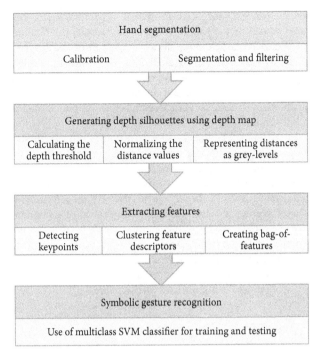

FIGURE 2: The architecture to recognize symbolic gestures.

with RGB-D Kinect sensor on robots [31]. SURF is the fast approximation of SIFT that uses box filter instead of Gaussian filter. However, SURF is not good at different illumination conditions [29]. To improve the time complexity of SIFT several alternatives were proposed, such as Binary Robust Independent Elementary Features (BRIEF) [32] and Oriented FAST and Rotated BRIEF (ORB) [33] that uses binary descriptor instead of floating point descriptor to achieve faster performance suitable for real-time applications.

In [34], the authors showed the comparisons among different image matching algorithms, such as SIFT, SURF, and ORB. They have manually performed transformation and deformation on the images in respect to rotation, scaling, fish eye distortion, noise, and shearing. The comparison was done based on different evaluation parameters, such as the number of keypoints in images, execution time, and matching rate. For most of the scenarios they have found SIFT performed best. The researchers in [35] tried to use depth map to perform smoothing process in the scale-space. They smoothed the scene surface considering smoothing quantity as a function of the distance given by the depth map so that 'the further a given pixel is, the less it is smoothed'. They tried to inject the smoothing filter in the SIFT algorithm and determined the repeatability score to evaluate the keypoint detection performance. Their goal was to find the keypoint repeatability under viewpoint position changes. However, the dataset we have used in our research was generated using single depth camera without changing the viewpoint positions.

Bag-of-Feature (BoF) representation was used in [36] to obtain a global information of visual data out of arrays of local point descriptors generated by SIFT algorithm. SIFT algorithm can extract higher dimensional feature points from the images even with lower resolutions but compromises

the efficiency in terms of computation. To address this problem, BoF approach has been applied in reducing feature dimensions, redundancy elimination, and extracting global information from local SIFT features [36]. Moreover, the BoF approach has been considered as an efficient method to represent visual contents in hand gesture recognition [37]. The local feature points extracted from SIFT are fed into clustering algorithm to learn visual codebook and then each feature vector is mapped to a visual codeword represented by a sparse histogram. We have applied this technique to depth images for the classification using a multiclass SVM.

3. Proposed System

The proposed system consists of (1) hand segmentation and depth silhouette generation, (2) SIFT keypoints extraction, (3) clustering keypoints and generating BoF descriptors, and (4) symbolic gesture recognition using SVM.

The architectural diagram of the proposed approach is shown in Figure 2. The standard dataset [15] has considered 640×480 image resolution to capture the RGB image and the depth map of gesturing hand using Microsoft Kinect. Depth values are stored in millimeters. After calibration, we have applied the segmentation process as described in [15], except generating grey-scale variations on depth images.

3.1. Hand Segmentation. Segmentation is the process of removing the noninteresting area from the pertinent object. Many of the techniques in hand region segmentation worked on color space-based detection like skin-color detection, YCbCr/HSV color space filtering, and so on. These color-based techniques have limitations due to the noise, lighting variations, and background complexities. However, utilizing depth map information combined with color information improves the segmentation process which in turns gives better recognition accuracy.

Before segmenting the hand shape or region of interest (ROI), some preprocessing is performed. This involves calibrating the RGB and Depth Images. The RGB image is also converted into grey-scale. To extract the region of interest, first, we locate the smallest depth value from the depth image. This corresponds to the closest point of the hand from the camera plane. We call this value minimum distance. Next, an empirical threshold value is added to the minimum distance to give the segmentation threshold. This segmentation threshold is then used to segment the hand region from the rest of the image. This approach has proven to be robust in cluttered and noisy environments [38]. It is important to note that the hand should be the closest object to the camera for proper segmentation. The segmentation threshold is the sum of a minimum distance and a depth threshold. The minimum distance is easily obtained from the depth image as the minimum value in the depth matrix. The depth threshold is estimated based on different possible orientations of the hand shape.

After multiple measurements and testing, an upper bound is chosen as the depth threshold, such that the sum of the depth threshold and the minimum distance will allow us to isolate or segment the hand shape including the black belt from the rest of the image. In our scenario, the depth threshold was estimated at 200 mm. The depth threshold is useful for filtering cluttered background containing an overlapped image (e.g., gesturing hand is overlapped with the face having the same color). We followed the same segmentation process as described in our previous work in [39]. However, in this research, the segmentation process is applied to a larger and challenging dataset [15]. Earlier, we used smaller dataset containing only 5 (five) static hand gestures representing numeric symbols 1 to 5 in a restricted environment, collected from a limited number of users.

3.1.1. Generating Depth Silhouettes Using Depth Map. The images from the Kinect depth stream are in 640×480 resolution which does not show enough contrast variations. Keypoints with low contrast will not give enough gradient variations to identify finger bending information. If we can generate contrast variation according to the depth values,

then we can get more discriminative keypoints. These keypoints would be the salient features to improve the recognition accuracy. So, we have done some preprocessing where the depth values of gesturing hands were used to produce grey-scale levels. The closer a point is, the brighter its shade is. To do that, we cropped out depth values of the hands and got an m-by-n matrix with depth values of hands and its background.

Let $dist(x, y)$ be the distance of a point in the millimeter at (x, y). $f(x, y)$ is the corresponding grey level of the generated image used in extracting the key features by SIFT. Now, we select η as the number of grey levels between $greyLevel_{min}$ and $greyLevel_{max}$. We also selected η number of distance segments between $dist_{min}$ (minimum distance) and $(dist_{min} + dist_{th})$; where $dist_{th}$ is the distance, we assumed the hand would be from $dist_{min}$ and the depth threshold. We let the background be black in the generated image to get the better result using SIFT. We have applied (1) to generate the grey-scale image using only the depth values.

$$
f(x, y)
$$
$$
= \begin{cases} 0, & \text{if } dist(x, y) > dsit_{min} + dist_{th} \\ greyLevel_{min} + \left(\left\lfloor \left(\frac{dist(x, y) - dist_{min}}{dist_{th} - dist_{min}} \times \eta \right) + 0.5 \right\rfloor \times \left\lfloor \frac{greyLevel_{max} - greyLevel_{min}}{\eta} \right\rfloor \right), & \text{Otherwise} \end{cases} \quad (1)
$$

We can see from the equation that any point in the depth image within the threshold distance is going to be a nonblack pixel depending on the grey levels determined from depth information. To assign grey levels to those pixels we segmented the depth values in η levels. Any distance value under the threshold is rounded off and normalized. The normalized distance values are converted into appropriate grey levels. After that, we find a grey-scale image which is the depth silhouette of a hand with the dark background and the grey levels corresponding to the depths of different parts of the subject hand. To emphasize the contrasts, the η number of segments was used. If we had used all the 256 levels of the grey image, the contrasts would not be prominent enough to get fair results. We considered $\eta = 10$ grey-scale levels from 155 to 255, dividing the levels equally to get a good contrast ratio. The number of levels was heuristically determined based on the assumption that more levels of grey will mean that the hand segments' contrast will be low. Thus, one of our main focuses (to represent distances in distinctive grey levels) would be undermined. Representing the distances using fewer grey levels would have the similar effect as the binary images. The shape would be distinct but the local features would be lost. Moreover, the grey-scale images with proper contrast are useful enough to distinguish the curves and angles of finger joints in different gestures. Both of the characteristics helped the SIFT to generate feature descriptors for the gestures, indifferent of the orientation of the hands.

For each gesturing image, we have extracted depth values within 200 from the depth image of the resolution 640×480.

Actually, the 200 region contains the gesture information which we have used to generate the depth silhouettes. The process of segmentation and grey-scale varying depth silhouette generation are shown in Figure 3.

3.2. Feature Extraction. Features to be extracted by the feature extraction algorithm should present a high degree of invariance to scaling, translation, and rotation. Feature representation depends on the algorithm to be used for classification. We have used SIFT algorithm to represent the features as 128-dimensional feature points that are extracted from the depth images.

3.2.1. SIFT Features. The SIFT algorithm detects keypoints from a multiscale image representation consisting of blurred images at different scale. The keypoint location and the scale values of each keypoint are accurately determined using the Difference of Gaussian (DoG). Then the key points are filtered by eliminating edge points and low contrast points. After that, the orientation of the keypoint is determined based on the local image gradient within an image patch. Finally, the keypoint descriptor is computed which defines the center, size, and orientation of normalized patch [4]. We have used the SIFT implementation code as in [40].

Features generated by SIFT algorithm are invariant to scales and robust against changing position of object, slight rotation of object, and object in noisy and varying illumination condition in different images. These feature points can be found in the high-contrast regions and we have generated those contrast varying images based on depth values of the

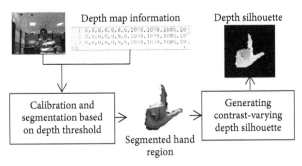

FIGURE 3: Hand gesture segmentation.

gesturing hand. SIFT algorithm effectively determines the keypoints on those depth images and represent them as feature descriptors.

The main objective of our approach is to improve the recognition accuracy for static gestures using depth information compared to binary and time-series representation of the images. We have utilized depth information and generated depth silhouettes which can be fed to any keypoint detector and descriptor-based algorithm, such as SIFT, SURF, and ORB. However, we have chosen SIFT to generate training and testing images. The training images with corresponding keypoints mapped over the gesturing image are shown in Figure 4. The first and third columns in Figure 4 represent the depth silhouette generated using depth map information of the gestures 1-10 (G1-G10) of the numeric symbols 0-9. The second and fourth columns in Figure 4 represent the corresponding hand gestures G1-G10 with 27, 41, 51, 61, 77, 101, 55, 56, 32, and 80 SIFT keypoints, respectively.

While extracting the keypoints we have found that the number of keypoints varies according to the type of gestures. As different symbolic gestures consist of a different number of fingers to be articulated, hence we got these variations. We captured 100 images per gesture as the candidates to generate keypoint descriptors and we got 41273 keypoints by considering 1000 images in total training images. The distribution of the number of keypoints per gesture is shown in Figure 5.

The keypoint descriptors that we have found are 128-dimensional feature vectors. Due to the changes in orientation, scale, and illumination of the same gesturing image by multiple persons the number of keypoints varies. Moreover, the dimensions of the gesturing images become larger which increases computations. Hence, we have used the strategy of a bag-of-visual-words and clustering technique to reduce dimensions.

3.2.2. Clustering Feature Descriptors.

The dimension of the feature vector in each gesturing image varies based on the number of keypoints found for each gesture. The problem is that we need unified dimensional feature vectors as the training set to classify using multiclass SVM [41]. For the depth image that has 27 keypoints, the dimension of that image becomes $27 \times 128 = 3456$ and if another image from the same gesture contains 80 keypoints then the dimension becomes $80 \times 128 = 10240$. So, we have used the bag-of-word for which we need clustering to reduce the dimensions.

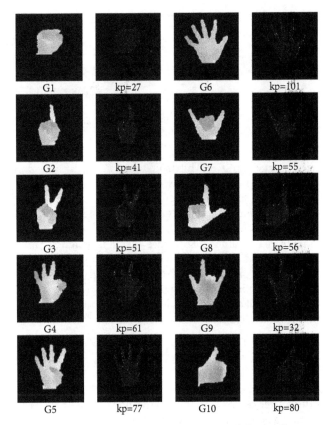

FIGURE 4: Example images containing generated depth silhouettes (first and third columns) and the corresponding SIFT keypoints mapped in to depth images (second and fourth columns) showing numeric symbols (0-9) representing the gestures (G1-G10).

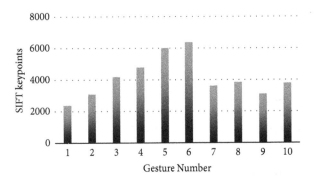

FIGURE 5: Number of SIFT keypoints at $\sigma = 1.8$.

The basic k-means clustering served our purpose because k-means converge faster than hierarchical-based clustering approaches. It also gives efficient performance for larger datasets. The keypoint distributions for different gestures are found to be almost Gaussian and distinctive as shown in Figure 5. In the concept of bag-of-word, the clusters are defined as codebooks and the size of the cluster determines the convergence property of the clustering technique. If we took smaller codebook size then bag-of-word vectors may not contain all the important keypoints. The larger codebook size may raise the overfitting problem. As the keypoints in

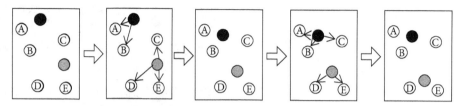

FIGURE 6: Demonstration of k-means clustering.

depth images are well distributed containing information about opening finger parts as well as bending finger parts, intuitively, we should get better accuracy.

To build our k-means clustering model, we have chosen 1600 as the cluster size which is the size of the visual vocabulary. An individual feature vector is assigned based on the nearest mean value while partitioning the feature vectors. After that, the code vectors were updated to reform the clusters until the grouping stops.

The goal of the k-means clustering approach is to minimize total intracluster distance using the following.

$$J = \sum_{j=1}^{k} \sum_{i=1}^{n} \left\| x_i^{(j)} - c_j \right\|^2 \qquad (2)$$

where k is the cluster size, n is the number of instances, and c is the cluster centroid of cluster j. An illustration of k-means clustering is shown in Figure 6 for five keypoints, A, B, C, D, and E, to form two clusters.

We develop the cluster model from each of the training images consisting feature vectors and encoded each of the keypoints with the clustered index. Keypoint and the cluster centroid are mapped according to the minimum distance criteria based on Euclidean distance measurement.

We got k disjoint subgroups of keypoints after assigning the keypoints to the corresponding cluster centers. So, the dimension of each training image consisting of n keypoints ($n \times 128$) reduced to $1 \times k$. k determines the cluster numbers.

3.2.3. Creating Bag-of-Features. We have created the bag-of-feature representation of each training image from the SIFT feature extracted. In order to learn visual vocabulary, we have built the k-means clustering model. Keypoints from each training image are mapped to the centroid of the corresponding cluster to represent visual vocabulary, known as feature vector quantization (VQ) process [42]. After that, we have represented each training image by the frequencies of visual words and found a unified dimensional histogram vector. The histogram representations of images of each gesture are ready for the classification. The process of creating Bag-of-features is shown in Figure 7

We updated the feature extraction process which is applied to two types of images; one is the depth image and the other one is the edge image, generated from the same dataset [15]. This is because we tried to establish more reliability in our approach through experimental evaluation compared to our previous work [39].

3.3. Recognition of Gestures Using SVM Classifier. The bag-of-feature vectors are now the input feature vectors for the

classification algorithm. In order to recognize the performed symbolic gestures, we have applied a multiclass SVM training algorithm which is a supervised machine learning algorithm. It performs nonlinear mapping and transforms the training dataset into higher dimensional datasets. The algorithm tries to find out an optimal hyperplane which is linear.

SVM determines that the support vectors are closest to the separating hyperplane. The margins are also defined by those support vectors. Maximum separation is ensured by the maximum margin hyperplane.

We have applied the one-against-all approach to implement the SVM classifier [41] that built the model with respect to the training set supplied with group vector (class label indicator from gesture classes 1 to 10).

4. Experimental Evaluation

In order to evaluate the symbolic gesture recognition results, we have considered NTU hand gesture recognition dataset [15] which is a benchmark dataset in static hand gesture recognition. The dataset was collected using Kinect depth camera from 10 subjects. Each subject has performed 10 symbolic gestures 10 times. So, the dataset contains total of 1000 instances. Each gesturing instance contains a color image and the corresponding depth map. The dataset was prepared in a very challenging real-life environment containing the situations like the cluttered background and pose variations in terms of rotation, scale, orientation, articulation, changing illumination, etc.

We have conducted the 5-fold cross-validation process to evaluate our results. In each fold 4 of the image groups were used as training set and one of them was used as validation testing set. Each fold contains 20 images and we permuted the process, calculating the accuracy of SVM classifier. All the experiments were executed on an Intel Core I7 2.60 GHz CPU having 16 GB RAM.

Our system is robust to cluttered background due to the process of segmentation where the depth threshold and minimum hand-finger distance from the depth camera are used to determine the segmentation threshold. Good contrast varying depth silhouettes guarantee SIFT keypoints to be extracted in different scale-rotation-orientation changing conditions as shown in Figure 8.

SIFT extracted local features which produce good recognition results compared to global features considered in FEMD-based approach [15]. We tested our results in two types of images produced from the same dataset: binary images and image with edge information. The former was generated along with depth silhouette by converting the

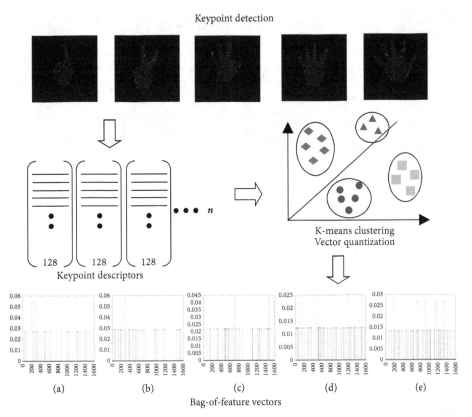

FIGURE 7: Generating bag-of-feature for training. (a)-(e) Bag-of-feature generated of gesture 2-6 from individual depth silhouette for 1600 clusters.

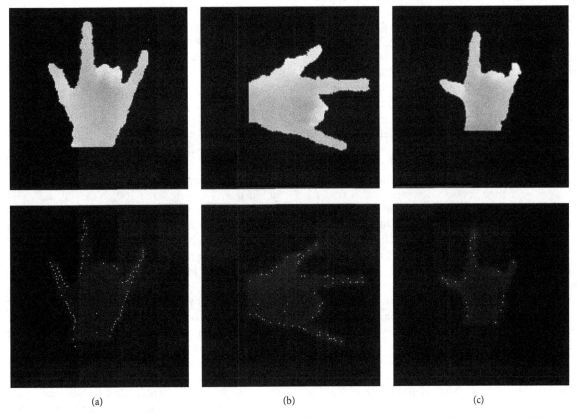

FIGURE 8: SIFT features are robust to orientation changes (b) and scale changes (c) along with normal pose (a).

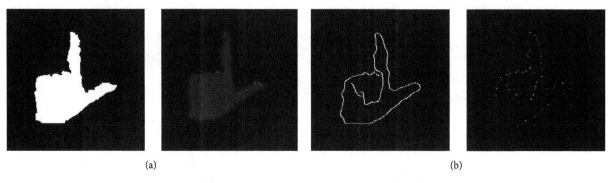

(a)   (b)

FIGURE 9: SIFT keypoints on binary image (a) and edge image (b).

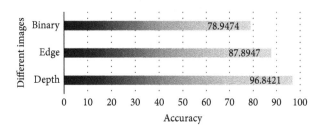

FIGURE 10: Accuracy comparison among different images.

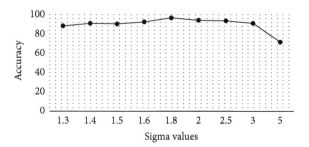

FIGURE 11: Accuracy at different sigma values.

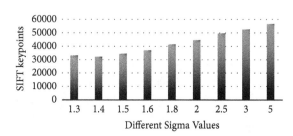

FIGURE 12: Number of SIFT keypoints at different Sigma values.

depth silhouettes into binary images and the latter was generated applying Canny's edge detection algorithm [25] on depth silhouettes. Example binary and edge images are shown in Figure 9. The image contains internal finger bending edge overlapped with palm and the external hand shape edge, but this information is not present in binary image or time-series images. So, the accuracy of our approach should vary on these different datasets.

Previously in [39], we demonstrated that the SIFT works better on depth images rather than binary images for static hand gesture recognition consisting of symbolic gestures (numeric symbol 1-5). The dataset used in the previous work was generated by us in a constrained environment. To create the dataset, we considered a limited number of hand gestures from a limited number of users. The comparison of experimental results was not performed among depth images, binary images, and edge images. However, in this research work, we have compared our experimental results among all the images and also compared the result with FEMD-based approach [15] and got higher accuracy for depth images (recognition accuracy is shown in Figure 10). Moreover, we elaborated the processes of depth silhouette generation with equations which illustrates the fact that the intensity of a pixel in grey-scale depends on the distance of that pixel from the depth camera. This, in turn, determines the contrast of the image based on depth values suitable for key point detector and descriptor-based algorithms.

To evaluate the accuracy of our approach, we generated different SIFT keypoints by varying the sigma (scaling parameter) value and found the highest accuracy at $\sigma = 1.8$. The mean accuracy at different σ values is shown in Figure 11.

With the increased value of sigma, we found more keypoints (Figure 12) which results in spurious DoG extrema

considered as less stable and not linked to any particular structure in the image. These cause the differences in accuracy.

We evaluated the accuracy with the different number of clusters. We considered 100, 200, 400, 800, 1200, 1600, and 2000 clusters to validate our proposed method and compared the results for depth, binary, and edge images. The comparison result is shown in Figure 13. We observed that the accuracy increments commensurate with the higher number of clusters. The highest accuracy we attained has been with a cluster size of 1600. This phenomenon can be traced back to depth images which significantly contribute to the salient keypoints identification for it is the depth images from which we can distinguish the positions of each fingers. However, the same cannot be said for binary images or images containing only edge information. FEMD has considered the shape distance metric which matches only opening finger parts or finger shapes, not the whole hand. While making a pose the bending finger parts are also important to distinguish slightly varying gestures, which can be found in the local features. To avoid local distortion we have chosen the correct scale factor.

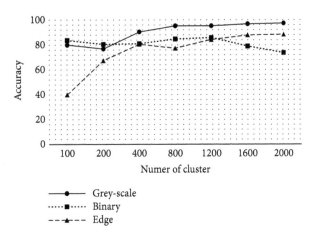

FIGURE 13: Overall accuracy comparison among different images.

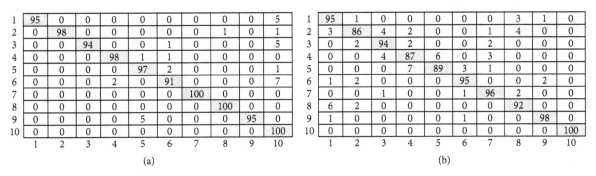

(a)

(b)

FIGURE 14: Confusion matrix of (a) proposed approach and (b) FEMD-based approach.

We have presented the input hand as a contrast varying grey-scale image depending on the depth map information but FEMD has presented the hand image as a global feature using time-series curves. Shape contour presentation introduces lower accuracy in terms of scale, rotation, or orientation changes which we have overcome through depth images and got accuracy up to 96.8421% whereas the FEMD has produced 93.2%. The confusion matrix of our approach and FEMD is given in Figure 14.

We have also calculated True Positive (TP), True Negative (TN), False Positive (FP), and False Negative (FN) and based on these the F-Score values using the following.

$$F - Score = \frac{2 \times TP}{2 \times TP + FP + FN} \quad (3)$$

The class-wise F-Score comparison between our approach and FEMD is given in Figure 15.

From Figure 14(a), we find that the accuracy of gestures 2, 4, 5, 7, and 8 has been improved significantly as expected because SIFT features are found more robust in the benchmark dataset. Moreover, we prove this by comparing the results with binary and edge images. In binary or edge images, a small variation in the shape may cause significant changes on the tangent vectors at the points on the shape. Since we are considering local hand-finger features for the hand

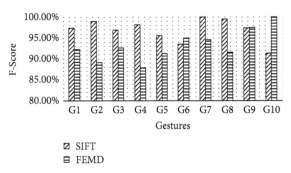

FIGURE 15: F-Score comparison between proposed approach and FEMD [15].

poses we are getting better results. Shape changes over time-series data are not required to be considered. Recognition accuracy of gestures 4 and 5 has increased to 98% and 97%, respectively, compared to FEMD-based approach. In gestures 6 and 10, we are getting most confusing results. Gesture 6 is all finger open gesture and contains a maximum number of keypoints (6374) as shown in Figure 5 and includes no bending finger information. The same is for gesture 10 and it is the only gesture in the dataset which contains no bending finger information like other gestures. The pose was given by the user opposite to other gestures; the bending fingers were facing towards the user, not the camera.

5. Conclusion

This paper describes a symbolic hand gesture recognition system and presents an effective way of utilizing depth map information. The use of depth value in determining grey-scale levels to generate contrast varying depth images is one of the significant contributions to this research. Moreover, hand-finger's context information of the gesturing hand represented by local invariant feature descriptors has contributed the recognition accuracy up to 96.84% which is better compared to binary images, images containing edge information, and images represented in time-series curves.

Preparing depth silhouettes of the gesturing hand is one the factors that affect the accuracy of gesture recognition system. With the help of depth map information, we were able to produce those gesturing images using fast and effective segmentation process. Choosing the right cluster size is also important. Our empirical results indicate that 1600 is the most desirable number of clusters to attain the best accuracy. This large number of clusters is contributed by the fact that images with only edge information or binary images contain far less keypoints than that of depth images. The number of training samples that we have taken was sufficient to develop the cluster model as well as the SVM classification model.

In future, we will analyze gesture recognition accuracy in terms of variations in cluster size using the principal component analysis (PCA), adaptive grey-scale levels, combining local, and global features (containing contour information) using hierarchical classification techniques. We will also try to compare the performance result of different detector and descriptor-based algorithms, such as SURF, BRIEF, and ORB.

References

[1] H. Hasan and S. Abdul-Kareem, "Human-computer interaction using vision-based hand gesture recognition systems: a survey," *Neural Computing and Applications*, vol. 25, no. 2, pp. 251–261, 2013.

[2] Y. Park, J. Lee, and J. Bae, "Development of a wearable sensing glove for measuring the motion of fingers using linear potentiometers and flexible wires," *IEEE Transactions on Industrial Informatics*, vol. 11, no. 1, pp. 198–206, 2015.

[3] J. Suarez and R. R. Murphy, "Hand gesture recognition with depth images: A review," in *Proceedings of the 2012 RO-MAN: The 21st IEEE International Symposium on Robot and Human Interactive Communication*, pp. 411–417, Paris, France, September 2012.

[4] D. G. Lowe, "Distinctive image feature from scale-invariant keypoints," *International Journal of Computer Vision*, vol. 60, no. 2, pp. 91–110, 2004.

[5] S. Zhang, W. He, Q. Yu, and X. Zheng, "Low-cost interactive whiteboard using the Kinect," in *Proceedings of the 2012 International Conference on Image Analysis and Signal Processing (IASP)*, pp. 1–5, Hangzhou, November 2012.

[6] Y. Chang, S. Chen, and J. Huang, "A Kinect-based system for physical rehabilitation: a pilot study for young adults with motor disabilities," *Research in Developmental Disabilities*, vol. 32, no. 6, pp. 2566–2570, 2011.

[7] A. Ramey, V. Gonzalez-Pacheco, and M. A. Salichs, "Integration of a low-cost RGB-D sensor in a social robot for gesture recognition," in *Proceedings of the 6th ACM/IEEE International Conference on Human-Robot Interaction (HRI '11)*, pp. 229-230, Lausanne, Switzerland, March 2011.

[8] M. Van Den Bergh, D. Carton, R. De Nijs et al., "Real-time 3D hand gesture interaction with a robot for understanding directions from humans," in *Proceedings of the 20th IEEE International Symposium on Robot and Human Interactive Communication, RO-MAN 2011*, pp. 357–362, USA, August 2011.

[9] D. Xu, Y. Chen, C. Lin, X. Kong, and X. Wu, "Real-time dynamic gesture recognition system based on depth perception for robot navigation," in *Proceedings of the 2012 IEEE International Conference on Robotics and Biomimetics (ROBIO)*, pp. 689–694, Guangzhou, China, December 2012.

[10] Z. Zafrulla, H. Brashear, T. Starner, H. Hamilton, and P. Presti, "American sign language recognition with the kinect," in *Proceedings of the 2011 ACM International Conference on Multimodal Interaction, ICMI'11*, pp. 279–286, Spain, November 2011.

[11] O. M. Mozos, H. Mizutani, R. Kurazume, and T. Hasegawa, "Categorization of indoor places using the Kinect sensor," *Sensors*, vol. 12, no. 5, pp. 6695–6711, 2012.

[12] G. Azzari, M. L. Goulden, and R. B. Rusu, "Rapid characterization of vegetation structure with a microsoft kinect sensor," *Sensors*, vol. 13, no. 2, pp. 2384–2398, 2013.

[13] P. K. Pisharady and M. Saerbeck, "Recent methods and databases in vision-based hand gesture recognition: A review," *Computer Vision and Image Understanding*, vol. 141, pp. 152–165, 2015.

[14] W. Lin, Y. Wu, W. Hung, and C. Tang, "A Study of Real-Time Hand Gesture Recognition Using SIFT on Binary Images," in *Advances in Intelligent Systems & Applications, SIST 21*, pp. 235–246, Springer-Verlag, Berlin Heidelberg, 2013.

[15] Z. Ren, J. Yuan, J. Meng, and Z. Zhang, "Robust part-based hand gesture recognition using kinect sensor," *IEEE Transactions on Multimedia*, vol. 15, no. 5, pp. 1110–1120, 2013.

[16] T. D'Orazio, R. Marani, V. Renò, and G. Cicirelli, "Recent trends in gesture recognition: How depth data has improved classical approaches," *Image and Vision Computing*, vol. 52, pp. 56–72, 2016.

[17] C. Wang and K. Wang, *Hand Gesture Recognition Using Adaboost With SIFT for Human Robot Interaction*, vol. 370, SpringerVerlag, Berlin, Germany, 2008.

[18] Q. Chen, N. Georganas, and E. Petriu, "Real-time vision-based hand gesture recognition using Haar-like features," in *Proceedings of the IEEE Instrumentation and Measurement Technology Conference Proceedings (IMTC '07)*, pp. 1–6, Warsaw, Poland, May 2007.

[19] P. Viola and M. Jones, "Robust real-time object detection," *International Journal of Computer Vision*, vol. 2, no. 57, pp. 137–154, 2004.

[20] D. Lisin, M. Mattar, M. Blaschko, E. Learned-Miller, and M. Benfield, "Combining Local and Global Image Features for Object Class Recognition," in *Proceedings of the 2005 IEEE Computer Society Conference on Computer Vision and Pattern Recognition (CVPR'05) - Workshops*, pp. 47-47, SanDiego, CA, USA.

[21] K. Siddiqi, S. Bouix, A. Tannenbaum, and S. W. Zucker, "Hamilton-Jacobi skeletons," *International Journal of Computer Vision*, vol. 48, no. 3, pp. 215–231, 2002.

[22] S. Belongie, J. Malik, and J. Puzicha, "Shape matching and object recognition using shape contexts," *IEEE Transactions on Pattern Analysis and Machine Intelligence*, vol. 24, no. 4, pp. 509–522, 2002.

[23] H. Ling and D. W. Jacobs, "Shape classification using the inner-distance," *IEEE Transactions on Pattern Analysis and Machine Intelligence*, vol. 29, no. 2, pp. 286–299, 2007.

[24] K. Matusiak, P. Skulimowski, and P. Strumillo, "Depth-based descriptor for matching keypoints in 3D scenes," vol. Volume 64, Issue 3, pp. 299–306, 2018.

[25] J. Canny, "A computational approach to edge detection," *IEEE Transactions on Pattern Analysis and Machine Intelligence*, vol. 8, no. 6, pp. 679–698, 1986.

[26] X. J. Meng, Y. L. Yin, G. P. Yang, and X. M. Xi, "Retinal identification based on an improved circular gabor filter and scale invariant feature transform," *Sensors*, vol. 13, no. 7, pp. 9248–9266, 2013.

[27] S. Zhao, X. Xu, W. Zheng, and J. Ling, "Registration of Depth Image and Color Image Based on Harris-SIFT," in *Proceedings of the IEEE 2012 Second International Conference on Electric Information and Control Engineering (ICEICE, 2012.*

[28] Y. Ke and R. Sukthankar, "PCA-SIFT: a more distinctive representation for local image descriptors," in *Proceedings of the IEEE Computer Society Conference on Computer Vision and Pattern Recognition (CVPR '04)*, vol. 2, pp. II-506–II-513, July 2004.

[29] H. Bay, A. Ess, T. Tuytelaars, and L. Gool, "SURF: Speeded up robust features," *Computer Vision and Image Understanding*, vol. 110, no. 3, pp. 346–359, 2008.

[30] K. Mikolajczyk and C. Schmid, "A performance evaluation of local descriptors," *IEEE Transactions on Pattern Analysis and Machine Intelligence*, vol. 27, no. 10, pp. 1615–1630, 2005.

[31] L. Zhang, P. Shen, G. Zhu, W. Wei, and H. Song, "A fast robot identification and mapping algorithm based on kinect sensor," *Sensors*, vol. 15, no. 8, pp. 19937–19967, 2015.

[32] M. Calonder, V. Lepetit, C. Strecha, and P. Fua, "BRIEF: Binary robust independent elementary features," *Lecture Notes in Computer Science (including subseries Lecture Notes in Artificial Intelligence and Lecture Notes in Bioinformatics): Preface*, vol. 6314, no. 4, pp. 778–792, 2010.

[33] E. Rublee, V. Rabaud, K. Konolige, and G. Bradski, "ORB: an efficient alternative to SIFT or SURF," in *Proceedings of the IEEE International Conference on Computer Vision (ICCV '11)*, pp. 2564–2571, Barcelona, Spain, November 2011.

[34] E. Karami, S. Prasad, and M. Shehata, "Image Matching Using SIFT, SURF, BRIEF and ORB: Performance Comparison for Distorted Images," in *Proceedings of the 2015 Newfoundland Electrical and Computer Engineering Conference, St, johns, Canada, November 2015.*

[35] M. Karpushin, G. Valenzise, and F. Dufaux, "Keypoint detection in rgbd images based on an anisotropic scale space," *IEEE Transactions on Multimedia*, vol. 18, no. 9, pp. 1762–1771, 2016.

[36] S. Lazebnik, C. Schmid, and J. Ponce, "Beyond bags of features: spatial pyramid matching for recognizing natural scene categories," in *Proceedings of the IEEE Computer Society Conference on Computer Vision and Pattern Recognition (CVPR '06)*, pp. 2169–2178, June 2006.

[37] D. A. Leite, J. C. Duarte, J. C. Oliveira, V. d. Thomaz, and G. A. Giraldi, "A System to Interact with CAVE Applications Using Hand Gesture Recognition from Depth Data," in *Proceedings of the 2014 XVI Symposium on Virtual and Augmented Reality (SVR)*, pp. 246–253, Piata Salvador, Bahia, Brazil, May 2014.

[38] Y. Li, "Hand gesture recognition using Kinect," in *Proceedings of the 2012 IEEE 3rd International Conference on Software Engineering and Service Science, ICSESS 2012*, pp. 196–199, China, June 2012.

[39] H. Mahmud, M. K. Hasan, A. A. Tariq, and M. A. Mottalib, "Hand Gesture Recognition Using SIFT Features on Depth Image," in *Proceedings of the the Ninth International Conference on Advances in Computer-Human Interactions (ACHI)*, pp. 359–365, Venice, Italy, 2016.

[40] C. Naveen, *SIFT algorithm*, vol. 11, MATLAB Central File Exchange, 2018, https://www.mathworks.com/matlabcentral/fileexchange/43723-sift-scale-invariant-feature-transform-algorithm.

[41] "Multiclass Support Vector Macine Classifier," http://www.mathworks.com/matlabcentral/fileexchange/33170-multi-class-support-vector-machine/.

[42] A. Bosch, X. Muñoz, and R. Martí, "Which is the best way to organize/classify images by content?" *Image and Vision Computing*, vol. 25, no. 6, pp. 778–791, 2007.

2

Usability Studies on Mobile User Interface Design Patterns

Lumpapun Punchoojit and Nuttanont Hongwarittorrn

Department of Computer Science, Faculty of Science and Technology, Thammasat University, Pathum Thani, Thailand

Correspondence should be addressed to Lumpapun Punchoojit; l.punchoojit@gmail.com

Academic Editor: Thomas Mandl

Mobile platforms have called for attention from HCI practitioners, and, ever since 2007, touchscreens have completely changed mobile user interface and interaction design. Some notable differences between mobile devices and desktops include the lack of tactile feedback, ubiquity, limited screen size, small virtual keys, and high demand of visual attention. These differences have caused unprecedented challenges to users. Most of the mobile user interface designs are based on desktop paradigm, but the desktop designs do not fully fit the mobile context. Although mobile devices are becoming an indispensable part of daily lives, true standards for mobile UI design patterns do not exist. This article provides a systematic literature review of the existing studies on mobile UI design patterns. The first objective is to give an overview of recent studies on the mobile designs. The second objective is to provide an analysis on what topics or areas have insufficient information and what factors are concentrated upon. This article will benefit the HCI community in seeing an overview of present works, to shape the future research directions.

1. Introduction

The emergence of computers into workplaces and home during the 1970s has brought attention to the interaction between people and computer systems; and, thus, the field of Human-Computer Interaction (HCI) began to emerge during the same period [1]. HCI encompasses extensive areas and designing effective user interface (UI) is one of the areas that has always been emphasized, as effective interfaces provide potential to improve overall system performance [2]. It is a great challenge to design an effective UI, as it requires understanding of different disciplines; for example, user's physical and cognitive capabilities, sociological contexts, computer science and engineering, graphic design, and work domain [2, 3]. An effective user interface would be created based upon perspectives from the disciplines.

HCI consistently evolves in response to technological changes. At the first stage, HCI focused on how to facilitate convenient means for a single user to use a computer on a fixed platform, such as desktop computers. At the second stage, HCI was no longer confined to stationary computers. Mobile innovation started in the late 1990s. Many actions and

feedback under small-sized screen and a limited number of buttons became an area of focus in the HCI community [4]. In 2007, many companies, such as LG, Apple, and HTC, released new models of mobile devices. The new models were no longer equipped with keypads; instead, they were replaced by touchscreens. This caused a major shift on research attention ever since [5, 6].

There are more than billion smartphone users worldwide which include a large proportion of nongeneric users—children, the elderly, and users with disorders or disabilities. Although mobile platforms are becoming an indispensable part of daily lives, true standards for mobile UI design patterns do not exist. Seemingly, most of the designs are based on the desktop paradigm [7]. The desktop paradigm may be applicable, but there are notable differences between mobile devices and desktops, including the lack of tactile feedback, limited screen size, and high demands of visual attention. Apart from differences in physical qualities, contexts of use between desktop computers and mobile devices are different. Desktop computers are stationary, whereas mobile devices can be used anywhere or even while users are walking, carrying objects, or driving. Thus, desktop designs do not fully fit mobile context.

There is a need to see an overview of usability studies on mobile UI design, to ascertain the current state of knowledge and research and to comprehend research gaps. This article provides systematic review of the existing studies on mobile UI design patterns. The first objective is to give an overview of recent studies on mobile designs. The second objective is to provide analyses on what topics or areas have insufficient information and what factors are concentrated upon. This article will benefit the HCI community in seeing an overview of present works and knowledge gaps, to shape the future research directions.

2. Theoretical Backgrounds

2.1. Usability. Usability is a core terminology in HCI. It has been defined as "the extent to which a product can be used by specified users to achieve specified goals with effectiveness, efficiency, and satisfaction in a specified context of use" [8]. The term usability was coined in the early 1980s to replace "user-friendly," which was vague and contained subjective connotation [9]. Usability is crucial to any products because if the users cannot achieve their goals effectively, efficiently, and in satisfactory manner, they can seek for alternative solutions to achieve their goals [10]. A usable product seeks to achieve three main outcomes: (1) the product is easy for users to become familiar with and competent in using it during the first contact, (2) the product is easy for users to achieve their objective through using it, and (3) the product is easy for users to recall the user interface and how to use it on later visits [11].

Usability criteria ensure that the products meet the three outcomes. There are several usability criteria mentioned in literature, for instance, effectiveness, efficiency, satisfaction, safety (error tolerance), utility, learnability (easy to learn), memorability, and engaging [11, 12]. The objective of usability criteria is to enable the assessment of product usability in terms of how the product can improve user's performance [12]. Some of the usability criteria are very much task-centered, where specific tasks are separated out, quantified, and measured in usability testing [13]. For example, efficiency which refers to how fast the user can get their job done [10] can be measured by time to complete a task or learnability can be measured by time to learn a task [12]. These criteria can provide quantitative indicators of how productivity has improved [12]. Some of the usability criteria can hardly be measured by using quantitative measurement, such as satisfaction and engagement, as they are subjective and basically involve human emotion. There are several factors which contribute to overall satisfaction, and the factors may include entertaining, helpfulness, aesthetically pleasing, and rewarding, or there are some negative qualities such as boring, frustrating, and annoying [12]. When it comes to evaluation whether users have pleasant or terrible experience, it is difficult to objectively measure. This is where user experience has become another core terminology in HCI.

2.2. User Experience. User experience (UX) has been defined as "the combined experience of what a user feels, perceives, thinks, and physically and mentally reacts to before and during the use of a product or service" [14]. Basically, an important concept in UX is the process by which users form experiences since they first encounter the product and as the product is used throughout a period [15]. UX can be explained by three characteristics. The first one is the holistic nature of UX. What is meant by holistic nature is that UX encompasses a broad range of qualities and includes not only the visual, tactile, auditory aspects of the system but also how the system functions under an appropriate usage environment or context [4]. The second characteristic is that UX focus is heavily tilted towards user's perspective. UX is often misunderstood for UI (user interface), as their abbreviations are similar. UI tends to tilt towards computer side, and UI evaluations are often subjected to quantitative measurement or usability testing. UX, in contrast, concerns how users think, feel, and behave [4]. The third characteristic is that UX has strategic value in firm's development of a product or service. UX has recently become an important topic worth consideration by top executives [4].

The goal of designing for UX is to encourage positive feelings (e.g., satisfying, enjoyable, exciting, motivating, and fun) and minimizing negative feelings (e.g., boring, frustrating, annoying, and cutesy) towards the product. Unlike usability goals, UX goals are subjective qualities and concerned with how a product feels to a user. There were attempts to utilize quantitative measurements to measure user's emotion. The measurements were adopted from medical applications, such as measuring pulse and blood pressure, or using facial electromyography (EMG) and electroencephalography (EEG) to reflect computer frustration [13]. However, its validity in measuring user experience remains questionable. Although usability and UX are different, they are not completely separated. In fact, usability is part of user experience. For example, a product that is visually pleasing might evoke positive first-contact experience; however, if its usability was inadequate, it could damage overall user experience. Apart from usability, other core components of UX include useful and desirable content, accessibility, credibility, visually pleasing, and enjoyment [15].

2.3. User Diversity. One of the most important design philosophies in HCI is the universal design. It is the process of creating products that can be accessed by as many people as possible, with the widest possible range of abilities, operating within the widest possible range of situations [16]. To make products that can be used by everyone is impossible; however, designers can try to exclude as few people as possible, by ensuring that the products are flexible and adaptable to individual needs and preferences [17]. To accomplish universal design goals, the understanding of user diversity is needed. There are several dimensions of user diversity that differentiate groups of users.

The first dimension is disabilities. Much of experimental research has been conducted to understand how disabilities affect interaction with technology. The main efforts of studies were to study the users themselves, their requirements for interaction, appropriate modalities, interactive devices, and techniques to address their needs [18]. The research includes visual impairments, auditory impairments, motor and physical impairments, and cognitive impairments [18]. Visual impairments greatly affect human interaction with technology, as human relies on vision to operate computer systems. Visual impairments encompass a wide range of vision problems related to acuity, accommodation (ability to focus on objects at different distances from the eyes), illumination adaption, perception of depth, and color vision [19]. Minor visual impairments can usually be addressed by magnifying the size of interactive elements, increasing color contrast, or selecting appropriate color combinations for color-blinded users [18]. Unlike visual impairments, blindness refers to a complete or nearly complete vision loss [20]. Blind users benefit from audio and haptic modality for input and output. They are supported by screen readers, speech input and output, and Braille displays [18]. Auditory impairments (or hearing impairments) can also affect interaction with technology. The impairments may vary in degree, from slight to severe. Majority of people with hearing impairments have lost their hearing usually through aging. They have partially lost perception of frequency (cannot discriminate between pitches), intensity (need louder sounds), signal to noise (distracted by background noise), and complexity (can hardly perceive speech) [19]. Some people were prelingually deaf, either were born deaf or had lost their hearing before they can speak [21]. Some strategies to address hearing impairments are to provide subtitles or captions to auditory contents or to provide sign-language translation of the contents [21]. Motor and physical impairments interfere with interaction with technology. Although causes and severity of motor impairments vary, the common problems faced by individuals with motor impairments include poor muscle control, arthritis, weakness and fatigue, difficulty in walking, talking, and reaching objects, total or partial paralysis, lack of sensitivity, lack of coordination of fine movement, and lack of limbs [18, 19]. The main strategy to address motor impairments is to minimize movement and physical effort required for input, for instance, using text prediction, voice input, switch control devices, and eye-tracking [18, 19]. Besides the aforesaid impairments, cognitive impairments can also limit user's interaction with technology. Cognitive impairments can be the result of brain injury, Alzheimer's disease and dementia, dyslexia, Down's syndrome, and stroke [18, 19]. Cognitive disabilities limit user's capacities to think, to remember (either long-term or short-term), to sequence thoughts and actions, and to understand symbols [18, 19]. The strategies are to keep user interface simple, provide simple methods for remembering, provide continuous feedback about position in the system, provide longer time to complete task, and support user's attention [19].

The second dimension is age. Age influences physical qualities and abilities, cognitive abilities, and how a person perceives and processes information. The elderly and children are the two major age groups that have age-dependent requirements [18]. There are several definitions of children. Some studies include adolescence (13–18 years) into childhood, whereas some studies focus only on children under the age of 12 [18, 22]. Like the children group, there is no consensus on the cut-off point of old age. Most researchers

regard 55 years as the beginning of old age. Nevertheless, there are enormous differences in abilities and problems within elderly group; for example, people aged 55 and people aged 90 are extremely different [19]. Therefore, the age range is further divided into two or three groups: young-old (ages 55 to 75) and old-old (over 75) or young-old (ages 65 to 74), old-old (ages 75 to 85), and oldest-old (over age 85) [19]. Old age is associated with declines in vision, hearing, motor function, and cognition [19]. Elderly people commonly have problems with vision acuity, depth of perception, color vision, hearing high frequency sounds, controlling coordination and movement, short- and long-term memory, and information processing speed [19]. Children have unique characteristics. They do not possess the same levels of physical and cognitive capabilities as the adults. They have limited motor abilities, spatial memory, attention, working memory, and language abilities. Thus, the general characteristics of the elderly and children need to be considered when developing products for these two age groups.

The third dimension is culture. Cultural differences include date and time format, interpretation of symbols, color meaning, gestures, text direction, and language. Thus, designers must be sensitive to these differences during the development process and avoid treating all cultures the same [18].

The fourth dimension is computer expertise. Some groups of users are unfamiliar with technology, for example, older adults and those with minimal or no education. Some strategies to address differences in expertise level include providing help options and explanations, consistent naming convention to assist memory, and uncluttered user interface to assist attention [18].

2.4. Mobile Computing. The first era of mobile devices dated back to the late 1970s and early 1980s. The models during this era were precursor to present time's laptops and were originally intended for children. The focus of this era was to reduce the size of computer machine to support portability [23]. Mobile phones introduced during this period were still large and required enormous batteries [24]. Around ten years later, mobile devices reached the point where the sizes were small enough to be fit in a pocket. During the same time, the network shifted to 2G technology and cellular sites became denser; thus, mobile connectivity was easier than before. This led to the increase in consumer demand for mobile phones. Increased demand meant more competition for service providers and device manufacturers, which eventually reduced costs to consumers [24]. In the late 1990s, feature phones were introduced to the market. The phones were equipped with several "features," such as cameras, games, wallpapers, and customizable ringtones [24]. Smartphone era started around 2002. Smartphones have the same capabilities as the feature phones; however, the smartphones use the same operating system, have larger screen size, and have a QWERTY keyboard or stylus for input and Wi-Fi for connectivity [24]. The most recent era starts in 2007 when Apple launched the iPhone [23, 24]. It was like smartphones; however, it presented a novel design of mobile interactions. It introduced multitouch display with simple touch gesture (e.g., pinching, swiping), and physical keyboard was completely removed from the phone. The iPhone was also equipped with context-awareness capabilities, which allowed the phone to detect orientation of the phone, or even the location of the users. It took a couple of years later for the competitors to match up with the Android operating system, mobile devices, and associated application store [23].

The challenges of mobile interaction and interface design have evolved over time. Early mobile interaction design involved physical design, reducing physical size while optimizing limited screen display and physical numeric keypads [23]. Later, the challenges evolved to the development add-on features, for example, digital cameras and media player. However, today challenges may have moved to a completely new dimension. Physical shape and basic size of mobile phones have remained unchanged for many years. The challenges may have shifted to the development of software application or designing mobile interaction [23].

3. Previous Reviews

There have been several previous reviews of mobile user interface; however, they did not focus on user interface design patterns. Instead, the focus was primarily on certain application domain of mobile devices. For instance, Coppola and Morisio [25] focused on in-car mobile use. Their article provided an overview of the possibilities offered by connected functions on cars, technological issues, and problems of recent technologies. They also provided a list of currently available hardware and software solutions, as well as the main features. Pereira and Rodrigues [26] made a survey on mobile learning applications and technologies. The article provided an analysis of mobile learning projects, as well as the findings of the analysis. Becker [27] surveyed the best practices of mobile website design for library. Monroe et al. [28] made a survey on the use of mobile phones for physical activities (e.g., exercising, walking, and running) and approaches for encouraging and assessing physical activities using mobile phones. Donner [29] reviewed mobile use in the developing world. His article presented major concentrations of the research, the impacts of mobile use, and interrelationships between mobile technology and users. Moreover, the article also provided economic perspective on mobile use in the developing world.

Some review articles concentrated on technical approach of mobile devices and user interface. For instance, Hoseini-Tabatabaei et al. [30] surveyed smartphone-based systems for opportunistic (nonintrusive) user context recognition. Their article provided introduction to typical architecture of mobile-centric user context recognition, the main techniques of context recognition, lesson learned from previous approaches, and challenges for future research. Akiki et al. [31] provided a review on adaptive model-driven user interface development systems. The article addressed the strengths and shortcomings of architectures, techniques, and tools of the state of the art. Summary of the evaluation, existing research gaps, and promising improvements were also stated. Cockburn et al. [32] provided a review of interface

schemes that allowed users to work at focused and contextual views of dataset. The four schemes were overview + details, zooming, focus + context, and cue-based techniques. Critical features of the four approaches and empirical evidence of their success were provided.

Some previous reviews focused on mobile use in some user groups. For instance, Zhou et al. [33] made a survey on the use and design of mobile devices for older users, focusing particularly on whether and why older users accept mobile devices and how to design the elderly-friendly mobile devices. Their article provided a summary on technology acceptance of the elderly users, input devices, menus and functions, and output devices.

Some more reviews concerned the impact of mobile use. Moulder et al. [34] reviewed the evidence concerning whether radiofrequency emitted from mobile phones were a cause of cancer. The article provided summary from relevant medical research. Nevertheless, the evidence for a causal association between cancer and radiofrequency was weak and unconvincing.

4. Research Questions

This article surveys literature on usability studies on mobile user interface design patterns and seeks to answer the following two research questions:

RQ1: in each area, what factors were concentrated?

RQ2: what areas of mobile user interface design patterns had insufficient information?

5. Literature Search Strategy

Four phases were used to systematically survey literature: (1) listing related disciplines, (2) scoping databases, (3) specifying timeframe, and (4) specifying target design elements.

5.1. Listing Related Disciplines. The first phase was to list out HCI related disciplines, to cover user interface research from all related disciplines. Based on [3, 35], the related disciplines are as follows: computer science and engineering, ergonomics, business, psychology, social science, education, and graphic design.

5.2. Scoping Databases. The articles for review were retrieved from 24 online databases, based upon access provided by authors' affiliation. The databases covered all disciplines mentioned in Section 5.1, and they were listed in Table 1.

5.3. Specifying Timeframe. The current article was confined to the papers published from 2007 to 2016. As stated, many companies released new touchscreen mobile devices in 2007, which was a turning point of research attention [5, 6].

5.4. Specifying Target Design Elements. The categories of major design patterns defined in the book *Designing Mobile Interfaces*, by Hoober and Berkman [7], were used to scope literature search. The categories were listed in Table 2.

TABLE 1: Database list.

Number	Database name
(1)	ABI/Inform
(2)	Academic Search complete
(3)	ACM
(4)	Annual Reviews
(5)	Business Monitor
(6)	Business Source Complete
(7)	Cambridge Journal Online
(8)	Computer & Applied Science Complete
(9)	CRCnetBase
(10)	Credo Reference
(11)	Education Research Complete
(12)	Emerald Management
(13)	EBSCOhost
(14)	ERIC
(15)	GALE
(16)	H. W. Wilson
(17)	IEEE
(18)	Ingenta
(19)	JSTOR
(20)	PsycINFO
(21)	SAGE
(22)	ScienceDirect
(23)	SpringerLink
(24)	Taylor & Francis

Note. Items are ordered alphabetically.

There were altogether 10 categories of mobile UI design patterns. Some of them contained subelements; for instance, in input mode and selection, the subelements of this category were gesture, keyboard, input area, and form.

5.5. Inclusion Criteria. For each category of the design patterns, the papers which contained any of these keywords: mobile, user, and interface as well as the name of the category were retrieved; for instance, keywords used in retrieving papers about icons were "icon"; "mobile"; "user"; and "interface". The subelements in the categories were also included in retrieval keywords.

The abstracts of all retrieved papers were initially read through. The papers which contained the input keywords but did not discuss or were not related to mobile user interface were omitted; for instance, papers related to networking were often retrieved in "navigation" category, as they contained the keywords "link" and/or "navigation." Once the related papers were identified, their main contents were read through. The number of primary search results and the remaining papers in each category were listed in Table 3.

From Table 3, the input mode and selection category had the highest remaining papers—27—followed by icons (14 papers), information control (9 papers), buttons (7 papers), page composition, display of information, and navigation (4 papers each). The control and confirmation, revealing more information, and lateral access categories had no relevant

papers. In each category, the papers which shared the common ground were grouped together, to posit research theme in each design pattern.

6. Research Overview

This section provided an overview of prior research and studies on each category of mobile UI design pattern conducted since 2007.

6.1. Page Composition. Page composition is a very broad term for interface design. A composition of a page encompasses various components, including scrolling, annunciator row, notification, title, menu patterns, lock screen, interstitial screen, and advertising [7]. Only menu was discussed in this section. The other elements that were overlapped with other topics would be discussed later (i.e., scrolling) or out of the scope of this current article (i.e., annunciator row, notification, title, lock screen, interstitial screen, and advertising).

Menu method is a popular alternative to traditional form of retrieving information [36]. It plays a significant role in overall satisfaction of mobile phones [37]. The primary function of menus is to allow users to access desired functions of applications or devices. Early research on menus was carried out on many topics. The research primarily examined effectiveness of menu patterns and relevant components on desktop platform. The research included 2D and 3D menus, menu structures (depth versus breadth), menu adaptation, item ordering (categorically and alphabetically), item categorization, task complexity, menu patterns (hierarchical and fisheye), help fields, methodological studies, and individual differences [36].

The first few studies of menus on mobile devices are due to small screen of devices. The guidelines or principles that are generally applied from menus on personal computers should be reexamined. Early studies on desktops show that 3D menus can convey more information than 2D menus. In mobile context, superiority of 3D menus can be inconclusive as the screen size is more limited. In Kim's study [36], 2D menu (i.e., list menu) was compared with three types of 3D menus (i.e., carousel, revolving stage, and collapsible cylindrical trees) on mobile phone. The performance of menus was measured by task completion time, satisfaction, fun, and perceived use of space. The results partially substantiated previous studies. With respect to overall metrics, 3D menus outperformed 2D menus; however, the 2D menus surpassed 3D in high breadth level [36]. In fact, there are more types of 2D and 3D menus that have not been examined, and they can be further studied.

Besides menu components, prior research showed that user factors had influences on menu usability. The topics included user language abilities, spatial abilities, visual characteristics, and user expertise [36]. The scope became narrower and it examined primarily on age and cultural differences since 2007.

Prior research highlighted cultural influences on usability. The research was mostly at superficial level (e.g., text,

TABLE 2: Design patterns and subelements.

Number	Design patterns	Subelements
(1)	Page composition	Menu
(2)	Display of information	List, classify, order
(3)	Control and confirmation	Sign on, confirmation, time-out
(4)	Revealing more information	Pop-up, prompt, hierarchical list
(5)	Lateral access	Tab, pagination
(6)	Navigation	Link, navigation
(7)	Button	No subelements
(8)	Icon	No subelements
(9)	Information control	Zoom, search, filter
(10)	Input mode and selection	Gesture, keyboard, input area, form

TABLE 3: Primary search results and remaining papers in each category.

Number	Design patterns	Primary search results	Remaining
(1)	Page composition	116 (menu = 116)	4
(2)	Display of information	286 (list = 215, classify = 41, order = 30)	4
(3)	Control and confirmation	220 (pop-up = 0, confirmation = 0, time-out = 220)	0
(4)	Revealing more information	524 (pop-up = 6, prompt = 500, hierarchical list = 2)	0
(5)	Lateral access	15 (tab = 15, pagination = 0)	0
(6)	Navigation	1287 (link = 516, navigation = 771)	4
(7)	Button	167	7
(8)	Icon	2436	14
(9)	Information control	839 (zoom = 102, search = 552, filter = 185)	9
(10)	Input mode and selection	1157 (gesture = 886, keyboard = 239, input area = 0, form = 32)	27
Total			68

number, and date and time format), whereas that at implicit cognition level was rare. Moreover, they were mostly conducted in desktop environment [38]. Thus, applying the findings from desktop research to mobile environment remained unsettled. Kim and Lee [38] examined correlation between cultural cognitive styles and item categorization scheme on mobile phones. They found different user preferences towards categorization of menu items. Dutch users (representing Westerners) preferred functionally grouped menus, for instance, setting ringtones and setting wallpaper, as they shared a common function—setting. In contrast to Dutch users, Korean users (representing Easterners) preferred thematically grouped menu, for instance, setting wallpaper and display, as they shared a common theme—pictorial items. Menus should be optimized to fit user's cognitive styles and preferences to enhance system usability [38].

Apart from cultural differences, influence of age differences on menu usability was also studied. As people aged, there are changes and decline in sensation and perception, cognition, and movement control, for instance, decline in vision acuity, color discrimination, hearing, selective attention, working memory, and force controls [39]. These changes influence computer use. Thus, user interface must be designed to support the unique needs of older users. A study found that aging had influences on menu navigation. Menu navigation is an important concern when designing a menu, as an effective menu leads users to correct navigational path. Effective menu is related to several components, including the structure of the menu, its depth and breadth, and naming and allocation of menu items. Menu navigation is also associated with individual factors: spatial ability, verbal memory, visual abilities, psychomotor abilities, and self-efficacy, and these individual factors are age-related [40]. Menu navigation is more challenging on mobile devices, as the menus are implemented on limited screen space and users can partially see the menus; thus, users need to rely on working memory more than on desktops. Arning and Ziefle [40] studied the menu navigation on mobile environment with younger (average age = 23.8) and older users (average age = 56.4), all of whom were experienced computer users. The performance of menu navigation was measured by task completion time, number of tasks completed, detour steps, and node revisited. Prior to navigation tasks, preliminary tests were conducted to measure user's spatial ability, verbal memory, and self-efficacy. The results of the preliminary tests indicated that spatial ability, verbal memory, and self-efficacy of younger users were significantly higher than older users. The navigation tasks found differences on user's performance. Task completion time, number of tasks completed, detour steps, and nodes revisited of older users were significantly greater than those of younger users; in other words, younger users outperformed older users on mobile menu navigation [40]. However, further analysis found that the variable which had the best predictive power for navigation performance was not age but spatial ability; age was only a carrier variable that was related to many variables which changed over the lifespan. Although all older users in their study were experienced computer users, the study found that more than half of them were not able to build a mental model of how the system was constructed. Their study also found that both verbal memory and spatial ability were related to strategies employed in menu navigation. Users with high spatial ability navigated through information structure based on their spatial representation of menu structure, while users with high verbal memory referred to memorization of function names in navigation [40].

With many individual factors and diversity of users, one-size-fits-all system is impossible to achieve, and tailoring product to fit all segments of users is very costly. An alternative solution is to allow users to adapt the interface (adaptable interface) or to allow the interface to adapt itself (adaptive interface). Both types of interfaces locate frequently used items in a position that can be easily selected by the users; thus, menu selection time can be reduced [41]. However, each of them has its own weaknesses. On adaptive interface, no special knowledge of users is required, as the interface can adapt itself; however, users can have difficulty in developing mental model of the system due to frequent change of item location. On adaptable interface, users can autonomously manipulate location of items, but users need to learn how to move items to intended position [42]. Prior studies on desktops show that adaptive interfaces have potential for reducing visual search time and cognitive load, and adaptive interfaces can be faster in comparison to traditional nonadaptive interfaces [43]. Nevertheless, these two approaches have been less studied on mobile devices. Park et al. [44] examined conventional adaptive and adaptable menus, adaptive and adaptable menus with highlights on recently selected items, and traditional menu. The study found that the traditional menu had higher learnability as the menu items did not change their positions. However, the traditional menu did

not provide support for frequently selected items, and this type of menus became less efficient when the number of items was large. Adaptable menus were more robust but required a significant amount of time to learn adaptation and to memorize which items to adapt. The adaptable menu with highlights on recently selected items helped users recognize which items should be adapted. Performance of the adaptive menus was similar to the adaptable one; however, constantly changing item locations made it difficult for users to develop stable mental representation of the system. In sum, the results showed that adaptable menu with highlights were in favour by most users, as the highlights could reduce memory load for adaptation [44].

6.2. Display of Information. On desktops, users are constantly surrounded by ocean of information. Many information display patterns help users in filtering and processing relevant visual information. Examples of information display patterns include different types of lists, including vertical list, thumbnail list, fisheye list, carousel, grid, and film stripe [7]. Effective patterns should reflect user's mental models and the way users organize and process information.

Limited screen size has caused a design challenge to information display patterns and effectiveness of applying desktop designs to mobile platform unsettled. Since 2007, research has been directed to reassessment of display pattern usability, specifically on efficiency, error rate, and subjective satisfaction. In [45], the fisheye list was compared to the vertical list on satisfaction and learnability, which was measured in terms of task execution time in this study. The study was carried out with 12 participants, aged 10 to 39. The results showed that the vertical list was better than the fisheye menu in task execution time; thus, the vertical list was superior to the fisheye list in terms of learnability. Despite being more efficient, the vertical list was less preferred as the fisheye menu was more visually appealing [45]. Another study compared a list-based to a grid-based interface on click-path error and task execution time. The two layouts were very common on mobile devices [46]. The prototypes in Finley's study were mobilized versions of the existing website of a university. He ran the experiment with 20 participants, who were experienced mobile phone users, and all of them were students, staffs, or faculty members of the university. The results showed that grid-based interface was significantly more efficient, and it was rated as more appealing and more comfortable by the users [46].

Besides the layouts, there has been an argument that interaction concepts established on desktops work only with restrictions [47]. Due to limited screen size, list scrolling and item selection can be more demanding on mobile devices than on desktops. Breuninger et al. [47] compared seven different types of touch screen scrolling lists on three metrics: input speed, input error, and user subjective rating. The seven types of list included (1) scrollbar, (2) page-wise scrolling with arrow buttons, (3) page-wise scrolling with direct manipulation, (4) direct manipulation of a continuous list with simulated physics, (5) direct manipulation of a continuous list without simulated physics, (6) direct manipulation of a continuous list with simulated physics and an alphabetical index bar, and (7) direct manipulation of a continuous list without simulated physics and with an alphabetical index bar. The results indicated that there were variations in efficiency of different list scrolling mechanisms. The input speed and error rate of "page-wise scrolling with direct manipulation without physics" were significantly higher than other interaction types. Although the differences between other interaction types were not significant, participants most preferred direct manipulation with simulated physics [47].

To compensate difficulty of input precision, interaction with mobile devices was sometimes done through a stylus, pressure sensing, or alternative interaction styles. Quinn and Cockburn [48] proposed "Zoofing," which was a list selection interface for touch or pen devices. The experiment asserted that the Zoofing technique outperformed conventional scrolling interaction on selection time and input errors [48].

6.3. Control and Confirmation. Physical and cognitive limits of human users often cause unwanted errors that can be trivial to drastic. On computer systems, control and confirmation dialogues are being used to prevent errors, typically user errors. A confirmation dialogue is used when a decision point is reached and user must confirm an action or choose between options. Control dialogue is used to prevent against accidental user-selected destruction, for example, exit guard and cancel and delete protection [7]. Since 2007, there has been no research regarding control and confirmation dialogues on mobile devices.

6.4. Revealing More Information. Two common types for revealing more information are to display in a full page and revealing in a context. Revealing in a full page is generally part of a process, where large amounts of content will be displayed. Revealing in context is generally used when information should be revealed quickly and within a context. Some of the patterns for revealing more information include pop-up, window shade, hierarchical list, and returned results [7]. Since 2007, there has been no research regarding patterns in revealing more information on mobile devices.

6.5. Lateral Access. Lateral access components provide faster access to categories of information. Two common patterns for lateral access are tabs and pagination. There are several benefits of using lateral access, including limiting number of levels of information users must drill through, reducing constant returning to a main page, and reducing the use of long list [7]. Since 2007, there has been no research regarding lateral access on mobile devices.

6.6. Navigation (Links). A link is a common element available on all platforms. It supports navigation and provides access to additional content, generally by loading a new page or jumping to another section within the current page [7]. Early research was primarily conducted on desktop environment and mainly supports web surfing.

Navigation on small screen of mobile devices can be more challenging. Typical web navigation technique tends to support depth-first search. In other words, users select a link on a page, then a new page would be loaded; and the

process would repeat until the users find the information they need [49]. This method is more difficult on mobile environment, as the navigation is constrained by small screen size. It was found that search behavior on mobile device was different from that on desktop. Most mobile users used mobile devices for directed search, where the objective was to find a predetermined topic of interest with minimum divergence by unrelated links [49, 50]. Some alternative solutions to tackle this issue were to show a thumbnail of the page [51]. However, the thumbnail approach may benefit only desktops. Thumbnail is a scaled down version of the target page. Thus, it contains exceeded unnecessary amount of information when displayed on mobile screen. An alternative method may be needed for mobile devices. Setlur et al. [49] and Setlur [50] proposed context-based icons "SemantiLynx" to support navigation on mobile devices. SemantiLynx automatically generated icons that revealed information content of a web page, by semantically meaningful images and keywords. User studies found that SemantiLynx yielded quicker response and improved search performance [49, 50].

Another challenge to navigation on mobile devices is to display large amount of information on a small screen. Large amount of information makes it more difficult for users to navigate through pages and select information they need. Early research on desktop employed gaze tracking technique to utilize navigation; however, peripheral devices and software were required in this approach [52]. Cheng et al. [53] proposed a new method for gaze tracking which utilized the front camera of mobile devices. The performance on the prototype was satisfactory; however, comparison to conventional navigation technique was still lacking.

Another challenge for mobile interaction is the need for visual attention [54]. As stated, contexts of use of desktop computers and mobile devices are different. Desktop computers are always stationary, whereas mobile device is ubiquitous. Users can use mobile devices while doing some other activities, such as walking, carrying objects, or driving. This brings about inconvenience when users cannot always look at the screen. Aural interface or audio-based interface is an alternative solution. Users can listen to the content in text-to-speech form and sometimes look at the screen. However, it is difficult to design aural interface for large information architecture. Backtracking to previous pages is even more demanding, as users are forced to listen to some part of the page to recognize the content. Yang et al. [54] proposed topic- and list-based interface to support backnavigation on aural interface. In topic-based backnavigation, the navigation went back to visited topic, rather than visited pages. In list-based backnavigation, the navigation went back to visited list of items, rather than visited pages. The study found that topic-based and list-based backnavigation enabled faster access to previous page and improved navigation experience.

6.7. Buttons. Button is one of the most common design elements across all platforms. It is typically used to initiate actions (i.e., standalone button) or to select among alternatives (i.e., radio button) [7]. Early research covered several topics, including button size and spacing, tactile and audio feedback, and designing for users with disabilities [55–58].

Since 2007, research direction has been strongly influenced by touchscreen characteristics. Touchscreen enabled more versatility in interface designing as a large proportion of the device is no longer occupied by physical buttons; however, this brings about a new design challenge—the lack of physical response and tactile feedback. Without physical responses, users have less confidence on the consequences of their actions which eventually compromise system usability [59]. Studies indicated that tactile feedback improved efficiency, error rate satisfaction, and user experience [60]. Nevertheless, not all types of the feedback are equally effective. There are certain factors that contribute to tactile feedback quality. The first factor is the realistic feel of physical touch. Park et al. [59] compared different styles of tactile effects, to evaluate perceived realism of physical response and user preference. The varied styles of tactile effects included slow/fast, bumpy/smooth, soft/hard, weak/strong, vague/distinct, light/heavy, and dull/clear responses. The results found that participants preferred the clear or smooth tactile clicks over dull ones for virtual buttons [59]. Besides the realistic feel of physical touch, simultaneity of touch-feedback and the effects of latency is another factor that influences tactile feedback quality. In [58], latency was varied from 0 to 300 ms. for tactile, audio, and visual feedback modalities. The results showed that long latency worsened perceived quality. The perceived quality was satisfactory when latency was between 0 and 100 ms. for visual feedback and between 0 and 70 ms. for tactile and audio feedback. When the latency condition was 300 ms., quality of the buttons dropped significantly for all modalities of feedback [58]. Koskinen et al.'s study [60] considered user preference towards different tactile feedback modalities. They compared three conditions of virtual button feedback—(1) Tactile and audio, (2) tactile and vibration, and (3) nontactile—to find the most preferred style of feedback. The results suggest the using nontactile feedback was least preferred by the users. It also yielded the lowest user performance which was measured by time to complete tasks and error rate. Tactile and audio feedback was more pleasant and better in user performance than the tactile and vibration one; however, the differences were not significant [60].

Another challenge is the high demand for visual attention. As stated, mobile devices are designed for ubiquity. Users may need to do some other activities simultaneously while using the devices. Pressing virtual buttons can be more difficult, and incorrect operations can occur more frequently as users need to divide their attention to the environment. To compromise high error rate, studies on spatial design of virtual buttons were carried out to explore the appropriate button size, spacing between buttons, and ordered mapping of buttons [55–57]. Conradi et al.'s study [56] investigated the optimal size (5×5 mm, 8×8 mm, 11×11 mm, and 14×14 mm.) of virtual buttons for use while walking. The results found significant differences on errors and time on task between the smallest size (5×5 mm) and all other button sizes. Walking also had a significant influence on errors for all button sizes. The influence was magnified with smaller buttons. The findings of this study suggested that larger buttons were recommended for the use while walking [56]. Haptic

button is another approach to tackle the challenge. Pakkanen et al. [61] compared three designs for creating haptic button edges: simple, GUI transformation, and designed. The stimuli in the simple design were accompanied with single bursts, and identical stimuli were utilized whether towards or away from the buttons. GUI transformation stimuli were combined with several bursts. When moving over the edge, the burst raised from the minimum to maximum, and the burst decreased from maximum to minimum when moving away from the edge. In designed stimuli, when moving off the button, there was a single burst which simulated slipping off the buttons. The results indicated that simple and designed stimuli were most promising. Furthermore, stimuli with fast, clear, and sharp responses were good choice for the haptic button edge. Another complementation for the demand for visual attention is to utilize physical buttons, such as a power-up button [62]. Spelmezan et al. [62] showed a prototype that can use a power-up button to operate functions, such as clicking, selecting a combo box, and scrolling a scrollbar. Even though the preliminary experiment yielded promising results, the prototype required the installation of additional sensors: proximity sensor, and pressure sensor [62].

Besides the lack of tactile feedback and demand for visual attention, touching gesture can be hard for users with fine motor disabilities. Pressing a small size button requires high precision in fine motor control, and different contact time on buttons may alter actions (e.g., touching and pressing). Sesto et al. [55] investigated the effect of button size, spacing, and fine motor disability on touch characteristics (i.e., exerted force, impulses, and dwell time). The results showed that touch characteristics were affected by the button size, but not spacing. The users with fine motor disability had greater impulses and dwell time when touching buttons than nondisabled users. The findings of this study can guide designers in designing an optimal size and touch characteristics to enhance accessibility of virtual button [55].

6.8. Icons. An icon is a visual representation that provides users with access to a target destination or a function in a cursorily manner [7]. Icons serve altogether three different functions. Those functions are (1) an access to a function or target destination, (2) an indicator of system statuses, and (3) a changer of system behaviors [7]. The topics of early research extended to various areas, including the use of icons to convey application status; interpretation of icon meaning, icon recognition, and comprehensibility of icons; appropriate size of an icon; and influences of cultural and age differences on icon interpretation [63–65].

Since 2007, research has been directed to two major areas: icon usability and influences of individual differences (age and culture). Research on icon usability examined several icon qualities and how they affected system usability. Usability of an icon is usually determined by findability, recognition, interpretation, and attractiveness [66]. On mobile devices, the usability measurement criteria can be different. Touch screen allows direct manipulation using a finger. Interactive elements became smaller on a mobile touchscreen; thus, the finger occlusion often occurs. Touchable area is one of the mobile usability components that dictates an activation area of an interactive element. Im et al. [67] studied the suitable touchable area to improve touch accuracy for an icon. The study looked into the icon width-to-height ratio (0.5, 0.7, and 0.9) and the grid size (3 × 4, 4 × 5, 5 × 6, and 6 × 8). User performance was determined by input offset, hit rate, task completion time, and preference. The study found that 3 × 4 and 4 × 5 grid sizes and the icon ratio of 0.9 had better performance than the others [67]. In addition to touch accuracy, shape and figure-background ratio of icons had the effect findability. In a vast array of icons, visual search time must be minimized to assure system usability and user satisfaction. Luo and Zhou [68] investigated the effects of icon-background shape and the figure-background ratio on findability. Seven background shapes in Luo and Zhou's study [68] included (1) isosceles triangle, (2) isosceles trapezoid, (3) regular pentagon, (4) regular hexagon, (5) rounded square, (6) square, and (7) circle. Five figure-background ratios were 90%, 70%, 50%, 30%, and 10%. The results showed that unified background yielded better findability. The optimal ratio was, however, related to a screen size; the smaller the screen, the higher the figure-background ratio [68].

Being aesthetic is another criterion of icon usability, and color contributes to aesthetic quality of an icon. However, preference towards colors and color combinations can be difficult to measure objectively. Huang [69] explored the degree of agreement of subjective aesthetic preferences for different icon-background color combinations. In total, 3306 color combinations were rated. The results showed that 30 color combinations consistently had high preference scores. The rating was consistent between male and female participants; specifically, there was no significant effect of gender differences. Thus, it was suggested to use certain color combinations to create appealing aesthetics. Besides aesthetic values, colors are also used to convey messages [69]. Ju et al. [70] conducted a study to find out whether there was a relationship between the change of icon colors and the implicit message behind the changes. The study found that participants could perceive the relationship between application status and the change of colors [70].

The second research direction on icons was to investigate the effects of individual differences on icon usability. The focus was on cultural differences [63, 70, 71] and age differences [64, 65, 72–76]. The studies on cultural differences primarily concerned icon interpretation and whether it was affected by culture. The results, however, were not consistent. Only some of the studies found cultural influences on icon interpretability, whereas some did not. Ghayas et al. [72] compared the user performances from two different cultures: Malaysian and Estonian. The results found that Malaysian users could interpret more concrete icons than abstract icons, whereas Estonian users performed better with abstract icons [72]. Chanwimalueng and Rapeepisarn [77] compared performances of Easterners (Thai, Malaysian, and Indonesian users) and Westerners (Finnish and German users). In contrast to Ghayas et al. [72], no cultural differences on icon recognition, interpretation, and preference were found in Chanwimalueng and Rapeepisarn's study [77]. Rather, icon recognition was influenced by icon concreteness and abstractness. Pappachan and Ziefle [71] investigated the

cultural effects on icon interpretation as well. The results showed that icon interpretability greatly depended on icon complexity and concreteness. The results of Chanwimalueng and Rapeepisarn [77] and Pappachan and Ziefle [71] imply that culture may have only small effect, and icon interpretation should be regarded as cultural-unspecific. Abstractness causes larger effect and deteriorates icon usability.

Similar to the studies on cultural differences, the primary concern of the studies on age differences focused on icons interpretation. Since 2007, several studies have been conducted, and their results were consistent. Gatsou et al. [65] carried out a study to find any differences in recognition rate among age groups. The participants underwent the recognition test on sample icons that were selected from different mobile device brands. Although the participant's recognition rate varied among icons, the recognition rate dropped as age increased. Kim and Cho [76] conducted an evaluation study to evaluate multiple cognitive abilities of different age groups, including button comprehension, icon interpretation, vocabulary comprehension, menu comprehension, perceived icon size, and perceived text size. The study found that performance time and error rate increased as age increased. Koutsourelakis and Chorianopoulos [75] also studied whether typical mobile phone icons could be interpreted by senior users. Younger and older participants underwent the icon recognition test. There were significant differences in icon recognition and interpretation performance of younger and older users. The results of Gatsou et al. [65], Kim and Cho [76], and Koutsourelakis and Chorianopoulos [75] suggested that the older participants had more problems using mobile icons. More studies looked into what factors contribute to icon usability for senior users. Leung et al. [64] found that the factors included semantically close meaning (i.e., natural link between icon picture and associated function), familiarity with icons, labelling, and concreteness [64]. Ghayas et al. [72] also found that visual complexity affected icon usability for senior users. Apart from icon interpretation, icon color is another important icon characteristic that assists icon discrimination. Kuo and Wu [73] studied the discrimination of colors and no-saturation icons and color combination between icons and interface background. The results showed that colored icons were more distinguishable than no-saturation icons for elder users. Some color combinations were more difficult for older users to differentiate, such as green and blue. Salman et al. [74] proposed the participatory icon design that could reduce system complexity and increase usability. The results of participatory approach in icon design were successful.

The studies of Gatsou et al. [65], Leung et al. [64], Ghayas et al. [72], and Koutsourelakis and Chorianopoulos [75] show the effect of age on icon usability. The older users have problems in interpreting icons, probably because of technological inexperience. Icon characteristics—complexity, concreteness, semantic closeness, and labelling—contributed to icon usability. These should be regarded as age-unspecific.

6.9. Information Control. Limited size of mobile devices constraints the amount of information to be displayed on the screen. Information control mechanisms such as zooming and scaling, searching, and sorting and filtering have been utilized to assist users in finding, accessing, and focusing on intended information while minimizing unrelated information [7].

Zooming and scaling provide the ability to change the level of detail in dense information, such as charts, graphs, or maps [7]. There are several techniques used in zooming, for instance, on-screen buttons, hardware buttons, interactive scale, and on-screen gesture. Early studies on zooming covered several areas, including screen size, readability, font size, selection precision, and designing for visual-impaired and senior users [78, 79].

Since 2007, research direction on zooming is influenced by the limited screen size. Zooming methods are determined by device manufacturers, and there was no evaluation carried out to examine their usability. Garcia-Lopez et al. [78] examined the most efficient, effective, and satisfying zooming methods by comparing zooming techniques from 19 different devices. The study found no significant differences on efficiency and effectiveness among zooming techniques. Nevertheless, users preferred using links to zoom in and zoom out.

Zooming on a touchscreen relies on gesture. Children at very young age have limited fine motor skills; thus, they can probably face difficulty in manipulating gestures. Hamza [80] carried out research to examine children ability to perform touch screen gestures. The results showed that young children (aged 4 and 5) were able to do gestures; however, older children were more accurate in the interaction with the screen. Although children were able to interact with the screen, the size of the targets had significant effect on accuracy [80].

Searching is another information control function which allows users to quickly access specific information within a long list or huge data array [7]. Early studies on search covered several topics, including load and query, full-text search, and voice input [81, 82]. Research direction on search function since 2007 is also influenced by the limited screen size. Search function normally requires user-supplied text to query the results; however, the limited screen size constrains text input convenience and precision [83]. Thus, searching on mobile devices can be more demanding. An alternative solution to tackle the challenge is by minimizing a demand for user-supplied text. Shin et al. [82] proposed a semantic search prototype, to reduce the amount of full-text search. Semantic approach enables keyword-based search where users can search for intended information without entering exact search terms. A preliminary experiment revealed better user experience results using the proposed prototype compared with full-text search [82]. Church and Smyth [83] suggested that context information, such as time and location, should be integrated to mobile search to help search engine in retrieving more relevant information. For instance, when users in a shopping mall searched by the word "Apple", the users would be more likely to look for an Apple Store than the nearest apple farm. In this approach, users would be less likely to experience a long list of irrelevant search results. However, no preliminary experiment was conducted to compare the context-based search with the conventional one. Gesture-based interaction is also utilized to enable

fast mobile search. Li [81] proposed a gesture-based search technique which enabled a fast access to mobile data such as contacts, applications, and music tracks by drawing gestures. A longitudinal study showed that gesture search enabled a quicker way for accessing mobile data, and users reacted positively to the usefulness and usability of gesture search technique [81].

The previous paragraph discussed how limited screen size constrained user text entry and how that affected the design of information search and retrieval. Apart from that, limited screen size also influences the amount of search results to be displayed at a time. Early web design guidelines suggested that the number of search results per page should be around 30–40 sites, as users usually do not look at the search results that are not in top 30 [84]. The study was intended for desktop platform and carried out only with adult participants. Zhou et al. [85] conducted a study to investigate how many search results should be displayed on mobile device for older users. Older adults have decline in their selective attention [39]; thus, they may be able to grasp limited amount of information at a time. The results showed that most of the participants in the study preferred 30–40 search results per page, which was consistent with the existing guideline.

Sorting and filtering is another important information control function used on mobile devices. Sorting and filtering aids exploratory search by disclosing search options to narrow relevant results [7]. Early studies on sorting and filtering focused on data organizational patterns. Sorting and filtering criteria are usually predefined and cannot be changed, and the system generally allows users to apply only one criterion at a time. However, in practice, multiple criteria could be applied in sorting and filtering. Panizzi and Marzo [86] proposed that the users should be enabled to sort items by using multiple criteria. However, no preliminary experiment was conducted to evaluate the proposed framework, and the authors did not highlight how the proposed idea was related to mobile-specific context.

6.10. Input Mode and Selection. Input and selection concern the methods by which users communicate to computer devices. On desktops, user input is received from major peripheral devices, such as keyboards and mice, and output is displayed through different channels. In contrast, a touch-screen works as both input and output channels. This has brought about changes to input methods; for instance, mouse gestures are replaced by touch gestures, and physical keys are replaced by virtual miniature keys. This has made data inputting on mobile devices more challenging task.

Prior to 2007, research objectives can be classified into two main areas. The first one was to study factors that affected input accuracy, for instance, visual distraction, user's sensorimotor coordination, blindness, and aging [87–91]. The second one was to improve input accuracy, for instance, changing keyboard layouts and increasing input feedback [92, 93]. Since 2007, research objectives are becoming more diverse. The objectives can be classified into seven areas: effects of finger and thumb on input accuracy, user factors, novice users, external factors, eye-free interaction, large form input techniques, and alternative input methods.

A number of studies were carried out to examine how finger and thumb interaction affected input accuracy. When entering text, users preferred to use their finger than a stylus [94, 95]. As the size of the keys is too small, finger occlusion often occurs. A small size of a key can also induce the lack of visual perception; in other words, a finger can block user's perception while they are pressing the key. This consequently affects input accuracy. It has been suggested that the appropriate size for a key that guaranteed a greater hit rate was 9.2 mm, with 95% touchable area [96]. A touchable area is an area around the key that could activate the respective key. An intended key might not be selected if the touchable area is too small (e.g., 90%), but larger touchable area (e.g., 99%) does not necessarily yield more precise selection as it could activate unintended neighboring keys. These numbers, however, were based on touch interaction tests with an index finger [96]. On actual usage, some users prefer using their thumb, while other users prefer using their finger. Compared to finger-based interaction, research found that thumb-based interaction on virtual keyboards showed a 30% drop in throughput, as well as a significant drop in speed and accuracy. Furthermore, thumb-based interaction had lower stability in hand gripping [97]. Despite apparent drawbacks of thumb-based interaction, users prefer using it [98]; perhaps thumb-based interaction freed the other hand from the screen to attend to other events [99]. A few studies looked into designs for thumb-based interaction and found that there were four factors that impacted accuracy of thumb-based interaction: the size of the key, key location, thumb length, and user age [100, 101]. Similar to index finger interaction, input accuracy of thumb interaction increased as the size of the key increases, and the key must be located within the areas that can be easily reached by a thumb, which were the bottom-left, the center, and the upper-right area [100]. Thumb coverage area was also influenced by users' thumb length and their age. Older users and users with longer thumbs were likely to leave unreached space around the bottom-right corner and the bottom edge of the screen [101]. This suggested consideration for positioning interactive elements for generic and older users. The studies, however, did not discuss handedness and thumb lengths of different ethnicity.

Besides effects of finger and thumb, other aspects of user factors were examined. Major interest was on elderly users. Usability assessment and accessibility issues have always come after technology. Seemingly, there is a necessity of establishing design guidelines for elderly users, as it was reported that elderly users faced difficulties in using mobile phones as the phones were not properly designed for them [102]. To tackle difficulties, there were applications that modified default interface into a more accessible and friendly interface for elderly users. Diaz-Bossini and Moreno [87] compared sample interface-modifying applications against accessibility guidelines, but they found that the applications did not meet requirements for accessibility. The study was, however, based on accessibility guidelines for websites (e.g., W3C, WDG) as there was a lack of guidelines for mobile context [87]. A set of design recommendations for elderly users was presented by De Barros et al. [88]. The recommendations covered navigation, interaction, and visual design,

but the recommendation did not address specific differences between desktop and mobile devices. Moreover, they were based merely on observation [88]. This illustrates the need of empirically based guidelines to assist designers in designing accessible applications in mobile context.

More studies were carried out to assess usability of the existing input methods. Stößel [103] compared younger and older users on gestures with variation in familiarity (i.e., familiar versus unfamiliar gestures). In general performance, older users performed accurately as younger users; however, the older users were significantly slower (1.3 times slower) and less accurate with unfamiliar gesture [103]. This suggests consideration for choosing gesture and specifying gesture timeout time for older users. Text entry is another challenging task for elderly users. The lack of haptic feedback and small key size make it harder for the elderly to accurately select targets [104]. Several input controls, such as autocompletion, word prediction, drop-down list, and using locally stored data, are adopted from desktops to facilitate manual text entry [7]. However, the input controls were not as efficient as on desktops. Rodrigues et al. [104] presented five keyboard variants to support manual text entry. These variants were different in color, width, size, and touch area of most probable letters or displaying predicted words. Although all variants slightly improved input errors, there were variations in their efficiency. Color, width, and predicted word variants were more visually distracting, and they were slower than size and touch area variants and QWERTY keyboard. This suggested consideration for choosing appropriate keyboard variant and text-entry support for elderly users [104]. Input usability assessment studies for children users were rarer. A study by Anthony et al. [89] investigated usability of visual feedback for adult and children users. They found that participants of both age groups seemed confused by the absence of feedback, but the results were magnified for children [89]. Anthony et al.'s study [89] was one of a few studies that investigated children users and input on mobile devices. Yet, many areas were left unexamined for children users, and it could be an opportunity for future research.

Besides age differences, the research focus was on users with disorders or disabilities. The most popular topics were in users with blindness. The lack of tactile buttons obstructed blind users in locating interactive components and inputting commands. A common practice is to use audio augmentation techniques, such as voice-over (a.k.a. screen reader) and speech recognition [90, 91]. However, audio augmentation techniques can be interfered with by background noise [90], and the performance of audio augmentation techniques is also influenced by algorithm recognition accuracy. Recent studies have designed and developed a gesture-based set of commands [90] and tangible bendable gestures for blind users [91]. The studies highlighted that the gestures designed for blind users should be logical and easy to learn and remember, as blind users rely much on their memories [91]. Other topics on user factors include users with upper extremity disabilities [105], users with ALS [106], and users with Down's syndrome [107]. This group of users face difficulties in precisely controlling their hands; thus, designers should consider selecting simple gestures (e.g., tapping) and flexible error handling and avoiding gestures that involve a great degree of hand-eye coordination (e.g., dragging and rotating).

A few studies looked into novice users. Mobile input methods could spell trouble for inexperienced users. Standard QWERTY keyboard bombarded users with many keys, and touch gestures had no standards or guidelines to show the users what they could do or how they could interact with the systems [92, 93]. Geary [93] proposed alternative keyboard layouts to assist novice users. The more frequently used characters, based on MacKenzie and Soukoreff [108] and NetLingo.com [109], were arranged closer to the center of the keyboard, as it was the area that can be easily reached when users used one or two thumbs to type. However, the results of the experiments in Geary's study indicated no significant improvement from standard QWERTY was found. Lundgren and Hjulström [92] proposed visual hinting for touch gestures. However, the idea of visual hinting was not empirically verified, and it was not tested whether visuals were the best way to hint interaction [92].

Apart from user factors, external factors also influenced input efficiency. Durrani [110] found that environmental condition, cognitive load, and communication load had effects on input efficiency.

Eye-free interaction was another research interest. Besides the absence of tangible buttons, environmental contexts of use of mobile devices were also different. Desktop computers were stationary, whereas mobile devices were ubiquitous. When users used mobile devices, they may simultaneously move or do other activities. This could turn input and selection into demanding tasks. While users needed to focus on mobile screen which required high visual attention, they also needed to pay attention to their environment at the same time [111]. Ng et al. [112] found that input accuracy for tapping interaction dropped to 65% while users were walking and to 53% while they were carrying objects. Input accuracy for tapping was noted as the highest among other touch gestures. Eye-free interaction can be optimal solution to increase accuracy. Nevertheless, there were no empirical studies that may lead to establishing design guidelines for eye-free interaction. Touch screen interface is also gaining popularity in in-car interactive systems. This can be a great design challenge. As stated, a touch screen highly demands visual attention; however, when using in-car touch screen, the touch screen can minimally distract user (i.e., driver) from the main task which was driving. Otherwise, it could lead into an accident. Louveton et al. [111] assessed three different interface layouts and interaction: binary selection (e.g., yes/no), list selection, and slide bar. The results indicated that the binary selection was most efficient and demanded the lowest eye fixation, whereas the slide bar was least efficient and demanded the highest eye fixation [111]. However, more usability studies are needed to identify appropriate layouts and interaction for in-car interactive systems.

A form input can be a design challenge, as it can be too complex to display or to navigate on a small screen. There were only few studies that compared different input forms. Balagtas-Fernandez et al. [113] assessed two layouts (i.e., scrolling list and tabs), two input methods (i.e., keyboard and modal dialogue), and two menu designs (i.e., device menu and context menu). The results indicated that the scrolling, modal dialogue, and the device menu were more efficient [113]. El Batran and Dunlop [114] compared two form navigation methods: tabbing and pan and zoom. The results showed that the pan and zoom technique was more efficient. Nevertheless, there are more styles of input forms and navigation techniques that can be subjected to usability assessment.

Alternative input methods were another research interest. The main objective of the studies in this category was to propose novel techniques to improve input accuracy. As the key size was very small, finger occlusion usually occurred. One solution to compensate finger occlusion was the regional correction. Regional correction was a dictionary-based predictive text-entry method that activated not only the intended key but also neighboring keys. This method selected valid words available in a dictionary for automatic input correction. A study found that the regional correction method reduced time and the number of touches required to complete text entry, but only when the keys were small (i.e., 18 pixels). No significant differences were found between using and not using the regional correction when the keys were large (i.e., 26 and 34 pixels) [115]. Some novel techniques were also proposed to deal with input imprecision. Koarai and Komuro [116] proposed a system which used two cameras in combination with a touch panel to track user input. The preliminary experiment revealed a lower number of errors when the proposed technique was used, comparing to nonzoomed text entry. However, the proposed technique required the installation of additional equipment [116]. Some mobile gears, such as a smart watch, had a very compact-size screen; thus, entering text from such devices is even more difficult. Oney et al. [79] proposed an interaction called zoom-board to enable text entry from ultrasmall devices. The proposed technique used the iterative zooming to enlarge tiny keyboard to comfortable size. The preliminary experiment showed promising input rate from zoom-board interaction [79]. Some other novel techniques include lens gestures [117], multistroked gesture [118], ambiguous keyboard input [119, 120], effect of key size [115], and five-key text-entry technique [121]. Nevertheless, these novel techniques required empirical evaluation, to validate their usability with collected evidence.

7. Findings

To recapitulate, this article seeks to answer two research questions:

RQ1: in each area, what factors were concentrated?

RQ2: what areas of mobile user interface design patterns had insufficient information?

This section elaborates the findings from surveying the literature.

Table 4 shows the information about page composition research. The range of research on page composition since 2007 was narrower than before 2007. The concentration on this area was whether limited screen size affected menu

TABLE 4: Page composition research.

Research topics prior to 2007	Research topics since 2007	Factors of interest since 2007	Unexamined/other possible topics
(i) 2D and 3D menus (ii) Depth and breadth (iii) Menu adaptation (iv) Item ordering (v) Item categorization (vi) Task complexity (vii) Menu patterns (viii) Help fields (ix) Methodological studies (x) Language abilities (xi) Spatial abilities (xii) Visual characteristics (xiii) User expertise	(i) 2D and 3D menus (ii) Age differences (spatial ability, verbal memory, visual abilities, psychomotor skills, self-efficacy) (iii) Cultural differences (Westerners versus Easterners) (iv) Menu adaptation	(i) Whether limited screen size affect menu usability (ii) Efficiency (iii) User preference (iv) Satisfaction	(i) Depth and breadth (ii) Item ordering (iii) Item categorization (iv) Task complexity (v) Menu patterns (vi) Help fields (vii) Methodological studies (viii) Language abilities (ix) Spatial abilities (x) Visual characteristics (xi) User expertise (xii) User with unique need (e.g., children, disabled users, user with impairments)

usability, efficiency, user preference, and satisfaction. There were several topics that were unexamined by experimental studies.

Table 5 shows the information about display of information research. The range of research since 2007 was wider than before 2007. However, the topics were still very limited. The concerns in this area were if limited screen size affects list access, efficiency, selection errors, and satisfaction. Several topics were unexamined by experimental studies.

Table 6 shows the information about control and confirmation research. There has been no research on control and confirmation. There were several topics that were unexamined by experimental studies. This demonstrates a huge research gap in this area.

Table 7 shows the information about revealing more information research. There has been no research on revealing more information. There were several topics that were unexamined by experimental studies. This demonstrates a huge research gap in this area.

Table 8 shows the information about lateral access research. There has been no research on lateral access. There were several topics that were unexamined by experimental studies. This demonstrates a huge research gap in this area.

Table 9 shows the information about navigation research. The range of research topics since 2007 was wider than before 2007. However, the topics were still very limited. The major concerns in this area were whether content navigation was affected by screen size and how to tackle the demand for visual attention in navigation, efficiency, selection errors, and satisfaction. There were several topics that were unexamined by experimental studies.

Table 10 shows the information about button research. The topics of research since 2007 were greater than before 2007. The concerns in this area were to simulate realistic feeling of physical buttons on touchscreen. The factors of interest include user preference, experience, accuracy, errors, efficiency, exerted force, impulse, and dwell time. There were several topics that were unexamined by experimental studies.

Table 11 shows the information about icon research. The major concerns in this area were influences of cultural and age differences on icon interpretation, aesthetic qualities of icons, and touchable areas of icons. The factors of interest include icon recognition and interpretation.

Table 12 shows the information about information control research. The major concerns in this area were how small screen size of mobile devices affects zooming, searching, and filtering. The factors of interest include efficiency, effectiveness, and precision.

Table 13 shows the information about input mode and selection research. The range of research topics since 2007 was wider than before 2007. The factors of interest include input accuracy, efficiency, errors, key size, touchable area, location of interactive elements, and eye fixation.

8. Discussion, Conclusions, and Limitations

Mobile platforms have called for attention from HCI community. Although there are several studies investigating dimensions related to mobile user interface, a standard of mobile user interface design patterns has not been established. This current article provides an overview of the existing studies on mobile UI design patterns and covers altogether 10 different categories.

8.1. Discussion. The research on page composition (menu) was quite narrow. Since 2007, the topics included usability assessment of 2D and 3D menus, adaptive menus, influence of cultures on item categorization scheme, and influence of aging on menu navigation. The primary concern was whether the limited screen size affected menu usability. The factors of interest included menu efficiency, user preference, and satisfaction, as it is important for users to promptly select the target menu item and complete intended tasks in timely manner. This positively affects users' preference and satisfaction towards the system. In menu navigation study, verbal memory and spatial abilities were also subjected to investigation, as they were related to navigation performance. The review showed that data from menu research are insufficient to establish guidelines for mobile menu patterns. Empirical-based knowledge of what type of menus should be

TABLE 5: Display of information research.

Research topics prior to 2007	Research topics since 2007	Factors of interest since 2007	Unexamined/other possible topics
(i) Evaluation of list patterns	(i) Applying desktop design to mobile (ii) Evaluation of list scrolling styles (iii) Evaluation of list patterns (iv) Novel scrolling techniques	(i) Whether list access was affected mobile screen size (ii) Efficiency (iii) Selection errors (iv) Satisfaction	(i) Other list patterns (ii) User with unique need (e.g., the elderly, children, disabled users, user with impairments)

TABLE 6: Control and confirmation research.

Research topics prior to 2007	Research topics since 2007	Factors of interest since 2007	Unexamined/other possible topics
(i) N/A	(i) N/A	(i) N/A	(i) Designing error message for mobile screen (ii) Error prevention (iii) Error recovery (iv) Users with difficulties in controlling fine muscles (e.g., the elderly, children, upper extremities impaired users)

TABLE 7: Revealing more information research.

Research topics prior to 2007	Research topics since 2007	Factors of interest since 2007	Unexamined/other possible topics
(i) N/A	(i) N/A	(i) N/A	(i) Applying desktop techniques of revealing more information to mobile screen

TABLE 8: Lateral access research.

Research topics prior to 2007	Research topics since 2007	Factors of interest since 2007	Unexamined/other possible topics
(i) N/A	(i) N/A	(i) N/A	(i) Applying desktop techniques of lateral access to mobile screen

TABLE 9: Navigation research.

Research topics prior to 2007	Research topics since 2007	Factors of interest since 2007	Unexamined/other possible topics
(i) Web surfing on desktops	(i) Displaying contents on mobile screen (ii) Previewing content (iii) Gaze tracking (iv) Aural interface	(i) Whether content navigation was affected by mobile screen size (ii) How to tackle high demand for visual attention in navigation (iii) Efficiency (iv) Selection errors (v) Satisfaction	(i) Evaluation of other list patterns (ii) User with unique need (e.g., the elderly, children, disabled users, user with impairments)

TABLE 10: Button research.

Research topics prior to 2007	Research topics since 2007	Factors of interest since 2007	Unexamined/other possible topics
(i) Button size (ii) Button spacing (iii) Tactile feedback (iv) Audio feedback (v) Users with disabilities	(i) Simulating realistic response of physical buttons on touchscreen (ii) Latency of response (iii) Usability of feedback modalities	(i) User preference (ii) Experience (iii) Accuracy (iv) Errors (v) Efficiency (vi) Exerted force (vii) Impulse (viii) Dwell time	(i) Applying desktop techniques of lateral access to mobile screen

TABLE 11: Icon research.

Research topics prior to 2007	Research topics since 2007	Factors of interest since 2007	Unexamined/other possible topics
(i) Interpretation of icon meaning (ii) Icon recognition (iii) Comprehensibility (iv) Appropriate size of icon (v) Cultural differences on icon interpretation (vi) Age differences on icon interpretation (vii) Using icon to convey application status	(i) Touchable area of icon (ii) Effect of icon-background shape on findability (iii) Aesthetic (iv) Cultural difference on icon interpretation (v) Age differences on icon interpretation	(i) Icon recognition (ii) Icon interpretation	(i) N/A

TABLE 12: Information control research.

Research topics prior to 2007	Research topics since 2007	Factors of interest since 2007	Unexamined/other possible topics

(i) Zooming
  (a) Screen size
  (b) Readability
  (c) Font size
  (d) Selection precision
  (e) Designing for visual-impaired and senior users
(ii) Searching
  (a) Load and query
  (b) Full-text search
  (c) Voice input
(iii) Sorting and filtering
  (a) Data organization patterns
	(i) Zooming
	  (a) Evaluation of zooming technique
	  (b) Evaluation of zooming gestures with children users
	(ii) Searching
	  (a) Minimizing user input
	  (b) Integration of context information in search
	(iii) Sorting and filtering
	  (a) Enable multiple sorting criteria
		(i) Zooming
		  (a) Efficiency
		  (b) Effectiveness
		(ii) Searching
		  (a) Efficiency
		  (b) Precision
		(iii) Sorting and filtering
		  (a) N/A
			(i) Novel techniques still need validation and evaluation

TABLE 13: Input Mode and Selection Research.

Research topics prior to 2007	Research topics since 2007	Factors of interest since 2007	Unexamined/other possible topics

(i) Factors affecting input accuracy
  (a) Visual distraction
  (b) Sensorimotor coordination
  (c) Blindness
  (d) Aging
(ii) Improving input accuracy
  (a) Alternative keyboard layouts
  (b) Increase input feedback
	(i) Finger and thumb interaction
	(ii) User factors
	  (a) Elderly users
	  (b) Disabilities (blindness, ALS, Down's syndrome)
	(iii) Novice users
	(iv) External factors
	(v) Eye-free interaction
	  (a) Walking
	  (b) Driving
	(vi) Large form input
	(vii) Alternative input methods
		(i) Accuracy
		(ii) Efficiency
		(iii) Errors
		(iv) Key size
		(v) Touchable area
		(vi) Location of interactive elements
		(vii) Eye fixation
			(i) Effect of handedness
			(ii) Effect of finger and thumb lengths
			(iii) Children users
			(iv) Evaluation of interaction elements in in-car usage
			(v) Novel techniques need validation and evaluation

used in what context is still lacking. Many important elements of menu composition were unexamined, for example, menu depth and breadth, item ordering, task complexity, and assessment of other menu layouts. Other user groups with unique needs, such as children and user with disabilities or disorders, were also uninvestigated.

The research on display of information was limited and covered only a few areas. The research included usability evaluation of list scrolling styles and different list patterns (i.e., fisheye and vertical list and grid and vertical list). The key issue was whether list access and usability were affected by a limited screen size. A novel list scrolling technique was also proposed. The factors of interest were efficiency, selection errors, and satisfaction, as it is important for users

to promptly access the target item with minimum errors. This positively affects their preference and satisfaction towards the system. The review showed that empirical data are not sufficient to draw a guideline for display patterns of information. Other list layouts and possible effect of number of items are left unexamined. Moreover, the number of participants in the research was considerably low. Other user factors that may have potential effects, such as elderly users, children, and user with disabilities, were not studied. Clearly, the knowledge of what type of display should be used in what context and for which group of users is still lacking.

There has been no research on control and confirmation, revealing more information, and lateral access categories. These categories are important design elements on mobile devices. The primary function of control and confirmation is to prevent errors, especially user errors. There is an enormous knowledge gap which needs to be filled. For example, error message design cannot be directly adopted from desktop platform; they must be adjusted to fit small size dialogue. Touch screen is also prone to user errors, in particular with users that have difficulties or have not fully developed the control of their fine muscles (e.g., the elderly, children, and user with upper extremity disabilities). Error prevention and error recovery mechanisms needed to be designed for these groups of users. The function of revealing more information is to display larger information for users. With limited screen size, adopting information revealing techniques from desktops can be ineffective. Moreover, the knowledge of what revealing techniques should be used in what context is still lacking. Nevertheless, these issues have not been empirically examined. Lateral access is another important design element. Some examples of lateral access are pagination and tabs. Lateral access provides a faster access to intended information and reduces the use of long lists. With limited screen size of mobile devices, it is still unexamined whether adopting lateral access techniques from desktops is practical.

The research on navigation (links) was limited and covered only some areas. The research included previewing content of web pages, gaze tracking, and designing aural interface. The key concerns were motivated by limited screen size and high demand for visual attention. The factors of interest were efficiency, accuracy, and navigation experience, since it is important for users to accurately and promptly access the target link and find intended information as quick as possible. This positively affects their experience of using the system. More empirical studies are needed to establish guidelines for navigation on mobile screen. Other user factors that may have potential effects are also needed to be examined.

The research on buttons was motivated by the lack of physical response and tactile feedback. The lack of tactile feedback makes users unconfident of their actions which consequently deteriorates system usability. Thus, the primary objective was to simulate realistic response of physical buttons. The research topics included characteristics of response that gave realistic feeling of buttons, latency of response, and usability of different feedback modalities. Unlike other categories that focus on efficiency, the factors of interest of button research primarily concern user preference and experience since it is important for users to experience the realistic response that resembles physical button. Some other studies looked into spatial design of buttons (i.e., button size and spacing), in order to find optimal design that needed less visual attention and match the fine motor abilities of users. The array of factors of interest include accuracy, errors, and efficiency for generic users and exerted force, impulse, and dwell time of pressing for users with fine motor difficulties.

Unlike other categories, the research on icons was almost platform-unspecific. The topics heavily focused on influence of age and culture on icon usability. The factors of interest were icon recognition and icon interpretation, as it is crucial for users to correctly identify and select the right function that

they want. Senior users faced greater problem recognizing and interpreting icons; however, it was due to technological inexperience. It was found that, regardless of culture or age, the factors that contribute to icon usability were icon concreteness, low visual complexity, close semantic distance, user familiarity with icons, and sensible labelling. More studies examined visual qualities of icons, namely, color combination, shape and size of icons, and their influence on icon usability. Only icon study can be regarded as mobile-specific. The study examined optimal touchable area of an icon since it is important for users to select the intended icons, without activating neighboring functions.

Information control encompasses zooming, searching, and sorting and filtering. The research topics were influenced by limited screen size of mobile devices. Studies on zooming included evaluation of different zooming methods and zooming gesture performance of children users. The factors of interest of evaluation study concern efficiency and effectiveness as it is important for users to be able to zoom in and out and promptly select the target item and complete intended tasks in timely manner. The factor of interest of zooming and children study concerns only accuracy, but not efficiency. For children users, it is more important for them to understand gestures and accurately use their hand to do gestures than timely finish their task. Children users have exploratory behaviors; thus, measuring efficiency does not match their behavior. Studies on searching were new searching techniques, including semantic search, context-based search, and gesture-based search. The factors of interest were efficiency and precision, as it is important for users to quickly search for information from accurate and relevant search results. A new idea was proposed in sorting and filtering category; however, the idea was not demonstrated or verified.

As stated, input mode and selection contribute the highest number of papers; thus, the research topics were considerably diverse. The topics were motivated by limited screen size of mobile devices. The first area of topics concerned effects of finger and thumb on input accuracy. Although some mobile models were equipped with a stylus, users prefer using their finger. As the key size is small, finger occlusion often occurs. The factors of interest were accuracy, efficiency, and errors, since it is important for users to promptly and precisely supply input with minimum errors. Other factors include key size, touchable area size, and location of interactive elements as they also contribute to input accuracy and efficiency. However, no studies considered potential factors that would affect touch accuracy, such as handedness, and finger and thumb length of different ethnicity. The second area of topics concerned user factors. The key issue was to study whether and how user characteristics affect input. User groups that were included in the studies were mainly elderly users, blind users, and users with upper extremity disabilities or difficulties. Only one study focused on children. The factors of interest are accuracy and efficiency because it is important for users to promptly and precisely supply input. The third area of research focused on novice users. Mobile devices bombard novice users with many input keys and touch gestures are not visible. The factors of interest are accuracy and efficiency because it is important for novice users to quickly learn the system and precisely supply input. The fourth area concerned external factors. It was found that environmental condition, cognitive load, and communication load affect input accuracy and efficiency. The fifth area concerned eye-free interaction. The topics in this area were motivated by high demands for visual attention, and mobile ubiquity. Without physical buttons, users cannot rely on their touch to locate interactive elements. Moreover, users could attend some other activities (e.g., walking, carrying objects, and driving) while simultaneously using mobile devices. As a result, users cannot always fix their eyes on the screen. The factors of interest included accuracy, efficiency, and errors because it is important for users to promptly and precisely supply input with minimum errors. For in-car interaction, eye fixation was also a factor to study, as the interface cannot distract users from driving. However, more evaluations are needed to find out which input layouts and interaction are suitable for in-car interaction. The sixth area concerned complex input form, as an input form can be too complex to display on a small screen. Only a few studies examined and compared input forms. The factors of interest included accuracy, efficiency, and errors because it is important for users to quickly and correctly supply input with minimum errors. The last area of research topics concerned alternative input methods. The objective of the research in this area was to propose novel techniques to compensate input accuracy. Only some of them carried out experiment to assess the proposed techniques. Similar to other areas, the factors of interest included accuracy, efficiency, and errors because it is important for users to quickly and correctly supply input with minimum errors. Nevertheless, the proposed techniques still require empirical evaluation.

8.2. Conclusions. The review was made on 68 papers. Input mode and selection contribute the highest number of papers—27 papers. There were no papers discussing the designs of mobile user interface on three categories—(1) control and confirmation, (2) revealing more information, and (3) lateral access. Early research on mobile user interface was made with engineering approach, for instance, proposing new techniques, new interaction styles, and prototyping. Since 2010, the focus has gradually shifted to usability evaluation of design patterns and to studying user factors (e.g., age, culture, and disabilities).

To recapitulate, the review clearly shows that touch screen is the major factor that forms research directions of mobile user interface. Important touch screen qualities that shape research directions are limited screen size, lack of physical response and tactile feedback, invisible gesture, mobile ubiquity, and high demand for visual attention. The review also showed that there is an enormous knowledge gap for mobile interface design. There are some categories where no research can be found, despite their importance to mobile interface and interaction design. Several categories have insufficient empirical-based data to establish a solid design guideline, and there is still a need to assess more factors that influence its usability.

8.3. Limitations. During the review, inconsistency in terminologies used to refer to each design element was common. For example, list is also referred to as linear or vertical menu, and grid menu is also referred to as table-based menu. All papers with different terms that were considered by the authors of this article are included in the review. However, some papers may be missing due to the use of different terms.

References

[1] E. F. Churchill, A. Bowser, and J. Preece, "Teaching and learning human-computer interaction: past, present, and future," *Interactions*, vol. 20, no. 2, pp. 44–53, 2013.

[2] K. B. Bennett, A. L. Nagy, and J. M. Flach, "Visual display," in *Handbook of Human Factors and Ergonomics*, G. Salvendy, Ed., John Wiley & Sons, Hoboken, NJ, USA, 2012.

[3] A. Dix, J. Finlay, G. D. Abowd, and R. Beale, *Human–Computer Interaction*, 1993.

[4] J. Kim, *Design for Experience*, Springer International Publishing, Switzerland, 2015.

[5] S. C. Lee and S. Zhai, "The performance of touch screen soft buttons," in *Proceedings of the 27th International Conference Extended Abstracts on Human Factors in Computing Systems (CHI '09)*, pp. 309–318, Boston, MA, USA, April 2009.

[6] K. B. Perry and P. Hourcade, "Evaluation one handed thumb tapping on mobile touchscreen devices," in *Proceedings of the Graphics Interface (GI '08)*, pp. 57–64, Ontario, Canada, May 2008.

[7] S. Hoober and E. Berkman, *Designing Mobile Interfaces*, Ontario, Canada, O'Reilly Media, 2011.

[8] International Organization of Standardization (ISO), "Ergonomic requirements for office work with visual display terminals (VDTs)—part 11: guidance on usability," ISO 9241-11:1998, 1998, https://www.iso.org/obp/ui/#iso:std:iso:9241:-11:ed-1:v1:en.

[9] N. Bevan, "Usability is quality of use," in *Proceedings of the 6th International Conference on Human-Computer Interaction*, Yokohama, Japan, July 1995.

[10] Interaction-Design.org, Introduction to Usability, n.d., https://www.interaction-design.org/literature/article/an-introduction-to-usability.

[11] nteraction-Design.org, What is Usability?, n.d., https://www.interaction-design.org/literature/topics/usability.

[12] Y. Rogers, J. Preece, and H. Sharp, *Interaction Design: Beyond Human-Computer Interaction*, John Wiley & Sons, West Sussex, UK, 2007.

[13] J. Lazar, J. H. Feng, and H. Hochheiser, *Research Methods in Human-Computer Interaction*, John Wiley & Sons, West Sussex, UK, 2010.

[14] International Organization of Standardization (ISO), "Ergonomics of human-system interaction—part 210: human-centred design for interactive systems," ISO 9241-210: 2010, 2010, https://www.iso.org/standard/52075.html.

[15] Interaction-Design.org, User Experience (UX) Design, n.d., https://www.interaction-design.org/literature/topics/ux-design.

[16] G. C. Vanderheiden, *Application Software Design Guidelines: Increasing the Accessibility of Application Software for People with Disabilities and Older Users*, Trace Research and Development Center, Madison, Wis, USA, 1992.

[17] J. J. Abascal and C. Nicolle, "Why inclusive design guidelines?" in *Inclusive Design Guidelines for HCI*, pp. 3–13, Taylor & Francis, 2001.

[18] C. Stephandis, "Design for all," in *The Encyclopedia of Human-Computer Interaction*, Interaction Design Foundation, 2nd edition, 2014, https://www.interaction-design.org/literature/book/the-encyclopedia-of-human-computer-interaction-2nd-ed/design-4-all.

[19] H. Petrie, "Accessibility and usability requirements for ICTs for disabled and elderly people: a functional classification approach," in *Inclusive Design Guidelines for HCI*, C. Nicolle and J. Abascal, Eds., pp. 29–60, Taylor & Francis, Abingdon, UK, 2001.

[20] D. A. L. Maberley, H. Hollands, J. Chuo et al., "The prevalence of low vision and blindness in Canada," *Eye*, vol. 20, no. 3, pp. 341–346, 2006.

[21] H. Petrie, G. Weber, and J. Darzentas, "Designing for accessibility," in *Human-Computer Interaction—INTERACT 2017*, vol. 10516 of *Lecture Notes in Computer Science*, pp. 387–390, Springer International Publishing, Mumbai, India, 2017.

[22] J. C. Read, "Children participating in HCI research," in *Human-Computer Interaction—INTERACT 2017*, vol. 10516 of *Lecture Notes in Computer Science*, Springer International Publishing, Mumbai, India, 2017.

[23] J. Kjeldskov, "Mobile computing," in *The Encyclopedia of Human-Computer Interaction*, Interaction Design Foundation, 2nd edition, 2014, https://www.interaction-design.org/literature/book/the-encyclopedia-of-human-computer-interaction-2nd-ed/mobile-computing.

[24] B. Fling, *Mobile Design and Development*, O'Reilly Media, Sebastopol, Cali, USA, 2009.

[25] R. Coppola and M. Morisio, "Connected car: technologies, issues, future trends," *ACM Computing Surveys*, vol. 49, no. 3, article 46, 2016.

[26] O. R. E. Pereira and J. J. P. C. Rodrigues, "Survey and analysis of current mobile learning applications and technologies," *ACM Computing Surveys*, vol. 46, no. 2, article 27, 2013.

[27] D. A. Becker, "Best practices of library mobile website design: a literature review," *College and Undergraduate Libraries*, vol. 22, no. 2, pp. 167–187, 2015.

[28] C. M. Monroe, D. L. Thompson, D. R. Bassett, E. C. Fitzhugh, and H. A. Raynor, "Usability of mobile phones in physical activity—related research: a systematic review," *American Journal of Health Education*, vol. 46, no. 4, pp. 196–206, 2015.

[29] J. Donner, "Research approaches to mobile use in the developing world: a review of the literature," *The Information Society*, vol. 24, no. 3, pp. 140–159, 2008.

[30] S. A. Hoseini-Tabatabaei, A. Gluhak, and R. Tafazolli, "A survey on smartphone-based systems for opportunistic user context recognition," *ACM Computing Surveys*, vol. 45, no. 3, article 27, 2013.

[31] P. A. Akiki, A. K. Bandara, and Y. Yu, "Adaptive model-driven user interface development systems," *ACM Computing Surveys*, vol. 47, no. 1, article 9, 2014.

[32] A. Cockburn, A. Karlson, and B. B. Bederson, "A review of overview+detail, zooming, and focus+context interfaces," *ACM Computing Surveys*, vol. 41, no. 1, article 2, 2008.

[33] J. Zhou, P.-L. P. Rau, and G. Salvendy, "Use and design of handheld computers for older adults: a review and appraisal," *International Journal of Human-Computer Interaction*, vol. 28, no. 12, pp. 799–826, 2012.

[34] J. E. Moulder, K. R. Foster, L. S. Erdreich, and J. P. McNamee, "Mobile phones, mobile phone base stations and cancer: a review," *International Journal of Radiation Biology*, vol. 81, no. 3, pp. 189–203, 2005.

[35] N. Wagner, K. Hassanein, and M. Head, "Computer use by older adults: a multi-disciplinary review," *Computers in Human Behavior*, vol. 26, no. 5, pp. 870–882, 2010.

[36] K. Kim, *Derivation and evaluation of 3D menu designs for smartphones [Ph.D. thesis]*, Purdue University, West Lafayette, Indiana, 2011.

[37] C. Ling, W. Hwang, and G. Salvendy, "A survey of what customers want in a cell phone design," *Behaviour & Information Technology*, vol. 26, no. 2, pp. 149–163, 2007.

[38] J. Kim and K. Lee, "Culturally adapted mobile phone interface design: correlation between categorization style and menu structure," in *Proceedings of the 9th International Conference on Human Computer Interaction with Mobile Devices and Services (MobileHCI '07*, pp. 379–382, Singapore, September 2007.

[39] W. A. Rogers, A. J. Stronge, and A. D. Fisk, "Technology and aging," *Reviews of Human Factors and Ergonomics*, vol. 1, no. 1, pp. 130–171, 2005.

[40] K. Arning and M. Ziefle, "Effects of age, cognitive, and personal factors on PDA menu navigation performance," *Behaviour & Information Technology*, vol. 28, no. 3, pp. 251–268, 2009.

[41] J. Park, S. H. Han, Y. S. Park, and Y. Cho, "Adaptable versus adaptive menus on the desktop: performance and user satisfaction," *International Journal of Industrial Ergonomics*, vol. 37, no. 8, pp. 675–684, 2007.

[42] G. Fischer, "User modeling in human-computer interaction," *User Modeling and User-Adapted Interaction*, vol. 11, no. 1-2, pp. 65–86, 2001.

[43] L. Findlater and K. Z. Gajos, "Design space and evaluation challenges of adaptive graphical user interfaces," *AI Magazine*, vol. 30, no. 4, pp. 68–73, 2009.

[44] J. Park, S. H. Han, and Y. S. Park, "Human complementary menu design for mobile phones," *IFAC Proceedings Volumes*, vol. 40, no. 16, pp. 67–72, 2007.

[45] A. Osman, M. H. Ismail, and N. A. Wahab, "Combining fisheye with list: evaluating the learnability and user satisfaction," in *Proceedings of the 2009 International Conference on Computer Technology and Development (ICCTD '09)*, pp. 49–52, Kota Kinabalu, Malaysia, November 2009.

[46] P. Finley, *A study comparing table-based and list-based smartphone interface usability [Msc. thesis]*, Iowa State University, Ames, Iowa, USA, 2013.

[47] J. Breuninger, S. Popova-Dlugosch, and K. Bengler, "The safest way to scroll a list: a usability study comparing different ways of scrolling through lists on touch screen devices," *IFAC Proceedings Volumes*, vol. 46, no. 15, pp. 44–51, 2013.

[48] P. Quinn and A. Cockburn, "Zoofing!: faster list selections with pressure-zoom-flick-scrolling," in *Proceedings of the 21st Annual Conference of the Australian Computer-Human Interaction Special Interest Group - Design: Open 24/7 (OZCHI '09)*, pp. 185–192, Melbourne, Australia, November 2009.

[49] V. Setlur, S. Rossoff, and B. Gooch, "Wish I hadn't clicked that: context based icons for mobile web navigation and directed search tasks," in *Proceedings of the 15th ACM International*

Conference on Intelligent User Interfaces (IUI '11), pp. 165–174, Palo Alto, Claif, USA, February 2011.

[50] V. Setlur, "SemantiLynx: context based icons for mobile web navigation and directed search tasks," in *Proceedings of the 12th International Conference on Human-Computer Interaction with Mobile Devices and Services (MobileHCI '10)*, pp. 409-410, Lisbon, Portugal, September 2010.

[51] A. Woodruff, A. Faulring, R. Rosenholtz, J. Morrsion, and P. Pirolli, "Using thumbnails to search the Web," in *Proceedings of SIGCHI Conference on Human Factors in Computing Systems (CHI '01)*, pp. 198–205, Seattle, DC, USA, March 2001.

[52] X.-D. Yang, E. Mak, D. McCallum, P. Irani, X. Cao, and S. Izadi, "LensMouse: augmenting the mouse with an interactive touch display," in *Proceedings of the 28th Annual CHI Conference on Human Factors in Computing Systems (CHI '10)*, pp. 2431–2440, Atlanta, Ga, USA, April 2010.

[53] D. Cheng, D. Li, and L. Fang, "A cluster information navigate method by gaze tracking," in *Proceedings of the 26th Annual ACM Symposium on User Interface Software and Technology (UIST '13)*, pp. 61-62, Scotland, UK, October 2013.

[54] T. Yang, M. Ferati, Y. Liu, R. R. Ghahari, and D. Bolchini, "Aural browsing on-the-go: listening-based back navigation in large web architectures," in *Proceedings of the 30th ACM Conference on Human Factors in Computing Systems (CHI '12)*, pp. 277–286, Austin, Tex, USA, May 2012.

[55] M. E. Sesto, C. B. Irwin, K. B. Chen, A. O. Chourasia, and D. A. Wiegmann, "Effect of touch screen button size and spacing on touch characteristics of users with and without disabilities," *Human Factors: The Journal of the Human Factors and Ergonomics Society*, vol. 54, no. 3, pp. 425–436, 2012.

[56] J. Conradi, O. Busch, and T. Alexander, "Optimal touch button size for the use of mobile devices while walking," *Procedia Manufacturing*, vol. 3, pp. 387–394, 2015.

[57] K. Tanaka and K. Watanabe, "Interference between accustomed number-space mappings and unacquainted letter-space mappings in a button press task," *Human Factors: The Journal of the Human Factors and Ergonomics Society*, vol. 55, no. 6, pp. 1088–1100, 2013.

[58] T. Kaaresoja, S. Brewster, and V. Lantz, "Towards the temporally perfect virtual button: touch-feedback simultaneity and perceived quality in mobile touchscreen press interactions," *ACM Transactions on Applied Perception*, vol. 11, no. 2, article 9, 2014.

[59] G. Park, S. Choi, K. Hwang, S. Kim, J. Sa, and M. Joung, "Tactile effect design and evaluation for virtual buttons on a mobile device touchscreen," in *Proceedings of the 13th International Conference on Human-Computer Interaction with Mobile Devices and Services (MobileHCI '11)*, pp. 11–20, Stockholm, Sweden, September 2011.

[60] E. Koskinen, T. Kaaresoja, and P. Laitinen, "Feel-good touch: finding the most pleasant tactile feedback for a mobile touch screen button," in *Proceedings of the 10th International Conference on Multimodal Interfaces (ICMI '08)*, pp. 297–304, Crete, Greece, October 2008.

[61] T. Pakkanen, R. Raisamo, J. Raisamo, K. Salminen, and V. Surakka, "Comparison of three designs for haptic button edges on touchscreens," in *Proceedings of the IEEE Haptics Symposium (HAPTICS '10)*, pp. 219–225, Waltham, Mass, USA, March 2010.

[62] D. Spelmezan, C. Appert, O. Chapuis, and E. Pietriga, "Controlling widgets with one power-up button," in *Proceedings of the 26th Annual ACM Symposium on User Interface Software and Technology (UIST '13)*, pp. 71–74, Scotland, UK, October 2013.

[63] S. Ghayas, S. Sulaiman, J. Jaafar, S. Mahamad, and M. Khan, "Mobile phone Icons recognition and cultural aspects," in *Proceedings of the 2014 International Conference on Computer and Information Sciences (ICCOINS '14)*, Kuala Lumpur, Malaysia, June 2014.

[64] R. Leung, J. McGrenere, and P. Graf, "Age-related differences in the initial usability of mobile device icons," *Behaviour & Information Technology*, vol. 30, no. 5, pp. 629–642, 2009.

[65] C. Gatsou, A. Politis, and D. Zevgolis, "From icons perception to mobile interaction," in *Proceedings of the 2011 Federated Conference on Computer Science and Information Systems (FedCSIS '11)*, pp. 705–710, Szczecin, Poland, September 2011.

[66] A. Harley, Usability Testing of Icons, 2016, https://www.nngroup.com/articles/icon-testing/.

[67] Y. Im, T. Kim, and E. S. Jung, "Investigation of icon design and touchable area for effective smart phone controls," *Human Factors and Ergonomics in Manufacturing & Service Industries*, vol. 25, no. 2, pp. 251–267, 2015.

[68] S. Luo and Y. Zhou, "Effects of smartphone icon background shapes and figure/background area ratios on visual search performance and user preferences," *Frontiers of Computer Science*, vol. 9, no. 5, pp. 751–764, 2015.

[69] S.-M. Huang, "The rating consistency of aesthetic preferences for icon-background color combinations," *Applied Ergonomics*, vol. 43, no. 1, pp. 141–150, 2012.

[70] S.-W. Ju, K. Jeong, and H.-J. Suk, "Changing the color attributes of icons to inform of the application status," in *Proceedings of the 18th IEEE International Symposium on Consumer Electronics (ISCE '14)*, JeJu Island, South Korea, June 2014.

[71] P. Pappachan and M. Ziefle, "Cultural influences on the comprehensibility of icons in mobile-computer interaction," *Behaviour & Information Technology*, vol. 27, no. 4, pp. 331–337, 2008.

[72] S. Ghayas, S. Sulaiman, M. Khan, and J. Jaafar, "Qualitative study to identify icons characteristics on mobile phones applications interfaces," in *Proceedings of the 3rd IEEE Symposium on Wireless Technology and Applications (ISWTA '13)*, pp. 310–315, Kuching, Malaysia, September 2013.

[73] J. Kuo and F. Wu, "The elder's discrimination of icons with color discrimination on the cell phone," in *Advances in Cognitive Ergonomics*, D. Kaber and G. Boy, Eds., Advances in Human Factors and Ergonomics Series, pp. 176–185, CRC Press, Boca Raton, Fla, USA, 2010.

[74] Y. B. Salman, Y. Kim, and H. Cheng, "Senior—friendly icon design for the mobile phone," in *Proceedings of the 6th International Conference on Digital Content, Multimedia Technology and its Applications (IDC '10)*, South Korea, August 2010.

[75] C. Koutsourelakis and K. Chorianopoulos, "Icons in mobile phones: comprehensibility differences between older and younger users," *Information Design Journal*, vol. 18, no. 1, pp. 22–35, 2010.

[76] J. Kim and Y. Cho, "Evaluation of the cognitive ability among aging groups using mobile phone," in *Proceedings of the Pan-Pacific Conference on Ergonomics*, Kaohsiung, Taiwan, November 2010.

[77] W. Chanwimalueng and K. Rapeepisarn, "A study of the recognitions and preferences on abstract and concrete icon styles on smart phone from Easterners and Westerners' point of view," in *Proceedings of the 12th International Conference on Machine Learning and Cybernetics, ICMLC 2013*, pp. 1613–1619, Tianjin, China, July 2013.

[78] E. Garcia-Lopez, L. de-Marcos, A. Garcia-Cabot, and J.-J. Martinez-Herraiz, "Comparing zooming methods in mobile

devices: effectiveness, efficiency, and user satisfaction in touch and nontouch smartphones," *International Journal of Human-Computer Interaction*, vol. 31, no. 11, pp. 777–789, 2015.

[79] S. Oney, C. Harrison, A. Ogan, and J. Wiese, "ZoomBoard: a diminutive QWERTY soft keyboard using iterative zooming for ultra-small devices," in *Proceedings of the 31st Annual CHI Conference on Human Factors in Computing Systems: Changing Perspectives (CHI '13)*, pp. 2799–2802, Paris, France, May 2013.

[80] Z. Hamza, *Study of touch gesture performance by four and five year-old children: point-and-touch, drag-and-drop, zoom-in and zoom-out, and rotate [Msc. thesis]*, Minnesota State University, Mankato, Minn, USA, 2014.

[81] Y. Li, "Gesture search: a tool for fast mobile data access," in *Proceedings of the 23rd Annual ACM Symposium on User Interface Software and Technology (UIST '10)*, pp. 87–96, New York, NY, USA, October 2010.

[82] S. Shin, J. Ko, D.-H. Shin, J. Jung, and K.-H. Lee, "Semantic search for smart mobile devices," in *Proceedings of the 18th International Conference on Intelligent User Interfaces (IUI '13)*, pp. 95-96, Santa Monica, Calif, USA, March 2013.

[83] K. Church and B. Smyth, "Who, what, where & when: a new approach to mobile search," in *Proceedings of the 13th international conference on Intelligent user interfaces (IUI '08)*, pp. 309–312, Gran Canaria, Spain, January 2008.

[84] U.S. Department of Health and Human Service, Research-based web design & usability guidelines, 2007, https://guidelines.usability.gov/.

[85] R. Zhou, H. Sato, Q. Gao et al., "Mobile search: how to present search results for older users," in *Proceedings of the IEEE International Conference on Industrial Engineering and Engineering Management (IEEM '07)*, pp. 457–461, Singapore, December 2007.

[86] E. Panizzi and G. Marzo, "Multidimensional sort of lists in mobile devices," in *Proceedings of the 12th International Working Conference on Advanced Visual Interfaces (AVI '14)*, pp. 375-376, Como, Italy, May 2014.

[87] J. Diaz-Bossini and L. Moreno, "Accessibility to mobile interfaces for older people," *Procedia Computer Science*, vol. 27, pp. 57–66, 2014.

[88] A. C. De Barros, R. Leitão, and J. Ribeiro, "Design and evaluation of a mobile user interface for older adults: navigation, interaction and visual design recommendations," *Procedia Computer Science*, vol. 27, pp. 369–378, 2014.

[89] L. Anthony, Q. Brown, J. Nias, and B. Tate, "Children (and adults) benefit from visual feedback during gesture interaction on mobile touchscreen devices," *International Journal of Child-Computer Interaction*, vol. 6, pp. 17–27, 2015.

[90] N. K. Dim and X. Ren, "Designing motion gesture interfaces in mobile phones for blind people," *Journal of Computer Science and Technology*, vol. 29, no. 5, pp. 812–824, 2014.

[91] M. Ernst and A. Girouard, "Bending blindly: exploring bend gestures for the blind," in *Proceedings of the 34th Annual CHI Conference on Human Factors in Computing Systems (CHI EA '16)*, pp. 2088–2096, San Jose, Calif, USA, May 2016.

[92] S. Lundgren and M. Hjulström, "Alchemy: dynamic gesture hinting for mobile devices," in *Proceedings of the 15th International Academic MindTrek Conference: Envisioning Future Media Environments (MindTrek '11)*, pp. 53–60, Tampere, Finland, September 2011.

[93] M. S. Geary, *A quasi-experiment study comparing the gradual introduction of alternative soft keyboard on a smartphone versus the immediate introduction of an alternative soft keyboard on a smartphone [Msc. thesis]*, Colorado Technical University, Colorado Springs, Colo, USa, 2015.

[94] A. K. Karlson, B. B. Bederson, and J. L. Contreras-Vidal, "Studies in one-handed mobile design: habit, desire and agility," HCIL-2006-02, Computer Science Department, University of Maryland, College Park, Md, USA, 2006.

[95] D. Vogel and P. Baudisch, "Shift: a technique for operating pen-based interfaces using touch," in *Proceedings of the 25th SIGCHI Conference on Human Factors in Computing Systems (CHI '07)*, pp. 657–666, San Jose, Calif, USA, May 2007.

[96] E. S. Jung and Y. Im, "Touchable area: an empirical study on design approach considering perception size and touch input behavior," *International Journal of Industrial Ergonomics*, vol. 49, pp. 21–30, 2015.

[97] I. Kim and J. H. Jo, "Performance comparisons between thumb-based and finger-based input on a small touch-screen under realistic variability," *International Journal of Human-Computer Interaction*, vol. 31, no. 11, pp. 746–760, 2015.

[98] S. Hoober, How do users really hold mobile devices?, 2013, http://www.uxmatters.com/mt/archives/2013/02/how-do-users-really-hold-mobile-devices.php.

[99] J. Bergstrom-Lehtovirta, A. Oulasvirta, and S. Brewster, "The effects of walking speed on target acquisition on a touchscreen interface," in *Proceedings of the 13th International Conference on Human-Computer Interaction with Mobile Devices and Services (MobileHCI '11)*, pp. 143–146, Stockholm, Sweden, September 2011.

[100] Y. S. Park and S. H. Han, "One-handed thumb interaction of mobile devices from the input accuracy perspective," *International Journal of Industrial Ergonomics*, vol. 40, no. 6, pp. 746–756, 2010.

[101] J. Xiong and S. Muraki, "Effects of age, thumb length and screen size on thumb movement coverage on smartphone touchscreens," *International Journal of Industrial Ergonomics*, vol. 53, pp. 140–148, 2016.

[102] A. Holzinger, G. Searle, and A. Nischelwitzer, "On some aspects of improving mobile applications for the elderly," in *Proceedings of the International Conference on Universal Access in Human-Computer Interaction (UAHCI '07)*, pp. 923–932, Universal assessment in Human-Computer Interaction, Coping with Diversity, Beijing, China, July 2007.

[103] C. Stößel, "Familiarity as a factor in designing finger gestures for elderly users," in *Proceedings of the Proceedings of the 11th International Conference on Human-Computer Interaction with Mobile Devices and Services (MobileHCI '09)*, Bonn, Germany, September 2009.

[104] É. Rodrigues, M. Carreira, and D. Gonçalves, "Developing a multimodal interface for the elderly," *Procedia Computer Science*, vol. 27, pp. 359–368, 2014.

[105] K.-S. Choi and T.-Y. Chan, "Facilitating mathematics learning for students with upper extremity disabilities using touch-input system," *Disability and Rehabilitation: Assistive Technology*, vol. 10, no. 2, pp. 170–180, 2015.

[106] S. Raupp, *Keyboard layout in eye gaze communication access: typical vs. als [Msc. thesis]*, East Carolina University, Greenville, NC, USA, 2013.

[107] M. G. Alfredo, J. A. R. Francisco, M. G. Ricardo, A. E. Francisco, and M. A. Jaime, "Analyzing learnability of common mobile gestures used by Down syndrome users," in *Proceedings of the 16th International Conference on Human Computer Interaction*

(INTERACCION '15), Vilanova i la Geltrú, Spain, September 2015.

[108] I. S. MacKenzie and R. W. Soukoreff, "Phrase sets for evaluating text entry techniques," in *Proceedings of the Conference on Human Factors in Computing Systems (CHI EA '03)*, pp. 754-755, Ft. Lauderdale, Fla, USA, April 2003.

[109] NetLingo.com, NetLingo List of Chat Acronyms & Text Shorthand, n.d., http://www.netlingo.com/acronyms.php.

[110] S. K. Durrani, *Data entry error in mobile keyboard device usage subject to cognitive, environmental, and communication workload stressors present in fully activated emergency operations [Msc thesis]*, University of Central Florida, Orlando, Fla, USA, 2009.

[111] N. Louveton, R. McCall, V. Koenig, T. Avanesov, and T. Engel, "Driving while using a smartphone-based mobility application: evaluating the impact of three multi-choice user interfaces on visual-manual distraction," *Applied Ergonomics*, vol. 54, pp. 196–204, 2016.

[112] A. Ng, J. Williamson, and S. Brewster, "The effects of encumbrance and mobility on touch-based gesture interactions for mobile phones," in *Proceedings of the 17th International Conference on Human-Computer Interaction with Mobile Devices and Services (MobileHCI '15)*, pp. 536–546, Copenhagen, Denmark, August 2015.

[113] F. Balagtas-Fernandez, J. Forrai, and H. Hussmann, "Evaluation of user interface design and input methods for applications on mobile touch screen devices," in *Human-Computer Interaction—INTERACT 2009*, vol. 5726 of *Lecture Notes in Computer Science*, pp. 243–246, 2009.

[114] K. El Batran and M. Dunlop, "Improved form navigation on mobile devices," in *Proceedings of the 6th International Conference on Computer Science and Information Technology (CSIT '14)*, pp. 96–99, Amman, Jordan, March 2014.

[115] S. Kwon, D. Lee, and M. K. Chung, "Effect of key size and activation area on the performance of a regional error correction method in a touch-screen QWERTY keyboard," *International Journal of Industrial Ergonomics*, vol. 39, no. 5, pp. 888–893, 2009.

[116] N. Koarai and T. Komuro, "A zooming interface for accurate text input on mobile devices," in *Proceedings of the CHI '13 Extended Abstracts on Human Factors in Computing Systems*, pp. 1299–1340, Paris, France, May 2013.

[117] X. Xiao, T. Han, and J. Wang, "LensGesture: augmenting mobile interactions with back-of-device finger gestures," in *Proceedings of the 15th ACM International Conference on Multimodal Interaction (ICMI '13)*, pp. 287–294, Sydney, Australia, December 2013.

[118] O. P. González, S. España, and O. Pastor, "Including multi-stroke gesture-based interaction in user interfaces using a model-driven method," in *Proceedings of the XVI International Conference on Human Computer Interaction (Interacción '15)*, pp. 1–8, Vilanova i la Geltrú, Spain, September 2015.

[119] J. Wang, K. Zhao, X. Zhang, and C. Peng, "Ubiquitous keyboard for small mobile devices: Harnessing multipath fading for fine-grained keystroke localization," in *Proceedings of the 12th Annual International Conference on Mobile Systems, Applications, and Services (MobiSys '14)*, pp. 14–27, Bretton Woods, NH, USA, June 2014.

[120] Y.-C. Huang and F.-G. Wu, "Visual and manual loadings with QWERTY-like ambiguous keyboards: Relevance of letter-key assignments on mobile phones," *International Journal of Industrial Ergonomics*, vol. 50, pp. 143–150, 2015.

[121] B. Millet, *Design and evaluation of three alternative keyboard layouts for five-key text entry technique, doctoral dissertation [Msc. thesis]*, University of Miami, Miami-Dade County, Fla, USA, 2009.

Computational Intelligence in Sports

Robson P. Bonidia ⓘ,[1] **Luiz A. L. Rodrigues,**[2] **Anderson P. Avila-Santos,**[3] **Danilo S. Sanches,**[1] **and Jacques D. Brancher**[2]

[1]*Bioinformatics Graduate Program, Federal University of Technology-CP (UTFPR), Paraná, Brazil*
[2]*Computer Science Department, State University of Londrina (UEL), Londrina, Paraná, Brazil*
[3]*Technology College, National Service Industrial Learning of Paraná (SENAI), Londrina, Paraná, Brazil*

Correspondence should be addressed to Robson P. Bonidia; robservidor@gmail.com

Guest Editor: Aida Mustapha

Recently, data mining studies are being successfully conducted to estimate several parameters in a variety of domains. Data mining techniques have attracted the attention of the information industry and society as a whole, due to a large amount of data and the imminent need to turn it into useful knowledge. However, the effective use of data in some areas is still under development, as is the case in sports, which in recent years, has presented a slight growth; consequently, many sports organizations have begun to see that there is a wealth of unexplored knowledge in the data extracted by them. Therefore, this article presents a systematic review of sports data mining. Regarding years 2010 to 2018, 31 types of research were found in this topic. Based on these studies, we present the current panorama, themes, the database used, proposals, algorithms, and research opportunities. Our findings provide a better understanding of the sports data mining potentials, besides motivating the scientific community to explore this timely and interesting topic.

1. Introduction

The advent of computing has produced a society that feeds on information. Most of the information is in its raw form, known as data [1]. Data are collected and accumulated at an increasing rate [2]. The government, corporate, and scientific areas have promoted significant growth in their databases, overcoming the usual ability to interpret and analyze data, thus, generating the need for new tools and techniques for automatic and intelligent evaluation [2–4].

Therefore, the data mining technique is one of the most competent alternatives to help in the knowledge extraction from large data volumes, discovering patterns, and generating rules for predicting and comparing data, which can help institutions in decision-making and achieve a greater degree of confidence [5, 6].

Historically, the technique of finding useful patterns in data has been named with a variety of names, including data mining, knowledge extraction, identification information,

data archeology, and data processing standard [3]. Basically, this technique is a process of exploring significant correlations and trends and discovering intriguing and innovative patterns, as well as descriptive models and comprehensible and predictive data, using statistical and mathematical techniques [4, 7].

Data mining is used to generate knowledge in many scientific, industrial, and mainly business sectors [3]. Moreover, it has been used mostly by statisticians, data analysts, and management information systems. This is because information is the most relevant asset for these organizations, becoming fundamental to gain competitiveness among small, medium, and large companies [8]. Nevertheless, the effective use of data in some areas has gradually developed, as is the case with sports, known for a large amount of information collected from each player, training session, team, games, and seasons [1, 9, 10].

Hence, connoisseurs and experts have dedicated to predict and discuss sporting results. With a large amount of data available (especially since the advent of the Internet), it was natural for statisticians and computer scientists to show interest in discovering patterns and making predictions using these data. The processing of sports data with data mining techniques can not only reduce manual workload and errors, but also improve fairness and development of sports games, assisting coaches and managers in predicting results, assessing players' performance, identifying talents, sporting strategy, and mainly making decision [11].

Based on these assignments, this article aims to perform a Systematic Literature Review (SLR), with the purpose of identifying researches using data mining in the sports field and describes the techniques and algorithms applied and possible research opportunities. Moreover, the current panorama of research, temporal distribution, themes, databases used, and proposals of these works will be presented.

This paper is organized as follows: Section 2 discusses the systematic review methods. Section 3 reports research planning. Sections 4 and 5 present how the SLR was conducted and the results obtained. Finally, Section 6, described the final considerations.

2. Systematic Review Methods

This study used the systematic review method which , according to Brereton et al. [12], allows a rigorous and reliable evaluation of the research carried out within a specific topic. This type of investigation presents a summary of evidence through comprehensible systematic search methods and synthesis of selected information [13]. Moreover, this methodology has been widely used [12–15]. Thus, we based our research on previous works recommendations, which is to divide this process into three stages: planning, conducting, and analysis of results. Therefore, the following sections describe how we approached each one of these stages.

3. Research Planning

The planning stage addressed the scientific questions definition, the intervention of interest specification, databases identification, keywords definition, search strategies, criteria for inclusion and exclusion, and articles quality [12, 16]. Therefore, the following issues were defined as research questions (RQn):

(i) RQ1: What is the current researches overview?

(ii) RQ2: What are the most used techniques?

(iii) RQ3: What is the temporal distribution of the works?

(iv) RQ4: What are the most cited research papers?

(v) RQ5: What are the datasets?

(vi) RQ6: What was the result of the researches?

(vii) RQ7: What are the algorithms and methods applied?

(viii) RQ8: What are the research opportunities?

Usually, inclusion, exclusion, and quality criteria are determined after the definition of research questions [17]. Hence, Table 1 establishes the criteria used in this study.

TABLE 1: Inclusion, exclusion, and quality criteria.

	Criteria
Inclusion	Studies in English
	Article, Conference or Methodology paper
	Studies relevant to the sports data mining techniques
Exclusion	Researches that do not accomplish the quality criteria
	Studies outside the context of work
	Studies written in another language than English
	Studies published before 2010
Quality	Studies with full results
	Studies with different proposals/results

Aspects of this process may include decisions about the type of revisions that should be included in the research, which is used to manage the selection criteria in a subset of primary studies [16, 18]. Therefore, in order to ensure the quality of this review, every article found will be analyzed according to Title, Abstract, Keywords, Proposed Mechanism, Results, and Conclusion. Furthermore, this article used the following electronic databases to find papers:

(i) *ACM Digital Library*: dl.acm.org

(ii) *IEEE Xplore Digital Library*: ieeexplore.ieee.org

(iii) *Science Direct*: www.sciencedirect.com

(iv) *Semantic Scholar*: www.semanticscholar.org

Finally, the selected method to search in these databases was boolean recovery. Essentially, it divides a search space, identifying a subset of documents in a collection, according to the criteria of consultation [19]. In our case, the key is the following string: *(("sports" OR "sport" OR "sports science") AND ("data mining" OR "mining" OR "computational intelligence" OR "machine learning" OR "deep learning" OR "artificial intelligence"))*.

4. Execution Plan

This stage involves five steps: (1) performing the search in the selected databases; (2) comparison of searches results to exclude repeated papers; (3) application of inclusion, exclusion, and quality criteria; (4) evaluation of all studies that passed the initial review; and (5) data synthesis [12, 16].

Figure 1 displays this flow for our SLR. Basically, the first phase consisted of executing the search strings in all databases, which found a large set of 1582. Thus, to aid the review and achieve better accuracy and reliability, the StArt tool (State of the Art through Systematic Reviews) was used. This tool has the purpose of supporting researchers in their systematic analysis [20–22].

It uses BibTeX extensions (bibliographic formatting file used in LaTeX documents) to perform these analyses. Therefore, these extensions were extracted from the aforementioned databases as well. It is important to note that the BibTeX files were exported without any filter, which explains the number of researches returned.

Thereafter, works published before 2010 were eliminated, returning an amount of 1172 titles (410 rejected articles).

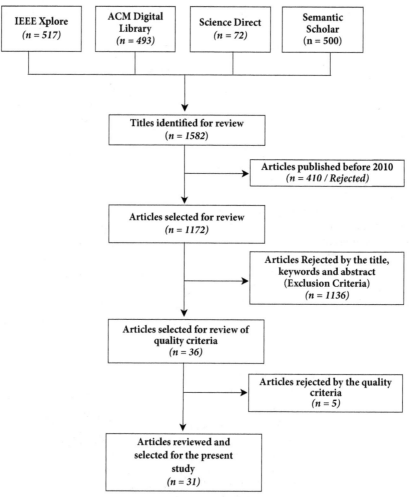

FIGURE 1: Systematic review research flow.

Nevertheless, in order to refine the search and eliminate articles that were outside the scope of this review, a careful analysis was applied in the titles, keywords, and abstracts, according to the exclusion criteria (see Table 1). It eliminated 1136 works, remaining a preselection set of 36 titles for quality analysis. It is important to emphasize which queries using keywords return several titles that are far from the context of this article; this justifies the amount of rejected research.

Finally, after the works preselection, a synthesis of the data was performed, with the objective of applying an evaluation based on the stated quality criteria. Thereby, of the 36 articles, 5 were eliminated (they have not demonstrated the methods or techniques applied), leading to a final set of 31 articles with relevant information about data mining in sports.

5. Results

In this section, the results of this SLR are presented. Thus, each subsequent subsection will answer the issues raised at the beginning of the research.

5.1. RQ1: Current Researches Overview. The works selected by this SLR are presented in Table 2. Examining them, we will provide a report regarding the current panorama of sports data mining.

Therefore, to provide an overview of the thematic types that have been proposed in the articles, they were categorized in nine classes: Motion Analysis; Performance Evaluation; Sports Data Capture; Generating Eating Plans; Training Planning; Strategic Planning; Predicting Results/Patterns; Sports Data Analytics; and Decision-Making Support. For a better understanding of these categories Table 3 introduces them.

(i) **Motion Analysis**: themes focused on strategies for the recognition and classification of patterns and skills through the motion analysis.

(ii) **Performance Evaluation**: guide coaches or athletes on how to improve performance and eliminate errors through data mining.

(iii) **Sports Data Capture**: category presenting the papers that developed or studied sports information extraction systems.

(iv) **Generating Eating Plans**: articles reporting research on the automatic generation of optimal food plans for athletes through artificial intelligence.

TABLE 2: Selected papers (IDs and references).

ID	Reference	ID	Reference
1	[23]	17	[24]
2	[25]	18	[26]
3	[27]	19	[28]
4	[29]	20	[30]
5	[31]	21	[32]
6	[33]	22	[34]
7	[35]	23	[36]
8	[37]	24	[38]
9	[39]	25	[40]
10	[41]	26	[42]
11	[43]	27	[44]
12	[45]	28	[46]
13	[47]	29	[48]
14	[49]	30	[50]
15	[51]	31	[52]
16	[53]		

TABLE 3: Thematic types.

Theme	Articles
Motion Analysis	[23, 27]
Performance Evaluation	[31, 33]
Sports Data Capture	[35]
Generating Eating Plans	[37]
Training Planning	[39, 41, 43, 45, 47, 49]
Strategic Planning	[24, 51, 53]
Predicting Results/Patterns	[26, 28, 30, 32, 34, 36, 38, 40, 42]
Sports Data Analytics	[25, 29, 44]
Decision Making Support	[46, 48, 50, 52]

(v) **Training Planning**: intelligent studies for planning sports training sessions, techniques to support the definition of training sessions and quick feedback systems.

(vi) **Strategic Planning**: researches developed from systems to support strategic planning in sports using data mining modules, tactical analysis techniques, and computational intelligence.

(vii) **Predicting Results/Patterns**: topics predicting game results in sports such as college football, elite soccer, basketball, and golf.

(viii) **Sports Data Analytics**: data mining platforms that aid the diagnosis of sports records.

(ix) **Decision-Making Support**: articles that investigated the potential of data mining or computational intelligence with the purpose of support in the decision-making process.

Papers distribution between the aforementioned categories is exposed in Table 3. As can be seen, the growth of sports data mining, even if limited, presents relevant works

aiming to automate empirical tasks and improve the reliability of strategies, predictions, and training decisions. Moreover, it is noted that the category Predicting Results/Patterns presents the greatest amount of works (9), followed by Training Planning (6), Decision-Making Support (4), Strategic Planning and Sports Data Analytics (3), Motion Analysis and Performance Evaluation (2), and finally Sports Data Capture and Generating Eating Plans (1).

5.2. RQ2: Most Used Techniques. A words cloud is demonstrated in Figure 2, where the size of each word reflects its frequency of occurrence. This cloud is based on words contained in the titles of the selected articles.

The preponderance of words suggests that these are the most used techniques to create computational intelligent systems in sport's field. Thus, as can be seen in the figure, data mining and machine learning are the most used, considering that words related to these techniques often appear in the papers, based on their size in this figure.

5.3. RQ3: Papers Temporal Distribution. Analyzing the temporal distribution of included articles, it was noticed that years 2014 and 2016 reported the highest amount of publications, with 12 articles (6 each year), representing 38.71% of the works reviewed. The years 2010, 2013, and 2017 together presented the same total number of articles (12-38.71%), but with only 4 works in each year. The year of 2012 had 3 (9.68%) articles, whereas 2015 and 2018 had only 2 (12.90%). This distribution is shown in Figure 3.

5.4. RQ4: Most Cited Researches. In total, the top 5 articles contributed 133 citations related to sports data mining, as can be seen in Table 4. The research of Novatchkov [43] published in Journal of sports science (2013) was the most cited (36 times). The remaining papers were published in Intelligent Systems and Informatics ([42], 31 times), Computational and Business Intelligence ([47], 26 times), Procedia Computer Science ([40], 23 times), and IFAC Proceedings Volumes ([27], 14 times).

5.5. RQ5/RQ6: Analyzed Datasets. This section presents the proposals or results as well as datasets used by the selected works in Tables 5 and 6, respectively. We highlight that data mining depends on the quality and quantity of data in order that algorithms yield satisfactory results. Furthermore, another limitation is to find a safe source and select relevant attributes to investigate the problem. Therefore, it is relevant to SLR report datasets used in the literature.

It is observed in Table 5 that the great majority seeks to find patterns to predict results, strategies, training sessions, and mainly support in decision-making. Other papers discuss the motion analysis, generating eating plans and data extraction tools. Nonetheless, the SLR demonstrated that the last 3 citation topics feature little-explored sports field. Furthermore, a great need that we perceive during the review is the data extraction. According to [35], text data related to sports are semistructured or even unstructured. Essentially, these texts contain relevant information and are available on the web; however, extracting data and useful knowledge of

FIGURE 2: Frequently occurring words in articles under review.

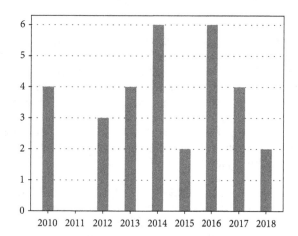

FIGURE 3: Work's temporal distribution.

TABLE 4: Top 5 articles according to citation frequency.

Article	Journal/Conference	Year	Citation
[43]	Journal of sports science & medicine	2013	39
[42]	Intelligent Systems and Informatics	2010	31
[47]	Computational and Business Intelligence	2013	26
[40]	Procedia Computer Science	2014	23
[27]	IFAC Proceedings Volumes	2012	14

these documents adequately is difficult and costly. This is confirmed in the datasets exposed in Table 6, which reflect the lack of model data to work with sports data mining.

5.6. Data Mining Techniques. Here, we present a brief description of the data mining techniques used by the surveyed papers in this SLR. Five main techniques were identified: classification, clustering, association, regression, and heuristics.

(i) **Classification:** consists of developing a model that can be applied in the prediction of events with a predefined number of outcomes (e.g., is the player's arm moving? Will my team win this game?). Fundamentally, this technique has a wide range of applications, including medical diagnosis, fraud detection, credit approval, target marketing, and prediction of sports results [54].

(ii) **Clustering:** analyzes data to find groups of items that are similar to each other according to some similarity metric. Essentially, this technique is used for unsupervised learning, when we do not know the answer to the investigated problem (e.g., finding players with similar skills or team using similar tactics without a direct indicator of these characteristics) [55].

(iii) **Association:** consists of identifying which attributes are related, extracting associations between a large set of items or events (e.g., players who are good in one task are also good in another) [7, 54, 56].

(iv) **Regression:** determines the relationship between a dependent variable (target field) and one or more independent variables. The dependent variable is the one whose values you want to predict, while the independent ones are the variables based on the prediction. In this case, the predicted values are continuous (e.g., how old is this player? How many points will my team score?) [7].

(v) **Heuristic:** the heuristic term means to discover. This technique is inspired by intuitive processes, whose purpose is to find a good solution at an acceptable computational cost. Fundamentally, heuristic algorithms seek viable solutions to optimization problems in which the complexity and time available for their solution do not allow the exact result [57, 58].

Furthermore, Table 7 shows, for each theme, the techniques that have been employed to address it. As can be seen, the classification was the most used (51.28%), followed by clustering, heuristics, and association with 17.95%, 15.39%, and 12.82% applications, respectively, while that the regression was adopted by a single research (2.56%).

5.7. RQ7: Applied Algorithms by the Articles. This section aims to explore the algorithms used in the revised works, as in Table 8 (Table follows as order the thematic types), in addition to making a brief introduction to the most used algorithms.

(i) **Bat algorithm:** this algorithm was developed in 2010 by Yang. The Echolocation process that bats use during their flight was the inspiration. Besides being used for orientation this mechanism helps the bats to find their prey. Essentially, the bat algorithm is based on the population of individuals where each one represents the candidate solution [49].

(ii) **Differential Evolution:** this algorithm was proposed in 1995 by Storn and Price [59]. The DE is a technique of the stochastic research efficient and powerful. It was based on population to solve the problem of continuous space optimization that has been largely applied in the most several scientific fields [60].

TABLE 5: Proposals/results of the works.

Paper	Proposal/Result
[27]	Research of strategies most used for the recognition and classification of human movement patterns.
[23]	Analysis of sports skills data with temporal series image data retrieved from films focused on table tennis.
[33]	Guide the athletes on how to improve their performance and how to eliminate errors related to the selection of the proper running strategy through the differential evolution algorithm.
[31]	Proposes a new clustering algorithm based on ant colony optimization.
[35]	Proposed the development of an information extraction system wherein its purpose was to obtain data frames of multiple sports performance documents.
[37]	Automatic generation of optimal food plans for athletes, through the particle swarm optimization algorithm.
[47]	Proposed an automated personal trainer.
[49]	Solution for automatic planning of training sessions.
[39]	A new solution capable of adapting training plans.
[41]	A framework to automatically analyze the physiological signals monitored during a test session.
[43]	Implementation of artificial intelligence routines for automatic evaluation of exercises in weight training.
[45]	Presented three geometric/temporal features of pen trajectories used in a cognitive skills training application for elite basketball players.
[24]	An data mining algorithm to soccer tactics using association rules mining.
[53]	Discussed the application of the association rule mining in sports management, especially, in cricket.
[51]	Presented a relational-learning based approach for discovering strategies in volleyball matches based on optical tracking data.
[36]	A generalized predictive model for predicting the results of the English Premier League.
[30]	A data analysis to identify important aspects separating skilled golfers from poor.
[38]	Compared the performance of algebraic methods to some machine learning approaches, particularly in the field of match prediction.
[40]	A sports data mining approach, which helps discover interesting knowledge and predict results from sports games such as college football.
[42]	Data mining techniques for predicting basketball results in the NBA (National Basketball Association).
[28]	Developed a tool COP (Cricket Outcome Predictor), which outputs the win/loss probability of a match.
[32]	Classify players into regular or All-Star players from the National Basketball Association and identify the most important features that make an All-Star player.
[26]	Designed and built a big data analytics framework for sports behavior mining and personalized health services.
[34]	Provides a prediction model of sports results based on knowledge discovery in database.
[25]	A machine learning system with unsupervised learning and supervised learning components to analyze chess data.
[44]	Concluded that the most important elements in basketball are two-point shots under the arch and defensive rebound.
[29]	A data mining approach for classification and identification of golf swing from weight shift data.
[52]	Describes machine learning techniques that assist cycling experts in the decision-making processes for athlete selection and strategic planning.
[46]	Predict match outcomes in the 2015 Rugby World Cup.
[48]	Presented a visualization system that uses statistics and movement analysis. Basically, the type of pattern of attack and play can be understood dynamically and visually.
[50]	Conducted a study on a decision support system for techniques and tactics in sports.

(iii) **Particle Swarm Optimization**: it is a bioinspired computational algorithm in the social behavior metaphor about the interaction between individuals (particles) of a group (swarm), developed in 1995 by Kennedy and Eberhart. This algorithm was implemented based on the observation of flocks of birds and shoals of fish in search of food in a certain region [61–63].

(iv) **Ant Colony Optimization**: the Ant Colony Optimization (ACO) is a bioinspired algorithm by the foraging behavior of some species of ants. Essentially, this technique applies the pheromone method that the ants deposit on the ground to demarcate a more favorable path and that must be followed by other members of the colony. The ACO uses a similar method to solve optimization problems [64, 65].

TABLE 6: Datasets.

Paper	Dataset
[27]	-
[23]	Moving images of 15 male college tennis players.
[33]	Data of Laguna Poreč half-marathon (2017) and Ormož half-marathon (2017).
[31]	A set of sports performance data of college students.
[35]	-
[37]	Training plan generated by an Artificial Sports Trainer and a list of potential nutrition.
[47]	-
[49]	Used exercise datasets for training.
[39]	Sports training plans generated by an Artificial Sport Trainer.
[41]	Training data and competitions of a cycling mode athlete.
[43]	Used sensors attached to various exercise equipment, allowing the collection of characteristics during the workout.
[45]	-
[24]	A football match data from European Cup 2008's final match - Spain vs Germany.
[53]	Data of matches played by India.
[51]	The data from the FIVB Volleyball World Championships finals that were held in Poland and Italy in 2014.
[36]	Data from 2005 to 2016, spanning 11 seasons of the English Premier League.
[30]	Data from 275 male golfers.
[38]	Website data http://www.football-data.co.uk/.
[40]	Real-life statistical data from cfbstats.com for past college football games.
[42]	A dataset comprising 778 games from the regular part of the 2009/2010 NBA season.
[28]	Data from One Day International (DOI) matches during the time period 2001-2015 for each team - http://www.cricinfo.com
[32]	An NBA men basketball dataset that is publicly available at open source sports in the period 1937 till 2011.
[26]	-
[34]	-
[25]	Data from 500 games from each of the 10 grandmaster chess players, a total of 5000 chess games.
[44]	Data from the First B basketball league for men in Serbia, from seasons 2005/06, 2006/07, 2007/08, 2008/09 and 2009/2010.
[29]	Weight shift data from golf experiments conducted by the research team.
[52]	Competition results for senior riders including the Australian Championships 2009, World Championships 2007–2010, UCI World Cup Melbourne 2010, UCI World Cup Cali 2011, UCI World Cup Beijing 2011, UCI World Cup Manchester 2011 and Oceania Championships 2010.
[46]	History of statistical data, ranking, and points of 20 rugby teams.
[48]	American football game data.
[50]	-

TABLE 7: Classification of thematic types by techniques.

Theme	Classification	Clustering	Association	Regression	Heuristic
Motion Analysis	[23, 27]	-	-	-	-
Performance Evaluation	-	[31]	-	-	[31, 33]
Sports Data Capture	[35]	-	-	-	-
Generating Eating Plans	-	-	-	-	[37]
Training Planning	[43, 47]	[41, 47]	[45]	-	[39, 49]
Strategic Planning	[51]	-	[24, 53]	-	-
Predicting Results/Patterns	[28, 30, 32, 34, 36, 38, 40, 42]	[26]	[34]	-	-
Sports Data Analytics	[25, 29, 44]	[25]	-	-	[29]
Decision Making Support	[46, 48, 52]	[50, 52]	[50]	[50]	-

TABLE 8: Algorithms.

Paper	Algorithm
[27]	Artificial Neural Networks, Statistical Classifiers and Hidden Markov Models.
[23]	C4.5, Random Forest and Native Bayes Tree.
[33]	Differential Evolution.
[31]	k-means, Ant Colony Optimization.
[35]	Naive Bayes.
[37]	Particle Swarm Optimization.
[47]	-
[49]	Bat Algorithm.
[39]	Particle Swarm Optimization.
[41]	K-Means.
[43]	Artificial Neural Networks.
[45]	AISReact.
[24]	Association Rule Mining Algorithms.
[53]	Association Rule Mining Algorithms.
[51]	Inductive Logic Programming
[36]	Gaussian Naive Bayes, Support Vector Machine and Random Forest.
[30]	Random Forest and Classification and Regression Trees.
[38]	Linear Algebra Methods, Artificial Neural Networks and Random Forest.
[40]	Decision tree, Artificial Neural Networks and Support Vector Machine.
[42]	Naive Bayes, Decision tree, Support Vector Machine and K Nearest Neighbors.
[28]	Naive Bayes, Support Vector Machine and Random Forest.
[32]	Random Forest.
[26]	K-means.
[34]	Artificial Neural Networks.
[25]	Hierarchical Clustering.
[44]	Artificial Neural Networks.
[29]	Particle Swarm Optimization, Support Vector Machine, C4.5.
[52]	Bayesian Belief Networks, Naive Bayes and K-means.
[46]	Random Forest.
[48]	-
[50]	-

(v) **Artificial Neural Networks:** Artificial Neural Networks (ANN) are widely used in machine learning. Fundamentally, this brain-inspired tool is meant to replicate the way humans learn. ANNs are excellent tools for finding patterns that are complex or numerous [66, 67].

(vi) **Support Vector Machine:** the SVM algorithms are based on the theory of statistical learning, developed by Vapnik [68] from studies initiated in [69]. This method establishes some principles that must be followed in obtaining classifiers with good generalization, defined as their ability to correctly predict the class of new data from the same domain in which learning occurred.

(vii) **CART Algorithm:** the CART algorithm is based on classification and regression trees. Basically, the algorithm builds a binary decision tree that divides a node into two child nodes repeatedly, starting with the root node that holds all the learning samples. The CART algorithm search all possible variables and values with the goals to detect the best one [70].

(viii) **Neural Network Ensemble:** it is a kind of modular neural network encompassing a set of whole problem classifiers where individual decisions are combined to classify new examples. It is a paradigm of learning where many neural networks are used together to solve a problem. This demonstrates that the generalization capacity of a neural network can be significantly improved through the use of several neural networks [71].

(ix) **Bayesian Classifier:** Bayesian classifiers use the Bayes theorem to perform probabilistic classification. They are statistical classifiers that classify an object into a given class based on the probability that the element belongs to this class. This theorem produces results quickly. It has great accuracy when applied on a big data if compared to the results produced by decision trees and neural networks. Then it is defined by the formula $P(H \mid E) = P(E \mid H)P(H)/P(E)$, where $P(H \mid E)$ is the probabilistic of some hypotheses H which are true whereas the evidence E is noticed. $P(H)$ is the probability that the hypothesis is true regardless of the evidence and $P(E)$ is the prior probability that the evidence will be observed [72].

(x) **Random Forest**: it was proposed in 2001 by Breiman with the goals to combine the classifiers created for several decision trees. This classifier is computationally efficient when each tree is built individually. Therefore, it is a combination of predictive trees which one depends on the vector of random values. This vector has the same distribution for all of the trees in the forest [73, 74].

(xi) **C4.5 Algorithm**: this algorithm builds a decision tree with a division and conquest strategy. Each node in the tree is associated with a set of cases. Furthermore, the cases are weights assigned to take into account the values of unknown attributes. The decision trees generated by it can be used for classification and are known as statistical classifiers [75].

(xii) **K-means Algorithm** this is a simple unsupervised learning algorithm that solves the known clustering problem. The procedure follows a simple way of classifying a given set of data across a number of groups [76, 77].

(xiii) **Hierarchical Clustering**: it is an approach of clustering analysis which has the purpose of building a hierarchy of groups. Strategies for hierarchical grouping are usually divided into two types. Bottom-up: in this method, each observation is assigned to its own group. Then, the similarity between each of the agglomerates is calculated and joined together the two most similar agglomerates. These procedures are repeated until there is only one group. Top-down: in this method, all observations are assigned to a single group; after that the group is divided into two less similar ones. Finally, it proceeds recursively in each group, until there is one for each observation [78].

It is important to emphasize that the revised works cited other algorithms for sports data mining. However, Table 8 is formed only by the algorithms applied in the surveys. Therefore, some of the algorithms mentioned are as follows:

(i) **A Priori Algorithm**: it is a classic algorithm used for data mining for association and learning rules that were proposed in 1994 by Agrawal and Srikant. This algorithm does a recursive search in the database seeking the frequent sets. It presents three phases: generation of candidate sets, pruning of candidate sets, and support calculation [79].

(ii) **Backpropagation Algorithm**: this algorithm was developed in the 70s; however it was fully appreciated after a famous article about the 80s. This article was written by David Rumelhart, Geoffrey Hinton, and Ronald Williams who described several neural networks in a scenario where backpropagation worked faster than previous approaches, making it possible to use neural networks to solve previously unsolvable problems. This algorithm is a multilayer network that uses an adjustment weight based on sigmoid function, such as delta rule. Backpropagation is a supervised learning method, where the function goals are known [80].

(iii) **Multilayer Perceptron Network**: this algorithm uses the backpropagation learning mechanism that is normally used for pattern recognition. Fundamentally, MLP is a multilayer feedforward network that uses a supervised learning mechanism based on the adjustment of its parameters according to the error between the desired and calculated output [7, 81].

(iv) **Levenberg-Marquardt Algorithm**: the Levenberg-Marquardt (LM) Algorithm is an iterative technique that identifies the minimum of a multivariate function, which is exposed with the sum of squares of real nonlinear functions. It is a standard technique for nonlinear least squares problems widely adopted [82, 83].

5.8. RQ8: Research Opportunities. Topics related to sports data mining are relevant. However, this domain still has several branches to be explored. Thus, in Table 9, we mapped the sports modalities or application field in which data mining was applied to papers addressing the topics. The goal of this table is to demonstrate possible gaps and future works to be investigated.

According to Table 9, general applications present 29.03% (9) of the papers. Essentially, this topic refers to surveys that were developed without a fixed scope in any sporting modality or field. Nevertheless, studies selected in the literature used more frequently basketball and football/soccer, covering 12.90% (4) and 9.67% (3), respectively. Table tennis, weight training, cycling, cricket, and golf were only 6.46% (2) each. Running, volleyball, American football, chess, and rugby were addressed in a single work each (3.22%). Thereby, there are distinct gaps to be explored since, considering high-quality works published from 2010 to 2018, few areas have been explored while there are many fields that could benefit from these applications, such as swimming, athletics, hockey, boxing, fencing, and tennis. That is, even with the growth sports data mining, there are still numerous fields of application to be studied. Therefore, seeking to aid researchers that intend to contribute to the community on these topics, a set of open hypothesis that could be examined in future studies are shown:

(i) **Analysis of sports performances**: helping to highlight good and bad techniques, beyond the team performance, through data mining, would assist coaches in decision making.

(ii) **Quick feedback systems**: data mining tools using systems that incorporate feedback sensors, to acquire values of biomechanical, physiological, cognitive, and

TABLE 9: Sports modalities or application field.

Modalities/Field	Articles
Table Tennis	[23, 50]
Running	[33]
Weight Training	[43, 49]
Cycling	[41, 52]
Basketball	[32, 42, 44, 45]
Volleyball	[51]
Football/Soccer	[24, 36, 38]
Cricket	[28, 53]
Golf	[29, 30]
American Football	[40]
Chess	[25]
Rugby	[46]
General Application	[26, 27, 31, 34, 35, 37, 39, 47, 48]

behavioral parameters of the training, could help to improve the performance of athletes in competition.

(iii) **Methods for talent detection**: systems capable of crossing information from athletes and find performance and development patterns can assist in detecting potential talents.

(iv) **Artificial Trainers**: smart tools to plan training sessions, specifying requirements, constraints, and goals, can present positive effects on athletes.

Finally, it is important to emphasize that the sports domain presents several others subjects in which data mining can be applied. Nevertheless, the objective of this section was to report themes and to highlight some hypotheses for future studies, based on the reviewed papers.

6. Final Considerations

In recent years, sports data mining has evolved. Consequently, many sports organizations have noticed that there is a wealth of unexplored knowledge in the data extracted by them. This is because even a small additional view of the variables can decide several factors, thus increasing the competitive advantage of the teams over their rivals. That is, data mining transfers to sports a higher degree of professionalism and reliability. Therefore, this article covered the last eight years (2010-2018) of papers available in relevant databases. The review issues considered methods, information, and applications. Thereby, the current panorama, temporal distribution, themes, the datasets used, proposals, and results of these revised works were presented. Moreover, techniques, algorithms, methods, and research opportunities have been reported.

As a result, we find 31 articles relevant that were separated into nine thematic types, whose highest frequency of publication was in the years 2014 and 2016. We also present the most cited articles, their datasets, and results. Regarding data mining techniques, the classification was most applied. Finally, possible areas to be explored were reported, such as swimming, athletics, hockey, boxing, fencing, and tennis. It

is expected that this article provides an important source of knowledge for future researches, beyond encouraging new studies.

Acknowledgments

The authors thank the Federal University of Technology, Paraná (UTFPR, Grant: April/2018), and Coordenação de Aperfeiçoamento de Pessoal de Nível Superior, Brasil (CAPES), Finance Code 001, for their financial support.

References

[1] E. Colantonio, "Detecção, seleção e promoção de talento esportivo: Considerações sobre a natação," *Revista Brasileira de Ciência e Movimento*, vol. 15, no. 1, pp. 127–135, 2007.

[2] M. J. Zaki and W. Meira Jr., *Data Mining And Analysis: Fundamental Concepts and Algorithms*, Cambridge University Press, UK, 2018.

[3] U. Fayyad, G. Piatetsky-Shapiro, and P. Smyth, "From data mining to knowledge discovery in databases," *AI Magazine*, vol. 17, no. 3, pp. 37–53, 1996.

[4] J. Han, J. Pei, and M. Kamber, *Data Mining: Concepts and Techniques*, Elsevier, 2011.

[5] O. N. Cardoso and R. T. Machado, "Gestão do conhecimento usando data mining: estudo de caso na Universidade Federal de Lavras," *Revista de Administração Pública*, vol. 42, no. 3, pp. 495–528, 2008.

[6] N. D. Galvão and H. D. F. Marin, "Técnica de mineração de dados: uma revisão da literatura," *Acta Paulista de Enfermagem*, vol. 22, no. 5, pp. 686–690, 2009.

[7] D. T. Larose, *Discovering Knowledge in Data: An Introduction to Data Mining*, John Wiley & Sons, Hoboken, NJ, USA, 2014.

[8] E. R. G. Dantas, J. C. Almeida, P. Júnior, D. S. de Lima, and J. Pessoa-UNIPÊ, "O uso da descoberta de conhecimento em base de dados para apoiar a tomada de decisões," in *V Simpósio de Excelência em Gestão e Tecnologia-SEGeT*, vol. 1, pp. 50–60, 2008.

[9] L. G. Castanheira, *Aplicação de técnicas de mineração de dados em problemas de classificação de padrões*, UFMG, Belo Horizonte, Brazil, 2008.

[10] J. McCullagh et al., "Data mining in sport: a neural network approach," *International Journal of Sports Science and Engineering*, vol. 4, no. 3, pp. 131–138, 2010.

[11] J. Lin, "Application of computer technology in sport data statistics," in *Proceedings of the Second International Conference on Innovative Computing and Cloud Computing*, pp. 248–250, ACM, Wuhan, China, December 2013.

[12] P. Brereton, B. A. Kitchenham, D. Budgen, M. Turner, and M. Khalil, "Lessons from applying the systematic literature review process within the software engineering domain," *The Journal of Systems and Software*, vol. 80, no. 4, pp. 571–583, 2007.

[13] B. Kitchenham, *Procedures for Performing Systematic Reviews*, Department of Computer Science, Keele University and National ICT, Australia Ltd, 2011.

[14] W. K. Bong, W. Chen, and A. Bergland, "Tangible user interface for social interactions for the elderly: a review of literature," *Advances in Human-Computer Interaction*, vol. 2018, 2018.

[15] R. P. Bonidia, J. D. Brancher, and R. M. Busto, "Data Mining in Sports: A Systematic Review," *IEEE Latin America Transactions*, vol. 16, no. 1, pp. 232–239, 2018.

[16] B. Kitchenham, *Procedures for Performing Systematic Reviews*, vol. 33, Keele University, Keele, UK, 2004.

[17] V. Smith, D. Devane, C. M. Begley, and M. Clarke, "Methodology in conducting a systematic review of systematic reviews of healthcare interventions," *BMC Medical Research Methodology*, vol. 11, no. 1, p. 15, 2011.

[18] S. L. Menezes, R. S. Freitas, and R. S. Parpinelli, "Mining of massive data bases using hadoop mapreduce and bio-inspired algorithms: A systematic review," *Revista de Informática Teórica e Aplicada*, vol. 23, no. 1, pp. 69–101, 2016.

[19] S. Karimi, S. Pohl, F. Scholer, L. Cavedon, and J. Zobel, "Boolean versus ranked querying for biomedical systematic reviews," *BMC Medical Informatics and Decision Making*, vol. 10, no. 1, p. 58, 2010.

[20] S. Fabbri, E. M. Hernandes, A. Di Thommazo, A. Belgamo, A. Zamboni, and C. Silva, "Managing literature reviews information through visualization," *ICEIS*, pp. 36–45, 2012.

[21] S. Fabbri, C. Silva, E. Hernandes, F. Octaviano, A. Di Thommazo, and A. Belgamo, "Improvements in the StArt tool to better support the systematic review process," in *Proceedings of the 20th International Conference on Evaluation and Assessment in Software Engineering*, p. 21, ACM, June 2016.

[22] E. Hernandes, A. Zamboni, A. Di Thommazo, and S. Fabbri, "Avaliação da ferramenta start utilizando o modelo tam e o paradigma gqm," in *Proceedings of the 7th Experimental Software Engineering Latin American Workshop (ESELAW 2010)*, p. 30, 2010.

[23] T. Maeda, M. Fujii, and I. Hayashi, "Sport motion picture analysis as time series data," in *Proceedings of the 2014 13th IEEE International Workshop on Advanced Motion Control, AMC 2014*, pp. 530–535, IEEE, Japan, March 2014.

[24] W. Puchun, "The application of data mining algorithm based on association rules in the analysis of football tactics," in *Proceedings of the 2016 International Conference on Robots & Intelligent System (ICRIS)*, pp. 418–421, IEEE, 2016.

[25] J. A. Brown, A. Cuzzocrea, M. Kresta, K. D. Kristjanson, C. K. Leung, and T. W. Tebinka, "A Machine Learning Tool for Supporting Advanced Knowledge Discovery from Chess Game Data," in *Proceedings of the 2017 16th IEEE International Conference on Machine Learning and Applications (ICMLA)*, pp. 649–654, Cancun, Mexico, December 2017.

[26] V. S. Tseng, C. Chou, K. Yang, and J. C. Tseng, "A big data analytical framework for sports behavior mining and personalized health services," in *Proceedings of the 2017 Conference on Technologies and Applications of Artificial Intelligence (TAAI)*, pp. 178–183, Taipei, December 2017.

[27] A. Baca, "Methods for Recognition and Classification of Human Motion Patterns – A Prerequisite for Intelligent Devices Assisting in Sports Activities," *IFAC Proceedings Volumes*, vol. 45, no. 2, pp. 55–61, 2012.

[28] N. Pathak and H. Wadhwa, "Applications of modern classification techniques to predict the outcome of ODI cricket," *Procedia Computer Science*, vol. 87, pp. 55–60, 2016.

[29] Y. Liu, Y. Y. Chung, and W. C. Yeh, "Simplified swarm optimization with sorted local search for golf data classification,"

[30] U. Johansson, R. Konig, P. Brattberg, A. Dahlbom, and M. Riveiro, "Mining trackman golf data," in *Proceedings of the International Conference on Computational Science and Computational Intelligence, CSCI 2015*, pp. 380–385, IEEE, December 2015.

[31] W. Jian, Z.-H. Hong, and Z.-Y. Zhou, "Clustering analysis of sports performance based on ant colony algorithm," in *Proceedings of the 2014 5th International Conference on Intelligent Systems Design and Engineering Applications, ISDEA 2014*, pp. 288–291, IEEE, 2014.

[32] G. Soliman, A. El-Nabawy, A. Misbah, and S. Eldawlatly, "Predicting all star player in the national basketball association using random forest," in *Proceedings of the 2017 Intelligent Systems Conference (IntelliSys)*, pp. 706–713, London, UK, September 2017.

[33] I. Fister, D. Fister, S. Deb, U. Mlakar, J. Brest, and I. Fister, "Post hoc analysis of sport performance with differential evolution," *Neural Computing and Applications*, pp. 1–10, 2018.

[34] B. Zhao and L. Chen, "Prediction model of sports results base on knowledge discovery in data-base," in *Proceedings of the 2016 International Conference on Smart Grid and Electrical Automation, ICSGEA 2016*, pp. 288–291, IEEE, China, August 2016.

[35] F. Simões, F. Matsunaga, A. Toda, J. Brancher, A. Junior, and R. Busto, "SSIE: An automatic data extractor for sports management in athletics modality," in *Proceedings of the 15th IEEE International Conference on Computer and Information Technology, CIT 2015, 14th IEEE International Conference on Ubiquitous Computing and Communications, IUCC 2015, 13th IEEE International Conference on Dependable, Autonomic and Secure Computing, DASC 2015 and 13th IEEE International Conference on Pervasive Intelligence and Computing, PICom 2015*, pp. 144–151, IEEE, October 2015.

[36] R. Baboota and H. Kaur, "Predictive analysis and modelling football results using machine learning approach for English Premier League," *International Journal of Forecasting*, 2018.

[37] D. Fister, I. Fister, and S. Rauter, "Generating eating plans for athletes using the particle swarm optimization," in *Proceedings of the 2016 IEEE 17th International Symposium on Computational Intelligence and Informatics (CINTI)*, pp. 000193–000198, IEEE, 2016.

[38] G. Kyriakides, K. Talattinis, and S. George, "Rating systems vs machine learning on the context of sports," in *Proceedings of the 18th Panhellenic Conference on Informatics*, pp. 1–6, ACM, Athens, Greece, October 2014.

[39] I. Fister Jr, A. Iglesias, E. Osaba, U. Mlakar, and J. Brest, "Adaptation of sport training plans by swarm intelligence," in *23rd International Conference on Soft Computing*, vol. 2017, pp. 56–67, Springer.

[40] C. K. Leung and K. W. Joseph, "Sports data mining: predicting results for the college football games," *Procedia Computer Science*, vol. 35, pp. 710–719, 2014.

[41] Y. Li and Y. Zhang, "Application of data mining techniques in sports training," in *Proceedings of the 2012 5th International Conference on Biomedical Engineering and Informatics, BMEI 2012*, pp. 954–958, IEEE, China, October 2012.

[42] D. Miljković, L. Gajić, A. Kovačević, and Z. Konjović, "The use of data mining for basketball matches outcomes prediction," in *Proceedings of the 8th IEEE International Symposium on

Intelligent Systems and Informatics, SIISY 2010, pp. 309–312, September 2010.

[43] H. Novatchkov and A. Baca, "Artificial intelligence in sports on the example of weight training," *Journal of Sports Science and Medicine*, vol. 12, no. 1, pp. 27–37, 2013.

[44] Z. Ivanković, M. Racković, B. Markoski, D. Radosav, and M. Ivković, "Analysis of basketball games using neural networks," in *Proceedings of the 11th IEEE International Symposium on Computational Intelligence and Informatics, CINTI 2010*, pp. 251–256, Hungary, November 2010.

[45] N. Ruiz, Q. Q. Feng, R. Taib, T. Handke, and F. Chen, "Cognitive skills learning: Pen input patterns in computer-based athlete training," in *Proceedings of the 1st International Conference on Multimodal Interfaces and the Workshop on Machine Learning for Multimodal Interaction, ICMI-MLMI 2010*, p. 41, Association for Computing Machinery, China, November 2010.

[46] A. Pretorius and D. A. Parry, "Human decision making and artificial intelligence: a comparison in the domain of sports prediction," in *Proceedings of the Annual Conference of the South African Institute of Computer Scientists and Information Technologists, (SAICSIT '16)*, vol. 32, pp. 1–32, ACM, New York, NY, USA, September 2016.

[47] I. Fister Jr., I. Fister, D. Fister, and S. Fong, "Data mining in sporting activities created by sports trackers," in *Proceedings of the 2013 International Symposium on Computational and Business Intelligence (ISCBI '13)*, pp. 88–91, IEEE, August 2013.

[48] T. Tani, H.-H. Huang, and K. Kawagoe, "Sports play visualization system using trajectory mining method," in *Proceedings of the International workshop on Innovations in Information and Communication Science and Technology*, IICST-Innertech Institute Of Computer Science and Technology, Warsaw, Poland, September 2014.

[49] I. Fister, S. Rauter, X.-S. Yang, K. Ljubič, and I. Fister, "Planning the sports training sessions with the bat algorithm," *Neurocomputing*, vol. 149, pp. 993–1002, 2015.

[50] L. Yu, P. Ling, and H. Zhang, "Study on the decision support system of techniques and tactics in net sports and the application in Beijing Olympic Games," in *Proceedings of the 2010 2nd WRI Global Congress on Intelligent Systems, GCIS 2010*, vol. 1, pp. 170–174, China, December 2010.

[51] J. Van Haaren, H. B. Shitrit, J. Davis, and P. Fua, "Analyzing volleyball match data from the 2014 world championships using machine learning techniques," in *Proceedings of the 22nd ACM SIGKDD International Conference on Knowledge Discovery and Data Mining, KDD 2016*, pp. 627–634, USA, August 2016.

[52] B. Ofoghi, J. Zeleznikow, C. Macmahon, and D. Dwyer, "Supporting athlete selection and strategic planning in track cycling omnium: A statistical and machine learning approach," *Information Sciences*, vol. 233, pp. 200–213, 2013.

[53] K. A. A. D. Raj and P. Padma, "Application of association rule mining: A case study on team india," in *Proceedings of the 2013 3rd International Conference on Computer Communication and Informatics, ICCCI 2013*, pp. 1–6, IEEE, India, January 2013.

[54] N. Ye et al., *The Handbook of Data Mining*, vol. 24, Lawrence Erlbaum Associates, Publishers, Mahwah, NJ, USA, London, 2003.

[55] É. B. Marques, L. H. Raimann, A. de Oliveira, and A. J. H. Zamberlam, "Anais do VII Simpósio de Informática da Região Centro do RS - SIRC/RS 2008 - ISBN 978-85-88667-89-1, Santa Maria - RS," in *Proposta de um módulo de data mining para um sistema de scout no voleibol*, 2008.

[56] J. Hipp, U. Güntzer, and G. Nakhaeizadeh, "Algorithms for association rule mining—a general survey and comparison," *ACM SIGKDD Explorations Newsletter*, vol. 2, no. 1, pp. 58–64, 2000.

[57] D. S. Johnson, "Approximation algorithms for combinatorial problems," *Journal of Computer and System Sciences*, vol. 9, pp. 256–278, 1974.

[58] R. L. Rardin and R. Uzsoy, "Experimental evaluation of heuristic optimization algorithms: A tutorial," *Journal of Heuristics*, vol. 7, no. 3, pp. 261–304, 2001.

[59] R. Storn and K. Price, "Differential evolution—a simple and efficient heuristic for global optimization over continuous spaces," *Journal of Global Optimization*, vol. 11, no. 4, pp. 341–359, 1997.

[60] A. K. Qin, V. L. Huang, and P. N. Suganthan, "Differential evolution algorithm with strategy adaptation for global numerical optimization," *IEEE Transactions on Evolutionary Computation*, vol. 13, no. 2, pp. 398–417, 2009.

[61] M. Clerc, *Particle Swarm Optimization*, vol. 93, John Wiley & Sons, 2010.

[62] Y. Shi et al., "Particle swarm optimization: developments, applications and resources," in *Proceedings of the 2001 Congress on Evolutionary Computation*, vol. 1, pp. 81–86, IEEE, 2001.

[63] I. C. Trelea, "The particle swarm optimization algorithm: convergence analysis and parameter selection," *Information Processing Letters*, vol. 85, no. 6, pp. 317–325, 2003.

[64] M. Dorigo, M. Birattari, and T. Stützle, "Ant colony optimization," *IEEE Computational Intelligence Magazine*, vol. 1, no. 4, pp. 28–39, 2006.

[65] V. Maniezzo and A. Carbonaro, "Anais do VII Simpósio de Informática da Região Centro do RS - SIRC/RS 2008 - ISBN 978-85-88667-89-1, Santa Maria - RS," in *Essays and Surveys in Metaheuristics*, vol. 15, pp. 469–492, Springer, 2008.

[66] R. J. Schalkoff, *Artificial Neural Networks*, vol. 1, McGraw-Hill, New York, NY, USA, 1997.

[67] B. Yegnanarayana, *Artificial Neural Networks*, PHI Learning Pvt. Ltd., 2009.

[68] V. N. Vapnik, *The Nature of Statistical Learning Theory*, Springer, 1995.

[69] V. N. Vapnik and A. Y. Chervonenkis, "On the uniform convergence of relative frequencies of events to their probabilities," in *Measures of Complexity*, pp. 11–30, Springer, 2015.

[70] D. G. Denison, B. K. Mallick, and A. F. Smith, "A bayesian cart algorithm," *Biometrika*, vol. 85, no. 2, pp. 363–377, 1998.

[71] Z. Zhou, J. Wu, and W. Tang, "Ensembling neural networks: many could be better than all," *Artificial Intelligence*, vol. 137, no. 1-2, pp. 239–263, 2002.

[72] L. Smith, B. Lipscomb, and A. Simkins, "Data mining in sports: predicting cy young award winners," *Journal of Computing Sciences in Colleges*, vol. 22, no. 4, pp. 115–121, 2007.

[73] P. O. Gislason, J. A. Benediktsson, and J. R. Sveinsson, "Random forests for land cover classification," *Pattern Recognition Letters*, vol. 27, no. 4, pp. 294–300, 2006.

[74] C. A. B. Segundo, A. A. de Abreu, and A. A. Esmin, "XII Encontro Nacional de inteligência Artificial e Computacional," in *Previsão de resultados de jogos do campeonato brasileiro de futebol: Uma abordagem de mineração de dados*, pp. 1–6, SBC, 2015.

[75] S. Ruggieri, "Efficient C4.5 [classification algorithm]," *IEEE Transactions on Knowledge and Data Engineering*, vol. 14, no. 2, pp. 438–444, 2002.

[76] R. Adderley, M. Townsley, and J. Bond, "Use of data mining techniques to model crime scene investigator performance," *Knowledge-Based Systems*, vol. 20, no. 2, pp. 170–176, 2007.

[77] J. A. Hartigan and M. A. Wong, "Algorithm as 136: A k-means clustering algorithm," *Journal of the Royal Statistical Society. Series C (Applied Statistics)*, vol. 28, no. 1, pp. 100–108, 1979.

[78] M. Steinbach, G. Karypis, V. Kumar et al., "A comparison of document clustering techniques," in *Proceedings of the KDD Workshop on Text Mining*, vol. 400, pp. 525-526, Boston, Mass, USA.

[79] Y. Ye and C.-C. Chiang, "A parallel apriori algorithm for frequent itemsets mining," in *Proceedings of the Fourth International Conference on Software Engineering Research*, pp. 87–94, IEEE, 2006.

[80] R. Rojas, "The backpropagation algorithm," in *Neural Networks*, pp. 149–182, Springer, Berlin, Germany, 1996.

[81] D. Delen, D. Cogdell, and N. Kasap, "A comparative analysis of data mining methods in predicting NCAA bowl outcomes," *International Journal of Forecasting*, vol. 28, no. 2, pp. 543–552, 2012.

[82] M. I. Lourakis, "A brief description of the levenberg-marquardt algorithm implemented by levmar," *Foundation of Research and Technology*, vol. 4, pp. 1-6, 2005.

[83] A. Ranganathan, "The levenberg-marquardt algorithm," *Tutorial on LM Algorithm*, vol. 11, no. 1, pp. 101–110, 2004.

4

A Case Study of MasterMind Chess: Comparing Mouse/Keyboard Interaction with Kinect-Based Gestural Interface

Gabriel Alves Mendes Vasiljevic, Leonardo Cunha de Miranda, and Erica Esteves Cunha de Miranda

Department of Informatics and Applied Mathematics, Federal University of Rio Grande do Norte (UFRN), 59078-970 Natal, RN, Brazil

Correspondence should be addressed to Gabriel Alves Mendes Vasiljevic; gabrielvasiljevic@outlook.com

Academic Editor: Thomas Mandl

As gestural interfaces emerged as a new type of user interface, their use has been vastly explored by the entertainment industry to better immerse the player in games. Despite being mainly used in dance and sports games, little use was made of gestural interaction in more slow-paced genres, such as board games. In this work, we present a Kinect-based gestural interface for an online and multiplayer chess game and describe a case study with users with different playing skill levels. Comparing the mouse/keyboard interaction with the gesture-based interaction, the results of the activity were synthesized into lessons learned regarding general usability and design of game control mechanisms. These results could be applied to slow-paced board games like chess. Our findings indicate that gestural interfaces may not be suitable for competitive chess matches, yet it can be fun to play while using them in casual matches.

1. Introduction

As computational systems advance in processing power and become more present in people's lives, new types of interaction arise. Touch screen and voice user interfaces, for example, are being widely used as interaction interfaces for smartphones, as they provide more usability than onscreen keyboards. Electronic entertainment systems, for example, video games, are also experimenting new forms of interaction to better immerse the player in the game, such as Virtual Reality (VR) and gestural interfaces. Regarding the latter, many current video games already utilize this type of interaction to control games, for example, Microsoft Xbox and Nintendo Wii.

Apart from video games, which explore a wide range of gestural interaction possibilities in game genres such as dance and sports, this technology is also starting to be used to control other systems, such as a PC itself. Regarding video games, as gestural interfaces are a relatively new kind of interaction paradigm, their usability has not yet been deeply investigated for many other genres such as board or turn-based games.

Gestural-based games began to increase in number and popularity with the advent of modern video games' built-in gesture technologies, such as the Kinect for Xbox One (http://www.xbox.com/en-US/xbox-one/accessories/kinect-for-xbox-one). At first, sports [1] and the dance [2] genres were dominant due to their straightforward mapping of gestures or body movements to game controls, but more games of different styles began to appear as this new form of interaction became more popular. However, one particular genre of game that has not gained popularity in gesture-based systems is board games, such as chess or checkers. A possible reason for the gaming industry's and developers' lack of interest in board games might be that, as a gaming platform that uses the whole body as a controller, it is expected that the player uses a lot of movement from their body to perform an action or complete an objective.

In typical board games, the only physical action that a player needs to perform is to move a piece, which requires much less effort than, for example, fighting an enemy with a sword. Nevertheless, this does not exclude the possibility that a gestural board game could be designed and still be fun to play, as it adds more interaction and movement to the game. Even if this type of control could possibly increase fatigue or discomfort, players could feel more motivated to play due to the enjoyment that this interface may bring [3]. Moreover, it could arouse the interest of users that do not like slow-paced board games due to their lack of body movement. Although there is no official gestural chess game available for the Kinect platform, some researches and developers are already exploring this particular genre.

This gestural interface is not easy to either conceive or implement, as this kind of interface brings many usability and gameplay issues [4, 5]. To help in this task, an online and multiplayer chess game was adapted to use gestural input based on the investigation of related gestural board games and the current available gestural technologies. To test the implementation, a case study was performed with chess players using the principles of experimental research [6, 7], and the findings were discussed.

There are a very few implemented board games that use gestural interaction. More importantly, there is no actual evaluation of this kind of control in this specific type of game, making it hard to define whether a gestural control fits or not into the context of the game and how it performs in comparison to the traditional mouse and keyboard input. These factors highlight the importance of this evaluation.

This paper is organized as follows: we briefly present related work of gesture-based computer board games in Section 2, proceed with detailing our Kinect-based gestural interface and its implementation in Section 3, showcase a case study using the gestural interface with chess players and its results in Section 4, and synthetize and discuss the results in Section 5. Finally, conclusions and future work are outlined in Section 6.

2. Related Work

We performed a search for gesture-based computer board games within the digital libraries of ACM, IEEE, and Google Scholar as well as in Kinect project communities, such as KineckHacks (http://www.kinecthacks.com/) and Develop Kinect (http://www.developkinect.com/). Based on the related games that were found, it is clear that there are a very limited number of implemented and reported on-computer board games using gestural interaction, both academic and commercial/hobbyist.

Although the use of gestural input for board games is not very popular, there are a few researches that explore this direction. Sriboonruang et al. [8], for example, developed a visual gestural interface for board games, which measures the distance between the player's thumb and index finger to determine whether the player is in a state of holding a piece. If so, the system then tracks the hand until the action of holding the piece is no longer executed and puts the previously selected piece on the destination square. Li and Hong [9], using a stereo camera, developed a real-time hand gesture recognition system. This system can recognize up to five different hand gestures and was used as a controller for a Korean chess game, in which the player was able to move the pieces using those gestures.

Kalpakas et al. [10] developed a system that recognizes 2D gestures using a web camera on the top of a wood chess board. The user can select a piece and choose a destination spot by pointing the location on the board using the index finger. The system tracks the position of the user's fingertip on the board to determine where to move the piece.

We also found projects in different Kinect developer communities. In [11], for example, the user controls the pieces by using the hands as in real life, that is, taking a piece with the hand and putting it on the destination square. The difference is that the computer's artificial intelligence responds by actually moving a physical piece in a board using a mechanical hand. In [12], a gestural-based game of checkers was developed, where the user can select, drag, and drop the pieces using hand gestures. Even though it does not use direct gestures to control the pieces, in [13] a Kinect-based accessible system was developed to allow visually impaired users to play chess against the computer. The Kinect, positioned on top of the board, recognizes the hand of the user as s/he performs a movement. Then, the computer gives audible feedback, for the player to know to what square the piece has moved and what the next movement of the computer is.

In Robot Chess (http://apps.leapmotion.com/apps/robot-chess/windows), the most recent gesture-based chess computer game when the search was performed, the player uses a Leap Motion (https://www.leapmotion.com/) to control a robotic hand in a virtual environment, against a robot. The pieces are controlled by hovering the hand-cursor over them and grabbing using the fingers. All menus are also controlled using exclusively the hand and the Leap Motion device. The system is also fully operational with the Oculus Rift (https://www.oculus.com/en-us/rift/), making the user capable of playing the game in a VR environment, also using the Leap Motion to control moves.

It appears that no further significant investment was made in the research, development, and/or evaluation of this kind of game in the past few years. It also appears that there are a very small number of researches with actual users in this particular genre; therefore it may be hard to have conclusive results regarding the application of gestural technology in slow-paced board games, such as chess. Being so, it is clear that researches using actual players, in order to evaluate the use of gestural interface in this specific genre—especially in comparison to the traditional platforms—are needed to investigate this application.

3. MasterMind Chess

Chess is one of the most famous and most-played board games in the world. Its popularity makes it a valuable candidate to test this kind of interaction in turn-based board games and to evaluate whether it makes sense to adapt this kind of game for gestural input. To this purpose, the MasterMind Chess game (available for free download at http://www.mastermindchess.pairg.ufrn.br) [14], an online, multiplayer, and multilanguage chess game, was adapted to handle gestural input and enable users to play chess using only the movement of one hand. This adaptation was possible due to the development of a gestural interface for the MasterMind Chess game, that is, the MasterMind Chess Kinect Module. The programming language used for this implementation was C#, due to the integration with the Kinect platform.

The MasterMind Chess game supports two more game modes, apart from the traditional, classic game, composed of the classic pieces in an 8 × 8 board. The first is Capablanca chess, where the traditional 8 × 8 board is exchanged for a larger 8 × 10 board, with two additional types of pieces. The other game mode is Fischer Random Chess. In this mode, the game still occurs in an 8 × 8 board, but the starting positions of the pieces of the same color, apart from the pawns, are permuted with each other. The Kinect Module gestural interface for the MasterMind Chess also allows the users to play these game modes using gestural input.

Many factors led to the choice of using the Kinect for Windows (https://developer.microsoft.com/en-us/windows/kinect) over other candidates—for example, Leap Motion and Asus Xtion (http://www.asus.com/3D-Sensor/Xtion/)—of gestural devices in the implementation of a nonperceptual gesture-based interface [15]. It is a well-grounded technology that has been on the market for years, with both theoretical and practical background supported by a great number of scientific researches, not only for entertainment, but also in the medical field [16, 17]. Although it is not as accurate as recent technologies, it is more accessible, in terms of ease of acquisition in comparison to the other available devices, and already has all the necessary drivers and programming libraries to fully support its functionalities. This decision was as a result of an investigation of the available gestural technologies that exist nowadays and the availability of these technologies to the authors.

The main purpose of the gestural module is to map the position of the player's hand, in Kinect's skeleton coordinates, to the screen of the MasterMind Chess game. The module offers the option to the players to choose if they want to use the right or left hand to control the game. After tracking the chosen hand's position, the gestural module sends the information in packets to the MasterMind Chess application. The Kinect device was positioned below the monitor, facing towards the player. Other approaches use the Kinect above the monitor, facing down, as in [18]; however, for our particular application, it was found that the Kinect performed better in this position and require less calibration to recognize the players' hands.

These packets containing the mapped position of the user's hand to the screen are organized in a seven-bit array and sent to the game through the UDP protocol. This packet is then read and translated to an action in the game, such as moving the cursor or selecting a piece, for example. The gestural interaction is not limited to the game itself; that is, it can also be used to navigate through the main screen of the software and the other menus. We found that using UDP for the communication between the application and the gestural module was easier to implement than using interprocess communication and shared-memory algorithms.

The action of clicking is represented by "holding the hand steady" at a position for a certain amount of time. In implementation terms, this means that if the user moves the hand in a radius of what corresponds to at most five pixels on the screen (or approximately 0.13 cm in space) during a period of 800 ms, this will be interpreted as a click. Furthermore, there is a 600 ms delay between two clicks, to try to avoid unintentionally clicking two times in a row.

A technical problem regarding Kinect's field of view occurs when the mapped position of the hands stands near the bounds of the game screen, as the Kinect starts to fail at recognizing a precise location for the hand and the cursor starts to tremble, making it hard to select or move a piece, since the clicking action requires a steady position of the cursor. To avoid this problem, the mapping function that translates the skeleton coordinates of the Kinect into screen coordinates in the MasterMind Chess application was adapted to fit the view, so the boundaries of Kinect's field of view remain out of the MasterMind Chess board range. This approach might cause a loss of precision regarding capturing the speed of the hand but avoids some of the imprecision caused by the hardware.

4. Case Study

In order to evaluate the user feedback regarding the new gestural interface, an activity was made using chess players with different levels of skill in the game. The users were asked to play the game using both the gestural and the mouse/keyboard interface and gave their opinions about the flaws and qualities of each one.

4.1. Research Questions. The general research question that this study presents and tries to answer is whether a gestural user interface is suitable for slow-paced board games. The specific research questions include the following:

(i) Is gestural interaction suitable for serious chess-playing?

(ii) What usability issues adding a gestural interface brings to the game? These issues can be overcome?

(iii) How the gestural interaction performs while compared to the mouse/keyboard interaction?

The evaluation process was composed of questionnaires, interviews, observation, and video analysis.

4.2. Methodology. For the application of the activity, there were two facilitators, one interviewer, two cameramen, and one background observer who overviewed the activity and only intervened when the facilitators required additional assistance. The interviewer performed the interview, recorded the audio, and made additional annotations to the answers. The cameramen filmed the entire sections of activities with users in different rooms. The facilitators resolved questions and problems of the chess players during the activities. They were also responsible for observing notable events and user reactions, in order to support the interviewer by indicating additional questions that should be posed to specific users.

4.2.1. Participants. A total of eight subjects participated in the activities, seven male and one female, with ages ranging from 19 to 25. The subjects were divided into three groups of four or two subjects each (U1, U2, . . ., U7, and U8), according to their skill levels in chess, that is, beginner, intermediate, and advanced. The beginner group (U1, U2, U3, and U4) was formed by the subjects with only basic knowledge of chess, sufficient enough to know how to move the pieces and end the game. The intermediate group (U5 and U6) was composed of the subjects that had a solid knowledge of basic chess strategy, such as famous opening and ending moves. The advanced group (U7 and U8) was formed by players who have a deep knowledge of chess, including advanced strategies and counterstrategies. These players had sound ELO (the ELO rating is a mathematical method to calculate the relative skill of a player in competitive games) and FIDE (the World Chess Federation, FIDE (Fédération Internationale des Échecs), is an international organization that regularizes and connects national chess federations all over the world) ratings and have prospects of a professional career in chess, such as participations in big tournaments. Only two volunteers were available for participating in the advanced and intermediate group each, so that there was a difference in the size of the groups.

All users are undergraduate or graduate students. None have any kind of special need. Table 1 summarizes the demographic data from all subjects.

4.2.2. Procedure. The activity was explained to the participants as the first step. The background observer explained each step and what the participants would have to do. The main features of the game were described and the users were given instructions on how to use the controls. To ensure that all participants received a comparable level of help and instructions, the same instructions were given to all participants, and each was aware that they could ask questions regarding the game and the experiment at any time. The experiment only began once the user stated that s/he comprehended the instructions.

Four questionnaires were used. The first questionnaire gathered essential demographic information about the subjects, such as the age, gender, if the user is right-handed or left-handed, their level of skill in chess, and how often they play the game. The second questionnaire addressed questions about the mouse/keyboard interaction with the game and was applied after the user played the first match using this interaction. The questions included whether the players used the keyboard to play (and if not, why), whether they tried to use any hotkey, whether they suggested any hotkey, and which was the preferred control device (mouse or keyboard).

The third questionnaire considered the gestural interaction and was applied after the users played the match using the gestural interface. Some of the questions included whether the users already used a gestural technology, such as the Kinect, whether they tried to use another body part to interact with the game other than a single hand, whether they felt that the performance in the game was affected by the gestural interaction, whether this mode of interaction

TABLE 1: Demographic data from subjects.

User	Age	Gender	Chess knowledge	Handedness	Chess matches per month
U1	25	M	Beginner	Right	0–3
U2	21	F	Beginner	Right	0–3
U3	25	M	Beginner	Right	0–3
U4	23	M	Beginner	Right	0–3
U5	23	M	Intermediate	Right	0–3
U6	23	M	Intermediate	Right	0–3
U7	22	M	Advanced	Right	10–15
U8	19	M	Advanced	Left	10–15

fit in the context of the chess game, whether they would use this type of interaction to play chess again, and whether they could satisfactorily perform all the desired movements. The fourth and last questionnaire was about the game in general. This included questions that regarded overall aspects of the game, such as if the visual elements of the game were presented in an intuitive way, if the user interface was enjoyable, if the current sounds of the game were sufficient, if the user missed some feature, and what kind of interaction, between mouse/keyboard and gestural, best fitted in the context of the game. This questionnaire was applied after the users had played both matches.

After the questionnaires, each user had a particular interview to probe any information left unanswered. The common questions of the interview were about how the users enjoyed playing the MasterMind Chess, whether they had any difficulties in interacting with the game and what these were, what interaction mode they liked most and why, whether they felt inhibited to play due to the fact of being filmed, how they were feeling during the match, and overall suggestions. Other questions were asked depending on the answers given by the users in the questionnaires. If an answer was too vague or required explanation, it was reinforced in the interview.

The activity's overall process is illustrated in Figure 1.

The facilitators observed the users in their activity and made annotations about their reaction and extraordinary events. Some examples of these reactions and events include whether the user talks during the match, if s/he makes comments or complains about the gameplay, if s/he shows any signs of disappointment or frustration, and whether s/he is having any kind of difficulties in playing the game.

Each group was divided into pairs of subjects, making a total of four pairs of equal level of skill between themselves. Each of these pairs was put to play for a total of two matches of 15 minutes for each player (i.e., 30-minute maximum time) against each other, in separate rooms, that is, one match using mouse/keyboard and another using only the gestural module. The second pair of beginner users played in the inverse order (i.e., first gestural interaction, then mouse/keyboard). For the users in intermediate and advanced levels, one of the matches (the first match in the advanced level and the second in the intermediate level) was in Capablanca mode, since its board is larger and the gameplay could be slightly different.

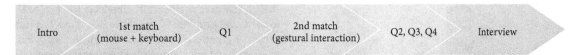

FIGURE 1: Activity flow.

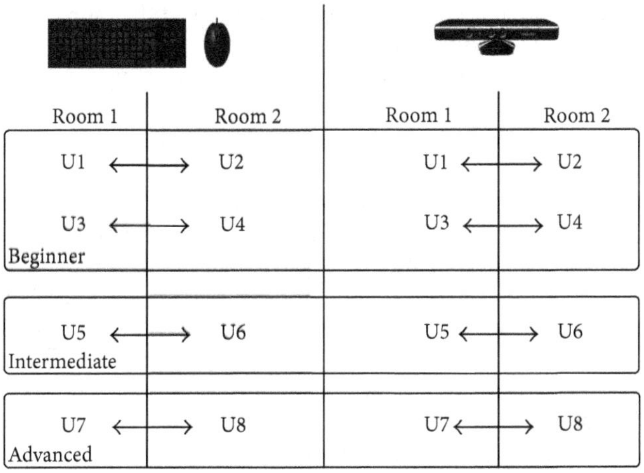

FIGURE 2: Activity's configuration.

In the mouse/keyboard match, the users were sitting on a chair and had only the mouse, keyboard, screen, and speakers (to hear the sound feedback of the game) available to interact. In the gestural match, the users were standing in front of the screen at an arbitrary distance. As the Kinect has a limited field of view, the sensor was adjusted to the person's height, for it to be able to capture all of the user's hands movements. The users were allowed to speak freely and make any commentary or observation during the match. After each match, they answered a questionnaire about the gameplay and usability of the type of interaction used and then a questionnaire about the game itself and then participated in a particular interview, to probe information left unanswered in the questionnaires. Figure 2 represents the configuration of the rooms and subjects for each match.

4.2.3. Design. In this case study, there were two independent variables:

   (i) *Game interaction*: mouse/keyboard and gestural.

   (ii) *User expertise in chess*: beginner, intermediate, and advanced.

Each user was tested on each interaction; therefore the study is a 3 × 2 within-subject design [19]. A 2 × 2 balanced Latin square [20] was used as a counterbalance in the beginners group to alternate the order of the interaction (i.e., users U3 and U4 played first with the gestural interaction mode). No counterbalance was used in the intermediate and advanced groups, as only two matches were played by each group.

4.3. Results. The activity revealed some important details about the gestural interaction and how the participants understood the game. By observing how the participants behaved while playing with the gestural module and given their feedback on the questionnaires and the interview, it became clear what points should be changed and improved both in the game in general and in the Kinect interface.

Regarding the mouse/keyboard interaction, no user claimed to have difficulties using it. The mouse/keyboard questionnaire had seven questions that the users answered after playing the game using only this kind of interaction. The first one regarded the use of the keyboard to play the game, and seven users had not used the keyboard at all. Only one user (U5) used the keyboard instead of the mouse. This particular user said that the keyboard was more practical and accessible. All the others claimed that the mouse was faster and more precise, that they were used to the mouse to interact with user interfaces, and that they did not feel the need to use the keyboard.

Only one user (U1) found it to necessary to use hotkeys. He suggested using the Escape key to deselect a piece. No user had tried to use a hotkey while playing. This was somewhat expected, as there are almost no special commands that could be used in a regular chess game, except for chatting, for example. If the same command that is used to move the pieces is also used to control the other functions of the game and if this command is satisfactory to the users, the handling of these options tends to also be of easy use.

Only one user (U4) felt mental fatigue while playing, but no user felt physical fatigue. This particular user said that he felt "only a little" mental fatigue, in his words. As one user (U3) commented, for a player used to playing computer games and/or chess very frequently, remaining seated for half an hour to play hardly causes any type of physical fatigue. All users stated that the way of selecting and moving the pieces was adequate.

Regarding the gestural and Kinect technology, only two users (U2 and U7) had never used the Kinect before. No user tried to use any other part of the body than the hands to interact with the game. Seven users felt that their performance was impaired because of the gestural interface. From these users, four (U4, U6, U7, and U8) said it was because the interface was slower than the mouse/keyboard. The others found it difficult to move the piece using the gestures.

Only one user (U4) felt mental fatigue while using the gestural interface. Three users (U2, U4, and U7) had reported feeling pain or discomfort in a part of the body while playing. U2 and U4 felt pain or discomfort in the legs, U4 in the shoulders, and U7 in the hand.

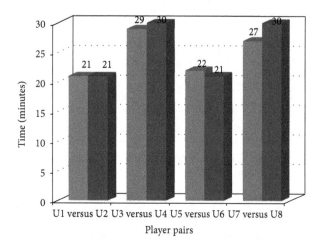

FIGURE 3: Chart of duration of the matches.

Regarding the movements, four users (U1, U2, U5, and U8) stated that they did not accomplish all the movements they wanted in a satisfactory way. Only one user (U5) said that he made an erroneous movement because of the interface; the others said that the precision in the corners of the board declined. Four users (U2, U5, U7, and U8) said that the gestural interaction disturbed the playability of the game; three users (U2, U3, and U8) stated that the gestural interaction fit in the context of a chess game.

In relation to whether the users would use the gestural module to play chess again, only two users (U5 and U8) would do so. The others stated that the reaction time of the game increased during gestural interaction and that the game would be best played while sitting but would consider using the gestural interaction again if those changes were made. Nevertheless, it is important to notice that these statements may have come from a good-subject effect or a novelty effect.

Figure 3 compares the match durations of different interaction types for each player pair. Reaching the 30-minute mark—gestural matches of U3 versus U4 and U7 versus U8—means that one of the players lost by timeout.

The great majority of the users had already used the Kinect technology, usually to play games on the Xbox 360, so they were habituated to using gestures to control the interface. In relation to other Kinect-based games, the MasterMind Chess gestural interface should be intuitive, as the user only uses a hand to control the cursor and click. Consistently with this conjecture, no user tried to use another body part to control the game. However, the majority of users felt that they had a lower-than-expected game performance, mainly because of the way used to select the pieces.

Two users (U7 and U8), the advanced ones, said that the time it took to select or deselect the piece consumed too much of the user's time. It takes around one and a half seconds to select and deselect a piece when the cursor is steady at the position, but if a user selects a piece and stays with the cursor at the same position for another 1,400 ms (800 ms standard time plus 600 ms of cooldown), the piece is selected again;

that is, the user accidentally deselects the piece. This points towards the problem of the timing: as chess is a time-critical game to competitive players, the time that a player loses by selecting a piece impacts their performance. This could perhaps be overcome by adding a time bonus to the gestural user's clock corresponding to the additional time it takes to move the piece in this mode or using an additional body movement to instantly click, for example, using the height of the other arm as reference; that is, the user would select the location of a piece with one arm and rise the other above the previous to select the piece.

Another issue caused by the timing for selecting a piece is that the users might accidentally move a piece to an undesired location, if they move the cursor too slowly. This caused some cases of the player moving the cursor much slower than expected, leading to unintentionally "clicking" in the middle of the path to the desired square and thus losing a piece or ruining the player's game strategy.

Yet another problem that the users reported and that influenced their performance was that it was hard to control the cursor in the borders of the screen, making it difficult to select a piece in the corners of the board that was close to those borders. However, this is a technical problem of the Kinect platform, which becomes imprecise on the limits of the field of view of Kinect's infrared camera. As stated before, one possible solution would be to adjust the calculation of the conversion of coordinates between the Kinect and the MasterMind Chess in a way in which a small movement of the hand causes larger displacement of the cursor on the screen. That way, the user would not require going to the borders of Kinect's field of view to reach the outer borders of the board. This occurs because the gestural interface converts the exact size of Kinect's view to the exact size of MasterMind Chess's view; that is, to move from one corner of the screen to another, the user has to move the hand all the way across Kinect's field of vision. However, as already mentioned, decreasing the necessary movement to move the cursor along the screen also decreases the precision; that is, the player must make more cautious movements.

One issue that most of the users reported was that it was at times difficult to recognize the pieces, since they needed to maintain a certain distance to the screen due to Kinect's minimum required distance for recognizing the person's body. As MasterMind Chess pieces have a 3D design that is seen from above, from a distance the pieces might look similar, especially the black ones. This forced most of the users to get closer to the screen to be able to distinguish the pieces, as shown in Figure 4.

While some of the users only approached to see the pieces and then got back to their original position to make a move, others tended to remain at a closer position to the screen as the game progressed, as shown in Figure 5. The figure also shows the time of each image.

Related to the fact that some users complained that they could not remain seated to play, one possible solution would be to develop a method in which the users could use the gestural module in the same way they use the mouse/keyboard input, that is, while sitting in front of the screen. This is virtually impossible using the Kinect platform,

FIGURE 4: Subject getting closer to the screen to better see the pieces.

FIGURE 5: Subjects tending to remain closer to the screen.

due to the minimum distance to recognize the person and the fact that the position of a sitting person is harder to identify. This could be solved by using another gestural technology that does not require seeing the entire player, but only the hands. A better approach in this case would be to use the Leap Motion technology, as it can be placed in front or at the side of the screen and recognizes the hands and fingers of the player in a volumetric field of view on top of it. Therefore, the player would be able to play the game while sitting, using the fingers to select the square and pushing it forward to click. A similar approach was used in Robot Chess (see Section 2), but no evaluation with users was yet made to compare the results.

When asked whether the gestural interaction fit into the context of the game, the opinions were divided. Some users said that the gestural interaction did not fit in because chess is the type of game that requires the players to stay seated while thinking and that it is unnecessary to stand while playing chess. When asked if they could have the option to play with the gestural module while sitting, the great majority of these players said that it would be much better.

Even not considering the gestural interface to be the best type of control for a chess game, some users stated that they would play again with the Kinect, for it is an interesting type of control that adds more interaction and movement to the game. This seems to be consistent with literature about tangible and natural interaction. Despite lower accuracy/precision and lower comfort/higher fatigue, users seem to be more motivated and to enjoy the interaction more. Others said that they would rather use the mouse, for it is more direct and precise and requires less time to

move a piece. The players that would rather use the gestural interface were the more casual players, while the users that preferred the mouse for its precise and faster input were more competitive players, that is, cared more about their game performance.

When asked for suggestions to improve the gestural interface, many opinions were put forward as a result of the mentioned issues. Most of the users recommended improving the precision of the clicking action and the borders of the screen. One user suggested that it should require less movement of the arm to move the cursor, that is, to increase the sensibility of the movement. Three users recommended that, instead of waiting for the gestural interface to recognize the click gesture just by holding the position steady, there should be a specific click command, such as using a specific gesture of staying in a pose, to avoid clicking in an undesired position. Two users suggested playing while sitting. Comparing the two forms of interaction, all users found that the mouse/keyboard best fit to the game context.

Although the players have complained that the reaction time was increased, no significant difference was noted in the total time of the matches, as seen in the chart of Figure 3. However, given the low number of participants, this result cannot be generalized. It is also important to notice that this slight difference in time can be more perceived by experienced players, as they want to spend the minimum amount of time to make their moves.

4.4. Lessons Learned. In the following, we present the main lessons we learned from the case study. These lessons are mainly related to MasterMind Chess for Kinect. However, some lessons might be generalized to gestural interaction for chess-like board games or to Kinect-like devices for chess-like board games (the difference between these two is that Kinect enables bodily interaction beyond gestures).

(i) Interaction Mode-Independent Usability Problems. During gestural interaction it was possible to detect usability problems that were not detected previously but that also affect the interaction with keyboard/mouse. The poor visibility and recognizability of certain chess pieces due to poor contrast and realistic icons were only detected during gestural interaction when users were more distant from the screen. Fixing this problem also benefits users of MasterMind Chess on smaller screens or in environments with bright lighting.

(ii) Kinect-Like Devices Are Not Very Adequate for Point-and-Click Interaction. The Kinect version of MasterMind Chess essentially emulates point-and-click actions of the mouse using gestures of the hand. These actions require a considerable accuracy of motor movements. Due to the limited accuracy of the Kinect sensors, users had a lower performance than when using the mouse. Furthermore some users experienced fatigue or discomfort. These two facts probably explain why only two of eight users stated that they would use the interaction mode again.

(iii) Kinect-Like Devices Might Not Be Adequate for "Serious" Chess-Playing. MasterMind Chess is essentially a chess game

for serious players playing tournament-like matches using time control. It does not use playful design elements such as Battle Chess (Battle Chess is a classic computer chess game where the pieces are animated, both in moving and in capturing others; each piece has its own animation) nor does it target novices who might need tutorials or other resources for learning chess. As a result, some players complained about the low accuracy of Kinect which resulted in moves taking more time. Other users suggested that the game should be played while sitting. Thus it seems that gestural interaction using Kinect-like devices might not be the best choice for tournament-like chess-playing. However, it is not clear whether this is also true for other variants of serious chess-playing [21] such as a simulation of open-air chess (open-air chess—or outdoor chess—is like a common game of chess but played with human-sized pieces on a very large board, usually located in an open space (thus its name)). Furthermore, it is also not clear to what extent this insight is generalizable to other slow-paced board games.

(iv) Gestural Interaction Is Not an "Add-On." The previous lessons made it clear that gestural interaction is not simply an additional input mode that can be added to an existing application. The direct mapping of mouse actions to hand gestures proved problematic due to technical limitations but also due to ergonomic considerations. Even if we had used the Leap Motion it would not have been clear whether users would have yielded higher performance or higher levels of satisfaction. Thus the game controls in the gestural mode should be redesigned to cope with the limited accuracy and to minimize fatigue and discomfort. For example, the second arm might be used for certain controls in order to provide more balance to body movements. Instead of point-and-click actions, the goal-crossing paradigm [22] could be used. Furthermore, when selecting the home square, only the target squares that constitute valid moves could be highlighted and enabled for selection. Goal-crossing might also benefit players with motor impairments. Highlighting and enabling only valid squares might benefit novices.

5. Discussion

One of the main results was that our activity revealed usability and design problems that were not detected during mouse/keyboard interaction but that also would affect users of these devices. Another important result was that gestural interaction is not just another input mode that can be easily mapped to existing controls. In order to leverage its benefits, application controls need to be adapted. Furthermore, we found that user satisfaction and perceived performance, and therefore overall acceptance of the gestural interaction mode, were lower than when interacting with mouse/keyboard. This result could be explained with technical limitations on the one hand and the framing of MasterMind Chess for Kinect as a serious chess game on the other hand. This also relates and brings the question of why a purely gestural interface may not be a natural choice for board games.

These games usually are almost always discrete, since it does not matter where a token was placed within a square,

as long as the correct square was selected. Games that are commonly used in gestural interfaces, such as the ones of dance and sports genre, are usually more continuous; that is, specific locations are taken into account when placing a token. As gestures provide good access to spatial information, it feels more natural to move or place tokens in such games rather than in discrete ones. However, the discrete part of the action in such games, such as picking up a token, may not be very suitable with gestures (as the activity showed), and this might explain why hybrid techniques such as the Wii controller perform well in these domains, as the gesture is used spatially and the button indicates an action. Other specialized controllers, like a dance mat, can be used to indicate discrete events. It is not clear whether this kind of hybrid control would perform in a casual or competitive chess game, and it is an interesting topic for research.

Since half of the participants reported a satisfactory interaction and since one of the two expert chess players stated that he would use the gestural interaction mode again, we are positive that gestural interaction with slow-paced board games such as chess provides an interesting topic area for future research, assuming that no good-subject or novelty effects took place.

Most of the lessons learned are related to the fact that the gestural interaction module was used as an add-on to an existing game that had not been redesigned to leverage the interaction potential of Kinect. As a result, players that focused on their chess performance expressed a somewhat lower satisfaction. Reframing the design problem as "designing a (playful) chess-like game that makes use of the interaction potential of Kinect-like devices" might yield different results. Two simple sources of inspiration might be the previously cited simulation of open-air chess or chess boxing, that is, the alternation between rounds of chess and boxing. Such a redesign would probably result in the user's reframing of the game as one the primary purpose of which is more playful and less focused on the chess game itself. This might lower expectations regarding accuracy and timing and increase overall satisfaction and acceptance, especially in more experienced users.

With these results, the research questions can be addressed. Regarding the first specific question "Is gestural interaction suitable for serious chess-playing?" it is clear from the case study that Kinect-like devices do not perform well for serious players, as their precision does not allow the fast movement that the players require. However, as some users reported that they liked the Kinect more as they had more fun playing with this interface, it is possible that, in a specifically designed playful chess game, the use of a gestural interface could be suitable.

As for the second question "What usability issues adding a gestural interface brings to the game? These issues can be overcome?" the study revealed that many usability issues that were not present in the mouse/keyboard interaction arise with the gestural interface. However, most of these issues can be addressed to factors that are not related to the gestural interaction itself; the chosen device has inline problems, such as low accuracy and the need to be standing, which affects the gameplay, and the game was originally designed for mouse/keyboard interaction. As in the first question, it is possible that most of these usability problems would not arise with a chess game designed specifically for this interface or using other kinds of gestural interfaces.

The answer for the third question "How the gestural interaction performs while compared to the mouse/keyboard interaction?" is also clear from the results. The mouse/keyboard interaction performed better in precision, accuracy, and preference of the users. Nevertheless, these results are valid for the context of Kinect-like devices and cannot be generalized to other gestural devices, such as the Leap Motion, which uses a different gesture recognition paradigm, or "wearable" gestural devices (e.g., [23–26]). Also, despite being used for a slow-paced board game, the result on the user preference could be different if a more playful game was used, such as an instance of open-air chess. Therefore, one should be careful while designing the game for using gestural interface for slow-paced board games using Kinect-like devices, as accuracy problems will arise and should be handled accordingly, as the playfulness of the game may not be enough to compensate this issue.

6. Conclusion

In this work, a case study of the MasterMind Chess computer game with a gestural interaction mode enabled by a Microsoft Kinect sensor was presented. We described an activity with eight users of three different chess-playing skill levels, comparing mouse/keyboard interaction with gesture-based interaction. The results of the activity allowed us to synthesize lessons learned. These results apply to the specific case of MasterMind Chess for Kinect but can also partly be generalized to gestural interaction with slow-paced board games and to slow-paced board games for Kinect-like devices.

Future work includes investigating other gestural technologies, such as the Leap Motion and Asus Xtion, for gestural interaction with "traditional" slow-paced board games, as well as designing slow-paced board games with gestural interaction enabled by Kinect-like devices.

Competing Interests

The authors declare that there are no competing interests regarding the publication of this paper.

Acknowledgments

This work was partially supported by the Brazilian National Council of Scientific and Technological Development (CNPq Grant no. 130158/2015-1) and by the Physical Artifacts of Interaction Research Group (PAIRG) at the Federal University of Rio Grande do Norte (UFRN), Brazil.

References

[1] L. Zhang, J.-C. Hsieh, T.-T. Ting, Y.-C. Huang, Y.-C. Ho, and L.-K. Ku, "A kinect based golf swing score and grade system using GMM and SVM," in *Proceedings of the 5th International Congress on Image and Signal Processing (CISP '12)*, pp. 711–715, Chongqing, China, October 2012.

[2] D. S. Alexiadis, P. Kelly, P. Daras, T. Boubekeur, and M. B. Moussa, "Evaluating a dancer's performance using Kinect-based skeleton tracking," in *Proceedings of the 19th ACM International Conference on Multimedia (MM '11)*, pp. 659–662, Scottsdale, Ariz, USA, December 2011.

[3] J. G. Posada, E. Hayashi, and M. Baranauskas, "On feelings of comfort, motivation and joy that GUI and TUI evoke," in *Design, User Experience, and Usability. User Experience Design Practice*, A. Marcus, Ed., vol. 8520 of *Lecture Notes in Computer Science*, pp. 273–284, Springer, 2014.

[4] D. A. Norman and J. Nielsen, "Gestural interfaces: a step backward in usability," *Interactions*, vol. 17, no. 5, pp. 46–49, 2010.

[5] J. Payne, P. Keir, J. Elgoyhen et al., "Gameplay issues in the design of spatial 3D gestures for video games," in *Proceedings of the Conference on Human Factors in Computing Systems (CHI EA'06)*, pp. 1217–1222, Montreal, Canada, April 2006.

[6] S. M. Ross and G. R. Morrison, "Experimental research methods," in *Handbook of Research on Educational Communications and Technology*, H. D. Jonassen, Ed., pp. 1021–1043, 2nd edition, 2004.

[7] J. Lazar, J. Feng, and H. Hochheiser, *Research Methods in Human-Computer Interaction*, John Wiley & Sons, Chichester, UK, 2010.

[8] Y. Sriboonruang, P. Kumhom, and K. Chamnongthai, "Visual hand gesture interface for computer board game control," in *Proceedings of the IEEE 10th International Symposium on Consumer Electronics (ISCE '06)*, pp. 508–512, Saint Petersburg, Russia, July 2006.

[9] X. Li and K.-S. Hong, "Korean chess game implementation by hand gesture recognition using stereo camera," in *Proceedings of the 8th International Conference on Computing Technology and Information Management (ICCM '12)*, pp. 741–744, Seoul, Republic of Korea, April 2012.

[10] A. C. Kalpakas, K. N. Stampoulis, N. A. Zikos, and S. K. Zaharos, "2D hand gesture recognition methods for interactive board game applications," in *Proceedings of the International Conference on Signal Processing and Multimedia Applications (SIGMAP '08)*, pp. 325–331, Porto, Portugal, July 2008.

[11] J. St. Jean, "Playing chess using Kinect controls versus robotic arm," Develop Kinect, 2012, http://developkinect.com/news/robotics/playing-chess-using-kinect-controls-versus-robotic-arm.

[12] Kinect Checkers, "Kinect Gesture Based Checkers Game," Kinect Hacks website, 2011, http://www.kinecthacks.com/kinect-gesture-based-checkers-game.

[13] P. Jetensky, "Accessible chess software for blind with audible feedback and physical chessboard interface," 2012, https://www.youtube.com/watch?v=Cz3Lt8JRbSc.

[14] G. A. M. Vasiljevic, L. C. Miranda, and E. E. C. Miranda, "MasterMind Chess: design and implementation of classic, capablanca and fischer modes with real time match observation," in *Proceedings of the 13th Simpósio Brasileiro de Jogos e Entretenimento Digital (SBGames '14)*, Porto Alegre, Brazil, 2014.

[15] A. C. de Carvalho Correia, L. C. de Miranda, and H. H. Hornung, "Gesture-based interaction in domotic environments: state of the art and HCI framework inspired by the diversity,"

in *Human-Computer Interaction—INTERACT 2013*, P. Kotzé, G. Marsden, G. Lindgaard, J. Wesson, and M. Winckler, Eds., vol. 8118 of *Lecture Notes in Computer Science*, pp. 300–317, Springer, Berlin, Germany, 2013.

[16] U. Z. S. Breton, B. G. Zapirain, and A. M. Zorrilla, "KiMentia: kinect based tool to help cognitive stimulation for individuals with dementia," in *Proceedings of the IEEE 14th International Conference on e-Health Networking, Applications and Services*, pp. 325–328, Beijing, China, October 2012.

[17] Y.-J. Chang, S.-F. Chen, and J.-D. Huang, "A Kinect-based system for physical rehabilitation: a pilot study for young adults with motor disabilities," *Research in Developmental Disabilities*, vol. 32, no. 6, pp. 2566–2570, 2011.

[18] F. Klompmaker, K. Nebe, and A. Fast, "dSensingNI—a framework for advanced tangible interaction using a depth camera," in *Proceedings of the 6th International Conference on Tangible, Embedded and Embodied Interaction (TEI '12)*, pp. 217–224, February 2012.

[19] G. Leroy, *Designing User Studies in Informatics*, Springer, Berlin, Germany, 2011.

[20] K. Hinkelmann and O. Kempthorne, *Design and Analysis of Experiments, Volume 1: Introduction to Experimental Design*, John Wiley & Sons, New York, NY, USA, 2nd edition, 2008.

[21] D. B. Pritchard, *The Encyclopedia of Chess Variants*, Games and Puzzles, London, UK, 1994.

[22] J. Accot and S. Zhai, "Beyond Fitts'law: models for trajectory-based HCI tasks," in *Proceedings of the ACM SIGCHI Conference on Human Factors in Computing Systems (CHI '97)*, pp. 295–302, ACM, Atlanta, Ga, USA, March 1997.

[23] P. Mistry and P. Maes, "Wearable Gestural Interface," U.S. Patent 2010/0199232 A1, Filed February 3, 2010, issued August 5, 2010.

[24] P. Mistry and P. Maes, "SixthSense: a wearable gestural interface," in *Proceedings of the ACM Special Interest Group on Computer Graphics and Interactive (SIGGRAPH '09)*, Yokohama, Japan, December 2009.

[25] L. C. Miranda and M. C. C. Baranauskas, "Artefato Físico de Interação de Televisão Digital," BR Patent PI 10134662-A2, October 2010.

[26] L. C. de Miranda, H. H. Hornung, and M. C. C. Baranauskas, "Adjustable interactive rings for iDTV," *IEEE Transactions on Consumer Electronics*, vol. 56, no. 3, pp. 1988–1996, 2010.

5

Dynamic Difficulty Adjustment (DDA) in Computer Games

Mohammad Zohaib ⓘ

Department of Computer Science, BMS College of Engineering, Bangalore 560 019, Karnataka, India

Correspondence should be addressed to Mohammad Zohaib; zohaib27may@gmail.com

Academic Editor: Hideyuki Nakanishi

Dynamic difficulty adjustment (DDA) is a method of automatically modifying a game's features, behaviors, and scenarios in real-time, depending on the player's skill, so that the player, when the game is very simple, does not feel bored or frustrated, when it is very difficult. The intent of the DDA is to keep the player engrossed till the end and to provide him/her with a challenging experience. In traditional games, difficulty levels increase linearly or stepwise during the course of the game. The features such as frequency, starting levels, or rates can be set only at the beginning of the game by choosing a level of difficulty. This can, however, result in a negative experience for players as they try to map a predecided learning curve. DDA attempts to solve this problem by presenting a customized solution for the gamers. This paper provides a review of the current approaches to DDA.

1. Introduction

The concept of the video game is continuously changing. The early games like Computer Space and Pong of the early seventies were limited to commercial arcades, but now they are seen in multiple platforms such as cell phones, tablets, computers, and other devices. People are spending in excess of 3 billion hours weekly on gaming [1], which goes to show the extent of change it has brought to our lives.

Entertainment is but one aspect; games are now moving into reality, and the invisible boundaries separating games and reality are now becoming increasingly obscure [2]. Video games now extend to realms of healthcare [3] and education [4]. Experts have studied methods to assess how playing video games affect motor learning and its scope of improving patient involvement with therapy, especially commercial games which could be linked with specialized controls [5].

Although technology in gaming continues to evolve, a general discontent of players with the existing games has been observed due to their limitations in offering challenge levels to suit individual traits of the player like dexterity, learning and adapting ability, and emotional characteristics [6, 7]. Static levels of difficulty that are selected manually can no longer avoid boredom in players as they, in all probability, would be unable to decide on the challenge level that matches their abilities [8]. Also, constantly calling out the players to select the difficulty levels could distract them and interrupt the game [9]. The fun factor in games depends on three factors: challenge, fantasy, and curiosity [10]. Creating an adequate level of challenge is not easy when players with varying skills are pitted against each other. When an opponent is beaten effortlessly, the game appears boring. Again, in the face of a vastly superior opponent, the game turns frustrating. These two extremes lessen fun, since an optimal challenge is not offered. Csikszentmihalyi [11] first proposed that players, when kept away from the states of boredom or frustration, travel through a "flow channel" (Figure 1) and this was incorporated into a gaming scenario by Koster [8].

This model indicates how the difficulty of a task directly relates to the performer's perception. The flow channel shows that the difficulty level can be gradually enhanced, as sufficient time exists for the players for learning and improvement to meet this challenge [11]. Thus, the model prevents the frustration of difficult situations and the boredom of simple ones. In a different study, Malone [10] suggested that if the fantasy, challenge, curiosity, and control in games could be

TABLE 1: DDA research studies since 2009.

Year	Journal Papers	Conference Papers	Theses	Books	Total
2009	1	2	1		4
2010	1	7	1		9
2011	2	5		1	8
2012	3	8	2		13
2013	2	5	3	1	11
2014	1	4	1	1	7
2015	1	5	1		7
2016	3	5	3		11
2017	5	7	2		14
2018	0	0	0	0	0

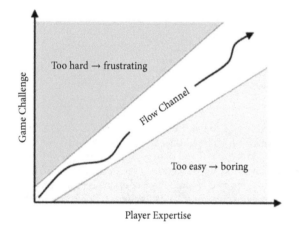

FIGURE 1: Flow channel concept proposed by Csikszentmihalyi.

balanced and associated with the gradual enhancement of difficulty level stated earlier, it could be possible that the ensuing game could keep the player entertained. Peeters [12] in her study suggested designing an automated platform for scenario-based training so that learners could engage in personalized autonomous training where agent-based notions such as beliefs, desires, and intentions can be used to deal with the gamer's competency and skills.

Numerous studies have been addressing the problems of static levels and have proposed the dynamic difficulty adjustment (DDA) technique that allows the automatic mapping of playing experience with the individual skills. DDA is a technique of automatic real-time adjustment of scenarios, parameters, and behaviors in video games, which follows the player's skill and keeps them from boredom (when the game is too easy) or frustration (when the game is too difficult). The essence of the DDA is to retain the interest of the user throughout the game and to offer a satisfactory challenge level for the player [13]. Andrade et al. suggested that DDA must cater the following three basic needs of games [14]:

(1) The game needs to automatically track the player ability and rapidly adapt to it

(2) The game must follow the player's improving or falling level and maintain a balance in accordance with the player's skill

(3) The process of adaptation must not be clearly perceived by the players, and successive game states need to have coherence with the earlier ones

Before applying the DDA, an understanding of the term "difficulty" is necessary. Though abstract, certain aspects need to be considered to assess and measure difficulty. Some of them are characteristics of design [15], number of resources [16], number of losses or victories [17], and so on. Nevertheless, DDA is not as easy as merely giving a player some healthier items in times of trouble. It needs an estimate of time and an entry at the right instant, as keeping the player absorbed is complicated in an interactive sense [16].

2. DDA Studies in the Last Ten Years

After 2009, there have been many research studies related to methods to develop or improve DDAs, including innovative applications in diverse fields. It is notable that the number of research papers in 2012 and 2017 is almost three times the number of research papers presented in 2009 (Table 1).

In this study, we have focused on DDA research studies undertaken after 2009 and have presented the important categories observed over the last decade (2009–2018). Going by the data presented in Table 1, we observe that, in the last decade, there has been a significant increase in the number of research papers on DDA over the years, and it was the highest in 2017.

Figure 2 depicts the DDA research studies carried out in the last ten years, including journal and conference papers, thesis work, and book chapters for every year.

3. Classification of DDA Approaches

Various methods for DDA are proposed in the literature (Table 2). The one common aspect in all methods is a requirement to measure (in a manner that may be implicit or explicit) the level of difficulty being faced by the player at any given instant. These measures are estimated by heuristic functions, also called challenge functions.

They assign a value for any game state that is indicative of the difficulty level of the game felt by the player at any given moment. Typical examples of heuristics in use are success rates of hits, numbers of pieces won and lost, life points,

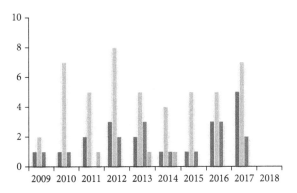

FIGURE 2: DDA studies over the past decade.

- Journal Papers
- Conference Papers
- Theses

TABLE 2: List of DDA approaches.

Author(s)	Approach
Xue et al.	Probabilistic Methods
Pedersen, Togelius, and Yannakakis	Single and multi-layered perceptrons
Spronck et al.	Dynamic scripting
Hunicke and Chapman	Hamlet System
Hagelback and Johansson	Reinforcement Learning
Li et al.	Upper Confidence Bound for Trees and Artificial Neural Networks
Ebrahimi and Akbarzadeh-T	Self-organizing System and Artificial Neural Networks

completion time for assigned tasks, or any other metrics for calculating game scores.

There are several ways we can classify approaches to DDA.

3.1. Probabilistic Methods. A study on a framework that sees DDA as a problem of optimization was carried out [18]. This approach maximized player engagement all through the game. They modeled the progression of the player on a probabilistic graph (Figure 3) that maximized engagement as a well-defined objective function.

A dynamic programming technique having high efficiency was utilized to solve it. They assessed the DDA implementation using a mobile game by Electronic Arts, Inc. The group treated by DDA showed a clear increase of core engagement metrics, e.g., total number of plays and duration of game, while being revenue neutral when evaluated with the control group that did not have enabled DDA. This framework can be extended to a variety of game genres. DDA can be successfully applied to other genres if an appropriate progression model is constructed. The states for level-based games can be established by two important facets: trial and level. For games that are more complex having multiple or nonlinear progressions (e.g., role-play games), too, the states having varied dimensions can be defined. The graph would

then be more complex since more states and links would be included.

Segundo et al. [19] proposed the creation of a parameter manipulating method for DDA, which aims to enhance the pleasure of gaming. The proposed method utilizes probabilistic calculations that could be deployed in a challenge function. A sample of students was provided with a questionnaire to assess whether a significant statistical difference existed in the understanding of game difficulty, game play, and the desire to play often with and without the method. The results indicated that the DDA version showed better results than the other versions with regard to game play and the desire to play often.

In a study [20], it was proposed that both online and offline learning techniques could be used for DDA. In the offline learning, a genetic algorithm was applied to create a fuzzy rulebase for game tactics during play to manipulate the computer-controlled adversaries. In the online learning, a probabilistic method was used for adapting the game strategies to the player. The level of difficulty of the game can be adjusted in accordance with the preference of the player seeking a challenge. The results demonstrated the superior capability of the evolved offline rulebases and the efficacy of the suggested online learning method for DDA.

Bunian et al. [21] developed a modeling technique by use of data gathered from players involved in a Role-Playing Game (RPG). The proposed technique has 2 features: (i) a player's Hidden Markov Model (HMM) tracking in-game traits for modelling individual differences and (ii) use of the HMM output to generate features of behaviors for classifying real-world characteristics of players that include expertise along with the big five personality traits. The results showed the prediction capability for some of personality traits, like conscientiousness and expertise. A logistic regression model was trained considering the composition of the freshly created behavioral features for 66 participants. A three-fold cross validation was used as the dataset was small. The prediction accuracy for conscientiousness and expertise category was 59.1% and 70.13%, respectively.

Bayesian optimization techniques were used in a study [22] to design games which maximize the engagement of users. Participants were paid to attempt a game for a short period, following which they could continue to play without payment or quit voluntarily. Engagement was measured by their persistence, estimates of duration of other players, and a survey after the game. Utilizing Gaussian surrogate-based process optimization, experiments were conducted to establish game design features, especially those affecting difficulty leading to maximum engagement. The converging outcomes indicated that overt difficulty manipulations were effectual in modifying engagement only with the covert manipulations, demonstrating the user's self-perception of skill as being critical.

Hintze, Olson, and Lehman [23] proposed the idea of orthogonal coevolution and verified its effectiveness in a game that was browser-based modified from a scientific simulation. The outcomes demonstrated that evolving adversaries together with evolved friends could lead to seamless DDA and permit gamers to experience more diverse

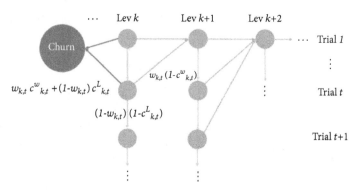

FIGURE 3: Probabilistic graph showing the player's progression model in a typical level-based game.

situations. They concluded that such an orthogonal coevolution could be of promise for adjusting gaming difficulties.

3.2. Single and Multilayered Perceptrons. In a study by Pedersen, Togelius, and Yannakakis [24], the relationship between parameters of level design of platform games, player experience, and individual characteristics of play were studied. The studied design parameters had relation to the size and placement of level gaps and the presence of direction changes; and the constituents of a player's experience comprised frustration, fun, and challenge. A neural network model, which mapped between characteristics of playing behavior, design parameters of levels, and player emotions, was trained utilizing game session data and evolutionary preference learning.

Data was gathered from the Internet. Users were inducted through messages on mailing lists and blogs and sent to a web page which contained a Java applet initiating the game and a questionnaire. After playing the games and completing the questionnaire, all the characteristics (gameplay, controllable, and player experience) were recorded in a repository on a server. After analyzing this data, they attempted a function approximation based on gameplay and controllable characteristics to record emotional choices utilizing neuroevolutionary preference learning. This data representing the function was full of noise, since the choices of the players were highly subjective and the style of playing varied. All of this, coupled with the meager training data amount, suggests the usage of a function approximator that is robust. An artificial neural network (ANN), being a nonlinear function, is a suitable option for the approximation in mapping between data and reported emotions. Therefore, a simple single-neuron (perceptron) was used to learn the relationship between characteristics (ANN data input) and the analyzed emotional choice. The primary purpose for the use of a single neuron rather than a multilayered perceptron (MLP) here was that the trained function approximator needed to be analyzed. Though MLP can approximate the function more accurately, it is simpler for us to visualize the derived function when presented by a single-neuron ANN. Learning was obtained by artificial evolution by adopting the preference learning method [25]. A generational genetic algorithm was deployed, utilizing a goodness-of-fit

function which measured the variation between the recorded emotional preferences and the corresponding model output. Results showed that there was high accuracy of prediction of challenge (77.77%), frustration (88.66%), and fun (69.18%) using a single-neuron model, which recommends using more elaborate nonlinear approximators. The study also discussed how the models generated could be used to generate game levels automatically, which would improve the player experience.

In another study, Shaker, Yannakakis, and Togelius [26] demonstrated the automatic generation of personalized levels for platform games. They built their model on the earlier work by Pedersen, Togelius, and Yannakakis [24]. At first, single layer perceptrons (SLP) were used to approximately evaluate the affective level of the players. The input subsets were selected by the sequential feature selection. To generate content customized to suit real-time player experience automatically in real-time, predicting emotions, to some extent, from controllable features is necessary. For this, the rest of the controllable features not already in the chosen feature subset were forcibly entered in the input of the multiple layer perceptron models, and the topology of the networks was made optimal for the highest accuracy of prediction.

In this study, dynamic adaptation to changes in playing styles was assessed. The model's capacity to generalize over players of various types was tested. To carry this out, two artificial intelligence (AI) agents were deployed for play in turns, while tracking the growth of the fun value. The experiment commenced from a level generated at random. The agents played 100 levels with an agent switch after every 20 levels. The result showing the variation in fun level across 100 levels is shown in Figure 4.

It is seen that the fun value is about 70% for the initial 20 levels when the first agent plays, increases to 80% when the next agent plays for 20 levels, and drops down to 70% when the first is brought back to the game. It clearly shows the model's capability to adjust to the player type. As a further test, the same trial was repeated on 4 human players in a reduced set of 12 levels. The result of this trial is illustrated in Figure 5, which shows the progress of fun over 48 levels. The results are similar to those obtained from the AI agents. It clearly indicates that the model robustly adapts to an individual player generalizing over various kinds of players.

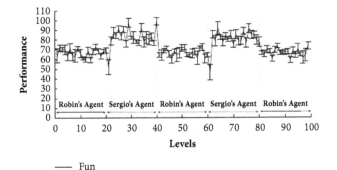

FIGURE 4: Two-agent optimized levels of fun.

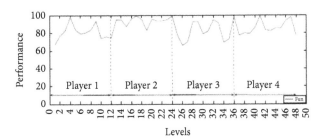

FIGURE 5: Four-player optimized levels of fun.

A study [27] constructed computational models of a player's experience derived from interaction in gameplay for use as fitness functions for content creation in games. A classic platform game's modified version was used for their experiments, and player data was collected from the Internet. They used the preference learning method for generating models of player experience. Feature selection was utilized to lower the features in the model. The data from training of nonlinear perceptrons was used to approximate the mapping functions between controllable features and selected gameplay. They presented the results of optimal construction of multilayer perceptrons (MLP) and the MLP model performances. They finally discussed the ways by which induced models could generate game content automatically.

Most DDA methods are based on the intuitions of designers, which do not reflect real-world playing patterns. Therefore, Jennings-Teats, Smith, and Wardrip-Fruin [28] created Polymorph that used methods from machine learning and level generation to analyze player skill and level difficulty, thereby dynamically creating levels in a 2D platformer game having continuously desired challenges. The DDA problem was addressed by generating a machine-learned difficulty model in a 2D platformer game using a model of the existing skill of the player. Multilayer Perceptrons accessed from play traces are used. These traces are gathered using a web-based tool which assigns users with various short-level components and rates them on a difficulty level. The Polymorph model utilizes the models of difficulty to choose the suitable level segment for the existing performance of the player.

Carvalho et al. [29] presented a method for generating gameplay sessions for endless games. This genre still remains largely unexplored in literature. The method uses a four-step process starting from the generation of required content to

placing the content through the gameplay sessions. A robust evaluation technique was also designed. This technique utilizes both features that can be adjusted by a designer and gameplay items gathered from gameplay sessions. The usage of 2 neural networks is a new technique that agrees with the idea of game as a service and supports it throughout the life cycle of the game. The two neural networks have different purposes: the first receives merely features that are controllable as input, and the other receives both non-controllable and controllable features as input. Both the neural networks adjust chunk (fixed-size segments of the game on which gameplay elements are placed) difficulty as their output. Thus, the first network is used in the initial development stages, where one has access to only controllable features of these chunks, and the other is used to periodically adjust the game once it is made available. Both neural networks are Multilayer Perceptrons, each having a hidden layer.

3.3. Dynamic Scripting. Dynamic scripting is an online unsupervised learning approach for games. It is computationally rapid, robust, efficient, and effective [30]. It operates many rulebases in the game, running one for every opponent type. These rules are designed manually utilizing domain-specific information. With the creation of a new opponent, the rules that constitute the script guiding the opponents are taken from the rulebase based on their type. The probability of a script rule selection depends on the weight value allotted to the rule. The rulebase adjusts by amending the values, reflecting the rates of failure or success of the related script rules.

In this approach, learning takes place progressively. On completing an encounter, the rule weights used in the encounter are treated depending on their effect on the result. The rules leading to success have their weights increased, while those leading to failure have their weights decreased. The remaining rules are adjusted accordingly so that the sum of all the rulebase weights remains constant. Dynamic scripting is used to generate fresh opponent tactics while increasing the level of difficulty of the game's AI to match the level of experience of the human player (Figure 6).

There are three different enhancements to this technique allowing the opponents to learn playing a balanced game:

(1) High-fitness penalizing: The weight balancing provides rewards in proportion to the fitness value. To obtain mediocre rather than optimal behavior, the weights can be amended to reward mediocre values of fitness and punish superior values.

(2) Weight clipping: The maximum value of weight decides the highest optimization level that a learned tactic can reach. A high value for the maximum permits the weights to increase to high values, so that soon the most effective rules will nearly always be chosen. This results in scripts having near to optimal values. Similarly, low values for the maximum hamper growth of weights. This creates a large variation in scripts generated, many of which would be nonoptimal. This method automatically varies the maximum value, thereby enforcing a balanced game.

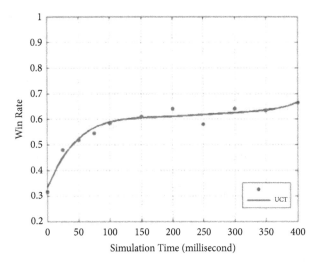

FIGURE 8: DDA from UST.

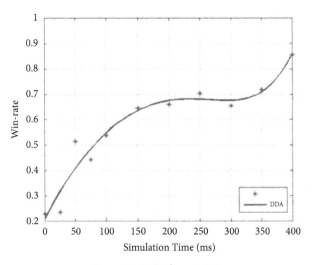

FIGURE 9: DDA from ANN.

3.6. Upper Confidence Bound for Trees and Artificial Neural Networks. Li et al. [36] developed a DDA technique using artificial neural networks (ANN) from data derived from the upper confidence bound for trees (UCT). The Pacman game was used as a test-bed for this study. Considering that UCT is a computing intelligence method, UCT performance significantly correlates with the duration of simulation [37]. Figure 8 illustrates DDA process from UCT-created data.

Here, the x-axis denotes simulation time, which is in the range 0–400 ms. The y-axis denotes win-rates of opponents (ghosts) which are in the range 30%–70%. The curve rises steeply in the period 0–100 ms; this period has a higher number of test data. After 100 ms, the curve flattens. The win-rate attains a maximum at 400ms. The reason for the stability of the win-rate is because of UCT being a stochastic simulation approach. In the interval 0–100 ms, the sample space is bigger and the stochastic outcomes become more accurate. Hence, the UCT performance is drastically improved. Also, after crossing 100 ms (threshold value), the accuracy of results is still fairly good so that the win-rate grows smoothly even at higher values of simulation time. UCT can be used as DDA in real-time games, too. By merely adjusting the UCT simulation time, we obtain game opponents of increasing difficulty levels.

ANN can be trained from UCT-created data. Even though the UCT approach can be deployed as DDA for games like Pacman, it is not practical to be used for complex online games because of UCT's computational intensiveness. But then since UCT's performance can be tweaked by varying the simulation time, ANN offline training becomes possible by running the UCT-created data with changed simulation times. Thus, DDA can be generated from UCT-created data, bypassing the computational intensiveness. In this study, the 3-Layered Feed-Forward Artificial Neural Network model in WEKA was used for the implementation.

DDA can also be created from ANN. The weights and bias of ANN are reserved in MDB files. Opponents are managed by ANN by loading MDB files.

Figure 9 illustrates the DDA from ANN. The x-axis ranging within 0–40ms is the same as Figure 7. The y-axis represents win-rate of opponents (ghosts) controlled by ANN from data created by UCT with changed simulation time ranging within 20%–86%. The curve rises steeply in the range 0–100ms. After 100ms, the curve rises steadily and the win-rate peaks at 400ms.

The performance of the opponent's neural network depends on the training data quality. With insufficient incidences for a certain route, the ANN training remains poor. With ample incidences for all routes, the trained ANN performs well. With the increasing growth of simulation time, the UCT data achieve greater precision, which in turn creates ANN that is better trained. Comparing the two curves, we note that the DDA curve tends to rise from a minimum to a maximum simulation time. Hence, a valid DDA curve can be derived by ANN training from UCT based data. Thus, UCT is a good computation intelligence algorithm which performs better when the simulation time increases. It can therefore be used as a DDA tool by tweaking the simulation time. UCT can also create data to train ANN.

A data-driven approach for DDA was proposed by Yin et al. [38]. The objective was to match the player's performance to the required conditions laid down by the designer. The data pertaining to dynamic game states and in-game player performance were used for taking decisions on adaptation. Trained ANNs were utilized to map the relationship between player performance, dynamic game state, adaptation decisions, and the game difficulty that resulted. The predicted difficulty enables effective adaptation of both magnitude and direction. An experiment on a training game application demonstrated the efficacy and stability of the suggested approach.

3.7. Self-Organizing System and Artificial Neural Networks. In another study [39], a self-organizing system (SOS) was developed, which is a group of entities that presents global system traits through local interactions while not having centralized control. This method proposes a new technique that tries to adjust the difficulty level by creating an SOS of

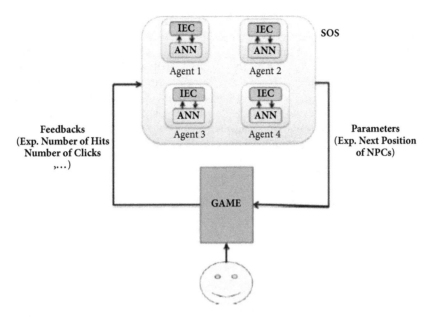

FIGURE 10: Illustration of self-organizing algorithm.

Non-Player Characters (NPCs) that are not in the player's control. To track human player traits, ANNs are used in the system. ANNs need to adapt to players having varied levels of skills and traits; therefore an evolutionary algorithm having adaptation skills was developed which modifies ANN weights (Figure 10).

Pacman game has been used as a test bed. There are two agents in the game: Pacman (the player) and ghost (opponent). The authors have considered four types of Pacmans having varying intelligence levels. The first is Cost-Based Pacman, a local agent who locates his subsequent location based on the position of his nearby ghosts. The second, named Distance-Based Pacman, is a global agent, who considers locations of all ghosts prior to deciding the next move. The third, neither fully global nor local, is named Nearest Distance-Based Pacman. The three Pacmans represent players having varying levels of skill. The fourth, Random Pacman, moves randomly and is not classified in any of these categories.

A neuroevolutionary controller for each Ghost was developed in order that they adapt to the different skill levels of the players. They decide the next position based on environmental precepts. Every ghost was given a feedforward neural network having a concealed layer. The topologies of the networks were decided during the game. Ghosts are first trained offline. This offline training helps to create chromosomes that perform better than random chromosomes. The Cooperative Coevolution Algorithm is used to train ghosts offline [40]. A subpopulation of chromosomes is considered for every ghost, which have neural network connection weights. The best performers in every subgroup are chosen as representatives. Next, to assess chromosomes of each subgroup, a game is arranged between the representatives and these chromosomes. On completion of the game, its fitness is assessed and assigned. This process is repeated till all the

chromosomes of every ghost are mapped. After assessment of all chromosomes in the subgroups is carried out, the genetic algorithm selects, crosses over, and mutates for producing new chromosomes. When the stop requirements are met, this sequence of events halts.

Next, online learning of the controllers takes place. Before the game starts, the required chromosomes are loaded in the ghost controllers. As the skill levels of the players are still unknown, intermediate chromosomes are selected for all ghosts. The subgroups are sorted on the basis of individual fitness; the median chromosomes are selected. The game begins when the chromosomes are loaded in the neural networks. The game runs for a short duration after which the system fitness is assessed. Neural controllers are trained using the Interactive Evolutionary Computation (IEC) where the fitness function replaces human evaluation [41]. As human evaluation results in fatigue, IEC optimizes systems effectively. System fitness is indirectly assessed using player feedback, e.g., number of keys pressed, occasions of key switches, and Pacman's wall hits. After each duration, these numbers are analyzed to assess fitness.

The results show that this system is capable of adapting to many skill levels by selecting proper factors that hasten convergence to the optimal requirements.

A study [42] explored the use of NEAT and rtNEAT neuroevolution techniques to create intelligent adversaries for games having real-time strategies. The primary objective is to convert the challenge created by the adversaries to match the recompetence of the player in a real-time situation, thereby resulting in a greater entertainment value experienced by the player. The study introduced the application of the neuroevolution techniques to Globulation 2 (G2), real-time strategy game for DDA. Initially, NEAT was used to optimize the functioning of G2 nonplayer characters and two suggested challenge factors were investigated by offline trials in G2. The results indicated that the aggressiveness factors and warrior numbers are contributors to challenge because neuroevolved agents obtained succeeded in outperforming all typical AI nonplayer characters available for playing the game.

3.8. Affective Modeling Using EEG. Earlier researchers studied heuristic approaches based on a game state. Generally, in a game that tracks an ongoing score, decisions on DDA application can be taken when the difference between the scores of the players exceeds a threshold value, i.e., when one player becomes stronger than the other, and assuming that this would result in boredom in the stronger and frustration in the weaker player.

Stein et al. [43] have proposed a different method—measuring the excitement of players and setting in motion the game levels when the level of excitement dips below a threshold value. They have attempted to address the main issue of gaming experience directly, rather than depending on heuristic scores to decide when they are bored with the game.

An affective-state regulation technique was implemented by using headsets to decipher electroencephalography (EEG) signals and the mechanism to modify the signal to an affective state.

Next, assessing this affective state, DDA is deployed by the game. Two studies were conducted. In the first, the relationship between the EEG signals and game events (GE) was investigated. The results showed a significant correlation between the indicator for short term excitement (STE) and GE. Playing experiences were attempted to be enhanced by maximizing STE. In the second study, this EEG-initiated DDA was compared to (1) a typical heuristic technique which used elapsed duration and game status and (2) a control game without DDA. A case study was presented for the EEG-initiated DDA approached in a customized version of the Boot Camp game. The study confirmed that (1) players preferred the EEG-initiated DDA to the two other choices and (2) this method greatly increased the excitement level of the players. The study also indicated that the option of the initiating strategy is significant and greatly impacts experience of the players.

Afergan, Mikami, and Kondo [44] used functional near-infrared spectroscopy for collecting passive brain-sensing information and detecting long durations of overload or boredom. Using these physiological signals, a simulation was adapted for optimizing real-time workload that permits the system to adjust the task for the user at each moment in a better manner. To demonstrate this concept, they conducted laboratory experiments where participants, in a simulation, were assigned path planning for several unmanned aerial vehicles. The task difficulty was varied based on their state by the addition or deletion UAVs and they found that errors could be decreased by 35% over and above a baseline level. The results indicated that fNIRS brain sensing can be used to detect real-time task difficulty and an interface constructed that enhances user performance by DDA.

Fernandez et al. [45] adapted the levels of difficulty of a basic 2D platform game, working on and building levels

automatically. The method proposed consisted of DDA and Rhythm-Group Theory, a procedural content development approach, along with attention levels gathered from EEG data. Trials were planned in a manner that players needed to perform 5 varied levels automatically created by their performances and EEG data collected through a biosensor during play. Results indicated that the method adapted successfully to the difficulty levels as per the status of the player. Additionally, the method calculated difficulty utilizing calculated real-time values to decide the level.

4. Future Work

There are many opportunities for higher research into DDA by creation of level structures. Researchers can go beyond the standard 2D platformer video game genre and apply the same DDA concepts to different genres. Also, more research is required in new search-based techniques for identifying optimal levels. Researching player models other than agent types could be another promising area for more research. As the fitness function is a crucial element in game design, increasing its complexity by the addition of more variables that could consider many other aspects of play is yet another promising area.

An interesting research could be to investigate the possibility of covering traits like playing style. The concept of mapping the human player and developing a player model accordingly is yet another possibility. A player model that includes more behavioral aspects could yield interesting observations.

Many player modeling techniques exist currently. Integrating a few of these with present DDA approaches could open up some possibilities of interest and yield more DDA techniques tailored to a gamer's preference.

5. Conclusions

DDA techniques have been proven in the literature to be useful tools for incorporation in complex and dynamic systems. This investigation has presented a review on DDA applications and directions in many diverse kinds of games in the past decade highlighting some of the most representative types for every application. There are numerous application studies of DDAs in various domains, including generalizations and extensions of DDAs. The number of approaches presented here is neither complete nor exhaustive but merely a sample that demonstrates the usefulness and possible applications of AI techniques in modern video games.

References

[1] J. McGonigal, *Reality Is Broken: Why Games Make Us Better and How They Can Change The World*, Vintage, London, UK, 2012.

[2] G. Calleja, "Digital games and escapism," *Games and Culture* vol. 5, no. 4, pp. 335–353, 2010.

[3] A. DeSmet, D. Thompson, T. Baranowski, A. Palmeira, M.

Verloigne, and I. De Bourdeaudhuij, "Is participatory design associated with the effectiveness of serious digital games for healthy lifestyle promotion? A meta-analysis," *Journal of Medical Internet Research*, vol. 18, no. 4, 2016.

[4] T. M. Connolly, E. A. Boyle, E. MacArthur, T. Hainey, and J. M. Boyle, "A systematic literature review of empirical evidence on computer games and serious games," *Computers & Education*, vol. 59, no. 2, pp. 661–686, 2012.

[5] K. Lohse, N. Shirzad, A. Verster, N. Hodges, and H. F. Van der Loos, "Video Games and Rehabilitation," *Journal of Neurologic Physical Therapy*, vol. 37, no. 4, pp. 166–175, 2013.

[6] P. Sweetser and P. Wyeth, "GameFlow," *Computers in Entertainment*, vol. 3, no. 3, 2005.

[7] K. M. Gilleade, A. Dix, and J. Allanson, "Affective videogames and modes of affective gaming: Assist me, challenge me, emote me," in *Proceedings of the 2nd International Conference on Digital Games Research Association: Changing Views: Worlds in Play (DiGRA '05)*, 20, 16 pages, Vancouver, Canada, June 2005.

[8] R. Koster, *A theory of fun for game design. Sebastopol (Cali.)*, OReilly Media, 2014.

[9] J. Chen, "Flow in games (and everything else)," *Communications of the ACM*, vol. 50, no. 4, pp. 31–34, 2007.

[10] T. W. Malone, "Toward a theory of intrinsically motivating instruction," *Cognitive Science*, vol. 5, no. 4, pp. 333–369, 1981.

[11] M. Csikszentmihalyi, *Flow: The Psychology of Optimal Experience*, Harper Row, New York, NY, USA, 2009.

[12] M. M. M. Peeters, *Personalized Educational Games-Developing agent-supported scenario-based training [Ph.D. thesis]*, The Dutch Graduate School for Information and Knowledge Systems, 2014.

[13] R. Hunicke and V. Chapman, "AI for Dynamic Difficulty Adjustment in Games," in *Proceedings of the Challenges in Game Artificial Intelligence AAAI Workshop*, pp. 91–96, San Jose, Calif, USA, 2004.

[14] G. Andrade, G. Ramalho, H. Santana, and V. Corruble, "Extending reinforcement learning to provide dynamic game balancing," in *Proceedings of the Workshop on Reasoning, Representation, and Learning in Computer Games, 19th International Joint Conference on Artificial Intelligence (IJCAI)*, 12, 7 pages, Edinburgh, United Kingdom, 2005.

[15] R. A. Bartle, *Designing Virtual Worlds*, New Riders, Berkeley, Calif, USA, 2006.

[16] R. Hunicke, "The case for dynamic difficulty adjustment in games," in *Proceedings of the ACM SIGCHI International Conference on Advances in Computer Entertainment Technology (ACE '05)*, pp. 429–433, Valencia, Spain, June 2005.

[17] S. Poole, *Trigger Happy Videogames and The Entertainment Revolution*, Arcade Publishing, New York, NY, USA, 2007.

[18] S. Xue, M. Wu, J. Kolen, N. Aghdaie, and K. A. Zaman, "Dynamic Difficulty Adjustment for Maximized Engagement in Digital Games," in *Proceedings of the the 26th International Conference*, pp. 465–471, Perth, Australia, April 2017.

[19] C. V. Segundo, K. Emerson, A. Calixto, and R. P. Gusmao, "Dynamic difficulty adjustment through parameter manipulation for Space Shooter game," in *Proceedings of SB Games*, Brazil, 2016.

[20] H. Hsieh, *Generation of Adaptive Opponents for a Predator-Prey Game*, Asia University, 2008.

[21] S. Bunian, A. Canossa, R. Colvin, and M. S. El-Nasr, "Modeling individual differences in game behavior using HMM," in *Proceedings of the 13th AAAI Conference on Artificial Intelligence and Interactive Digital Entertainment (AIIDE-17)*, 2017.

[22] M. M. Khajah, B. D. Roads, R. V. Lindsey, Y.-E. Liu, and M. C. Mozer, "Designing engaging games using Bayesian optimization," in *Proceedings of the 34th Annual Conference on Human Factors in Computing Systems, CHI 2016*, pp. 5571–5582, San Jose, Calif, USA, May 2016.

[23] A. Hintze, R. S. Olson, and J. Lehman, "Orthogonally evolved AI to improve difficulty adjustment in video games," in *European Conference on the Applications of Evolutionary Computation*, vol. 9597 of *Lecture Notes in Computer Science*, pp. 525–540, Springer International Publishing, Cham, Switzerland, 2016.

[24] C. Pedersen, J. Togelius, and G. N. Yannakakis, "Modeling player experience in Super Mario Bros," in *Proceedings of the 2009 IEEE Symposium on Computational Intelligence and Games (CIG)*, pp. 132–139, Milano, Italy, September 2009.

[25] G. N. Yannakakis and J. Hallam, "Game and player feature selection for entertainment capture," in *Proceedings of the 2007 IEEE Symposium on Computational Intelligence and Games*, pp. 244–251, Honolulu, Hawaii, USA, April 2007.

[26] N. Shaker, G. Yannakakis, and J. Togelius, "Towards automatic personalized content generation for platform games," in *Proceedings of the 6th AAAI Conference on Artificial Intelligence and Interactive Digital Entertainment, AIIDE 2010*, pp. 63–68, Stanford, Calif, USA, October 2010.

[27] C. Pedersen, J. Togelius, and G. N. Yannakakis, "Modeling player experience for content creation," *IEEE Transactions on Computational Intelligence and AI in Games*, vol. 2, no. 1, pp. 54–67, 2010.

[28] M. Jennings-Teats, G. Smith, and N. Wardrip-Fruin, "Polymorph: A model for dynamic level generation," in *Proceedings of the 6th AAAI Conference on Artificial Intelligence and Interactive Digital Entertainment, AIIDE 2010*, pp. 138–143, Stanford, Calif, USA, October 2010.

[29] L. V. Carvalho, A. V. M. Moreira, V. V. Filho, M. Túlio, C. F. Albuquerque, and G. L. Ramalho, "A Generic Framework for Procedural Generation of Gameplay Sessions," in *Proceedings of the SB Games 2013, XII SB Games*, São Paulo, Brazil, 2013.

[30] P. Spronck, I. Sprinkhuizen-Kuyper, and E. Postma, "Online adaptation of game opponent AI with dynamic scripting," *International Journal of Intelligent Games & Simulation*, vol. 3, no. 1, pp. 45–53, 2004.

[31] Z. Simpson, "The In-game Economics of Ultima Online," in *Proceedings of the Game Developers Conference*, San Jose, Calif, USA, 2000.

[32] J. Togelius, R. DeNardi, and S. M. Lucas, "Making racing fun through player modeling and track evolution," in *Proceedings of the Workshop Adaptive Approaches Optim. Player Satisfaction Comput. Phys. Games*, p. 70, 2006.

[33] J. Hagelback and S. J. Johansson, "Measuring player experience on runtime dynamic difficulty scaling in an RTS game," in *Proceedings of the 2009 IEEE Symposium on Computational Intelligence and Games (CIG)*, pp.46–52, Milano, Italy, September 2009.

[34] C. H. Tan, K. C. Tan, and A. Tay, "Dynamic game difficulty scaling using adaptive behavior-based AI," *IEEE Transactions on Computational Intelligence and AI in Games*, vol. 3, no. 4, pp. 289–301, 2011.

[35] Y. A. Sekhavat, "MPRL: Multiple-Periodic Reinforcement Learning for difficulty adjustment in rehabilitation games," in *Proceedings of the 5th IEEE International Conference on Serious Games and Applications for Health, SeGAH 2017*, Perth, Australia, April 2017.

[36] X. Li, S. He, Y. Dong et al., "To create DDA by the approach of ANN from UCT-created data," in *Proceedings of the 2010 International Conference on Computer Application and System Modeling (ICCASM 2010)*, pp. V8-475–V8-478, Taiyuan, China, October 2010.

[37] J. Yang, Y. Gao, S. He et al., "To Create Intelligent Adaptive Game Opponent by Using Monte-Carlo for Tree Search," in *Proceedings of the 2009 Fifth International Conference on Natural Computation*, pp. 603–607, Tianjian, China, August 2009.

[38] H. Yin, L. Luo, W. Cai, Y.-S. Ong, and J. Zhong, "A data-driven approach for online adaptation of game difficulty," in *Proceedings of the 2015 IEEE Conference on Computational Intelligence and Games, CIG 2015*, pp. 146–153, Tainan, Taiwan, September 2015.

[39] A. Ebrahimi and M.-R. Akbarzadeh-T, "Dynamic difficulty adjustment in games by using an interactive self-organizing architecture," in *Proceedings of the 2014 Iranian Conference on Intelligent Systems, ICIS 2014*, Iran, February 2014.

[40] M. A. Potter and K. A. de Jong, "Cooperative coevolution: an architecture for evolving coadapted subcomponents," *Evolutionary Computation*, vol. 8, no. 1, pp. 1–29, 2000.

[41] H. Takagi, "Interactive evolutionary computation: fusion of the capabilities of EC optimization and human evaluation," *Proceedings of the IEEE*, vol. 89, no. 9, pp. 1275–1296, 2001.

[42] J. K. Olesen, G. N. Yannakakis, and J. Hallam, "Real-time challenge balance in an RTS game using rtNEAT," in *Proceedings of the 2008 IEEE Symposium on Computational Intelligence and Games, CIG 2008*, pp. 87–94, Perth, Australia, December 2008.

[43] A. Stein, Y. Yotam, R. Puzis, G. Shani, and M. Taieb-Maimon, "EEG-triggered dynamic difficulty adjustment for multiplayer games," *Entertainment Computing*, vol. 25, pp. 14–25, 2018.

[44] D. Afergan, E. M. Peck, E. T. Solovey et al., "Dynamic difficulty using brain metrics of workload," in *Proceedings of the 32nd Annual ACM Conference on Human Factors in Computing Systems, CHI 2014*, pp. 3797–3806, Toronto, Ontario, Canada, May 2014.

[45] H. D. B., K. Mikami, and K. Kondo, "Adaptable game experience based on player's performance and EEG," in *Proceedings of the 2017 Nicograph International (NicoInt)*, pp. 1–8, Kyoto, Japan, June 2017.

6

With or against Each Other? The Influence of a Virtual Agent's (Non)cooperative Behavior on User's Cooperation Behavior in the Prisoners' Dilemma

Carolin Straßmann [ID],[1] **Astrid M. Rosenthal-von der Pütten,**[2] **and Nicole C. Krämer**[1]

[1]*Social Psychology: Media and Communication, University Duisburg-Essen, 47057 Duisburg, Germany*
[2]*Individual and Technology, RWTH Aachen University, 52062 Aachen, Germany*

Correspondence should be addressed to Carolin Straßmann; carolin.strassmann@uni-due.de

Academic Editor: Thomas Mandl

Most applications for virtual agents require the user to cooperate. Thus, it is helpful to investigate different strategies for virtual agents to evoke the user's cooperation. In the present work ($N = 80$), we experimentally tested the influence of an agent's (non)cooperative nonverbal behavior and actual decision-making behavior on user's cooperation in the Prisoners' Dilemma considering different age groups (students and seniors). Therefore, we used a 2 (nonverbal behavior) x 2 (age group) between-subjects design in Wizard-of-Oz study. Results show age differences with seniors cooperating more often than students do. The nonverbal behavior had no effect on the users' willingness to cooperate nor on the evaluation of the agent's cooperativeness. However, the agent's decision-making behavior in the game influenced the users' willingness to cooperate. In summary, the nonverbal behavior seemed to be too subtle, while the actions of the agent were important in terms of cooperation.

1. Introduction

The long-term goal of most endeavors regarding virtual agents is to create engaging experiences and interactions that are beneficial for the user. In most scenarios, however, the success of these systems depends on the user's willingness to cooperate with the virtual agent. In some scenarios this is even more crucial, for instance, with regard to interactions that are essential for the user's health. Systems supporting elderly users in their daily life, organizing appointments, and reminding them to take their medication rely on users who are willing to share information in order to keep record of all appointments or to guarantee successful medicinal treatment (see [1]). The challenge is to create interactions in which users do not feel patronized by the system but to facilitate cooperation. Interlocutors can show cooperation via different channels: (a) via nonverbal behavior signaling the intent for cooperation, (b) via direct verbal messages, and (c) via their actual cooperative or noncooperative decision-making behavior.

Since there is ample evidence that specific nonverbal behavior can lead to higher cooperativeness perception [2–6], the present study focuses on the effects of the agent's nonverbal behavior. In most situations, it is risky to trust and cooperate with a dishonest person. In order to avoid putting trust into the wrong person, interlocutors use nonverbal behavior as indicators for commitment and cooperation [7]. Nonverbal behavior might function as an indicator for cooperation in such a subtle way that the agent can evoke users' willingness to cooperate without making them feel forced to cooperate. Boone and Buck [3] claimed that nonverbal expressiveness plays an important role in the cooperation process. The authors further suggest testing this assumption by integrating nonverbal emotional displays (nonverbal expressiveness) within a social dilemma setting (e.g., Prisoner's Dilemma). In line with this claim, prior research demonstrated that interlocutors are sensitive to subtle facial expressions like smiling when they evaluate the other person's cooperativeness [5] and that smiling can evoke more cooperation behavior [6]. It has been shown that people who are more cooperative showed more expressive facial displays (both positive and negative) [8]. These facial expressions are assumed to signal honest intentions to cooperate [2]. Thus, a smiling agent should be perceived to signal cooperativeness and therefore users are more willing to cooperate with this agent in return. The effect of expressiveness on the perception of cooperativeness is not limited to facial expressions, but also expressiveness in body movements (large and high frequent gestures) was found to elicit higher perceptions of cooperativeness [4]. Moreover, gaze behavior and head-tilts are related to trust, a concept highly correlated to commitment and cooperation. Hence, gazing towards the user displaying a lateral head-tilt has also been found to evoke a more cooperative impression of the interlocutor [4].

In sum, prior findings suggest that specific nonverbal behavior (e.g., high expressiveness, gaze behavior, and head-tilt) will lead to the attribution of cooperativeness, which recursively fosters the cooperation behavior of the interlocutor. Therefore, we hypothesize the following:

H1: Users interacting with an agent showing cooperative nonverbal behavior cooperate more often with the agent.

Besides the nonverbal behavior of interlocutors, their actual decision-making behavior in the Prisoner's Dilemma is of course also a crucial indicator for trust and cooperation. Pletzer and colleagues [9] found that people are more willing to cooperate when they expect their counterpart to cooperate. Hence, once the trust between the interlocutors has been destroyed by not being cooperative, the perceived cooperativeness of the counterpart will also decrease. Following this we assume that if the agent decides not to cooperate, users' cooperative behavior will drop in return.

H2: The agent's actual decision-making behavior in the Prisoner's Dilemma influences users' willingness to cooperate. After choosing not to cooperate, user's cooperative decision-making behavior will decrease.

As mentioned above, especial applications for special target groups like seniors (e.g., daily life assistance) require the user to cooperate. However, these target groups have special needs due to their features and possibilities. It has been shown, that elderly people are more nervous during an interaction with a virtual agent [10] and, thus, it is especially important to calm them down and find a subtle way to gain their willingness to cooperate. One potential factor to evoke cooperation behavior might be nonverbal cues, but prior findings suggest that seniors showed a higher tendency to misinterpret emotional displays [11]. Hence, it is possible that seniors might also show a higher tendency to misinterpret nonverbal cooperation indicators. Since nonverbal behavior is assumed to be a good natural way to induce cooperation [3], it is a matter of concern whether this is also the case for elderly people, who would particularly benefit from it. Thus, this research aims to investigate age-related differences and the following research question will be examined:

RQ1: Are there age-related differences in the perception of the agent's cooperativeness and the users' willingness to cooperate?

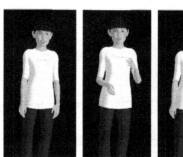

FIGURE 1: Examples of the presented nonverbal behavior smiling, expressive gesture, lateral head-tilt (cooperative nonverbal behavior), and avoiding gaze (noncooperative nonverbal behavior).

2. Materials and Methods

2.1. Experimental Design and Experimental Tasks. Depending on the experimental group, the virtual agent in this study showed either cooperative or noncooperative nonverbal behavior prior to and during the Prisoners' Dilemma game. The study was set up as Wizard-of-Oz scenario in a 2x2 between-subjects design with the independent factors "age group" (students versus seniors) and "nonverbal behavior" (cooperative versus noncooperative).

For the implementation of the two types of nonverbal behaviors, we rely on prior research [4] in which nonverbal behaviors were systematically tested with regard to how users perceived the virtual agent's expressivity and gaze behavior with regard to cooperativity. For the present study, we adopted these behaviors. Therefore, in the cooperative condition the agent ("Billie") showed expressive facial and body movements, turned the gaze towards the user, and showed a lateral head-tilt. Since expressiveness is one of the main indicators for cooperation, the agent in the noncooperative condition in contrast barely displayed nonverbal behavior and avoided the user's gaze more often. Figure 1 presents examples of these behaviors.

To test the impact of (non)cooperative nonverbal behavior we created situations in which cooperation is the key for the interaction. Participants played a virtual version of the well-established Prisoners' Dilemma (c.f. Figure 2). This version of the game is money-based. The players played four rounds in which both parties decided whether to place or to hold their money (10 €) without knowing in advance the decision of the other player. The gains in this game depended on the mutual decision to cooperate: when both parties cooperated and placed their money, they both doubled their placement (both gain 20 €). If just one player placed his or her money and the other player decided to hold, the cooperating player lost the placement (0 €) and the other tripled his or her stakes (30 €). When both players decided to hold their stakes nothing happens and both stakes remained (10 €). Within the four rounds, the virtual agent showed the same decision-making behavior for each participant: first, he cooperates, then he does not cooperate, and in the last two turns, he cooperates again.

FIGURE 2: Prisoner's Dilemma.

Before participants played the Prisoner's Dilemma, they had the chance to get to know the agent. Participants interacted with the virtual agent in a calendar setting, where they managed appointments and decided whether to follow suggestions of the virtual agent. In particular, participants planned three appointments together with the virtual agent Billie and entered the appointments into the virtual calendar by stating activity as well as date, starting time, and duration of the appointment. During this interaction, the agent already displayed the nonverbal behavior (either cooperative or noncooperative), so that participants also had the chance to perceive the manipulated cooperativity of the agent during this joint task and prior to the dilemma task.

2.2. Participants and Procedure. Overall 80 people participated in this lab experiment, 40 of which were students (age: $M = 22.03$, $SD = 2.61$; 24 female and 16 male) and 40 seniors (age: $M = 68.15$, $SD = 5.59$; 22 female and 18 male). Students received either course credits or 10 € and seniors received 10 € for participation. Upon arrival, participants read and signed informed consent. Afterwards, they first interacted with the agent in the calendar setting negotiating appointments and filled in a short evaluating questionnaire, in which they evaluated the agent's person perception. Subsequently, they were instructed about the mechanisms of the Prisoners' Dilemma and then they played four rounds of the game. After completion of the game, participants filled in questionnaires evaluating the agent and its abilities, the interaction, and the experimental tasks as well as scales assessing the explanatory variables.

2.3. Measurements

2.3.1. Cooperation Behavior. We analyzed users' behavior within the Prisoners' Dilemma. Participants could choose to cooperate or not during each of the four turns. We also calculated the sum score for all four decisions.

2.3.2. Person Perception. Participants were asked to evaluate the agent with regard to person perception on five dimensions (*Likability, Intelligence, Cooperativity, Dominance,* and *Autonomy*), indicating their agreement to 35 items on a 5-point Likert scale ranging from "I do not agree at all" to "I fully agree". The scales are based on a person perception scale previously used in human-agent/robot interaction studies [12]. Participants stated their evaluation of the agent's person perception twice: after the calendar interaction (T1) and after

the Prisoners' Dilemma (T2). The dimension *Autonomy* was measured only once at T2.

The dimension *Likability* was measured with eight items (e.g., friendly, likable; Cronbach's α $T1 =.911$; $T2 =.882$). Intelligence was measured using five items (e.g., dumb (rev), intelligent; Cronbach's α $T1=.820$; $T2 =.845$). *Cooperativity* was measured using seven items (e.g., ask Billie for advice, is cooperative, is supportive; Cronbach's α $T1 =.891$; $T2 =.859$). *Autonomy* was measured using six items (e.g., not autonomous (rev), self-dependent; Cronbach's α $T2 =.773$). *Dominance* was measured using nine items (e.g., dominant, submissive (rev)). Reliability was too low for this subscale and did not improve when using a subset of the items. Therefore, we decided to use only the single item dominant for further analyses.

2.3.3. Communicative Abilities. We assessed how participants rated the agent's verbal and nonverbal communicative abilities with regard to *mutual verbal understanding, dominance in conversation, nonverbal behavior production,* and *nonverbal behavior recognition/understanding.* Mutual verbal understanding was measured with nine items (e.g., Billie understood me well, did not hear me, did not understand me; Cronbach's α =.757; the item "the conversation with Billie was stiff" was omitted to enhance reliability). Dominance in conversation was measured using five items (e.g., I was able to control the conversation (rev), Billie was leading the conversation; Cronbach's α =.744). Nonverbal behavior production was measured with five items (e.g., I had the feeling that Billie's gestures were expressive, unambiguous; Cronbach's α =.832). Nonverbal behavior understanding was measured with six items (e.g., I had the feeling that Billie was able to recognize my gestures, was able to recognize my mimic; Cronbach's α =.888).

2.3.4. Physical Presence and Social Presence. We assessed participants' sense of copresence with the Nowak and Biocca Presence Scale [13], which contains 12 items on the concept of *"perceived other's copresence"* (e.g., my interaction partner was intensely involved in our interaction; Cronbach's α =.784) and 6 items on *"self-reported copresence"* (e.g., I was unwilling to share personal information with my interaction partner; Cronbach's α =.685), both rated on a 5-point Likert scale. Furthermore, we used Bailenson et al.'s *Social Presence* Scale [14] with 5 items rated on a 5-point Likert scale (e.g., I perceived the presence of another person in the room with me, Cronbach's α =.699). Since reliability of the Social Presence Scale and the subscale *"self-reported copresence"* was low, we excluded these measures from further analyses.

2.3.5. Perception of the Game. We asked participants about their perceptions of Billie and the Prisoners' Dilemma with fifteen ad hoc generated items. These items asked participants, for example, about the difficulty of the game (e.g., the game was easy to master), the perceived cooperation of the game (e.g., Billie and I were partners during the game), the trust towards the agent (e.g., Billie gave me the feeling that he knows better and I am better off not to trust him), or felt competitiveness (e.g., during the game I was mostly

TABLE 1: Means of participants' decision to cooperate for all four rounds.

	Students			Seniors			Σ		
	CO	NC	Σ	CO	NC	Σ	CO	NC	Σ
				Round $1_{a,b}$					
M	0.90	0.75	0.83	0.90	1.00	0.95	0.90	0.88	0.89
SD	0.31	0.44	0.38	0.31	0.00	0.22	0.30	0.33	0.32
				Round $2_{c,d}$					
M	0.85	0.75	0.80	0.85	0.95	0.95	0.85	0.85	0.85
SD	0.37	0.44	0.41	0.37	0.22	0.30	0.37	0.37	0.36
				Round $3_{a,c}$					
M	0.70	0.50	0.60	0.80	0.65	0.73	0.75	0.58	0.66
SD	0.47	0.51	0.50	0.41	0.45	0.45	0.44	0.50	0.48
				Round $4_{b,d}$					
M	0.40	0.55	0.48	0.65	0.75	0.70	0.53	0.65	0.59
SD	0.50	0.51	0.51	0.49	0.44	0.46	0.51	0.48	0.50

Note. Means in rows sharing subscripts are significantly different from each other. CO represents a cooperative nonverbal behavior, while NC is written for the noncooperative nonverbal behavior.

concerned with how I could maximize my own gains). All items were rated on a 5-point Likert scale ranging from "I do not agree at all" to "I do fully agree".

2.3.6. Future Usage of Agent System. Participants also indicated how likely they would use the virtual agent in the future (e.g., I can imagine interacting with Billie more often, Billie could help me also with other tasks in my everyday life; Cronbach's α =.955).

2.3.7. Moderating Variables. As moderating variables, we used the short version of the NEO-FFI Scale [15], the cooperation subscale of the Temperament and Personality Questionnaire [16], and the nonverbal immediacy scale [17].

3. Results

3.1. Decision-Making Behavior. A mixed-design repeated measures ANOVA was calculated with the agent's nonverbal behavior and age groups as between factors and users decision-making behavior during the game (user's decision to cooperate or not within the four rounds) as repeated measures. Greenhouse-Geisser correction (ε =.78) was used, since the assumption of sphericity has been violated. No main effect of the presented nonverbal behavior emerged, while there was a significant main effect for the age group ($F(1,76)$ = 9.438, p =.003, η^2 =.110) and a linear effect of the cooperation behavior itself ($F(2.35,178.63)$ = 9.852, p <.001, η^2 =.115). Post hoc tests indicated that participants cooperated in the first and second round significantly more often compared to the third and fourth round (cf. Table 1). Considering the overall cooperation behavior, an ANOVA with age and nonverbal behavior as independent and the frequency of cooperation (ranging from 0 to 4) as dependent variable was conducted. Analyses revealed only a significant difference regarding age ($F(1,76)$ = 9.438, p =.003, η^2 =.110): seniors cooperated more often than students (cf. Table 2).

3.2. Person Perception of Agent. Multiple ANOVAs were calculated, to investigate the effect of the nonverbal behavior and age group on the five subscales of person perception (after the interaction) revealing no significant effects on Cooperativity, Competence, and Autonomy. However, a significant main effect of the agent's nonverbal behavior on Likability was found, $F(1,79)$ = 5.04, p =.028, η^2 =.062. An agent showing noncooperative nonverbal behavior was evaluated as more likable than an agent who displayed cooperative nonverbal behavior.

Moreover, we tested whether users' perception of the agent prior to the dilemma influenced the user's cooperation behavior during the dilemma game. A multiple linear regression with the first evaluation of Likability, Cooperativity, and Competence as predictors and users' cooperation behavior during the game as dependent variable showed a valid regression model for Likability, b =.29, $t(78)$ = 2.56, p =.013. Initial Likability ratings also explained a significant proportion of variance in cooperation behavior, R^2 =.07, $F(1, 79)$ = 6.53, p =.013.

3.3. Communication Abilities. To examine the effect of age group and nonverbal behavior on the perceived communication abilities of the agent, we calculated two-factorial ANOVAs. However, the analyses for the four subscales did not result in any significant differences.

3.4. Future Usage. Results of an ANOVA showed no significant effect of age group or nonverbal behavior on the intended future usage of the agent.

3.5. Perception of the Game. The effect of nonverbal behavior and age group on the perception of the game based on single items was examined using two-factorial ANOVAs.

Significant main effects of age group were obtainable for the quality of the agent's arguments ($F(1,75)$ = 10.388, p =.002,

TABLE 2: Means for participants overall decision to cooperate.

| | Age group | | | | | |
| | Students | | Seniors | | Overall | |
Nonverbal behavior	M	SD	M	SD	M	SD
Coop	2.85	0.93	3.20	0.95	3.03	0.95
Non-coop	2.55	0.83	3.35	0.59	2.95	0.81
Overall	2.70	0.88	3.28	0.78	2.99	0.88

TABLE 3: Means of age group's game evaluation.

| | Age Group | | | | | |
| | Students | | Seniors | | Overall | |
Nonverbal behavior	M	SD	M	SD	M	SD
Billie provided good arguments for cooperation during the game	3.23	1.25	4.05	0.96	3.64	1.18
Billie gave me the feeling that he knows better and I am better off not to trust him	2.68	1.39	2.00	1.20	2.34	1.33
I perceived Billie as my opponent	2.65	1.33	1.90	1.24	2.28	1.33
During the game I was mostly concerned with how I could maximize my own gains	2.53	1.40	1.75	1.03	2.14	1.28
I often thought about how Billie would decide in this round	4.05	0.96	2.55	1.52	3.30	1.47

η^2 =.122), the perceived trust towards the agent ($F(1,75)$ = 4.731, p =.033, η^2 =.059), feelings of competitiveness ($F(1,75)$ = 6.140, p =.015, η^2 =.076), maximal gain ($F(1,75)$ = 7.50 p =.008, η^2 =.091), and the agent's decisions ($F(1,75)$ = 28.826, p <.001, η^2 =.278). Overall, the results showed the pattern that seniors felt less competitive, while students tried to maximize their gain and took into account the agent's potential future decision-making behavior more strongly during their own decision-making (c.f. Table 3).

Additionally, main effects of the agent's nonverbal behavior on the perceived difficulty of the game ($F(1,75)$ = 5.22, p =.025, η^2 =.063) and feeling of being confederates were found ($F(1,75)$ = 5.010, p =.028, η^2 =.063). On the one hand, users perceived the game as being easier when they interacted with an agent that displayed cooperative nonverbal behavior (CO: M = 1.20, SD = 0.46; NC: M = 1.75, SD = 1.32); on the other hand, participants perceived the agent more as a confederate when he showed noncooperative nonverbal behavior (CO: M = 2.63, SD = 1.28; NC: M = 3.23, SD = 1.10).

3.6. Physical and Social Presence. Further calculations demonstrated that age group and the agent's nonverbal behavior did not affect the perceived copresence of the agent.

3.7. Moderating Variables. We calculated multiple ANCOVAs with personality traits and nonverbal immediacy as moderating variables, but the presented pattern of results did not change.

4. Discussion, Limitations, and Future Work

In this study, we experimentally tested the influence of a virtual agent's (non)cooperative nonverbal behavior on users'

evaluation of the agent and their willingness to cooperate during a social dilemma game. Eliciting the perception of cooperativeness with nonverbal cues might be used as a subtle way in human-agent interaction to enhance users' willingness to cooperate without forcing them.

Surprisingly, our results did not demonstrate the expected influence of the agent's nonverbal behavior on participants' decision-making. In contrast to prior research and hypothesis H1, the user's willingness to cooperate during the Prisoner's Dilemma was not affected by the agent's nonverbal behavior. The scenario utilized for this study might have suppressed effects of nonverbal behavior, since the Prisoner's Dilemma is restricted in terms of the length of interaction and quality of interpersonal communication. Hence, participants' focus might have been more on the task than on the agent. In this regard, the manipulation of (non)cooperative nonverbal behavior might have been too subtle for the given scenario.

A manipulation check on whether participants consciously perceived the nonverbal behavior of the agent indeed indicated that participants were not able to report whether the agent showed cooperative behaviors or not. Therefore, participants stated how much the agent has moved, showed gestures, smiled, and looked towards them, and no significant differences between the conditions have been found. Since the mean values of all items were rather low (moved: M = 1.98, SD =.60; showed gestures: M = 1.85, SD =.66; smiled: M = 1.56, SD =.65; looked at me: M = 2.69, SD =.89), results indicate that the nonverbal behavior was not recognized by the participants in the way it was intended. This, however, is not automatically detrimental in our setting as nonverbal behavior might still be effective even if it is not consciously perceived. However, since the agent's nonverbal behavior had also no effect on the perceived cooperativeness of the agent, the presented behavior might have been too subtle or participants focused too much on the presented scenario. Therefore, hypothesis H1 was not supported. To investigate the role of the chosen scenario and its attracted attention in the recognition and perception of the nonverbal behavior, future studies may use eye-tracking methods to check participants eye-movements and focus during the interaction. That would be an objective way, to test whether participants looked at the agent and were able to obtain its nonverbal behavior. Further on, a more social scenario that ensures longer interactions between the agent and the user (as it is true for potential assistive applications, e.g., reviewing a schedule) and offers the option to test cooperation behavior should be used to examine the effect of nonverbal behavior in more detail.

Another possible explanation for our findings might be the context of the nonverbal behavior, because prior research has shown that emotional expressions are affected by the context in which they are presented. Melo and colleagues [18] showed that the morality of the nonverbal behavior is important. For instance, an agent who smiled after a user's loss was perceived as less cooperative than an agent showing empathy and displaying a sad facial expression when the user has lost. Although the agent followed the same scheme for cooperation during the game (yes, no, yes, yes), the cooperative behavior of the respective participant was not foreseeable. Hence, situations might have emerged where the agent displayed smiling behavior after a user's loss. The present study did not focus on the context of the nonverbal behavior, but on its mere exposure.

Besides the effect of the agent's nonverbal behavior, we investigated how the actual cooperation behavior of the agent influenced the user's decisions. We hypothesized that a noncooperative decision of the agent will be followed by a drop in cooperation on the side of the users (H2). Results indicate that the agent's actual decision-making behavior in the Prisoners' Dilemma influenced users' decision-making. While we observed a high initial willingness to cooperate, participants significantly cooperated less after the agent's noncooperative behavior in the second round of the game supporting our hypothesis. These findings are in line with prior research [9], demonstrating that persons are more cooperative when they expect their counterparts to cooperate as well. Thus, after the agent destroyed the participants' trust by being not cooperative, participants did not expect the agent to be cooperative anymore and therefore their own willingness to cooperate also decreases.

Additionally, likability ratings prior to the game predicted participants' willingness to cooperate. Participants who perceived the agent as more likable before they played the game cooperated more with the agent. The likability perception after the game was affected by the agent's nonverbal behavior, but not in the way as it was intended, since noncooperative behavior led to higher likability ratings. Although the nonverbal behavior was chosen based on prior research [4], where those behaviors evoked a higher cooperativeness and likability perception, this pattern could not be replicated in the present study. During the used scenario showing only little nonverbal behavior seemed to be perceived as more likable than being nonverbal expressive. Maybe the

cooperative behaviors were seen as not appropriate while gambling for money. However, this finding is contradicting to our assumptions and the empirical background.

Since applications of virtual agents for people in need of support (like the target group of seniors) are supposed to be beneficial and since cooperation in these contexts is regularly needed in order to provide benefits, we examined age-related differences in the perception of cooperativeness and the user's intention to cooperate. Our results demonstrate that seniors cooperated more often with the agent than students did. In addition, results regarding the evaluation of the game revealed that seniors showed unconditional trust and cooperation to the agent, since they stated to have less competitive thoughts. In contrast, students were more competitive and tried to maximize their win by considering the agent's behavior more carefully. No differences with regard to the perception of the agent's cooperativeness have been found. Seniors and students evaluated the agent similarly. Moreover, no interaction effects of age group and nonverbal behavior have been found. Therefore, the effect of the nonverbal behavior did not differ between the age groups and both groups perceived the agent in the same way.

5. Conclusion

It can be concluded that while actual cooperative behavior as well as the evaluation of the game was influenced by age, the perception and evaluation of the agent's nonverbal behavior were not. In summary, findings of the present study suggest that the actual decision-making behavior of a virtual agent is more important than the agent's nonverbal behavior—at least in this specific setting of the Prisoner's Dilemma. For a money-based game, the nonverbal behavior seemed to be too subtle to unfold full effect. An additional important finding with regard to future applications is that seniors cooperated more often with the agent and showed unconditional trust. This might be helpful with regard to future applications in which agents and humans cooperate to the human's benefit.

Acknowledgments

This work was part of the project KOMPASS (socially cooperative, virtual assistants as companions for people in need of cognitive support) [Grant no. 16SV7272] that is funded by the German Federal Ministry of Education and Research. The authors would like to thank Ramin Yaghoubzadeh, Katharina Suhre, Katharina Brockmann, and Sueyda Yüzer for their help with the scenario implementation and data collection.

References

[1] R. Yaghoubzadeh, M. Kramer, K. Pitsch, and S. Kopp, "Virtual agents as daily assistants for elderly or cognitively impaired people," in *Proceedings of the International Conference on Intelligent Virtual Agents*, pp. 79–91, 2013.

[2] L. I. Reed, K. N. Zeglen, and K. L. Schmidt, "Facial expressions as honest signals of cooperative intent in a one-shot anonymous Prisoner's Dilemma game," *Evolution and Human Behavior*, vol. 33, no. 3, pp. 200–209, 2012.

[3] R. Thomas Boone and R. Buck, "Emotional expressivity and trustworthiness: The role of nonverbal behavior in the evolution of cooperation," *Journal of Nonverbal Behavior*, vol. 27, no. 3, pp. 163–182, 2003.

[4] C. Straßmann, A. R. Von Der Pütten, R. Yaghoubzadeh, R. Kaminski, and N. Krämer, "The effect of an intelligent virtual agent's nonverbal behavior with regard to dominance and cooperativity," in *Proceedings of the 16th International Conference on Intelligent Virtual Agents (IVA '16)*, pp. 15–28, Los Angeles, Calif, USA, September 2016.

[5] E. Krumhuber, A. S. R. Manstead, D. Cosker, D. Marshall, P. L. Rosin, and A. Kappas, "Facial dynamics as indicators of trustworthiness and cooperative behavior," *Emotion*, vol. 7, no. 4, pp. 730–735, 2007.

[6] W. M. Brown and C. Moore, "Smile asymmetries and reputation as reliable indicators of likelihood to cooperate: An evolutionary analysis," *Advances in Psychology Research*, vol. 11, no. 3, pp. 59–78, 2002.

[7] J. Jahng, J. D. Kralik, D.-U. Hwang, and J. Jeong, "Neural dynamics of two players when using nonverbal cues to gauge intentions to cooperate during the Prisoner's Dilemma Game," *NeuroImage*, vol. 157, pp. 263–274, 2017.

[8] J. Schug, D. Matsumoto, Y. Horita, T. Yamagishi, and K. Bonnet, "Emotional expressivity as a signal of cooperation," *Evolution and Human Behavior*, vol. 31, no. 2, pp. 87–94, 2010.

[9] J. L. Pletzer, D. Balliet, J. Joireman, D. M. Kuhlman, S. C. Voelpel, and P. A. M. Van Lange, "Social value orientation, expectations, and cooperation in social dilemmas: a meta-analysis," *European Journal of Personality*, vol. 32, no. 1, pp. 62–83, 2018.

[10] N. C. Krämer, L. Hoffmann, and S. Kopp, "Know your users! Empirical results for tailoring an agent's nonverbal behavior to different user groups," in *Proceedings of the International Conference on Intelligent Virtual Agents*, vol. 6356, pp. 468–474, 2010.

[11] J. M. Beer, C. Smarr, A. D. Fisk, and W. A. Rogers, "Younger and older users' recognition of virtual agent facial expressions," *International Journal of Human-Computer Studies*, vol. 75, pp. 1–20, 2015.

[12] A. M. Rosenthal-Von Der Pütten, N. Bock, and K. Brockmann, "Not your cup of tea?: How interacting with a robot can increase perceived self-efficacy in HRI and evaluation," in *Proceedings of the 12th Annual ACM/IEEE International Conference on Human-Robot Interaction (HRI '17)*, pp. 483–492, March 2017.

[13] K. L. Nowak and F. Biocca, "The Effect of the Agency and Anthropomorphism on users' Sense of Telepresence, Copresence, and Social Presence in Virtual Environments," *Presence: Teleoperators and Virtual Environments*, vol. 12, no. 5, pp. 481–494, 2003.

[14] J. N. Bailenson, A. C. Beall, J. Blascovich, M. Raimundo, and M. Weisbuch, "Intelligent agents who wear your face: Users' reactions to the virtual self," in *Proceedings of the International Conference on Intelligent Virtual Agents*, vol. 2190, pp. 86–99, 2001.

[15] B. Rammstedt and O. P. John, "Measuring personality in one minute or less: a 10-item short version of the big five inventory in English and German," *Journal of Research in Personality*, vol. 41, no. 1, pp. 203–212, 2007.

[16] Black Dog Institute, "Temperament & personality (T&P) questionnaire information," BlackDog Insitution, 2012, http://www.blackdoginstitute.org.au/.

[17] V. P. Richmond, J. C. McCroskey, and A. D. Johnson, "Development of the nonverbal immediacy scale (NIS): Measures of self-and other-perceived nonverbal immediacy," *Communication Quarterly*, vol. 51, no. 4, pp. 504–517, 2003.

[18] C. M. De Melo, L. Zheng, and J. Gratch, "Expression of moral emotions in cooperating agents," in *Proceedings of the International Conference on Intelligent Virtual Agents*, pp. 301–307, 2009.

7

A Systematic Review of Modifications and Validation Methods for the Extension of the Keystroke-Level Model

Shiroq Al-Megren ⓘ**, Joharah Khabti, and Hend S. Al-Khalifa** ⓘ

King Saud University, Information Technology Department, Riyadh 12371, Saudi Arabia

Correspondence should be addressed to Shiroq Al-Megren; salmegren@ksu.edu.sa

Academic Editor: Thomas Mandl

The keystroke-level model (KLM) is the simplest model of the goals, operators, methods, and selection rules (GOMS) family. The KLM computes formative quantitative predictions of task execution time. This paper provides a systematic literature review of KLM extensions across various applications and setups. The objective of this review is to address research questions concerning the development and validation of extensions. A total of 54 KLM extensions have been exhaustively reviewed. The results show that the original keystroke and mental act operators were continuously preserved or adapted and that the drawing operator was used the least. Excluding the original operators, almost 45 operators were collated from the primary studies. Only half of the studies validated their model's efficiency through experiments. The results also identify several research gaps, such as the shortage of KLM extensions for post-GUI/WIMP interfaces. Based on the results obtained in this work, this review finally provides guidelines for researchers and practitioners.

1. Introduction

Human-computer interaction (HCI) simplifies reality with models of human behaviour to design and evaluate computer systems [1]. Within HCI, models of motor behaviour lie on a continuum of analogy and mathematical equations. Generally, the models are categorised as either descriptive or predictive. Descriptive models present a framework to describe a phenomenon by identifying its features within a computer system. At the other end of the continuum, predictive models are commonly used to provide analytical a priori estimations of human performance without user participation, thus reducing time and resource consumption.

A family of predictive models (GOMS) were developed to compare and evaluate goals, methods, and selection rules of skilled, error-free user performances [2]. GOMS techniques model goal hierarchies of defined unit tasks rendered as a composition of action and cognitive operators [3, 4]. The simplest member of the GOMS family is the keystroke-level model (KLM), which predicts the execution time of specific tasks in a desktop environment using a mouse and keyboard. The KLM has been widely utilised to evaluate

expert performances of various desktop interfaces, and its aptitude and usefulness have been well demonstrated.

The challenges of designing and developing computer systems and the emergence of new technologies have revealed a need for updated quality assessments. Revising predictive models for these challenges can help evaluate human performance a priori and reduce the need for time- and resource-intensive human studies. The KLM was developed from and intended for desktop systems but has continually been extended to model systems designed for other computer setups in various domains. These extensions involve adapting the original KLM operators, introducing or inheriting new operators, revising heuristics, and presenting new execution calculations or techniques to satisfy the extension's purpose.

A systematic review of KLM extensions provides an objective procedure for identifying the extent of the research that is available; to the best of the authors' knowledge no prior systematic review exists that focuses on KLM extensions. This paper extensively reviews KLM extensions between 1980 and 2016. The goal of this review is to summarise, analyse, and assess the empirical evidence regarding the purpose for each extension, the extension's application domains and setups,

TABLE 1: KLM operators and predicted execution times in seconds [6].

Type	Operator	Description	Time (s)
Physical		Keystroke or button press	
		Best typist (135 wpm)	0.80
		Good typist (90 wpm)	0.12
	K	Average skilled typist (55 wpm)	0.20
		Average non-skilled typist (40 wpm)	0.28
		Typing random letters	0.50
		Typing complex codes	0.75
		Worst typist	1.20
	P	Point with a mouse to a target on a display	1.10
	H	Home hands on the keyboard or other device	0.40
	D	Drawing n straight line segments with a total length of l	$0.90n_D + 0.16l_D$
Mental	M	Mental preparation for an action	1.35
System	$R(t)$	System response of t seconds	t

wpm: words per minute.

and the research methods used to create and validate extensions. Most importantly, this review investigates how the KLM has been extended within the new models by examining operators, heuristics, equations, and domain-specific metrics. The results of this review also outline relevant issues for designers, developers, and researchers who apply or extend the KLM.

The rest of this paper is organised as follows. Section 2 presents the background for the KLM by introducing the topic and its seminal publications. Section 3 describes the methodology and protocol used to systematically review the KLM extensions. Section 5 describes the results of the review. Section 6 discusses the principal findings, limitations, and implications for research and practice. Finally, Section 7 concludes the paper and suggests future directions.

2. Keystroke-Level Model: An overview

KLM [6] is the simplest and most practical GOMS method for evaluating the time performance of user-computer system interaction. Underlying the KLM is the assumption that user employs a series of small and independent unit tasks. These tasks support the decomposition of larger tasks into manageable units. The sum of the durations of these small units equals the time it takes to complete the task. Each unit task has two phases: task acquisition and task execution: the total time to complete a unit task is the sum of these two parts:

$$T_{task} = T_{acquire} + T_{execute} \qquad (1)$$

First, in the acquisition phase, the user conceptualises and develops a mental representation of the unit task. Then, during execution, the user invokes the appropriate system commands required to accomplish the unit task. The KLM predicts only the execution time of a unit task because that is the only phase over which a system designer has direct control.

Unit tasks in the KLM are described with a set of physical-motor, mental, and response operators (see Table 1). Operators are identified by a letter and include: K keystroking, P

pointing, H homing, D drawing, M mentally preparing, and R system response. K is the most frequently used operator and represents a keystroke or a button press. The operator P is the act of pointing to a target on a display with a mouse. P would typically be computed as a function of the distance to a target and its size (Fitts' law, [7]); however, for simplification it is assigned a constant time. In a typical computer setup, H is the action of moving the hand between keyboard and mouse and includes any fine hand adjustments on those devices. The physical operator, D, is restricted to the mouse and refers to manually drawing a set of straight-line segments within a constrained 0.56 cm grid. Before carrying out a physical action, the user has to mentally prepare for its execution. This preparation is represented by the M operator and a constant value of 1.35 seconds. The final operator, R, refers to the time it takes for the system to respond to a user's actions.

Unlike physical and system operators, M is not an observable user behaviour, yet it comprises a substantial fraction of the prediction. The occurrence of M is based on specific knowledge of user skills, and their placements are governed by a set of heuristics that embody psychological assumptions about users. Methods are a sequence of system commands that form a compiled segment of a user's behaviour when executing a unit task. A user cognitively organises a method according to cognitive chunks, and M typically occurs between chunks rather than within them. In Table 2, while Rule 0 identifies possible decision points within the methods, Rules 1 to 4 attempt to identify these method chunks.

Execution time is predicted by decomposing a unit task into a list of operators and then computing their summation:

$$T_{execute} = T_K + T_P + T_H + T_D + T_M + T_R \qquad (2)$$

$T_{operator}$ is an operator's total time, e.g., $T_K = n_K t_K$, where n_K is the number of keystrokes and t_K is the duration of each K. To illustrate how the KLM's equation and rules can be applied to predict user performance, consider the following example of a user renaming a folder to "klm" on a desktop. The user homes the hand on the mouse, H; points the mouse cursor at the object, P; double-clicks on the folder icon to

TABLE 2: Heuristic rules for M operator placement [6].

Rule 0	Insert Ms in front of all Ks that are not part of an argument string. Place Ms in front of all Ps that select commands.
Rule 1	When an operator following an M is fully anticipated in the operator just prior to M, remove the M.
Rule 2	When a string of MKs belongs to a cognitive unit, delete all Ms except the first.
Rule 3	When a K is a redundant terminator, delete the M prior to the K.
Rule 4	When a K terminates a constant string, delete the M prior to the K; however, do not delete the M when the K terminates a variable string.

allow for renaming, KK; homes hands on keyboard, H; keys new name "klm", KKK; and presses Enter, K

The KLM model without M and R (assuming an instantaneous response from the system) is $HPKKHKKKK$. Applying the heuristic rules for placing the M operators results in the final model $MHPKKHMKKKK$, where the first M is the time spent by user searching for the folder on the computer display, and the second M is the time the user requires to mentally prepare for typing. Therefore, (assuming K is 0.28 for average nonskilled typist):

$$T_{execute} = 2M + 2H + 1P + 6K = 5.8s \qquad (3)$$

KLM was validated against observed values to determine how well the model predicted performance times and was subsequently used to model typical tasks in various systems (text editors, graphic editors, and executive subsystems). K's value can be determined from a typing test prior to the test tasks. After a practice period, each expert user carried out test tasks and their keystroke times were logged. These times were then compared against the modelled predictions. The root-mean-square percentage error (RMSPE) was calculated as 21%. The developers of the KLM reported that this accuracy is the best that can be expected from the KLM and that it is comparable to the 20-30% previously obtained from more elaborate models [2, 6].

KLM inherits several limitations from GOMS. It assumes the user is an expert and does not account for user errors. This makes the model ill-suited for predicting average or novice system users. The model also assumes that the task is performed linearly; however, users often multi-task and are frequently interrupted. The KLM also does not consider individual differences in performance, such as mental workload and fatigue. In addition, the KLM predictive model is usually not generalizable because it is constructed to fit and evaluate a given interface.

3. Methodology

This systematic review of KLM extensions was carried out following the procedure given by Kitchenham and Charters [5, 8]. The review process consisted of three stages: planning, conducting, and reporting (see Figure 1). The review protocol was established after several meetings and discussions to reduce the risk of research bias. The rest of this section describes the research questions and the subsequent steps undertaken to conduct the review.

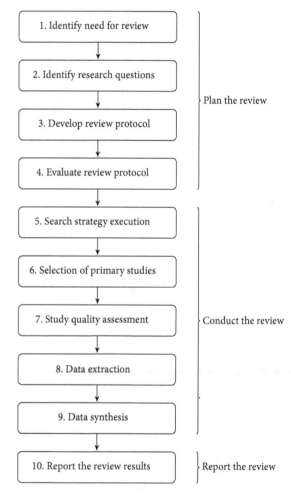

FIGURE 1: The systematic review process [5].

3.1. Research Questions. The goal of this review is to examine the current extensions of the KLM from the point of view of the following research question: "What extensions have been applied to the KLM and how have these extensions been developed and evaluated?" The question aims to summarise the current practices around extending the KLM to shed light on gaps in the current research, suggest areas for further investigation, and provide knowledge on the adoption of the KLM and its extensions to measure the performance of prototypes. Table 3 lists all the research questions and their motivations.

TABLE 3: Systematic review research questions and their motivations.

Research Questions	Motivation
RQ1: What was the purpose of extending the KLM?	Identify why the original KLM was modified, i.e., for which domain, application, or target user.
RQ2: What was the research method used to extend the KLM?	Identify research methods used to extend the original KLM, e.g., previous literature or user study.
RQ3: How was the original KLM extended?	Identify ways in which the original KLM was extended—specifically, how the operators and equations were affected. This includes, but is not limited to: original operators preserved, adapted or discarded, new operators and/or equations, updated M heuristics, and domain-specific metrics.
RQ4: What was the research method used to validate the extended KLM?	Identify research methods used to validate the extended KLM and the performance metrics utilised.

TABLE 4: Search string used to conduct the review search in the digital libraries. The wildcard * is used to signify any character to include variations for each term.

KLM	"keystroke level model" OR "keystroke-level model" OR "keystroke model" OR "KLM-GOMS"
	AND
Extension	exten* OR modif* OR enhanc* OR assess* OR evalu* OR revis* OR adapt* OR refin*

3.2. Data Sources.

The main electronic database sources used to search for primary studies included the ACM digital library, IEEE Xplore, Springer Link, Elsevier Science Direct, Web of Science, Scopus, Taylor and Francis online, and Google Scholar.

3.3. Search Strategy and Terms.

The search string consisted of two main parts: the KLM and its extensions (see Table 4). The first part relates to studies utilising the KLM for extension or evaluation, and the second part relates to extensions. The terms were extracted from textbooks and research papers on the KLM. The search string was formed by incorporating alternative terms and synonyms using the Boolean "OR" expression. The two main search terms were then combined using "AND".

The search was conducted by applying the search string to collections of article meta-data. The string syntax was adapted for application to each digital library and its restrictions. This review was restricted to the period from July 1980 (the first time KLM was presented in "The Keystroke-level Model for User Performance Time with Interactive Systems," [6]) to December 2016.

In addition to the primary search strategy, backward and forward searches were conducted. For each selected paper, the references were examined for a backward search, while the "cited by" links provided by some of the digital libraries were analysed for the forward search. Finally, publications citing the original KLM paper were also searched.

3.4. Study Selection Criteria.

Each primary study was evaluated for relevance against inclusion and exclusion criteria. A study was selected when it satisfied one of the following inclusion criteria:

(i) Studies explicitly extending the KLM.

(ii) Studies reporting evaluations that employed the KLM or its extensions in post-WIMP interfaces or new application domains.

(iii) Studies combining the KLM or its extensions with other models.

Studies were excluded from the review when they met one of the following exclusion criteria:

(i) Studies presenting KLM-like extensions that did not extend the KLM or an extended version.

(ii) Studies presenting extension recommendations.

(iii) Studies presenting KLM testing processes that were focused on determining the effectiveness of the KLM for evaluation.

(iv) Studies modifying the KLM to create composite operators.

(v) Studies presenting duplicate reports of the same study and that did not present new material.

(vi) Studies not written in English.

(vii) Unpublished studies, excluding technical reports and theses.

3.5. Quality Assessment.

The selected primary studies were assessed for relevance and strength using a three-point Likert-scale questionnaire consisting of the following subjective and objective closed-ended questions (see Appendix A):

(i) The study presents a clearly stated purpose for extending the KLM.

(ii) The study extends the KLM with new operators or modifications.

(iii) The study clearly defines the research method used to extend the KLM.

TABLE 5: Digital search results resulting from applying the search string to the selected digital libraries. The numbers in parentheses show the number of unique articles.

Digital Source	Potential	Preliminary Selection	Final Selection
ACM digital library	44	23	18
Scopus	62	29	17
Springer Link	212	22	16
Elsevier Science Direct	184	17	5
Web of Science	31	10	10
Taylor and Francis on-line	67	12	4
IEEE Xplore digital library	93	7	5
Google Scholar	1751	118	62
Total	2444	238 (149)	137 (66)

(iv) The extension methodology is adequate and repeatable.

(v) The extension results and findings are clearly stated.

(vi) The study clearly defines the research methods used to validate the extended KLM.

(vii) The extension validation methodology is adequate and repeatable.

(viii) The validation results and findings are clearly stated.

(ix) The study presents a comparative analysis of the extended KLM against the original KLM.

(x) The paper has been cited by other authors and/or contributes to the literature.

Each question is ranked 1 (yes), 0.5 (partly), and 0 (no). The final quality score is the sum of these values. The maximum score is 10 and the minimum score is 0. The quality of each primary study was ranked by two researchers. After thorough reviews, discussions were conducted to reach a final decision about the inclusion of each study in the review.

3.6. Data Extraction. The data extraction strategy was used to provide answers to the research questions in Table 3. An extraction form was developed to ensure that consistent extraction criteria were used (see Appendix A). The information extracted included:

(1) Title, author, year, and type of publication.

(2) RQ1: the purpose of the extension, device setup, application domain, and the intended users.

(3) RQ2: the research method used to extend the KLM.

(4) RQ3: how the KLM was extended, including adapted operator unit times, new operators or equations, updated M heuristics, and domain-specific metrics.

(5) RQ4: the research method used to validate the viability of the KLM extension, and the performance metrics used for validation, including any comparison of the extension's performance against KLM.

3.7. Data Synthesis. The objective of this step was to accumulate and combine facts and formulate responses to the research questions. The extracted information was grouped, summarised, and tabulated based on the six separate tables according to the elements identified in the data extraction process: general information, quality assessment, and RQ1–RQ4. Each primary study was assigned a code to identify the reviewed studies. Furthermore, extracted information concerning how the KLM was extended (RQ3) was collected in a table that lists and collates all the operators utilised.

4. Conducting the Review

Applying the review protocol yielded the preliminary results shown in Table 5. In total, 149 studies were selected. Using the defined inclusion and exclusion criteria, 62 primary studies (based on 66 articles) were identified. During this stage several issues were identified:

(i) Some studies document different stages of the same research; for this reason, we refer to a smaller number of studies based on a larger number of articles.

(ii) Some studies appeared in more than one source; these were considered based on the adopted search order (ACM, Scopus, Springer Link, Science Direct, Web of Science, Taylor and Francis on-line, IEEE Xplore, and Google Scholar).

The forward and backward search of the selected studies yielded only two relevant papers that were included. This low number indicates the thoroughness of the search terms used. The number of papers reviewed totalled 64 primary studies, based on 68 articles.

5. Systematic Review Results

This section summarises the results obtained after conducting the review and synthesis. First, an overview of the primary studies and their corresponding quality marks is presented. Next, the answers for three of research questions are addressed in separate subsections (RQ1, RQ2, and RQ4). Because research question RQ3 (see Table 3) is considered the most important, it is addressed in a separate section. Finally, a discussion and interpretation of the results is presented.

TABLE 6: Selected primary studies. The studies with a * were excluded based on the quality assessment results.

Study no.	Study	Study no.	Study
PS1	Roberts and Moran [9]	PS35	Dunlop and Montgomery Masters [10]
PS2	Kankaanpaa [11]*	PS36	Kulik, Kunert, Lux, and Fröhlich [12]*
PS3	Olson and Nilsen [13]	PS37	Sad and Poirier [14]
PS4	Edwards [15]	PS38	H. Li et al. [16]
PS5	Olson and Olson [17]	PS39	Liu and Räihä [18]
PS6	Lane, Napier, Batsell, and Naman [19]	PS40	Overill, Silomon, and Chow [20]*
PS7	Quintana, Kamel, and McGeachy [21]	PS41	Schrepp [22]
PS8	Haunold and Kuhn [23]	PS42	Pettitt and Burnett [24]
PS9	Haunold and Kuhn [25]	PS43	Schneegaß, Pfleging, Kern, and Schmidt [26]
PS10	Koester and Levine [27]	PS44	Gokarn, Lobo, Gore, Doke, and Kimbahune [28]
PS11	Lee [29]	PS45	F. C. Y. Li, Guy, Yatani, and Truong [30]
PS12	Glenstrup, Engell-Nielsen, and Hansen [31]*	PS46	Holleis, Scherr, and Broll [32]
PS13	Manes [33]	PS47	Chatterjee, Sinha, Pal, and Basu [34]
PS14	Manes [35]	PS48	Webster [36]*
PS15	Green [37]	PS49	Spalteholz [38]
PS16	Dunlop and Crossan [39]	PS50	Jung and Jang [40]*
PS17	Bälter [41]	PS51	Rendon, Estrada-Solano, and Granville [42]*
PS18	Nowakowski [43]	PS52	Kang, Lin, Green, Pettinato, and Best [44]
PS19	Kieras [45]*	PS53	Rice and Lartigue [46]
PS20	Maragoudakis and Tselios [47]	PS54	Thompson III [48]*
PS21	Mori, Matsunobe, and Yamaoka [49]	PS55	El Batran and Dunlop [50]
PS22	Andrew Sears and Zha [51]	PS56	Lee, Song, Ryu, Kim, and Kwon [52]
PS23	John, Salvucci, Centgraf, and Prevas [53]*	PS57	Erazo, Pino, and Antunes [54]
PS24	Myung [55]	PS58	Palilonis [56]*
PS25	Jassar [57]*	PS59	Erazo and Pino [58]
PS26	How and Kan [59]	PS60	Jones, Wray, Zaientz, Bachelor, and Newton [60]*
PS27	Jokela, Koivumaa, Pirkola, Salminen, and Kantola [61]	PS61	Green, Kang, and Lin [62]
PS28	Tonn-Eichstädt [63]	PS62	Elwart, Green, and Lin [64]
PS29	Hinckley et al. [65]	PS63	Burns and Ritter [66]
PS30	Holleis, Otto, Hussmann, and Schmidt [67]	PS64	Boring and Rasmussen [68]
PS31	Pettitt, Burnett, and Stevens [69]	PS65	Ginn [70]
PS32	Esteves, Komischke, Zapf, and Weiss [71]	PS66	Nasirinejad [72]
PS33	Hashizume, Kurosu, and Kaneko [73]*	PS67	Christensen, Pedersen, Bjerre, Pedersen, and Stuerzlinger [74]
PS34	Cox, Cairns, Walton, and Lee [75]	PS68	Erazo Moreta [76]

5.1. Descriptive Statistics. Table 6 shows the unique identifier assigned to each study and lists the associated reference. These identifiers will be used throughout the remainder of this review to refer to the primary studies.

5.1.1. Quality Assessment. Each quality assessment question was assigned a score of 1 (yes), 0.5 (partly), or 0 (no). The maximum score is 10 and the minimum score is zero. The quality scores were divided into categories:

(i) Very High: $8 \leq$ quality score ≤ 10

(ii) High: $5.5 \leq$ quality score ≤ 7.5

(iii) Medium: $3 \leq$ quality score ≤ 5

(iv) Low: $0 \leq$ quality score ≤ 2.5

Figure 2 demonstrates the quality-wise distribution of the primary studies. Of the 68 studies, 15 (22.06%) were

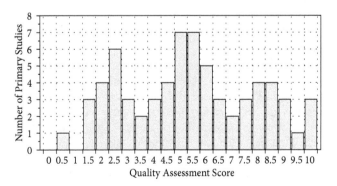

FIGURE 2: Quality-wise distribution of studies.

assessed as Very High, 20 (29.41%) were assessed as High, 19 (27.94%) were assessed as Medium, and 14 (20.59%) were

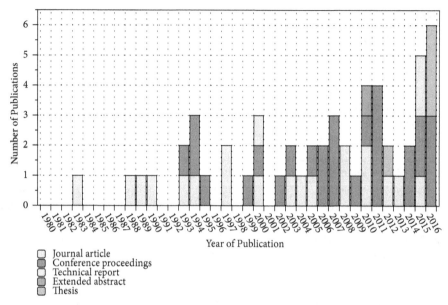

FIGURE 3: Year-wise distribution of studies and their publication type.

TABLE 7: Summary of top publications for KLM extensions.

Publication	Type	Number	Percentage
ACM Human Factors in Computing Systems	Conference	7	12.96%
University of Michigan Transportation Research Institute	Research centre	5	9.26%
HCI International	Conference	4	7.41%
HumanComputer Interaction	Journal	4	7.41%
Personal and Ubiquitous Computing	Journal	4	7.41%
IFIP Conference on Human-Computer Interaction	Conference	3	5.56%

assessed as Low. The primary studies PS3, PS14, and PS56 ranked at the top had quality scores of 10. Studies PS3 and PS56 were published in the journal of Human-Computer Interaction and Human Movement Science, respectively, and PS14 is a technical report from the University of Michigan Transportation Research Institute (UMTRI). The lowest score was 0.5 for PS48. The primary studies with low quality scores were excluded from analysis (PS2, PS12, PS19, PS23, PS25, PS33, PS36, PS40, PS48, PS50, PS51, PS54, PS58, and PS60), resulted in 54 primary studies with Medium, High, or Very High quality scores.

5.1.2. Publication Year. Figure 3 illustrates the distribution of published studies from July 1980 to December 2016. In the first decade after July 1980, only three (5.56%) journal papers were published in Communications of the ACM (PS1), Journal of Human–Computer Interaction (PS3), and the International Journal of Man-Machine Studies (PS4). The publication rate increased in the following decade (1990s), with 10 publications (18.52%, PS5-11, and PS13-15). This increase continued from 2000 to 2010, with 17 (31.48%) published studies (PS16-18, PS20-22, PS24, PS26-32, PS34-35, and PS37). A significant rise followed through the end of 2016 with 24 (44.44%) published studies (PS38-39, PS41-47, PS49, PS52-53, PS55-57, PS59, and PS61-68). This post-2010

spike in publications coincides with the resurgence of touch interactions and post-GUI configurations, which signalled a need for updated performance assessors.

5.1.3. Publication Sources. Table 7 summarises the details of the top publications for KLM extensions. Seven primary studies (12.96%) were published in ACM Human Factors in Computing Systems (CHI), this includes PS9, PS17, PS29-31, and PS38-39. Fewer than 10% of the primary studies were technical reports (PS13-14, PS18, PS52, and PS62) published through University of Michigan Transportation Research Institute (UMTRI). Just under 15% of the publications were journal articles: Human-Computer Interaction and Personal Ubiquitous Computing; the former had four primary studies published (PS3, PS5-6, and PS22) and the latter also had four (PS16, PS27, and PS34-35). HCI International published four studies for 7.41% (PS29, PS32, PS37, and PS67). Three studies (5.56%) were sourced from the IFIP Conference on Human-Computer Interaction (PS11, PS46, and PS59).

Figure 4 illustrates seven of the eight digital sources used to search for primary studies and the number of publications retrieved. Overlaps existed between the various sources, and the studies were considered based on the search order. The results from Web of Science were encountered in other sources and are not shown. The majority (40.74%) of the

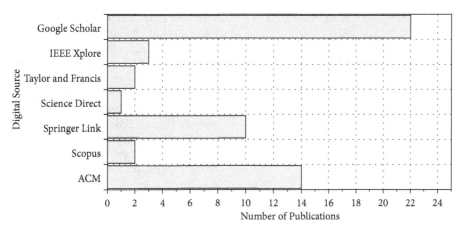

FIGURE 4: Distribution of primary studies across the seven digital sources utilised in this systematic review. The eighth digital source (Web of Science) is not shown due to overlapped content with earlier sources.

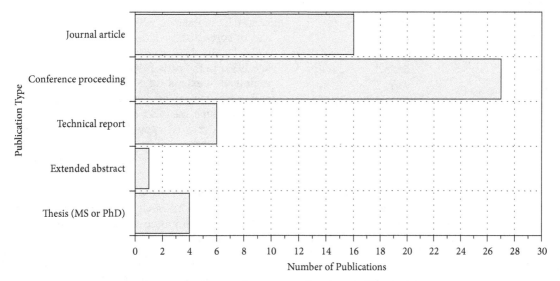

FIGURE 5: Distribution of primary studies across publication types.

studies were retrieved from Google Scholar. Fourteen studies (25.93%) were found in the ACM digital library. Springer Link produced 10 studies (18.52%), followed by IEEE Xplore with 3 studies (5.56%), Scopus and Taylor & Francis On-line with 2 studies (3.70%) each, and finally, a single publication from Science Direct (1.85%).

5.1.4. Publication Type. Publications were categorised as journal articles, conference proceedings, technical reports, extended abstracts, or theses. Figure 5 illustrates the distribution of primary studies across the five publication types. Statistics show that 50% (27 studies) of the studies were conference proceedings and 29.63% (16 studies) were in journals. The remainder of the studies were technical reports (6, 11.11%), theses (4, 7.41%), and one extended abstract (1.85%).

5.2. RQ1: What Was the Purpose of Extending the KLM? The motivation behind this research question was to identify why the KLM or one of its extensions was revised. This question encompasses several areas of interests: main purpose, hardware technology (i.e., device setup), application domain, and intended users.

5.2.1. Main Purpose for Creating Extensions. Several purposes for creating extensions were identified in the review. These were collated into six main reasons:

(P1) To fulfill a need for an updated quality assessment for new technologies, applications, techniques, or representations.

(P2) To test the applicability of the KLM or its extensions.

(P3) To extend the KLM to evaluate new technologies, applications, techniques, or representations.

(P4) To revise the original or extended operators and heuristics.

(P5) To extend the KLM or its extensions to describe additional interactions.

(P6) To integrate KLM or its extensions with other models.

TABLE 8: Summary of the identified purposes of the selected primary studies and median quality scores.

Purpose ID	Number	Percentage	Median Quality Score
(P1)	20	37.04%	6.00
(P2)	4	7.41%	7.75
(P3)	16	18.52%	4.24
(P4)	12	18.52%	6.00
(P5)	7	9.26%	7.50
(P6)	8	7.41%	5.25

TABLE 9: Summary of the distribution of primary studies' device setups.

Device Setup	Number	Percentage
Traditional	13	24.07%
Mobile or tablet	20	37.04%
Key-based	12	22.22%
Touch-based	8	14.81%
In-vehicle Information System	10	18.52%
Traditional	6	11.11%
Touch-based	4	7.41%
Specialised	7	12.96%
Post-GUI	4	7.41%
Television	1	1.85%

Studies with (P1) as a purpose were conducted to extend the model, and in some instances validation studies were also conducted to confirm the viability of the model. For (P2), research methods were often utilised to extend and validate the extended model. In (P3), the studies typically extended the KLM or one of its enhancements and used experiments to determine the performance of a certain device or application. The fourth purpose, (P4), revised operators and heuristics using research methods; however, validation was infrequent. (P5) extended the model to describe new interactions, and utilised research methods to extend and validate the enhancement. The final purpose, (P6), utilised short studies to extend the KLM or one of its extensions to better incorporate it with a larger model.

Table 8 summarises the results of analysing the number of publications for each purpose. The table shows that publications with purposes (P2) and (P5) had the highest median quality scores (7.75 and 7.50, respectively). This is because these studies usually carried out experiments to extend and validate KLM. Publications that extended the KLM for purpose (P3) obtained medium quality scores (median of 4.24), since validation was often not considered.

5.2.2. Device Setup. Table 9 summarises the device setups collated from the review of 54 primary studies. The majority of extensions (20, 37.04%) modified the KLM or one of its extensions to model mobile or tablet interactions. These extensions were further categorised as key-based (12, 22.22%) or touch-based (8, 14.81%) mobile devices, smartphones, or tablets. Fourteen studies (25.93%) extended the KLM for traditional configurations. The KLM was also extended for In-vehicle Information Systems (IVIS), which were categorised as either traditional (with knobs and dials, 11.11%) or touch-based (7.41.26%). Specialised configurations add features such as a digitized pad (PS8-9), Braille display (PS28), mouth-stick (PS10 and PS49), Leap Motion sensor (PS28), and specialised controls (PS64). Post-GUI configurations addressed extensions for natural user Interfaces (PS50, PS54, and PS68) and immersive projection (PS66). The KLM was also extended for web navigation on a television and for remote setup (PS47). Note that the percentages do not add up to 100% because one study (PS47) combined two setups.

5.2.3. Application Domain and Target Users. Several application domains were identified from the primary studies and grouped into high-level categories. Table 10 summarizes the recurrent domains. The most frequently examined domain relates to mobile or tablet applications (13 studies). Text and/or spreadsheet editing was the domain used to validate KLM [2, 6]; these studies were mainly conducted in the late 1980s to the early 1990s. Accessible interfaces were also examined to extend the KLM for interaction by blind users and users with motor disabilities. Navigating the web from various setups was also considered in the literature. IVIS setups were relatively popular (see Table 9) as a domain and considered tasks such as radio tuning, navigating lists, and using a global positioning system (GPS) for map navigation.

5.3. RQ2: What Was the Research Method Used to Extend the KLM? This research question examines the research methods used to modify the KLM or any of its extensions. The question is addressed in two ways:

(1) What was the research method used to extend the KLM operators and heuristics?

(2) What was the research method used to modify or compute the KLM operators' unit times?

Figure 6 demonstrates various research methods used to extend the KLM; these include experimentation, previous literature, observations, and several combinations of these methods. Twenty-seven (50%) of the studies did not use research methods to extend operators and modify heuristics. Observations were commonly conducted to identify or examine interactions (9 studies, 16.67%). Operators and heuristics were also extracted from previous literature (7 studies, 12.96%), and some studies used experiments (6 studies, 11.11%). Research methods were also combined. Several combinations were noted, including literature and experimentation, literature and observational studies, and observation and experimentation.

Figure 6 also illustrates the research methods used to modify the unit times of KLM operators. Of the 54 studies, only 12 (22.22%) did not utilise research methods. Over 50% of the primary studies (30 studies, 55.56%) conducted experiments to modify unit times. Eight studies (14.81%) relied on previous literature to adjust unit times. Additionally, research methods were also combined to extend unit times.

TABLE 10: Summary of recurrent domains from the primary studies.

Domain	Number	Studies
Accessibility	5	PS4, PS10, PS28, PS41, PS65
Games	1	PS56
Geographic Information Systems	2	PS8, PS9
In-vehicle Information Systems	10	PS13-15, PS18, PS31, PS42, PS43, PS52, PS6s, PS62
Medical	1	PS32
Mobile	13	PS16, PS20-22, PS24, PS26, PS30, PS35, PS35, PS37, PS39, PS45, PS46
Text and/or Spreadsheet Editing	4	PS1, PS3, PS4, PS6
Web navigation	4	PS11, PS17, PS47, PS49

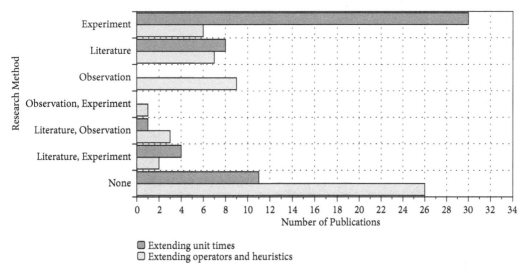

FIGURE 6: Research methods utilised to extend the KLM operators, heuristics, and unit times (RQ3).

These combinations include combining a literature search with either experimentation (4 studies, 7.41%) or observation (1 study, 1.85%).

5.4. RQ3: How Was the Original KLM Extended? The reviewed extensions demonstrated numerous ways in which KLM was revised:

(i) Adapting the original KLM operators: *K*, *P*, *H*, *D*, *M*, and *R*.

(ii) Inheriting operators from other KLM extensions or previous literature.

(iii) Introducing new operators.

(iv) Formulating new equations to calculate execution time.

(v) Updating *M* heuristics.

(vi) Computing domain-specific metrics.

It was also of interest to consider the operators that have been explicitly preserved in the extensions. The rest of this section discusses the operators, equations, heuristics, and metrics based on their intended device setup (see Section 5.2.2). Figure 7 collates the operators reported in the primary studies to identify their frequencies among the selected studies and device setups.

5.4.1. Traditional Setup. Thirteen studies were categorised as having a traditional setup: PS1, PS3-7, PS11, PS17, PS32, PS37, PS41, PS63, PS65. Figure 8 shows how the primary studies extended the KLM. The following sub-sections elaborate further on these operators, equations, and heuristics.

(1) Preserved Original Operators. K was the most popularly preserved of the original operators. PS6, PS32, PS11, PS65, PS41, and PS17 used the unit times associated with various typing skills. The majority of these used the time related to the speed of an average skilled typist (0.2 seconds), while others utilised the value 0.28 seconds (average non-skilled typist). *H* was preserved by PS1, PS11, PS32, and PS65, while *M* was used in three studies: PS1, PS17, and PS41. Four studies (PS1, PS32, PS41, and PS68) preserved the value of *P*. PS17 aimed to increase the accuracy of the *P* operator by utilising Fitts' Law. Operator *R* is system dependent and was often not utilised in the studies, yet it was still conserved.

(2) Adapted Original Operators. Some of the KLM operators were adapted through unit time adjustments or decomposition into finer tasks. PS7 updated the unit times of *H*, *K*, *M*, and *P*. PS63 dissected *H* into two actions: homing from the keyboard to the mouse and homing from the mouse to the keyboard. *P*'s unit time was updated in PS4, PS5, and PS7. A specialized *P*, PM(l), was introduced in PS11 to indicate

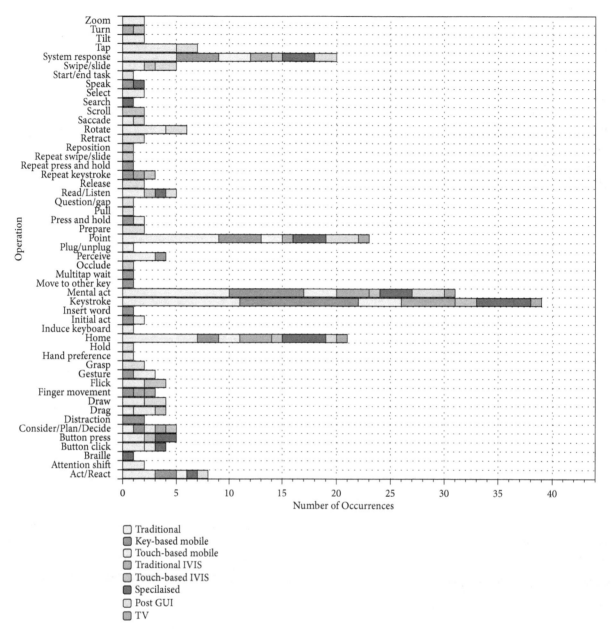

FIGURE 7: A bar chart of the collated operators and the frequency of adoption by the primary studies reviewed. The groups reflect the device setups previously discussed in Section 5.2.2: traditional, key-based mobile, touch-based mobile or tablet, traditional IVIS, touch-based IVIS, specialised, post-GUI, and TV.

pointing to the ith menu item. K and M were the two most frequently updated operators. K was updated in PS1, PS3, PS5, PS7, and PS63, while M was revised in PS3, PS5, PS6, PS7, and PS32. In PS5, M was decomposed into three mental actions: retrieval from memory, choosing among options, and executing a mental step. K was decomposed in PS3, where the unit times were 0.36 and 0.23 for two different spreadsheet tasks, respectively.

(3) Inherited Operators. PS11 inherited ten operators from previous extensions and prior literature: pressing a button B [45]; executing a mental step [17]; retrieving from memory, dragging to a menu item, and pointing to a menu item [77];

perceiving an image, reaction time of choosing an image, and eye movement [2]; menu search slope, intercept, and an overall value from an investigation into history tools for user support [52]; pressing a button and performing a button click [45].

(4) New Operators. New operators were introduced in 8 of the 13 traditional setup studies. PS1 identified several operators, including acquiring a task by looking at a certain manuscript A and using the arrow keys to point to a location Ps. PS7 introduced RW as the time required to read a word from the screen. PS4 identified several new operators: choosing a target, planning a route, moving to the next window, and

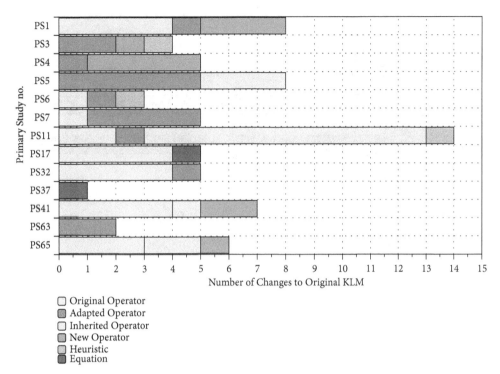

FIGURE 8: The number of original operators preserved, adapted, inherited from other extensions or prior literature, and newly introduced in the traditional setups category.

clicking the mouse. The symbol *S* was introduced in three studies (PS3, PS41, and PS51) to represent two different operations: mentally scanning/searching the display and pressing a keyboard shortcut. The time it takes to listen to a spoken word was utilised in PS64. PS41 also established a new operator for the time it takes to press a navigation key when navigating websites.

(5) Updated Heuristics. Heuristics are commonly updated when new operators are introduced to revise *M* placement. PS3 argues that commands issued through a series of menu choices involve a single *M* rather than one for each menu choice, because the command forms a single cognitive unit. Using a history tool, PS6 stated that switching from typing to using the history tool includes an additional long-term memory retrieval. For another history tool studied in PS11, *M* placement was extended for formula tasks. The study also offered guidance for placing the new mental scanning *S* operator.

(6) New Equations. In the KLM, task time is computed from the summation of the operators' unit times (see (2)). Some studies modified these equations to consider additional elements that may affect execution time. Both PS17 and PS37 introduced new equations in their extensions. PS17's authors formulated equations of various tasks that impact email archiving and retrieving. For word selection tasks, PS37 introduced equations to compute the time it takes to select a word given several variables, including scanning and scrolling time, word length, and the index of the selected word.

5.4.2. Key-Based Mobile. It was in the new millennium that interest in extending the KLM for mobile interaction and text entry became most evident. Twelve of the 54 selected studies modified the KLM to accommodate key-based mobile interactions (PS16, PS20, PS21, PS24, PS26, PS27, PS30, PS34, PS35, PS39, PS44, and PS46). Figure 9 illustrates these studies and the approaches they proposed to extend the KLM. The following subsections describe the changes made to extend the KLM.

(1) Preserved Original Operators. Several operators were preserved from the KLM: *H, K, M,* and *P*. PS16 utilised the original *H, K,* and *M* for predictive text entry on mobile phones. The KLM was further extended by the same authors in PS30 for five predictive text entry methods that preserved the original *M* and *R. R* was also used as is by PS21 and PS46. An extended KLM for modelling speech navigation and text entry preserved *K*.

(2) Adapted Original Operators. PS26 extended the KLM for SMS input by dissecting *K* into nine operators for various keys and repetitions. *K* was also decomposed in PS39 to reflect unique interactions with a Pinyin keyboard, an input method for Chinese text using the Pinyin method of romanisation. *K*'s unit time was revised in PS21, PS27, PS30, PS35, and PS44, the majority of which dissected the unit times based on the type of key and repetition. It should be noted that PS27 approached the KLM differently, assigning each key or repetition a score rather than a unit time. *P* has also been adapted and at times redefined. For instance, PS30 and PS46 modified *P* to reflect pointing with a device

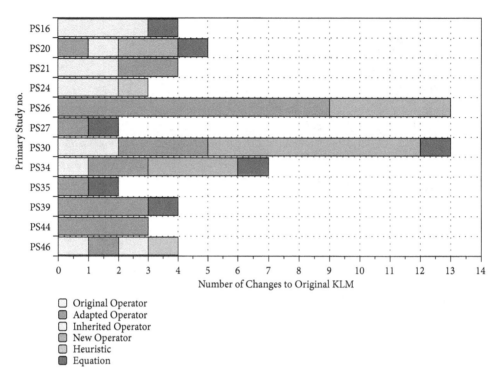

FIGURE 9: The numbers of original operators preserved, adapted, inherited from other extensions or prior literature, and newly introduced in the key-based mobile category.

to perform an action. PS44 considered P for pointing to a keypad. While PS21 preserved P's original meaning, M was adapted in both PS21 and PS44 and decomposed in PS34 to represent time delays during text entry and recognition. TPER from PS20 is also an adaptation of M for text entry perception. H was revised for PS30 to consider the time needed to switch between listening/speaking on the phone and reading from the screen.

(3) Inherited Operators. Only four operators from three studies were inherited from the literature or another extension. Two of these replaced the value of K, the third updated the unit time for M, and the last re-used a value from a previous model for complex actions. PS24 enhanced the KLM to evaluate Korean text entry on a mobile phone where the values for K and M were inherited from Kim, Kim, and Myung [78] and John and Newell [79]. K's unit time was also inherited from Silfverberg, MacKenzie, and Korhonen [80] to extend the KLM for message-text entry with a Greek corpus. Mobile KLM (PS30) was revised in PS46, which inherited the complex action operator to reflect tag-reading interactions.

(4) New Operators. Several new actions were recognised by half of the studies that extended the KLM for key-based mobile phones. PS20 introduced two new operators: waiting for the cursor to process when successive letters are entered from the same key in multi-tap text entry and the action of moving to another key. Similarly, PS26 utilised a wait operator for multitap entry. It also introduced MPHAlphaK (press and hold key), RPHAlphaK (repeat press and hold key), and InsertWord (insert word into corpus dictionary). Mobile

KLM (PS30) extended the KLM with several operators: attention shift for various focus shifts, complex actions, gesturing with phone, finger movement, initial act, and a multiplicative factor for distraction. PS34 extended the KLM for speech text entry and introduced an action that reflected the time needed to consider/recognise a command and utter a syllable.

(5) Updated Heuristics. A number of studies updated the placement of M and other perceptive actions to reflect interactions with a mobile phone. For Korean text entry (PS24), an M is expected to occur both before and after entering a syllable. Moreover, an M should not be placed before the next key since finger movement and the mental activity overlap. PS46 declared that M should appear before cognitive chunks and that an M is unnecessary before pointing at longer distances with respect to shorter ones.

(6) New Equations. When extending the KLM for text entry, new equations were commonly formulated based on the text entry techniques. Of the 12 studies, six modelled text entry on mobile phones (PS16, PS20, PS24, PS34, PS35, and PS39). PS16 introduced three new equations for traditional (multitap), predictive, and word-completion text entry with an English corpus. In PS35, the equation for predictive text entry from PS16 was reused for various word look-up techniques. For Greek text entry, PS20 formulated two equations to compare typical phone text entries against a newly developed approach. PS39 established an equation to compare the performances of two types of Chinese Pinyin input by integrating the KLM with other models. PS34 evaluated

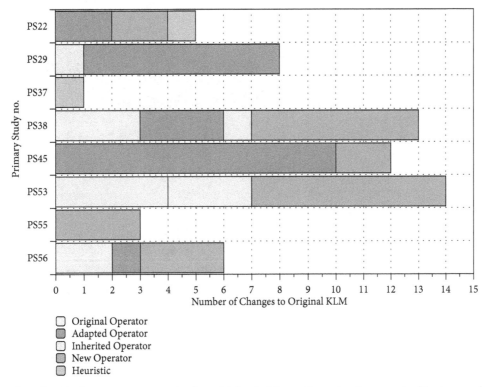

FIGURE 10: The number of original operators preserved, adapted, inherited from other extensions or prior literature, and newly introduced in the touch-based mobile or tablet category.

speech text entry compared with multitap and predictive text entry, in which several equations were constructed to consider time-out delays, number of words, and word options in predictive entry.

Two other studies formed equations in contexts other than text entry. The mobile KLM in PS30 proposed a new equation that took distractions of various severities into account. PS27 approached the KLM differently, presenting unit times as scores used to calculate the relative average efficacy, where the sum of the scores for each task is first divided by the number of tasks and finally multiplied by 100 to obtain a percentage.

5.4.3. Touch-Based Mobile or Tablet. Touchscreen interactions were considered in several KLM extensions as early as 2003. Eight studies from the selected 54 were identified (PS22, PS29, PS37, PS38, PS45, PS53, PS55, and PS56). Figure 10 illustrates how the new models were modified for extension. The following sub-sections describe the various updates applied to the KLM to represent touch-based mobile or tablet interactions.

(1) Preserved Original Operators. PS29 extended the KLM to measure the performance of a new interaction technique on a touch tablet under various conditions and with various styles. The model preserved R, as did PS53 and PS56. PS53 revised the KLM to accommodate a modern touchscreen interface, but preserved H, K, and M. The original operators D, H, and K were utilised by PS38 as an extended KLM for touch phone

mobile interactions. The primary studies PS53 and PS56 both preserved M, and PS53 also utilised the H and K operators.

(2) Adapted Original Operators. One KLM extension, developed to model the performance of a new interaction technique, decomposed P, D, and R. P was subdivided as follows: point stylus at segment, point to command, and point to end the mark. Dc and Dm symbolise drawing a circle around a dot and drawing a mark, respectively. R was divided into switching modes and the time it takes the system to respond. K was adapted by PS22 to consider both key repetition and movement between keys. In testing a new keyboard design for Chinese text input, 1 Line (PS45), K was dissected into a key for each finger on both hands. Similarly, M was modified in PS38 to reflect mentally initiating a task, deciding or choosing, retrieving, finding, and verifying. The extended model also adapts H into two actions: homing either a stylus or a finger to some location. PS56 modified P to reflect a relatively long movement from one position to another on a touch mobile phone in network gaming.

(3) Inherited Operators. PS53 inherited two operators from mobile KLM (PS30): initial act and distraction. Gesture actions were inherited but adapted to reflect the time needed to physically form specialised gestures with one or more fingers. The same operator was also used by PS38 to represent holding a gesture for a certain application.

(4) New Operators. Numerous operators have been created to represent touch interaction. PS53 extended the KLM

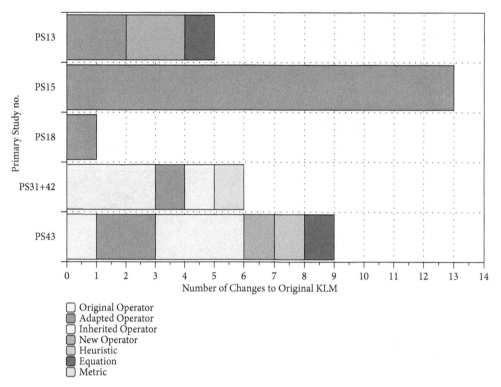

FIGURE 11: The number of original operators preserved, adapted, inherited from other extension or literature, and newly introduced in the traditional IVIS setup category.

to form a touch-level model (TLM) for touchscreen and mobile devices and introduced several new operators: tap, pinch/zoom to zoom in/out, swipe, rotate, drag element, and tilt device. Tapping is a common interaction in touch interfaces that was also introduced in PS38, PS55, and PS56. Swipe, zoom, and drag actions were also identified in PS55 and PS56. PS22 utilised two new operators that consider the decision and recovery times for data entry using a soft keyboard. Flick was established in PS56 to identify quick, short dragging actions. This action was decomposed in PS45 to distinguish between flick down and flick up. New operators introduced for finger/stylus touch mobile devices extended the model to include flipping or sliding a keyboard, continuously holding a key down, pressing a key on the side of the device, and plugging and unplugging other devices.

(5) New Equations. A quarter of the studies formulated new equations to compute the execution times of various tasks. PS22 formed a new equation for text entry on a soft keyboard that considers the number of characters, shifted characters, and a transition between keys. PS37 introduced a new equation that computes the time it takes to select a word from a list given several factors: scanning and scrolling time, word length, and the index of the selected word in the list.

5.4.4. Traditional In-Vehicle Information Systems. Traditional In-Vehicle Information Systems (IVIS) typically consist of a screen surrounded by a series of keys, buttons, and knobs indented to perform tasks such as: turning the radio on,

road navigation, navigating music lists, etc. Of the 54 primary studies, six were categorised as traditional IVIS (PS13, PS15, PS18, PS31, PS42, and PS43). Figure 11 shows how the operators were extended in the new models. The following subsections elaborate further on these operators, heuristics, equations, and metrics.

(1) Preserved Original Operators. Four of the five original KLM operators were preserved in the IVIS extensions. PS31 and PS42 document different stages of the same research that enhanced the original KLM for traditional IVIS systems; both studies preserved K, M, and P. One other study, PS43, provides a model for rapid user interface prototyping in the IVIS context and incorporates a modified KLM for that purpose. Of the original operators, only R was utilised from the KLM.

(2) Adapted Original Operators. H was modified from its original values in PS31 and PS42 to reflect new homing interactions between the IVIS and the steering wheel. Similarly, PS15 decomposed H into two operators, Rn and Rf, for reach-near (from the steering wheel to other parts of the wheel) and reach-far (from steering wheel to IVIS). It also presented age-adjusted unit times for older drivers. The study also dissected K and R into refined operators and replaced the original value of M with 1.50 seconds and an age-adjusted value of 2.70 seconds. M was also modified by PS43 with two new values based on its placement after R and their new turn operator. PS13 adapted K for an enter keystroke along with a down keystroke. K was also modified by PS43

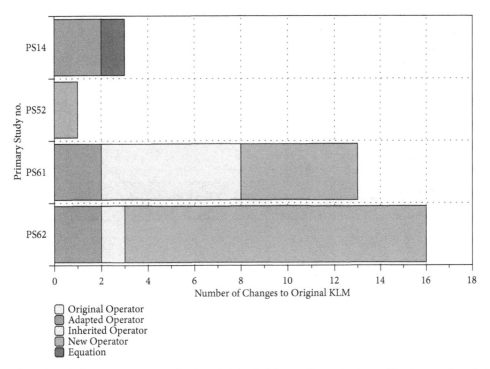

FIGURE 12: The number of original operators preserved, adapted, inherited from other extension or literature, and newly introduced in the touch-based IVIS category.

and PS18 by decomposing the original operator into specified actions.

(3) Inherited Operators. PS43 incorporated their extended the KLM with a prototyping model in which three operators were inherited from other extensions: H [69], F (move finger between controls), and attention shift from PS30. PS15's reach-far operator was inherited by PS31 and PS42.

(4) New operators. Only two new operators were introduced in two studies, PS13 and PS43. A reading/decision operator was identified by PS13 to represent the time needed to read an IVIS menu and decide upon actions based on the menu's depth and breadth. A turn operator was introduced in PS43 for tuning a dial (clockwise or counter-clockwise) at various degrees.

(5) Updated Heuristics. The placement of M was revised to incorporate the turn operator introduced in PS43. The new heuristic dictates that M should be placed in two different scenarios with two different values: after R and both before and after the user turns a knob.

(6) New Equations. The equation to compute the time required to execute a unit task was revised in PS43. Their new equation considered age as a factor as well as visual and non-visual periods that are characteristic of driving and IVIS interactions. PS13 updated the original equation to consider the number of menus encountered and the number of downward scrolls required to read a list item.

(7) Domain-Specific Metrics. The occlusion technique is used to simulate common driving distractions that occur when using IVIS systems. In occlusion, users are asked to conduct tasks with an IVIS while wearing computer-controlled goggles that open and shut at regular intervals. This condition imitates the glancing behaviour of drivers who cycle between looking at the IVIS (vision) and driving (non-vision or occlusion) periods. Two metrics are computed by PS31 and PS42:

(i) Total shutter open time (TSOT): the number of visual periods during occlusion trials with an IVIS.

(ii) Resumability ratio (R): the degree to which an IVIS task can be performed without looking.

PS31 and PS42's approach to modelling a unit task involved developing the model traditionally using their extended KLM, and then reassessing the sequence of operators by considering the vision/no-vision intervals.

5.4.5. Touch-Based In-Vehicle Information Systems. Touch-based IVIS systems feature a touch screen for navigating the IVIS. Of the selected studies, four extended the KLM for touch-based IVIS (PS14, PS52, PS61, and PS62). Figure 12 illustrates the various changes made to extend the KLM. These extensions did not explicitly preserve any of the original operators; thus, the following subsections discuss the adapted and original operators, inherited actions, new operators, and new equations.

(1) Adapted Original Operators. PS14 extended the KLM to revise the unit times previously measured in the literature.

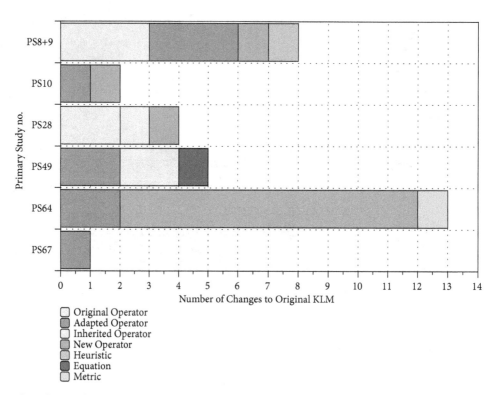

FIGURE 13: The number of original operators preserved, adapted, inherited from other extension or literature, and newly introduced in the specialised setup category.

They argue that the values misrepresented the evaluated IVIS *K* because the original values were based on a QWERTY keyboard. Therefore, in their study, *K* and *M* were revised. For *K*, several values were considered: letters, numbers, cursor keys, enter, shift, and space. The revision also considered key repetitions. *M* was adapted to 2.22 seconds in their extension method. *K* was divided in PS61 to represent function key actions and their repetition. PS61 also considered age-adjusted unit times for these operators. *R* was adapted by PS62 for wait-while-loading and wait-after-loading, each of which were age adjusted.

(2) Inherited Operators. PS15 was revised in PS61 to model interactions with a touch-based IVIS. PS61 inherited and revised the following actions: cursor key pressed once, cursor key after first press, letter key pressed once, letter key after first press, number key pressed once, and number key after first press. The unit times were also adjusted for age. A flicking operator was inherited by PS62 to represent the act of moving a finger in the flick direction (this operator was inherited and revised from PS52).

(3) New Operators. PS52 considered the new flick operator in the context of navigating lists of contacts or albums, each of which are age adjusted. Several new operators were introduced by PS61 to re-evaluate the traditional IVIS model, including scrolling through a list, pressing and holding a key, dragging, and first and subsequent slider actions. PS62 developed an extended KLM that overcome a noted shortcoming of the occlusion methods used by PS31 and

PS42. A variety of operators were introduced: flick/scroll return, pressing an on-screen button, quick flick, reach for button, reach for console, read instructions, reposition hand on knob, scroll, search, stop screen, turn knob, and wait for goggles in known and unknown locations to represent the time the user waits for a vision period.

(4) New Equations. PS14 determined the retrieval time of a destination from an IVIS, that involved keying in part of the destination name, scrolling through a list of names, or a combination of these approaches. Destination entry tasks were also considered that involved keying in a destination name or a longitude and a latitude. To aid in modelling the KLM extension, the study created a spreadsheet for both tasks in which predicted times were adjusted for age, lighting conditions, and destination. These spreadsheets were used to construct formulas used with equations to calculate the total predicted times for destination retrieval and entry tasks.

5.4.6. Specialised Setup. Specialised setups enhance a traditional device with domain-specific controls or involve more than one screen. Seven of the 54 primary studies were categorised as specialised setups (PS8, PS9, PS10, PS28, PS49, PS64, and PS67). Of these, PS8 and PS9 involve the same continuing study. These studies preserved/discarded/adapted original operators, inherited operators from the KLM or its extensions, introduced new operators or equations, updated the heuristics, and identified domain-specific metrics (see Figure 13). The remainder of this section describes the modifications applied to the KLM.

(1) Preserved Original Operators. Several operators were preserved from the KLM: *H*, *K*, *P*, and *M*. *H* was utilised by PS8, PS9, and PS28. PS28 also preserved the *K* value of an average non-skilled typist (0.28 seconds). In PS9, *M* was used as is; however, it was not considered in their earlier work (PS8). *P* was utilised from the original KLM in both PS8 and PS9.

(2) Adapted Original Operators. The majority of studies in this section adapted operators from the KLM. PS64 developed a GOMS-HRA to dynamically assess the reliability of human operators in nuclear plants. The study introduced two operators, Dp and Dw, that are analogues of *M* and represent the acts of making a decision based either on an existing procedure or without an existing procedure, respectively. *H* was adapted by PS67 to consider homing actions in hybrid interfaces—particularly for in-air devices such as the Leap Motion sensor. *K* was modified in PS8, PS9, PS10, and PS49. The first two of those studies also divided *R* to identify the time needed to select a new function from a command menu and the time it take the system to close a polygon in a manual map digitising task. PS49 adapted *P* for keyboard navigation by individuals with motor disabilities. An operator was identified by PS8 and PS9 that adapted *P* to quantify two specialised pointing actions.

(3) Inherited Operators. The button click-and-release *BB* operator was inherited by PS49 from PS19, a study that was excluded due its low score in the review's quality assessment phase. This was also the case for the *M* operator used in PS28 and PS49.

(4) New Operators. PS64 extended the KLM to assesses the reliability of nuclear plant operators and introduced several new operators: performing a physical action on the control board or in a field, looking up required information on the control board or in a field, obtaining required information on the control board or in a field, producing or receiving verbal or written instructions, and selecting or setting a value on the control boards for fields. A Braille operator was introduced by PS28 to evaluate blind users' interactions during web navigation. A new operator was identified by PS8 and PS9 to represent a button press on a specialised 16-button cursor used for map digitisation.

(5) Updated Heuristics. PS8 and PS9's KLM extensions for map digitisation updated the placement of the *M* operator to reflect their modifications to the original KLM operators. They suggested placing an *M* prior to digitising with a snap function before deciding on the next vertex to digitise as well as when deciding whether the digitising task should be ended. For a zooming task, they recommended being careful with the *M* operator because some users may require extra time.

(6) New Equations. PS47 provided a basis for an early comparison between keyboard navigation systems (including their newly devised KeySurf system)—particularly when used for tabbing and ID navigation—for people with motor disabilities. PS47 modelled the navigation system using updated

equations that reflected the unique navigation requirements for such systems.

(7) Domain Specific Metrics. Human error probability (HEP) was used in PS64 to quantify the KLM operators instead of unit time. Their model approached the KLM differently by arguing for what they declared to be a more important measure of the performance of nuclear plant operators.

5.4.7. Post-GUI. In this category, two studies (one of which involves three primary papers) modified the KLM for post-GUI systems. In particular, it extends the KLM for a natural user interface (NUI) (PS57, PS59, and PS68), and for an immersive interface with a projector and mobile navigation (PS66). The rest of this section describes the modified actions, updated heuristics, and new equations in the reviewed studies.

(1) Preserved Original Operators. *M* was preserved from the KLM by PS66 for modelling an immersive interface. The extended KLM for a NUI (PS59 and PS68) utilised the original *R*; however, during experimentation this value was ignored.

(2) Adapted Original Operators. *D*, while commonly discarded in other setup categories, was adapted by PS57 and modified to reflect drawing gestures in the air, as a user would in a NUI. *M* was adapted by PS59 and PS68, where its values were retrieved from earlier extensions [2, 45]. PS66 modified *P* depending on various user and mobile tracking devices.

(3) Inherited Operators. A number of operators were adapted in PS59 and PS68 from prior literature. Two *M* operators (Ms and Mp) were inherited from MacKenzie [81]. Both operators represent the mental act of preparing to execute subsequent physical actions in response to a stimulus or physical matching event. PS68 inherited *D* from their previous work in PS57. The value of *P* was inherited from Zeng, Hedge, and Guimbretiere [82] in PS59 and PS68 to denote the act of pointing to a target in a NUI.

(4) New Operators. Both main studies, as expected, introduced several operators to reflect the new interactions associated with their post-GUI interfaces. PS66's immersive interface required several new operators to represent tasks such as asking questions while using the interface and included start and end of task, question, gap between questions and mentally preparing a response, searching for an answer, reading, and physical movement operators. The NUI KLM also introduced several new operators, some of which were shared in two studies (PS59 and PS68), including holding a hand position, tapping by pushing or moving the hand towards the front, swiping and preparing to swipe, grasping, releasing an open hand, preparing to move the hand from a resting position to the position where a drawing stroke begins, and retracting the hand from the position where the stroke finishes. PS68 later introduced two new operators to reflect the act of pulling and a hand-preference factor.

TABLE 11: Summary of statistics used to evaluate the performance of predicted versus observed data.

Computation	Description	Number	Studies
Analysis of variance	The difference between two or more means	1	PS10
Contrast weight analysis	A specific comparison over scores or means.	1	PS34
Correlation analysis	The closeness of the relationship between two or more variables.	11	PS1, PS3, PS13, PS14, PS22, PS31, PS42, PS52, PS57, PS59, PS68
MAPE	Mean absolute percentage error.	1	PS11
Percentage difference	The difference between two values divided by the average of the two values. Shown as a percentage.	1	PS10
Percentage change	The change from one number to another expressed as a percentage increase or decrease.	5	PS8, PS9, PS30, PS46, PS65
Ratio	The ratio between observed and predicted values.	2	PS21, PS66
Regression analysis	The relationship between a dependent variable and one or more independent variables.	1	PS55
RMSPE	The percentage of the square root of the average of the square of all of the errors.	6	PS7, PS43, PS56, PS7, PS59, PS68
T-test	The comparison between the means of two populations to test the difference between the samples.	1	PS24

(5) New Equations. The extended model of PS59 and PS68 describes the execution of a NUI task using g-units. G-units are gesture units that identify the time between a hand movement and returning to rest. A single G-unit can contain several gesture phrases (g-phrases) as the hand moves into various position to achieve a stroke. The execution task of the model is the summation of the g-units, each of which is defined in several new equations. PS57 also introduced a new equation from the same study to represent the act of drawing gestures in the air.

(6) Updated Heuristics. PS68 updated the original heuristic rules for placing M. Rule 0 was updated from the original to consider preparation and P operators. Rule 2 was adapted to reflect that when a string of M's belong to a g-phrase, all subsequent Ms excluding the first one should be deleted. Their updated heuristics also suggest that when a P follows a preparation action, then M should be deleted (updated from Rule 4). Finally, t new rule was introduced (Rule 5) that stresses that when the model developed is unsure of placement, the number of operators should be emphasised over the placement of Ms.

5.4.8. Television. A single reviewed study (PS47) involved web navigation and text entry (both traditional and predictive) on a television set using a remote control. This study preserved three of the original KLM operators: K, H, and M and considered two different keyboard layouts for text entry. P was adapted to represent the different layouts. A finger movement and a dynamic mental operator were introduced into the extended KLM; the latter considers the additional cognitive load of using a word prediction system. To formulate these text entry tasks, two equations were introduced for the two text entry methods, traditional and predictive, respectively.

5.5. RQ4: What Was the Research Method Used to Validate a KLM Extension? The purpose of this research question is to identify the research methods used, if any, to validate the performance of an extended model. The original KLM publication conducted a user study to compare observed data and predicted the KLM's results [2, 6]. The model's performance was evaluated using root-mean-square percentage error (RMSPE), which was calculated as 21%. Of the primary studies, 51.85% (28 studies) conducted user experiments to validate their extended models.

Performance evaluations were commonly statistically analysed using several metrics (excluding PS41 and PS47). Table 11 summarises the statistics used to evaluate the performance of predicted data versus data observed from users. Correlation analyses were applied in 11 studies (39.29%), while RMSPE was adopted by 6 studies (21.43%). Other statistical measures utilised included contrast weights, mean absolute percentage error (MAPE), percentage difference, percentage change, ratio, regression analysis, and t-tests.

Some studies combined more than one statistical method to confirm their results.

Performance measured via correlation analysis ranged in value from 0.48 to 0.98 among the eleven primary studies. RMSPE values were generally within the suggested KLM bound of 21%, excluding one instance in PS7 where the RMSPE was 31%. The percentage change ranged from -15% to 11% in studies utilising this measure.

6. Discussion

This section summarises the principal findings of this systematic review of KLM extensions. It also addresses the limitations of this review that may threaten its validity. Finally, a discussion of the implications of this review for research and practice is presented.

6.1. Principal Findings. The goal of this systematic review was to examine the purposes for extending the KLM, the methods used to extend the model, how the KLM model was modified, and the techniques used to validate the extended models. The principal findings of this review are as follows:

(i) This review found diverse studies related to extending the KLM for various domains and device setups. However, the extent to which the KLM was rigorously extended varied based primarily on the purpose of the study.

(ii) Some studies exhaustively applied research methods for the prime purpose of extending the KLM to new domains or setups or to adapt the models to current situations and technologies. Other studies applied the original KLM to evaluate their applications or devices and included new operators to modify the KLM.

(iii) Many of the primary studies used controlled experiments to extend the unit times of the KLM or to create new operators.

(iv) The majority of the studies did not include any type of validation for their extended models. From the studies that did report model validation, controlled experiments were often reported. Performance measures varied; however, the majority utilised correlation analyses, and RMSE (the measure originally used to validate the KLM) was the next most common.

(v) Only a small number of papers compared the performances of their extended models against the original KLM to determine their effectiveness.

(vi) The majority of the primary studies were categorised as mobile or tablet, followed by traditional setups and IVIS systems.

(vii) Several software domains were modelled with extended KLMs; nevertheless, the majority were classified as mobile programmes.

(viii) *K* and *M* were two of the most commonly preserved and adapted operators, followed by *P*. *D* was almost entirely discarded by most extensions.

(ix) There is a shortage of studies that address the accessibility needs of disabled users, post-GUI, and Windows-Icons-Menus-Pointer (WIMP) interfaces.

(x) In the key-based mobile category, half the studies utilised the KLM to calculate text entry with various techniques such as multi-tap or predictive.

(xi) Two of the selected primary studies substituted the unit times with other measures. PS27 replaced them with scores for each operator and PS64 utilised a domain-specific measure, HEP.

6.2. Limitations. As with other systematic reviews, this review was limited by the search terms and digital databases used. The review was also impacted by selection bias, publication bias, improper or inaccurate data extraction, and data misclassifications. Efforts were taken to alleviate these limitations including the following:

(i) Setting a wider net with the search terms and digital databases. Database selection was influenced by the inclusivity of the databases, popularity, and recurrences of previous work related to predictive modelling.

(ii) Publication and selection bias was overcome to some extent by including technical reports and MSc/PhD theses, which comprised the selected primary studies.

(iii) Data extraction was repeatedly re-evaluated in weekly meetings by the reviewers to guarantee consensus and mitigate inaccurate data extraction and misclassifications.

6.3. Implications. The findings of this systematic review have implications for researchers who plan on refining current extensions or developing new extensions as well as for designers and developers who are considering using the KLM or one of its extensions to evaluate their computer systems.

For researchers, several gaps have been identified in the literatures that lend themselves to future revisions and investigations. Despite the spike in KLM extensions in the past two years (see Figure 3), much of the work done previously requires authentication and revisions for traditional setups and mobile phones. It is unlikely that the unit times measured in the early 2000s would still hold true with current processors and memories. Efforts should be made to re-evaluate useful models with the traditional setups utilised today as well as with mobile phones and tablets that are commonly used.

Tables 9 and 10 summarises the device setups and application domains of the 54 primary studies. While the summaries show a varied selection, several weak areas were identified. Device setups primarily focused on traditional setups, mobile, tablet, and IVIS systems. Despite efforts to develop post-GUI KLM extensions, a shortage still exists in studies that address new setups, including virtual and augmented reality, tangible user interfaces, physical interfaces, tabletops, large touch displays, and malleable interfaces. All of these setups have been in existence for at least a decade and are costly to develop; thus, they would certainly benefit from

TABLE 12: Summary of high-quality studies based on this review that can guide designers and developers to the most appropriate KLM extensions.

Study	Setup	Domain	Extension	Validation	Quality score
PS3	Traditional	Spreadsheet	Experiment	Experiment	10
PS8-9	Specialized	GIS	Observation, experiment	Experiment	8
PS10	Traditional	AAC	Experiment	Experiment	9
PS13	Traditional IVIS	IVIS	Experiment	Experiment	8.5
PS14	Touch-based IVIS	IVIS	Experiment	Experiment	10
PS24	Mobile	Text entry	Literature, experiment	Experiment	8.5
PS30	Key-based mobile	Mobile	Observation, experiment	Experiment	8.5
PS34	Key-based mobile	Voice text entry	Experiment	Experiment	9
PS43	Traditional IVIS	IVIS	Observation, experiment	Experiment	8
PS46	Key-based mobile	Mobile	Observation, experiment	Experiment	9.5
PS55	Touch-based mobile	Custom	Experiment	Experiment	8
PS56	Touch-based mobile	Games	Experiment	Experiment	10
PS68	NUI	Custom	Literature, observation, experiment	Experiment	8.5

predictive models to determine performance in early design phases. While a reasonable array of application domains were investigated, the distribution of studies across these domains was uneven. Concentrated efforts were directed toward mobile applications and IVIS systems, leaving considerable room for further research into domains such as medical IT setups.

Extensions to the KLM commonly occur as a result of experiments to extract new actions and unit times. Figure 6 illustrates the research methods utilised by the reviewed studies to extend the KLM operators, heuristics, and unit times. However, when extending operators and heuristics, the majority of studies did not conduct experiments. While this could be expected for setups similar to the one used to extend and validate the original KLM, it is not ideal for new domains or device setups. Operators determined from normative actions could be useful but may fall short of detecting actions (particularly those relating to mental acts M) that are best observed. It is essential for an appropriate research method to be adopted to develop operators to measure human behaviours. When extending operator unit times, the majority of studies conducted experiments to empirically assign values to their adapted or new operators. This approach is also advisable for future researchers because it ensures accurate and up-to-date measurements. It should also be noted that combinations of research methods strengthen the findings by taking full advantage of their combined benefits.

Of the 54 primary studies selected, only half conducted validation studies to confirm the efficacy of their proposed extended models (see Table 11). At times the same experimental results were used for both extending and validating the models, which clearly lends itself to bias. When a new extension is proposed, it is vital that experiments be conducted to provide empirical evidence of the extension's effectiveness. This calls for more controlled experiments to determine how well the proposed extensions perform. For extensions developed for traditional setups, a comparative assessment against the original KLM could be used to determine how well the new models perform against a stable usability model. Such a comparison might even be possible with setups that rely heavily on the original operators in the KLM.

TABLE 13: General information form.

Question	Answer
Reviewer name	
Primary study ID	
Primary study title	
Author name	
Year of publication	
Publication details	
Type of publication	○ Conference proceeding
	○ Journal article
	○ Technical report
	○ Thesis (MS or PhD)
	○ Extended abstract
	○ Other

A further finding was that the majority of reviewed extensions do not provide guidance or suggestions to help designers and developers apply the altered model to their product or computer system. Despite its simplicity, the application of the KLM or any of its extensions requires skill to ensure correct measurements of execution. Several tools (e.g., CogTool) have been developed to automate this process, but these are typically limited to traditional setups. Another observation from the review was that the expert level of users, in the case of most reviewed paper, was not disclosed; the users were merely declared as experts. However, what makes a user an expert? The answer to this question is highly subjective and depends on the perspective of the model developer. This in itself impacts the unit times collected for the operators and thus, the validity of the validation results. For researchers, we find that this issue could be mitigated by a clear definition of expertise that could be consistently applied across domains and device setups.

For designers/developers, we recommend the use of Table 12 to select an appropriate model given their products' domain and device setup. All the studies listed in the table

TABLE 14: Quality assessment form.

Quality Assessment	Mark		
	Yes	Partly	No
The primary study presents a clearly stated purpose for KLM extension	O	O	O
The primary study extends the KLM with new operators or modifications	O	O	O
The primary study clearly defines the research method used to extend the KLM	O	O	O
The extension study's methodology is adequate and repeatable	O	O	O
The extension study clearly states the results and findings	O	O	O
The primary study clearly defines the research method used to validate the extended KLM	O	O	O
The validation study's methodology is adequate and repeatable	O	O	O
The validation study clearly states the results and findings	O	O	O
The primary study presents a comparative analysis of the extended KLM against the original KLM	O	O	O
The paper has been cited by other authors and contributes to the literature	O	O	O
Quality score			

were ranked as Very High or High during the quality assessment phase and conducted experiments to extend and validate their models. It is also important to compare results from different extensions to determine the one best suited to the target users' actions and perceptions. It should be noted that, at times, the KLM or one of its extensions may be unable to address all the human behaviour anticipated in a product. In this case, combining two or more models is possible but not recommended without thorough investigation.

7. Conclusion and Future Work

KLM is popularly used in the literature to evaluate system design early in the development phase to determine probable performance times for skilled error-free tasks. Over the years, several extensions have been created that modify the original KLM to consider revisions of the original operators, varied device setups, and varied domains. This paper presented a systematic review that summarises the existing KLM extensions developed in the literature. From an initial 2,444 studies, 68 unique publications were selected for the review. Information was extracted from the selected studies, which allowed the reviewers to obtain conclusions to identify common techniques, find research gaps, and construct guidelines.

In future work, we intend to extend this systematic review and plan for future research in various ways:

(i) Perform a systematic review that addresses the research question "What publications have utilised the KLM or one of its extensions to evaluate the efficiency of their designs and how?" We intend to apply the information obtained from this review.

(ii) Develop a methodology with a formal protocol for extending the KLM that ensures an exhaustively assessed model.

(iii) Offer a guide for applying the KLM and its various extensions to guarantee correct application.

(iv) Review the term "expert" in an attempt to provide a unanimous definition for skilled user behaviour in the KLM and its extensions.

Appendix

A. Quality Assessment and Data Extraction Form

Tables 13, 14, and 15 demonstrate the respective forms used to extract general information, quality assessment, and data from the primary studies.

B. Practitioners Guide to KLM Extensions

Table 12 presents a summary of the high-ranking (based on this review's quality assessment) primary studies that utilised research methods to extend and validate their extensions in various domains and with various device setups. This list can help practitioners determine the best extension to use with their own products.

Authors' Contributions

Shiroq Al-Megren is an assistant Professor of Information Technology at King Saud University. She holds a Ph.D. in Computing Science from the University of Leeds and an MSc from Newcastle University. She has published numerous research papers on human-computer interaction and participated in several conference and workshops. Her areas of interest include accessibility, tangible user interfaces, touch interaction, and smart distributed systems. **Joharah Saeed Khabti** is a lecturer in the Information Technology Department with a specialisation in Security and Web Development at King Saud University. She is a Ph.D. student holding a Master's degree from George Washington University. Her research interests include image clustering, natural language

TABLE 15: Data extraction form.

RQ#	Research question	Answer
RQ1	What was the purpose of extending the KLM?	
RQ1	What was the intended device and setup?	
RQ1	What was the application domain?	
RQ1	Who were the intended users included in the experiment?	
RQ2	What research method was used to extend the KLM operators or modify heuristics?	○ Experiment ○ Literature ○ Observation ○ Other
RQ2	What research method was used to extend the KLM operators' unit times?	○ Experiment ○ Literature ○ Observation ○ Other
RQ2	What were the users' skill levels?	
RQ3	How was the original KLM extended?	○ KLM operators preserved ○ KLM operators discarded ○ Adapted operators ○ New operators ○ New equations ○ Updated heuristics ○ Application metrics
RQ4	What research method was used to validate the extended KLM?	○ Experiment ○ Literature ○ Observation ○ Other
RQ4	How was performance measured?	○ Correlation analysis ○ RMSPE ○ MAPE ○ Other
RQ4	What was the overall performance of the extended KLM?	
RQ4	Was the performance of the extended KLM better than that of the original?	○ Better ○ Worse ○ Unclear ○ Not measures ○ Other

processing, and human-computer interaction. **Hend S. Al-Khalifa** is a Professor at the Information Technology Department, King Saud University. She has contributed more than 120 research papers to symposiums, workshops, international conferences and journals. Moreover, Professor Hend has served as a program committee member at many national and international conferences and as a reviewer for several journals. Her areas of interest include semantic web technologies, computers for people with special needs, and Arabic NLP.

References

[1] I. S. MacKenzie, "Motor behaviour models for human-computer interaction," in *HCI Models, Theories, and Frameworks: Toward a Multidisciplinary Science*, J. M. Carroll, Ed., pp. 27–54, Morgan Kaufmann, San Francisco, CA, USA, 2003.

[2] S. K. Card, T. P. Moran, and A. Newell, *The Psychology of Human-Computer Interaction*, Lawrence Erlbaum Associates, Inc, Hillsdale, NJ, USA, 1983.

[3] B. E. John and D. E. Kieras, "The GOMS family of user interface analysis techniques: Comparison and contrast," *ACM Transactions on Computer-Human Interaction*, vol. 3, no. 4, pp. 320–351, 1996.

[4] B. E. John and D. E. Kieras, "Using GOMS for user interface design and evaluation: which technique?" *ACM Transactions on Computer-Human Interactions (TOCHI)*, vol. 3, no. 4, pp. 287–319.

[5] R. Malhotra, *Empirical Research in Software Engineering: Concepts, Analysis, and Applications*, Chapman and Hall/CRC, Boca Raton, FL, USA, 2015.

[6] S. K. Card, T. P. Moran, and A. Newell, "The Keystroke-Level Model for User Performance Time with Interactive Systems," *Communications of the ACM*, vol. 23, no. 7, pp. 396–410, 1980.

[7] P. M. Fitts, "The information capacity of the human motor system in controlling the amplitude of movement," *Journal of Experimental Psychology*, vol. 47, no. 6, pp. 381–391, 1954.

[8] B. Kitchenham and S. Charters, "Guidelines for performing systematic literature reviews in software engineering," Tech. Rep. EBSE-2007-01, Keele University and Durham University, 2007.

[9] T. L. Roberts and T. P. Moran, "The Evaluation of Text Editors: Methodology and Empirical Results," *Communications of the ACM*, vol. 26, no. 4, pp. 265–283, 1983.

[10] M. D. Dunlop and M. Montgomery Masters, "Investigating five key predictive text entry with combined distance and keystroke modelling," *Personal and Ubiquitous Computing*, vol. 12, no. 8, pp. 589–598, 2008.

[11] A. Kankaanpaa, "Fids A Flat-Panel Interactive Display System," *IEEE Computer Graphics and Applications*, vol. 8, no. 2, pp. 71–82, 1988.

[12] A. Kulik, A. Kunert, C. Lux, and B. Fröhlich, "The pie slider: Combining advantages of the real and the virtual space," in *Proceedings of the International Symposium on Smart Graphics*, pp. 93–104, 2009.

[13] J. R. Olson and E. Nilsen, "Analysis of the Cognition Involved in Spreadsheet Software Interaction," *Human—Computer Interaction*, vol. 3, no. 4, pp. 309–349, 1987.

[14] H. H. Sad and F. Poirier, "Modeling word selection in predictive text entry," in *International Conference on Human-Computer Interaction*, pp. 725–734, 2009.

[15] A. D. N. Edwards, "Modelling blind users' interactions with an auditory computer interface," *International Journal of Man-Machine Studies*, vol. 30, no. 5, pp. 575–589, 1989.

[16] H. Li, Y. Liu, J. Liu, X. Wang, Y. Li, and P.-L. P. Rau, "Extended KLM for mobile phone interaction: A user study result," in *Proceedings of the 28th Annual CHI Conference on Human Factors in Computing Systems, CHI 2010*, pp. 3517–3522, New York, NY, USA, April 2010.

[17] J. R. Olson and G. M. Olson, "The Growth of Cognitive Modeling in Human-Computer Interaction Since GOMS," *Human–Computer Interaction*, vol. 5, no. 2-3, pp. 221–265, 1990.

[18] Y. Liu and K. J. Räihä, "Predicting Chinese text entry speeds on mobile phones," in *Proceedings of the 28th Annual CHI Conference on Human Factors in Computing Systems, CHI 2010*, pp. 2183–2192, USA, April 2010.

[19] D. M. Lane, H. A. Napier, R. R. Batsell, and J. L. Naman, "Predicting the Skilled Use of Hierarchical Menus With the Keystroke-Level Model," *Human–Computer Interaction*, vol. 8, no. 2, pp. 185–192, 1993.

[20] R. E. Overill, J. A. M. Silomon, and K. P. Chow, "A complexity based model for quantifying forensic evidential probabilities," in *Proceedings of the 5th International Conference on Availability, Reliability, and Security, ARES 2010*, pp. 671–676, Poland, February 2010.

[21] Y. Quintana, M. Kamel, and R. McGeachy, "Formal methods for evaluating information retrieval in hypertext systems," in *Proceedings of the 11th Annual International Conference on SIGDOC '93*, pp. 259–272, October 1993.

[22] M. Schrepp, "GOMS analysis as a tool to investigate the usability of web units for disabled users," *Universal Access in the Information Society*, vol. 9, no. 1, pp. 77–86, 2010.

[23] P. Haunold and W. Kuhn, "A keystroke level analysis of manual map digitizing," in *Proceedings of the Conference on Spatial Information Theory*, pp. 406–420, 1993.

[24] M. Pettitt and G. Burnett, "Visual demand evaluation methods for in-vehicle interfaces," *International Journal of Mobile Human Computer Interaction*, vol. 2, no. 4, pp. 45–57, 2010.

[25] P. Haunold and W. Kuhn, "Keystroke level analysis of a graphics application: manual map digitizing," in *Proceedings of the CHI'94 Conference on Human Factors in Computing Systems*, pp. 337–343, April 1994.

[26] S. Schneegaß, B. Pfleging, D. Kern, and A. Schmidt, "Support for modeling interaction with automotive user interfaces," in *Proceedings of the 3rd International Conference on Automotive User Interfaces and Interactive Vehicular Applications, AutomotiveUI 2011*, pp. 71–78, December 2011.

[27] H. H. Koester and S. P. Levine, "Modeling the Speed of Text Entry with a Word Prediction Interface," *IEEE Transactions on Neural Systems and Rehabilitation Engineering*, vol. 2, no. 3, pp. 177–187, 1994.

[28] P. Gokarn, S. Lobo, K. Gore, P. Doke, and S. Kimbahune, "KLM operator values for rural mobile phone user," in *Proceedings of the 3rd International Conference on Human Computer Interaction*, pp. 93–96, Bangalore, India, April 2011.

[29] A. Lee, "Exploring user effort involved in using history tools through MHP / GOMS: Results and experiences," in *Human-Computer Interaction*, pp. 109–114, Chapman & Hall, 1995.

[30] F. C. Y. Li, R. T. Guy, K. Yatani, and K. N. Truong, "The 1Line keyboard: A QWERTY layout in a single line," in *Proceedings of the 24th Annual ACM Symposium on User Interface Software and Technology, UIST'11*, pp. 461–470, October 2011.

[31] A. Glenstrup, T. Engell-Nielsen, and J. P. Hansen, "Eye controlled media: Present and future state," Tech. Rep. DK-2100, University of Copenhagen, 1995.

[32] P. Holleis, M. Scherr, and G. Broll, "A revised mobile klm for interaction with multiple NFC-tags," in *Proceedings of the 13th IFIP TC 13 International Conference on Human-computer Interaction*, pp. 204–221, 2011.

[33] D. Manes, "Evaluation of a driver interface: Effects of control type (knob versus buttons) and menu structure (depth versus breadth)," Tech. Rep. UMTRI-97-42, The University of Michigan Transportation Research Institute, 1997.

[34] D. Chatterjee, A. Sinha, A. Pal, and A. Basu, "An Iterative Methodolgy to Improve TV Onscreen Keyboard Layout Design through Evaluation of User Studies," *Advances in Computing*, vol. 2, no. 5, pp. 81–91, 2012.

[35] D. Manes, "Prediction of destination entry and retrieval times using keystroke-level models," Tech. Rep. UMTRI-96-37, The University of Michigan Transportation Research Institute, 1997.

[36] B. M. Webster, *Implementing a Quantitative Analysis Design Tool for Future Generation Interfaces [Ph.D. thesis]*, Air-Force Institute of Technology, Wright-Patterson AFB, Dayton, OH, USA, 2012.

[37] P. Green, "Estimating Compliance with the 15-Second Rule for Driver-Interface Usability and Safety," *Proceedings of the Human Factors and Ergonomics Society Annual Meeting*, vol. 43, no. 18, pp. 987–991, 1999.

[38] L. Spalteholz, *KeySurf-A keyboard Web navigation system for persons with disabilities [PhD thesis]*, University of Victoria, Victoria, Canada, 2012.

[39] M. D. Dunlop and A. Crossan, "Predictive text entry methods for mobile phones," *Personal and Ubiquitous Computing*, vol. 4, no. 2-3, pp. 134–143, 2000.

[40] K. Jung and J. Jang, "A two-step click interaction for Mobile Internet on smartphone," *Communications in Computer and Information Science*, vol. 373, no. I, pp. 129–133, 2013.

[41] O. Bälter, "Keystroke level analysis of email message organization," in *Proceedings of the the SIGCHI conference*, pp. 105–112, The Hague, The Netherlands, April 2000.

[42] O. M. C. Rendon, F. Estrada-Solano, and L. Z. Granville, "A mashup ecosystem for network management situations," in *Proceedings of the 2013 IEEE Global Communications Conference, GLOBECOM 2013*, pp. 2249–2255, USA, December 2013.

[43] C. Nowakowski, "Navigation system destination entry: The effects of driver workload and input devices, and implications for SAE recommended practice," Tech. Rep. UMTRI-2000-20, The University of Michigan Transportation Research Institute, 2000.

[44] T.-P. Kang, B. T.-W. Lin, P. Green, S. Pettinato, and A. Best, "Usability of a prototype generation 4 Hyundai-Kia navigation-radio: Evidence from an occlusion experiment and SAE J2365 and Pettitt's method calculations," Tech. Rep. UMTRI-2013-11, The University of Michigan Transportation Research Institute, 2013.

[45] D. Kieras, *Using the keystroke-level model to estimate execution times*, Working paper, University of Michigan, 2001.

[46] A. D. Rice and J. W. Lartigue, "Touch-Level Model (TLM): Evolving KLM-GOMS for touchscreen and mobile devices," in *Proceedings of the 2014 ACM Southeast Regional Conference, ACM SE 2014*, Kennesaw, GA, USA, March 2014.

[47] M. Maragoudakis and N. K. Tselios, "Improving SMS usability using Bayesian networks," in *Proceedings of the Hellenic Conference on Artificial Intelligence*, pp. 179–190, 2002.

[48] F. V. III. Thompson, *Evaluation of a commodity VR interaction device for gestural object manipulation in a three dimensional work environment [PhD thesis]*, Iowa State University, Ames, IA, USA, 2014.

[49] R. Mori, T. Matsunobe, and T. Yamaoka, "A task operation prediction time computation based on GOMS-KLM improved for the cellular phone and the verification of that validity," in *Proceedings of the Asian Design International Conference (ADC'03)*, 2003.

[50] K. El Batran and M. D. Dunlop, "Enhancing KLM (Keystroke-Level Model) to fit touch screen mobile devices," in *Proceedings of the 16th ACM International Conference on Human-Computer Interaction with Mobile Devices and Services, MobileHCI 2014*, pp. 283–286, September 2014.

[51] A. Sears and Y. Zha, "Data Entry for Mobile Devices Using Soft Keyboards: Understanding the Effects of Keyboard Size and User Tasks," *International Journal of Human-Computer Interaction*, vol. 16, no. 2, pp. 163–184, 2003.

[52] A. Lee, K. Song, H. B. Ryu, J. Kim, and G. Kwon, "Fingerstroke time estimates for touchscreen-based mobile gaming interaction," *Human Movement Science*, vol. 44, pp. 211–224, 2015.

[53] B. E. John, D. D. Salvucci, P. Centgraf, and K. Prevas, "Integrating models and tools in the context of driving and in-vehicle devices," in *Proceedings of the Sixth International Conference on Cognitive Modeling: ICCCM 2004: Integrating Models*, pp. 130–135, 2004.

[54] O. Erazo, J. A. Pino, and P. Antunes, "Estimating production time of touchless hand drawing gestures," in *Human-Computer Interaction*, 569, p. 552, 2015.

[55] R. Myung, "Keystroke-level analysis of Korean text entry methods on mobile phones," *International Journal of Human-Computer Studies*, vol. 60, no. 5-6, pp. 545–563, 2004.

[56] J. A. Palilonis, *Active reading on tablet textbooks [PhD thesis]*, University-Purdue University Indianapolis, Indianapolis, IN, USA, 2015.

[57] S. Jassar, "The digital pen as a human computer interface," in *Proceedings of the 2004 IEEE International Symposium on Consumer Electronics - Proceedings*, pp. 629–634, September 2004.

[58] O. Erazo and J. A. Pino, "Predicting task execution time on Natural User Interfaces based on touchless hand gestures," in *Proceedings of the 20th ACM International Conference on Intelligent User Interfaces, IUI 2015*, pp. 97–109, April 2015.

[59] Y. How and M.-Y. Kan, "Optimizing predictive text entry for short message service on mobile phones," in *Proceedings of the HCII*, vol. 5, 2005.

[60] R. M. Jones, R. E. Wray, J. Zaientz, B. Bachelor, and C. Newton, "Using Cognitive Workload Analysis to Predict and Mitigate Workload for Training Simulation," *Procedia Manufacturing*, vol. 3, pp. 5777–5784, 2015.

[61] T. Jokela, J. Koivumaa, J. Pirkola, P. Salminen, and N. Kantola, "Methods for quantitative usability requirements: A case study on the development of the user interface of a mobile phone," *Personal and Ubiquitous Computing*, vol. 10, no. 6, pp. 345–355, 2006.

[62] P. Green, T.-P. Kang, and B. Lin, "Touch screen task element times for improving SAE recommended practice J2365: First proposal," Tech. Rep. ATLAS-2015-07, Center for Advancing Transportation Leadership and Safety (ATLAS Center), 2015.

[63] H. Tonn-Eichstädt, "Measuring website usability for visually impaired people - A modified GOMS analysis," in *Proceedings of the Eighth International ACM SIGACCESS Conference on Computers and Accessibility, ASSETS 2006*, pp. 55–62, October 2006.

[64] T. Elwart, P. Green, and L. Brian, "Predicting driver distraction using computed occlusion task times: Estimation of task element times and distributions," Tech. Rep. ATLAS-2015-01, Center for Advancing Transportation Leadership and Safety (ATLAS Center), 2015.

[65] K. Hinckley, F. Guimbretiere, P. Baudisch, R. Sarin, M. Agrawala, and E. Cutrell, "The Springboard: Multiple modes in one Spring-loaded control," in *Proceedings of the CHI 2006: Conference on Human Factors in Computing Systems*, pp. 181–190, April 2006.

[66] M. T. Burns and F. E. Ritter, "Using naturalistic typing to update architecture typing constants," in *Proceedings of the In Proceedings of the 14th International Conference on Cognitive Modeling*, pp. 169–174, 2016.

[67] P. Holleis, F. Otto, H. Hussmann, and A. Schmidt, "Keystroke-level model for advanced mobile phone interaction," in *Proceedings of the 25th SIGCHI Conference on Human Factors in Computing Systems 2007, CHI 2007*, pp. 1505–1514, May 2007.

[68] R. L. Boring and M. Rasmussen, "GOMS-HRA: A method for treating subtasks in dynamic human reliability analysis," in *Proceedings of the 2016 European Safety and Reliability Conference*, pp. 956–963, 2016.

[69] M. Pettitt, G. Burnett, and A. Stevens, "An extended keystroke level model (KLM) for predicting the visual demand of in-vehicle information systems," in *Proceedings of the 25th SIGCHI Conference on Human Factors in Computing Systems 2007, CHI 2007*, pp. 1515–1524, USA, May 2007.

[70] S. Ginn, *CLIsis: An Interface for Visu-ally Impaired Users of Apache Isis Applications [PhD thesis]*, University of Amsterdam, 2016.

[71] M. Esteves, T. Komischke, S. Zapf, and A. Weiss, "Applied user performance modeling in industry - A case study from medical imaging," in *Digital Human Modeling*, pp. 576–585, 2007.

[72] M. Nasirinejad, *Mobile focus+context: Exploring the combination of large overviews with high-resolution details in dynamic, mobile work environments [PhD thesis]*, Dalhousie University, Halifax, Canada.

[73] A. Hashizume, M. Kurosu, and T. Kaneko, "Multi-window system and the working memory," in *Proceedings of the International Conference on Engineering Psychology and Cognitive Ergonomics*, pp. 297–305, 2007.

[74] A. Christensen, S. A. Pedersen, P. Bjerre, A. K. Pedersen, and W. Stuerzlinger, "Transition times for manipulation tasks in hybrid interfaces," in *Proceedings of the International Conference on Human-Computer Interaction*, pp. 138–150, 2016.

[75] A. L. Cox, P. A. Cairns, A. Walton, and S. Lee, "Tlk or txt? Using voice input for SMS composition," *Personal and Ubiquitous Computing*, vol. 12, no. 8, pp. 567–588, 2008.

[76] E. Moreta, *A predictive model for user performance time with natural user interfaces based on touchless hand gestures [PhD thesis]*, Universidad de Chile, Santiago, Chile, 2016.

[77] I. S. MacKenzie, A. Sellen, and W. A. S. Buxton, "A comparison of input devices in element pointing and dragging tasks," in *Proceedings of the 1991 SIGCHI Conference on Human Factors in Computing Systems, CHI 1991*, pp. 161–166, May 1991.

[78] S.-h. Kim, G.-m. Kim, and R. Myung, "Hangul input system's physical interface evaluation model for mobile phone," *Journal of Korean Institute of Industrial Engineers*, vol. 28, no. 2, pp. 193–200, 2002.

[79] B. E. John and A. Newell, "Cumulating the science of HCI: from s-R compatibility to transcription typing," *ACM SIGCHI Bulletin*, vol. 20, no. SI, pp. 109–114, 1989.

[80] M. Silfverberg, I. Scott MacKenzie, and P. Korhonen, "Predicting text entry speed on mobile phones," in *Proceedings of the SIGCHI Conference on Human Factors in Computing Systems, CHI 2000*, pp. 9–16, Netherlands, April 2000.

[81] I. S. MacKenzie, *Human-Computer Interaction: An Empirical Research Perspective*, Elsevier, Waltham, MA, USA, 2013.

[82] X. Zeng, A. Hedge, and F. Guimbretiere, "Fitts' law in 3D space with coordinated hand movements," in *Proceedings of the Human Factors and Ergonomics Society 56th Annual Meeting, HFES 2012*, pp. 990–994, October 2012.

8

The Effect of Personality on Online Game Flow Experience and the Eye Blink Rate as an Objective Indicator

Pei-Luen Patrick Rau, Yu Chien Tseng, Xiao Dong, Caihong Jiang, and Cuiling Chen

Institute of Human Factors & Ergonomics, Department of Industrial Engineering, Tsinghua University, Beijing 100084, China

Correspondence should be addressed to Pei-Luen Patrick Rau; rpl@mail.tsinghua.edu.cn

Academic Editor: Pietro Cipresso

This study aimed to explore the effects of dominant and compliant personalities, on both flow experience and the external characteristics of flow experience. A total of 48 participants were recruited to play an online game and subsequently asked to recall the songs they had heard while they were playing the game. Eye blink rate was recorded. The results demonstrated that (1) the participant was immersed in the game more if he/she was relatively dominant or noncompliant; (2) the perceptions about the external environment declined remarkably while being in a flow state; and (3) eye blink rates decreased only when the flow happened at the beginning of the game, rather than throughout the whole process. The results suggested that gamers who tend to be dominant or noncompliant were more likely to experience flow. Eye blink rate and perceptions of the external environment could be objective indicators of flow experience.

1. Introduction

With the advent of Web 2.0, user experiences have become a significant topic of interest for researchers. Flow experience, the optimal user experience, has drawn the attention of many researchers, especially those studying topics within the virtual world. Many factors may influence an individual's flow experience. Personalities can influence the way we perceive and think about the world. However, how an individual's personality influences our flow experience in online games is still not clear. This is the first question that the present study sought to explore. In addition, we attempted to clarify the process of judging whether or not a person is in a flow state. Also, what indicators, especially those that are objective enough for us to evaluate flow, could be used to determine whether someone is in a flow state.

2. Literature Review

2.1. Flow Experience. Csikszentmihalyi (1975) first used the theory of flow to determine that people often do not need any prizes or punishment in order to push them to participate in activities they are interested in doing [1]. This phenomenon is especially applicable to artists, regardless of whether the art is related to work or leisure. Artists concentrate solely on their work and are willing to complete it without any external rewards or additional monetary costs or time. Csikszentmihalyi referred to this as "flow." According to Csikszentmihalyi, flow tends to occur when one's skills are fully involved in overcoming a challenge that is considered manageable. Optimal experiences usually involve a fine balance between one's ability to act and other available opportunities. Otherwise, the flow state will come to an end. There are three elements that best describe flow: antecedent conditions, characteristics, and consequences of experience [2]. Antecedent conditions refer to the balance of challenge and skills, the clear definition of goals, and immediate feedback. Characteristics include action awareness merging, effortlessness, intense concentration on the task at hand, a sense of control, and enjoyment. Consequences of experience are the loss of self-consciousness, transformation of time, and autotelic experiences.

2.2. Dominance/Compliance Personality and Flow Experience. Two distinct personalities, dominance and conformity, are thought to exert influence on an individual's flow experience. Dominance refers to controlling one's human environment, to influence or direct the behavior of others through suggestion, seduction, persuasion, or command, and to dissuade, restrain, or prohibit [3–5]. Dominant people are usually risk-takers, pugnacious, fearless, decisive, straight, innovative, dauntless, problem solvers, and self-inspired. They act as the leader in a group. These personal characteristics allow them to concentrate more on their own experiences and encounter more joy, which may indicate that people with high dominance may have a greater chance to experience flow compared to people with low dominance.

There is some empirical evidence to support that dominant people experience flow more easily, compared with nondominant people. Csikszentmihalyi and LeFevre (1989) have found that managers are more likely to experience flow at work, compared with blue-collar workers [6]. Managers are in a dominant position at work and demonstrate dominance through their leadership, while blue-collar workers passively accept tasks or directions from their supervisors or managers, because they are in a nondominant position [7]. Han and Yoo (2014) examined the effects of an autotelic personality on flow experience in cyclists. Their study found that people with an autotelic personality, which consisted of curiosity, persistence, altruism, independence, and vitality personality factors, could significantly influence levels of flow experience [8]. Heller et al. (2015) investigated the correlations between personality traits with Eysenck's Personality Profiler and flow experience by the Practice Flow Inventory, in 120 amateur vocal students. The results revealed that participants with high extraversion-scores experienced significantly more flow than less extraverted persons. Lesser flow experience levels were related to high neuroticism-scores. Heller et al. also found that the certainty in handling an instrument for singers is essential to arouse a feeling of flow [9], indicating that the feeling of control is vital for people to obtain flow. People with a dominant personality tend to control their environment and own a high degree of control [4, 5]. It was also reported that people with a strong internal control experienced more flow than people with weak internal control [10]. Based on the results referred to above, it is hypothesized that dominant people might experience more flow than nondominant people.

Myers (1987) defines conformity to be "a change in behavior or belief as a result of real or imagined group pressure." Myers stated that sometimes we conform without really believing in what we are doing and that this insincere outward conformity is called compliance. Other times we genuinely believe in what the group has convinced us to do. This sincere inward conformity is called acceptance. Compliance is the process of changing one's own idea passively, under the pressure of a group or society [11, 12]. When a person can be easily led or influenced by external factors, he or she may find it hard to concentrate on the task. But, one of the essential conditions required to experience flow is to fully focus on the task at hand. Thus, people with high compliance may be less likely to experience flow compared to people with low compliance. The empirical evidence for supporting this view is scarce. Ross and Keiser (2014) examined the effect

of personality, using the Five Factor Model of personality, and the flow propensity with the Dispositional Flow Scale 2 (DFS-2), in 316 young adults. They found that neuroticism, extraversion, agreeableness, and conscientiousness predicted global flow propensity, which accounted for 38% of the measured variance. Among these characteristics, extraversion (with dominance as a subdimension), positively predicted an individual's global flow propensity. But agreeableness (with compliance as a subdimension) negatively predicted an individual's global flow propensity [13]. These results may indicate that compliant people are negatively correlated with flow; that is, the more compliant characteristics that people have, the less flow they are likely to experience. Thus, we inferred that compliant people were less likely to experience flow than noncompliant people.

2.3. The External Expression of Flow Experience. People experiencing flow might display different behaviors compared to those not in a flow state. One important change is the perception of the external environment, while another factor is eye blink rate.

Perceptions of the External Environment. People in a flow state often focus their concentration on what he or she is doing, with almost all of their attention and resources absorbed by the current activity [6, 14]. A loss of self-awareness [15] may lead the external information to be poorly perceived. Perception of one's external environment begins with the activation of sensory receptors, with the information stored in a memory system. This process is referred to as the "sensory register," which is designed to store a record of the information received by receptor cells [16]. The sensory register is an important tool, as processing sensory information to obtain a meaning and adding information to the sensory pattern is not accomplished instantaneously. Yet, the ability of the brain to process multiple patterns of sensory information is limited. Thus, only part of the information can be selected by the working memory, to further enter into an individual's long-term memory. Most information is lost due to a lack of further processing. This process is called "attention filter theory." Flow theory also states that when a person goes into a flow status, brain activity usually focuses on the task, and thus the bandwidth of the information reception channel decreases [7]. Therefore, the amount of information from the external environment, which enters into an individual's working memory, is significantly reduced.

Eye Blink Rate. Currently, there is limited literature that has explored the adoption of eye tracking, as a means to evaluate computer games [17–19]. In these studies, eye fixation [20, 21], eye gaze [22], and saccades [23] are the key factors used to determine eye movement indicators. The eye blink rate, still called spontaneous eye blink in some studies, is also an important indicator in eye tracking studies. Some researchers have used eye blink rates as an indicator in some fields. Veltman and Gaillard (1998) reported that increases in visual information inhibited the eye blink, and in contrast, increasing the difficulty of a memory task led to an increase in the blink rate [24]. These results were consistent with a study by Acosta, Gallar, and Belmonte (1999) [25], who found that eye blink rates drop when people performed a task requiring strong visual attention. Wu, Begley, Zhang, Adebisi, and Simpson (2011) [26] confirmed these findings and reported that eye blink rates decreased with greater concentration. When investigating changes in the eye blink rates of children engaged in video games, researchers have demonstrated a decrease in blinking when the game was in progress [27]. Kim, Min, and Park (2013) also confirmed these findings. They found that the frequency of eye blink significantly decreased by 12%, when game playing participants were in high flow level compared with when they were in a low flow level [28]. Based on the studies above, we anticipated that the eye blink rate reduced when people were immersed in computer games, in other words, when people experienced flow.

Hypothesis. Based on the discussions above, a subsequent research framework was proposed (see Figure 1). The present study included two independent variables: personality (dominant/nondominant, compliant/noncompliant) and a participant's game status (flow versus nonflow). The dependent variables were the extent of flow experience, perception of external environment, and blink rate.

Four hypotheses were formulated.

Hypothesis 1 (H1). Compared with being nondominant, dominant individuals are more likely to experience flow.

Hypothesis 2 (H2). Compared with being compliant, individuals are more likely to experience flow if he/she is relatively noncompliant.

Hypothesis 3 (H3). A gamer's perceptions of their external environment will decline remarkably when he/she is in a flow state.

Hypothesis 4 (H4). A gamer's blink rate will decrease if he/she is experiencing flow.

3. Methodology

3.1. Participants. Firstly, we conducted a recruitment process in the city of Beijing for volunteers to take part in our study. We used posters to promote the study, with 129 students prepared to take part. Secondly, all volunteers were screened based on the following two criteria: (1) having at least three years of experience in playing *Warcraft* 3 and (2) a relatively high (dominant score is higher than 49 or compliant score is higher than 45) or low (dominant score is lower than 31 or compliant score is lower than 35) personality scale score. Finally, a total of 48 male participants with four personality types (dominance, nondominance, compliance, and noncompliance) were selected to take part in the study. Each personality type had 12 participants. All participants were undergraduate or graduate students from one of several universities in Beijing. The participants had little or no prior knowledge about the proposed tasks. The participant's ages ranged from 19 to 26 (M = 22, SD = 1.71) years. Participants

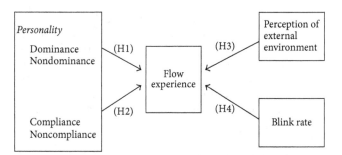

FIGURE 1: Research framework.

were allocated into four groups: dominant (range: 49–70) versus nondominant groups (range: 22–31) and compliant (range: 45–60) versus noncompliant (range: 20–35) groups, which were done according to the personality scale score.

Due to the limitation of the number of players, only 8 participants could play games simultaneously. As such, the 48 participants were assigned to six groups and each group consisted of four types of personalities (dominance, nondominance, compliance, and noncompliance) with two participants each. Each personality type had 12 participants. To preclude the effect of the degree of familiarity on the interaction frequency among them, each group of the participants (N = 8) were randomly selected from the 48 volunteers. The participants confirmed that they did not know each other. In addition, participants were asked to use their assigned code as their player name, to be sure that interactions with each other were objective.

3.2. Tasks

Task 1: Recording Eye Blink Films. All participants were twice asked to put on a head mounted device to record eye measurements. Both of the recordings were conducted in playing mode. The first eye recording was conducted for three minutes when participants were not in a flow experience status, and the second recording was conducted for 70 minutes when participants were in a flow state. After the experiment, the two films were loaded into the "Blink Statistic" program one by one. The blink rate of each film was counted separately.

Task 2: Playing Warcraft 3. The purpose of the game was to protect a basement. In the game, each of the participants chooses a character, and then control its actions with the objective to kill their enemies. Their accumulated money and experiences in the game increased with the number of enemies that they killed. Money could buy equipment, while experience could raise the player's abilities. A boss would appear at 60–70 minutes in games. Eight participants could communicate and cooperate with each other at any time in the game, unless their basement was breached and the game was over. If the game finished within 105 minutes, participants were asked to play another round until the time was up.

Task 3: Song Recognition Test. Participants were asked to answer ten questions without a time limitation. For each

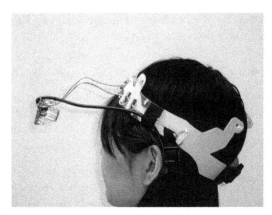
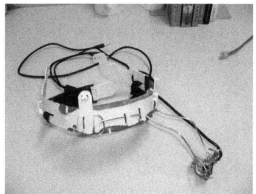

FIGURE 2: Head mounted device.

question, participants were required to listen to a song and recall whether they had heard it when they were playing *Warcraft* 3. They could adjust the scroll bar of the music player in order to listen to every part of the song. Once they had submitted an answer for each question, it could not be changed.

3.3. Experimental Design and Variables.

Personality was considered a between-subject variable and consisted of dominant/nondominant or compliant/noncompliant. Game stage (idle or playing game) was a within-subject variable. The dependent variables were blink rate, degree of flow experience, and perception of the external environment.

Flow experience was measured using a questionnaire with 28 questions [18], which were rated on a scale of 1 (*disagree strongly*) to 7 (*agree strongly*). Cronbach's alpha of the original questionnaire was between 0.79 and 0.94, implying a high level of reliability. Cronbach's alpha coefficient in this study was 0.92, indicating an excellent reliability.

The "Blink Statistic" program measured eye blink rates. When analyzing the blink rates during a flow experience, the normal condition of their eye blinks, which was found on the first recorded film for each participant, was used. Perception of the external environment was measured using the number of correct answers in the song recognition assessment.

3.4. Apparatus and System.

The study was conducted in a reserved room in a cybercafe. Each participant was equipped with two personal computers, one for the eye blink recording and the other for playing *Warcraft* 3.

Two Personal Computers. Two personal computers in the cybercafe were used for each participant. The detailed configuration of these computers were Pentium D 2.8 G CPU, 1 G RAM, Geforce Four 6600 display card, desktop monitor with a 17-inch LCD monitor with a display resolution 1024 × 768, and Windows XP Professional operating system.

Head Mounted Device. This was a piece of equipment used to measure the condition of the eye within a continuous period. The device was made up of a webcam and headgear (see Figure 2). The headgear was removed from a safety helmet

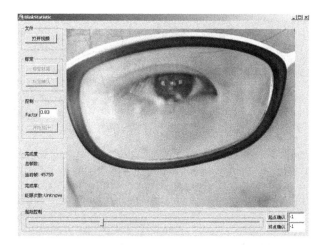

FIGURE 3: Interface of "blink statistic."

to keep the webcam stable on the head. The headgear was adjusted to suit the size of each of the participant's heads. The lens and chip were taken from a webcam with a resolution of five megapixels and plugged into a computer. At most, the webcam could process 30 frames, with a resolution of 640 * 480 per second. The webcam was tied with wire, fixed on the headgear, and stretched out. During the recording process, the webcam was adjusted to a distance of 8 cm and a 20° elevation degree to the front of the left eye.

Systems. The user interface of the experiment was designed as a webpage and developed using Macromedia Dreamweaver running on Windows XP SP2. The webpage would automatically save individual files for each subject. To avoid the effect of latency of the network transfer, this experiment was carried out without the use of Internet.

A self-written program called "Blink Statistic" was used for counting the number of eye blinks, as well as the blink rate over a long period of time (see Figure 3). The operating system platform for "Blink Statistic" was Microsoft Windows XP, DotNET Framework 1.1, and the display color quality was 32 bits. It was written in Microsoft Visual C++ language, developed by Microsoft Visual Studio.Net 2003.

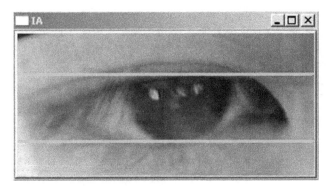

FIGURE 4: Demarcate the eye area.

After the experiment, all recorded films were loaded into "Blink Statistic." The researcher first needed to demarcate the spot of the eye manually, and then the system could scan the eyeballs in a limited area, ultimately deciding the position of the upper and lower eyelids (see Figure 4). Finally, the program automatically calculated and showed the total number of eye blinks and the blink rate of each film. The time taken to count the film takes only one-third of the original time span.

Game. Warcraft 3 was chosen for this experiment for the following reasons: (1) Internet games are highly self-centric and require a great deal of concentration for an individual to interact with virtual characters in a confined environment [29]; (2) it is a game conducted in real time with all players playing simultaneously, unlike card games that play in turn; and (3) the style of this game is rather simplistic and the participant's states can be easily controlled (players were all on the same side versus the computer). Participants could only choose one of the 21 characters, which were all at the same level at the beginning of the game. Finally, (4) this game takes advantage of the characteristics of online games, enabling participants to easily communicate. For example, a dialog box appears at the bottom left corner of the window after pressing "enter," and players can then communicate with each other by typing messages.

3.5. Procedure. The whole experimental study can be divided into three stages: before playing *Warcraft* 3; while playing *Warcraft* 3; and after playing *Warcraft* 3 (flow experience). Participants experienced all of these three stages. Finally, participants were asked to complete three questionnaires, the flow experience questionnaire, the satisfaction questionnaire, and a questionnaire regarding their self-evaluation of the games performance.

Before playing Warcraft 3 stage: an introduction to the study was provided to participants, informing them of how it would be conducted and what they would be required to do. All participants provided written informed consent and received financial compensation for their participation. The first eye recording was conducted during this stage. While playing Warcraft 3 stage: participants played the game during which time the eye recordings were performed. After

playing Warcraft 3 stage: a song recognition test and the flow questionnaire were completed.

4. Results

4.1. The Effect of Personality on Flow Experience. The results showed that the dominant personality had an overwhelming impact on flow experience, $F(1, 21) = 6.94$, $p < .05$. The dominant participants ($n = 12$) had a higher flow experience score (M = 131.58, SD = 24.49) than the nondominant group ($n = 12$; M = 100.42, SD = 25.32). These findings support (H1). The compliant personality type also had a significant effect on flow experience, $F(1, 21) = 4.51$, $p < .05$. The compliant group ($n = 12$) had a lower flow experience score (M = 108.17, SD = 22.98) compared with the noncompliant group ($n = 12$; M = 124.33, SD = 12.91). Hypothesis 2 was also supported.

4.2. The Effect of Different Flow States on Gamer's Perception of External Environment. In order to explore the effect of flow states on a gamer's perception of the external environment and blink rates, all the participant's flow scores ($n = 48$) were ranked in an ascending order. Twenty-five percent of the highest scores in the flow questionnaire were defined as the flow group (scores higher than 134; $n = 12$), and twenty-five percent of the lowest scores in the flow questionnaire were defined as the nonflow group (score lower than 98; $n = 12$).

An independent t-test was performed to examine the group differences regarding their perceptions of the external environment. The results demonstrated that the flow state had an overwhelming impact on a gamer's perceptions of their external environment ($t = 2.14$, df = 22, $p < .05$). The flow group (M = 1.50, SD = 1.17) had significantly lower scores on the song recognition test when compared with the nonflow group (M = 2.58, SD = 1.31), suggesting a decreased amount of perception of external information. Thus, (H3) was supported.

4.3. The Effect of Different Flow States on Gamer's Blink Rate. The ANOVA was performed on the gamer's blink rate with group (flow and nonflow) as between subjects factors and blink rate measurements as within subjects factors. The results showed that there was a significant difference between the flow group and the nonflow group on blink rate during the first 30 minutes of the game and when the boss appeared (at 60–70 minutes). The flow group had a significantly lower blink rate during the first ten minutes ($p < .05$), 10–20 minutes into the game ($p < .05$), 20–30 minutes into the game ($p < .05$), and when the boss appeared at 60–70 minutes ($p = 0.07$), compared to before the participants were immersed in the flow experience (see Figure 5). However, the nonflow group demonstrated no significant differences in blink rate over that time (see Figure 6). These results confirmed (H4).

5. General Discussion

The present study examined how two important personalities (dominance and compliance) affected people's flow experience and the external expressions of different flow

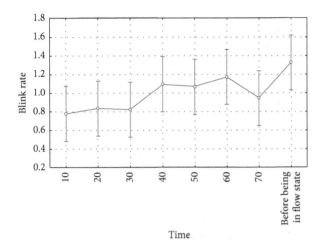

FIGURE 5: Blink rate result of flow group.

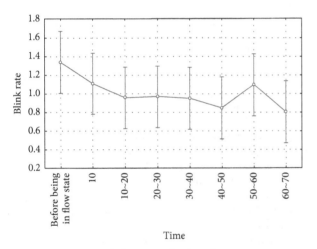

FIGURE 6: Blink rate result of nonflow group.

states. The results of our study confirmed all four hypotheses. People with dominant or noncompliant personalities experienced a much easier flow state compared to nondominant or compliant people. In addition, people in the flow state showed a decreased amount of perception of the external environment information, compared to people in the nonflow state. The most important result identified during the course of the study was that a reduced eye blink rate was found in the flow state, but this effect only appeared at the start of the game.

The results showed that dominant or noncompliant people were more immersed in the game than nondominant or compliant people, which was consistent with Mihaly's (1990) idea that the flow experience involves individual differences [7]. Mihaly found that some individuals relied upon their external environment and could not easily control their thinking. These people also could not easily enter into a flow status. The researcher suggested that self-perception could significantly affect flow. If one continuously worries about their surrounding environment, he/she will be afraid of making mistakes or creating a bad impression. As such, they are less likely to experience pleasure. Nevertheless, pleasure

or playfulness is some of the key elements for experiencing flow, an idea that was supported by a study conducted by Mauri et al. (2011) [30]. Mauri et al. found that a specific positive affective state experienced by users might be one of the key elements in the success of Facebook [30]. In the present study, dominant or noncompliant gamers always do things they want to do and their behaviors are less likely to be restricted by the group. As such, they are likely to enjoy the game much more. However, for nondominant or compliant gamers, who may be more likely to accept the tasks or directions passively experienced a higher level of group restriction on their behaviors, it was more difficult to enjoy the game. These gamers had a lower probability of experiencing flow.

The results demonstrated that people in a flow state had a decreased amount of perception of their external environment information, which conformed to our expectations. More importantly, the present study found that the eye blink rate also decreased when people were in the flow state. This finding was in accordance with previous studies [25], which revealed that the eye blink rate dropped when the task required strong visual attention. The findings were also consistent with flow theory, which considered that a loss of self-consciousness and action awareness were fundamental dimensions that described the mindset in a flow state [20]. This phenomenon might account for the attention filter theory [21], which suggests that attention selects certain pieces of incoming sensory information for conscious processing and filters out the remaining sensory information from conscious processing. In this study, participants who entered the flow experience might filter out information from the external environment, such as the song played on the computer. The reduction of eye blink frequency in the flow state elicited by computer games may be associated with the cortical impact on the pontine reticular formation neurons, which is considered to induce spontaneous blinking [31]. The suppressed input from peripheral afferents may partly explain this effect [25]. Therefore, the results of the present study may indicate that eye blink rate is an objective indicator of flow experience.

The present study contributed to the expanding theoretical base of understanding the elusive online flow, having implications for game designers and service providers. First, immersion is one of the main motivations for users to play online game [32]. People with dominant and noncompliant personalities more easily experience flow, so this finding indicates that game designers should develop more characters that gamers can easily control. This will maintain the gamers' optimal status, flow. Second, the study found that eye blink rates and perception tasks in the external environment could be objective indicators of flow experience. This provides scholars and service providers with objective and effective tools to investigate users' behaviors.

However, there are also some limitations in the present study. This research was an explorative study with the small sample size not large enough to represent all online gamers. Therefore, the conclusions derived from this study should be treated cautiously. Future studies should use a larger sample size to confirm the findings identified during the course of this study. In addition, the present study could not identify specific mechanisms of how personality influenced flow experience. Further research is needed to explore the underlying mechanisms.

6. Conclusions

The present study found that personality (dominance and compliance) had a significant impact on flow experience. People with dominant or noncompliant personalities experienced more flow than participants with nondominant or compliant personalities. More importantly, the present study found a decreased perception of the external environment and a decreased blink rate in the flow state compared to in the nonflow state. This suggests that perceptions of the external environment and blink rate could be objective indicators of flow experience.

Acknowledgments

This study was funded by a National Natural Science Foundation of China Grant 71661167006.

References

[1] M. Csikszentmihalyi, *Beyond Boredom and Anxiety*, Jossey-Bass, San Francisco, Calif, USA, 1975.

[2] T. P. Novak and D. L. Hoffman, "Measuring the flow experience among web users," *Interval Research Corporation*, vol. 31, pp. 1–36, 1997.

[3] P. H. Lindsay and D. A. Norman, *Human Information Processing: An Introduction to Psychology*, Academic Press, NY, USA, 1972.

[4] J. J. Fins and N. D. Schiff, *In the Blink of the Mind's Eye*, Wiley-Blackwell, Hoboken, NJ, USA, 2010.

[5] A. W. Lukaszewski and J. R. Roney, "Estimated hormones predict women's mate preferences for dominant personality traits," *Personality and Individual Differences*, vol. 47, no. 3, pp. 191–196, 2009.

[6] M. Csikszentmihalyi and J. LeFevre, "Optimal experience in work and leisure," *Journal of Personality and Social Psychology*, vol. 56, no. 5, pp. 815–822, 1989.

[7] C. Mihaly, *Flow: The Psychology of Optimal Experience*, Harper and Row, New York, NY, USA, 1990.

[8] S. H. Han and K. M. Yoo, "A study on the effects of autotelic personality on flow experience: focus on the bicycle riders," *Journal of Tourism Studies*, vol. 26, no. 5, pp. 45–72, 2014.

[9] K. Heller, C. Bullerjahn, and R. Von Georgi, "The relationship between personality traits, flow-experience, and different aspects of practice behavior of amateur vocal students," *Frontiers in Psychology*, vol. 6, Article ID 01901, 2015.

[10] J. Keller and F. Blomann, "Locus of control and the flow experience: an experimental analysis," *European Journal of Personality*, vol. 22, no. 7, pp. 589–607, 2008.

[11] D. G. Myers, *Social Psychology*, McGraw-Hill Education, New York, NY, USA, 1987.

[12] S. A. Hackley, M. Á. Muñoz, K. Hebert, F. Valle-Inclán, and J. Vila, "Reciprocal modulation of eye-blink and pinna-flexion

[13] S. R. Ross and H. N. Keiser, "Autotelic personality through a five-factor lens: Individual differences in flow-propensity," *Personality and Individual Differences*, vol. 59, pp. 3–8, 2014.

[14] C. Boersch and F. von Diest, *Flow: Das Geheimnis des Glücks*, Stuttgart: Klett-Cotta, Germany, 2010.

[15] M. Csikszentmihalyi and J. Nakamura, "Effortless attention in everyday life: a systematic phenomenology," in *Effortless Attention: A New Perspective in the Cognitive Science of Attention and Action*, B. Bruya, Ed., pp. 179–190, The MIT Press, Cambridge, UK, 2010.

[16] E. S. Reed, "Perception is to self as memory is to selves," in *The Remembering Self Construction And Accuracy in The Self-Narrative*, U. Neisser and R. Fivush, Eds., vol. 15, pp. 278–292, Cambridge University Press, Oxford, UK, 1994.

[17] S. Kühn, R. Lorenz, T. Banaschewski et al., "Positive association of video game playing with left frontal cortical thickness in adolescents," *PLoS ONE*, vol. 9, no. 3, Article ID e91506, 2014.

[18] S. Yan and M. S. El-Nasr, "Visual attention in 3D video games," in *Proceedings of the Symposium on Eye Tracking Research and Applications (ETRA'06)*, p. 42, San Diego, Calif, USA, March 2006.

[19] D. L. King, M. Gradisar, A. Drummond et al., "The impact of prolonged violent video-gaming on adolescent sleep: An experimental study," *Journal of Sleep Research*, vol. 22, no. 2, pp. 137–143, 2013.

[20] T. Strandvall, "Eye tracking in human-computer interaction and usability research," *Lecture Notes in Computer Science (including subseries Lecture Notes in Artificial Intelligence and Lecture Notes in Bioinformatics)*, vol. 5727, no. 2, pp. 936–937, 2009.

[21] G. Devetag, S. Di Guida, and L. Polonio, "An eye-tracking study of feature-based choice in one-shot games," *Experimental Economics*, vol. 19, no. 1, pp. 177–201, 2016.

[22] A. Kenny, H. Koesling, D. Delaney, S. McLoone, and T. Ward, "A preliminary investigation into eye gaze data in a first person shooter game," in *Proceedings of the 19th European Conference on Modelling and Simulation (ECMS'05)*, pp. 733–740, Riga, Latvia, June 2005.

[23] S. Alkan and K. Cagiltay, "Studying computer game learning experience through eye tracking: Colloquium," *British Journal of Educational Technology*, vol. 38, no. 3, pp. 538–542, 2007.

[24] J. A. Veltman and A. W. K. Gaillard, "Physiological workload reactions to increasing levels of task difficulty," *Ergonomics*, vol. 41, no. 5, pp. 656–669, 1998.

[25] M. C. Acosta, J. Gallar, and C. Belmonte, "The influence of eye solutions on blinking and ocular comfort at rest and during work at video display terminals," *Experimental Eye Research*, vol. 68, no. 6, pp. 663–669, 1999.

[26] Z. W. Wu, C. Begley, J. Zhang, L. A. Adebisi, and T. Simpson, "Does ocular surface stimulation oppose internal controls over blinking?" *ARVO Annual Meeting Abstract Search and Program Planner*, p. 3846, 2011.

[27] K. Iwanaga, S. Saito, Y. Shimomura, H. Harada, and T. Katsuura, "The effect of mental loads on muscle tension, blood pressure and blink rate," *Journal of Physiological Anthropology and Applied Human Science*, vol. 19, no. 3, pp. 135–141, 2000.

[28] J. Y. Kim, S. N. Min, and Y. D. Park, "Evaluation of flow experience by using psychophysiological visual feedbacks," *Journal of the Ergonomics Society of Korea*, vol. 32, no. 6, pp. 481–487, 2013.

[29] T. J. Chou and C. C. Ting, "The role of flow experience in cyber-game addiction," *CyberPsychology & Behavior*, vol. 6, no. 6, pp. 663–675, 2003.

[30] M. Mauri, P. Cipresso, A. Balgera, M. Villamira, and G. Riva, "Why is Facebook so successful? Psychophysiological measures describe a core flow state while using Facebook," *Cyberpsychology, Behavior, and Social Networking*, vol. 14, no. 12, pp. 723–731, 2011.

[31] C. N. Karson, "Blinking," *Bulletin of the Social Belge Ophthalmology*, vol. 237, pp. 443–457, 1989.

[32] N. Yee, "Motivations for play in online games," *CyberPsychology & Behavior*, vol. 9, no. 6, pp. 772–775, 2006.

9

Towards a Model of User Experience in Immersive Virtual Environments

Katy Tcha-Tokey,[1] **Olivier Christmann,**[1] **Emilie Loup-Escande** (ID),[2]
Guillaume Loup,[3] **and Simon Richir**[1]

[1]*Arts et Métiers ParisTech, LAMPA EA 1427, 2 bd du Ronceray, 49000 Angers, France*
[2]*Université de Picardie Jules Verne, CRP-CPO EA 7273, chemin du Thil, 80025 Amiens, France*
[3]*Université Bretagne Loire, LIUM EA 4023, avenue Olivier Messiaen, 72085 Le Mans, France*

Correspondence should be addressed to Emilie Loup-Escande; emilie.loup-escande@u-picardie.fr

Academic Editor: Salman Nazir

There are increasing new advances in virtual reality technologies as well as a rise in learning virtual environments for which several studies highlighted the pedagogical value, knowledge transfer, and learners' engaged-behaviors. Moreover, the notion of user experience is now abundant in the scientific literature without the fact that there are specific models for immersive environments. This paper aims at proposing and validating a model of User eXperience in Immersive Virtual Environment, including virtual learning environments. The model is composed of 10 components extracted from existing models (i.e., presence, engagement, immersion, flow, usability, skill, emotion, experience consequence, judgement, and technology adoption). It was validated in a user study involving 152 participants who were asked to use the edutainment application *Think and Shoot* and to complete an immersive virtual environment questionnaire. The findings lead us to a modified user experience model questioning new paths between user experience components (e.g., the influence of experience consequence on flow).

1. Introduction

The digital age has led to the emergence of digital games for learning [1]. These games are now too limited to conventional techniques such as Web, e-mail, or video conferencing [2]. So, new types of games known as "virtual learning environments" have succeeded in fully exploiting advanced technologies such as virtual reality. These virtual environments have opened up new perspectives in the field of education, increasing the number of stimuli by an immersive experience and then improving motivation [3].

Immersion should increase the motivation of users, and immersive virtual environments should provide a good User eXperience (UX) [4]. UX has been defined as "*the user's perceptions and responses resulting from the use of a system or a service [...]*" by the ISO 9241-210 (2009) norm. However, only few UX models are identified for immersive virtual environments (IVE) in the scientific literature. The UX approaches for virtual environments discussed in literature

focus on a single or a couple of components, particularly presence and immersion (i.e., [5–8]). Indeed, all of the UX components in IVE are not dealt with in the literature. The IVE should be useful, usable, and acceptable, provide a high level of presence, immersion, and flow, and cause little cybersickness. This led us to propose holistic model of the UX in IVE that considers the multiple components of the UX.

The aim of the present study is to propose and validate a conceptual model of the UX in IVE named *User eXperience in Immersive Virtual Environment Model* (*UXIVE Model*) in the field of edutainment. In Section 2, the *UXIVE* conceptual model is described in relation to UX models referenced in literature. An empirical study aiming at validating the *UXIVE Model* is detailed in Section 3. In Section 4, the validity of our model and component relationships with regard to the literature are discussed. In conclusion, suggestions on how to use our model to improve the UX in IVE, particularly in the field of edutainment, are evoked.

2. Proposition of a Model Measuring the UX in IVE

The *UXIVE Model* is based on four UX models [9–12]. These models are reviewed in Section 2.1. The hypothesized model was designed based on these four models and presented in Section 2.2. We chose these four precursor models for two reasons: they are—to our knowledge—the only ones to precisely identify and describe the relationships between components of the UX; they are suitable or adaptable immersive virtual environments in the field of edutainment. These models are complementary to more recent works but not specific to virtual environments as, for example, [13, 14].

2.1. User Experience Models Review

2.1.1. User Experience Based on Flow. The flow is defined as *"holistic sensation that people feel when they act with total involvement"* ([15], p. 36) as *"an enjoyable experience in which a participant feels an important level of behavioral control, happiness and enjoyment"* ([9], p. 174) when interacting within the virtual environment. These authors propose a model designed in a context of a virtual entertainment environment and its components are structured around the concept of flow in a virtual environment. Their model comprises 10 components identified as interactivity, involvement, vividness, skill, challenge, focused attention, flow, telepresence, positive effect, and loyalty. They consider that the user enters in a flow state when he interacts and perceives that the whole virtual environment is in his grip, when there is a balance between his skills and the challenge given, when he focuses on the current activity, and when he feels "telepresent". Moreover, this model suggests that vividness stimulates the sensory perceptions of the user improving his interactivity and enhancing the sense of telepresence. The model also reveals that higher level of involvement (expert/novice distinction, importance) increases the likelihood of forming positive telepresence, creates greater user challenge, and yields the user to develop stronger skills. The authors also found that mediated environment with higher interaction increases user attention (i.e., concentration) on the current activity, increases the perceived challenge for even the most experienced, and improves user perceptions of control skills. They observed that the user who focuses on stimuli in the virtual environment perceives a higher level of telepresence and that strong flow creates an emotional state in users and positively affects users' attitude and future usage desirability, thus, loyalty.

2.1.2. User Experience Based on Acceptance and Continuance. The technology acceptance is defined as the actions and decisions taken by the user for a future use of the virtual environment. The continuance intention is the intention of the user to continue using such system. A second model created in the virtual learning environment context is built on acceptance and continuance theories [10]. This model includes 9 components known as immersion, presence, flow, confirmation, satisfaction, perceived usefulness, perceived ease of use, previous experience, and intention. The authors

stated that the three constructs of flow, presence, and immersion coinfluence each other. They also revealed that users perceived immersion, flow, and presence as having impact on confirmation of what they expected regarding the technology. They observed that satisfaction, perceived usefulness, and perceived ease of use are influenced by the users' confirmation of the level of technology services and that user satisfaction is impacted by perceived usefulness, perceived ease of use, and confirmation. The author found that users' continuance intention is primarily determined by their satisfaction with prior technology use and that previous learning experience with technologies is a factor influencing intention directly.

2.1.3. User Experience Influenced by Virtual Environment Features. Lin and Parker [12] proposed a model designed in a context of virtual environment for entertainment which aims at identifying the virtual environment features (i.e., field-of-view, stereopsis, visual motion frequency, level of interactivity, and visual interventions predictability to visual motion) leading to an optimal UX. The authors define the UX through three components: presence, enjoyment, and simulator sickness. According to their model, there is a positive correlation between presence and enjoyment, a negative correlation between enjoyment and simulator sickness, no specific correlation between presence and simulator sickness, and a decline in presence or a growth in simulator sickness results from a decrease in enjoyment.

2.1.4. User Experience and Interaction. Mahlke [11] proposed a model which introduces the UX resulting from the interaction with a technical system. This model comprises 8 components defined as system properties, user characteristics, context parameters, human-technology interaction, perceptions of instrumental qualities, perception of noninstrumental qualities, emotional user reaction, and consequences of the UX. System properties, user characteristics, and context parameters are defined as categories of factors that determine the UX. The author observed that system properties lead to differences in objective measures of the interaction (e.g., number of accomplished tasks and time on task) as well as differences in UX (i.e., instrumental and noninstrumental quality perceptions as well as emotional user reactions) and in consequences of the experience (i.e., overall judgements and alternative choices). Their model suggests that user characteristics influence subjective feelings and context parameters influence overall judgement. The model also shows that emotional user reactions are assumed to be influenced by instrumental and noninstrumental quality perceptions. This suggests that consequences of UX are based on instrumental and noninstrumental quality perceptions as well as emotional user reactions.

2.2. Towards the UXIVE Model

2.2.1. Presence, Flow, and Experience Consequence. Presence is a component defined as the user's *"sense of being there"* in the virtual environment. Presence is achieved as soon as another reality is evoked, e.g., reading a book, watching

TV, and experiencing virtual reality [16]. The concept of presence can be divided into three categories: presence or telepresence, copresence, and social presence in a collective or collaborative virtual environment [9, 17, 18]. Experience consequence is a component we defined as the symptoms (e.g., the "simulator sickness", stress, dizziness, and headache) the user can experience in the virtual environment. As we saw previously in the user experience models review, for [9], the user enters in a flow state when he feels *"telepresent"*. Shin, Biocca, and Choo [10] have investigated the role of flow and presence and found that all two coinfluence each other; it can be said that they play enhancing roles for each other. As for [12], they investigated the degree of presence, enjoyment, and simulator sickness users experience in a virtual environment; they found that there is a positive correlation between presence and enjoyment, a negative correlation between enjoyment, and simulator sickness. Zhou and Lu [19] noted that flow experience includes perceived enjoyment and attention focus. Consequently, we may hypothesize that a low experience consequence and a high sense of presence greatly enhance the state of flow which influences back the two components (Hypothesis 1).

2.2.2. Presence, Immersion, and Engagement. Immersion is a component defined as the *"objective level of sensory fidelity a virtual reality system provides"* ([20], p. 38). The immersive dimension in a virtual environment is created by *"complex technologies that replace real-world sensory information with synthetic stimuli"* ([20], p. 36). Engagement is a component defined as *"a psychological state experienced because of focusing one's energy and attention on a coherent set of stimuli or meaningfully related activities and events"* ([21], p. 227). Following the Witmer and Singer's approach, immersion and engagement are two elements that contribute to the idea of presence [21]. Shin et al. [10] consider immersion as clearly related to the widely research concept of presence. Hence, we may hypothesize that the sense of presence enhances the degree of engagement and the feeling of immersion; the same way the two components enhance presence (Hypothesis 2).

2.2.3. Flow, Usability, Skill, and Emotion. Usability is a component defined as the ease of using (i.e., efficiency, effectiveness, and satisfaction) the virtual environment. Skill is a component defined as the knowledge the user gain in mastering his activity in the virtual environment. Emotion is a component defined as the subjective feelings (i.e., joy, pleasure, satisfaction, frustration, disappointment, and anxiety) of the user in the virtual environment that varies with his prior experience with virtual reality [22]. According to Shin et al. [10] users feeling present and in a state of flow may want to perceive what is useful and easy to use and thus feel satisfied. Given the widely accepted factors, perceived usefulness, perceived ease of use, and satisfaction can be indicators of perceived usability [10]. Cheng et al. [9] asserted that the user can derive emotions from the human-machine interaction experience and that strong flow creates this emotional state. They also suggest that skill affects flow. In fact, the state of flow results from an equilibrium between the user's perceived skill and the challenge given. Thus, we

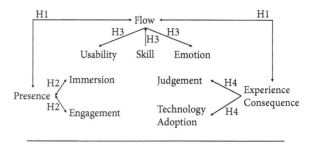

Flow	UX component
Hn	Influence of a component over another one (hypothesis n)

FIGURE 1: The hypothesized UXIVE Model.

may hypothesize that the perceived skills influence the state of flow which in turn influences the perceived usability and the emotion (Hypothesis 3).

2.2.4. Experience Consequence, Judgement, and Technology Adoption. Judgement is a component defined as the overall judgement (i.e., positive, indifferent or negative) of the virtual environment. Technology adoption is a component defined as the actions and decisions taken by the user for a future use or intention to use of the virtual environment. According to Shin et al. [10], experience consequence can alter the user's prior use and thus the intention to use the virtual environment. Indeed, as revealed by Lin and Parker [10], simulator sickness (i.e., a UX after effect) severity could make the users feel uncomfortable and even withdraw from a virtual environment exposure. Thus, simulator sickness could contribute negatively to UX. According to Mahlke [11] the consequence of the experience incorporates the acceptance of the system (overall judgement of the system), intention to use the system, and usage behavior. Consequently, we may hypothesize that the experience consequence influences the overall virtual environment judgement and the propensity of adopting the technology (Hypothesis 4).

These four hypotheses, justified by the literature, lead to a hypothesized model named *User eXperience in Immersive Virtual Environment Model* or *UXIVE Model (Figure 1)*. This model has been validated through an empirical study.

3. Validation of the User eXperience in Immersive Virtual Environment Model

After explaining the purpose of the study, methodology detailing participants, material, measures and the procedure, and results of the structural equation modelling analysis of the *UXIVE Model* are exposed.

3.1. Aim of the Study. This study aims at validating the theoretical *UXIVE Model* defining relationships between ten UX components specific to IVE: presence, immersion, engagement, skill, emotion, flow, usability, technology adoption, judgement, and experience consequence (*Figure 1*). In other words, this aim was to validate the following four hypotheses:

FIGURE 2: A participant (left) playing the "Think and Shoot" virtual environment (right).

(i) Hypothesis 1: a low experience consequence and a high sense of presence greatly enhance the state of flow which influences back the two components.

(ii) Hypothesis 2: the sense of presence enhances the degree of engagement and the feeling of immersion; the same way the two components enhance presence.

(iii) Hypothesis 3: the perceived skills influence the state of flow which in turn influences the perceived usability and the emotion.

(iv) Hypothesis 4: the experience consequence influences the overall virtual environment judgement and the propensity of adopting the virtual environment technology.

3.2. Method

3.2.1. Participants.
One hundred fifty-two participants (28 women and 124 men; 37 inexperienced and 115 experienced in virtual reality; students or professionals) had volunteered to take part in this study. The sample mean age was 23.96 years and the standard deviation was 6.93 (ranging from 18 to 63).

3.2.2. Material and Measures

Think and Shoot on Oculus DK2. Think and Shoot is an edutainment virtual environment aiming at familiarizing the participants with the notions of function and parameters. It consists of two main actions which are collecting balls and shoot on evil creatures. The participants are given instructions in a pseudo programming language where the action of shooting is represented by a function and the three parameters of the function are represented by the type of evil creature to shoot on (i.e., two different types of creatures), the type of ball to shoot (i.e., three different types of balls), and the remaining balls that can be used. An example of instruction could be *"Shoot (fire creature, ice ball, 0)" (Figure 2)*, the participant should understand that there is no ice ball left to shoot on the fire creature, and he must collect more.

This edutainment virtual environment was designed with the development tool UNITY © and ran on a Dell 64bits with 4 GB of RAM computer, an Intel® Xeon® processor, CPU E5-16030 2.80 GHz. A Logitech wireless gamepad and an Oculus development kit 2 (DK2) allowed the participant to collect balls and to shoot on three different sphere targets in the training session and on two different evil creatures in the regular session according the instructions given on a panel in the application. 3D spatialized sound was rendered in a Tritton AX 180 audio headset.

Questionnaires. Participants had to answer two questionnaires before and after the task.

The questionnaire filled in before the task contained 11 questions: four demographic items (age, gender, marital status, and occupation) and seven items on prior knowledge about programming and familiarity with virtual reality (e.g., *"Among the following devices (such as virtual reality headsets, data glove...), which ones have you used and how often (never, little, sometimes, often, very often)?"*).

The subjective questionnaire completed after the task was a UX questionnaire consisting of 84 items rated on 10-point Likert scales. It contained 12 items to measure presence taken from [21] (Cronbach's $\alpha = 0.76$; e.g., *"The virtual environment was responsive to actions that I initiated"*), 3 items to measure engagement translated from [21] (Cronbach's $\alpha = 0.74$; e.g., *"The sense of moving around inside the virtual environment was compelling"*), 7 items to measure immersion inspired by [21] (Cronbach's $\alpha = 0.74$; e.g., *"I felt stimulated by the virtual environment"*), 11 items to measure flow taken from [23] (Cronbach's $\alpha = 0.82$; e.g., *"I felt I could perfectly control my actions"*), 6 items to measure skill translated from [24] (Cronbach's $\alpha = 0.80$; e.g., *"I felt confident selecting objects in the virtual environment"*), 15 items to measure emotion taken from [25] (Cronbach's $\alpha = 0.72$; e.g., *"I enjoyed being in this virtual environment"*), 9 items to measure experience consequence inspired by [26] (Cronbach's $\alpha = 0.91$; e.g., *"I suffered from fatigue during my interaction with the virtual environment"*), 12 items (grouped in 4) to measure judgement taken from [27] (Cronbach's $\alpha = 0.82$; e.g., *"Personally, I would say the virtual environment is impractical/practical"*), and 9 items to measure technology adoption inspired by [28] (Cronbach's $\alpha = 0.75$; e.g., *"If I use again the same virtual environment, my interaction with the environment would be clear and understandable for me"*).

TABLE 1: The recommended value of fit indices for SEM analysis.

Fit index	Recommended value	Reference
CFI	> 0.9	Bagozzi and Yi (1988)
NFI	> 0.9	Bentler (1990)
RMSEA	< 0.08	Kline (2005)
$\chi 2$/df	< 5	Bagozzi and Yi (1988)

Note. CFI: Comparative Fit Index; NFI: Normed Fit Index; RMSEA: Root Mean Square Error of Approximation; $\chi 2$/df: the ratio between Chi square and degrees of freedom.

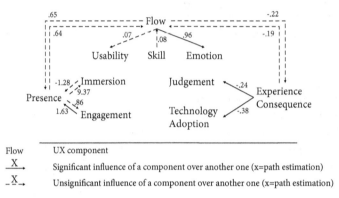

FIGURE 3: Standardized path estimation coefficient of the structural model of the hypothesized UXIVE Model.

Usability Measures. Usability was measured through level completion time, number of errors, total levels score, and level reached. Participants evolved from one level to the next after having eliminated all the creatures in the level. Level completion time is the time the users took to complete the level n°2 (i.e., level reached by all participants). The number of errors are the points the user had lost when he collided with a creature (i.e., one point was lost for every collision with a creature) during the whole session. The total levels score is the total score gained in all levels, and the level reached is the level the users reached at the end of the session.

3.2.3. Procedure. The experiment took place in a research laboratory in computer sciences. Once participant had filled in the pretask questionnaire (personal details), the experimenter introduced and gave the participant instructions about the experiment. The first one was an orally guided training session of about 5 minutes (the participants could ask for more or less training time if they felt more or less comfortable in the IVE). The second session was a regular session of 5 minutes. For each session, participants followed the instructions in a pseudo programming language written on a panel in the application. A questionnaire on UX completed the session. Each participant spent between 30 to 45 minutes in the experiment room.

3.2.4. Statistical Analyses. A Structural Equation Modelling (SEM) analysis was used to validate the hypothesized UXIVE Model. This statistical method has long been associated with the idea that a high sample size was necessary [29], recent studies show that the association between sample size and result is much more complex. For example, Wolf, Harrington,

Clark, and Miller (2013) indicate that the recommended minimum sample size may decrease if the number of components to be measured and the number of items per component is high (e.g., 8 items per component) [30]. Moreover, the reality on the field demonstrates the difficulty in obtaining the recommended minimum sample size. This gives rise to SEM studies with small samples [31]. According to these authors, our sample size (i.e., N = 152) and the complexity of the UXIVE Model (i.e., 10 components) are suitable for SEM analysis.

Scale scores of the UX questionnaire and usability measures (i.e., level completion time, the number of errors, the levels score, and the level reached) for all participants were both taken into account in the structural model designed on the IBM® SPSS® AMOS 24 software. To assess how well the model represented the data, four goodness-of-fit recommended indices were evaluated in a structural model: Comparative Fit Index (CFI), Normed Fit Index (NFI), Root Mean Square Error of Approximation (RMSEA), and the ratio Chi-square and the degree of freedom. The recommended fit indices of these analyses are presented in Table 1.

3.3. Results: From a Hypothesized UXIVE Model to a Modified UXIVE Model

Structural Model of the Hypothesized UXIVE Model. The structural model analysis—based on a SEM analysis—should reveal significance and fit of the components relations with the data collected. The test from the structural model (Figure 3) revealed three statistically significant relations and nine nonsignificant relations. We rejected these nine relations (Table 2).

TABLE 2: Evaluation of the structural model with supported and rejected paths estimations.

Hypothesis	From	To	Path estimation	Test Result
1	Presence	Flow	0.641	Reject
1	Flow	Presence	0.651	Reject
1	Flow	Experience consequence	-0.215	Reject
1	Experience consequence	Flow	-0.193	Reject
2	Presence	Engagement	0.860	Reject
2	Engagement	Presence	1.627**	Support
2	Presence	Immersion	9.368	Reject
2	Immersion	Presence	-1.279	Reject
3	Flow	Usability	0.067	Reject
3	Flow	Emotion	0.962***	Support
3	Skill	Flow	0.078	Reject
4	Experience consequence	Judgement	-0.236*	Support
4	Experience consequence	Technology adoption	-0.381***	Support

*P<0.05; **P<0.01; ***P<0.001.

TABLE 3: Evaluation of the modified UXIVE Model.

H	From	To	Estimate	S.E.
		Previous relations		
1	Flow	Presence	.168*	.066
1	Experience consequence	Flow	-.098*	.046
2	Engagement	Presence	.365***	.082
3	Skill	Flow	.190*	.093
3	Flow	Emotion	1.427***	.298
4	Experience consequence	Technology adoption	-.158**	.054
4	Experience consequence	Judgement	-.092*	.044
		Added relations		
	Skill	Experience consequence	-.694***	.208
	Skill	Usability	.328***	.078
	Experience consequence	Emotion	-.283***	.061
	Engagement	Immersion	.924***	.154
	Engagement	Technology adoption	.147*	.074
	Flow	Technology adoption	.288*	.128
	Presence	Emotion	.791***	.237
	Presence	Judgement	1.128***	.293
	Usability	Technology adoption	.430***	.130

H: hypothesis; S.E.: Standard Error; *p < 0.05; **p < 0.01; ***p < 0.001.

Furthermore, the model fit according to the SEM fit indices indicated that CFI is 0.539, NFI is 0.390, and RMSEA is 0.086 which also indicate poor fit of our hypothesized UXIVE Model. However, χ^2/df falls into the acceptable range (i.e., 2.098). Indeed, Kline (1998) suggested that there should be a minimum of four indices that are acceptable and compatible with the model fit, we only have one acceptable index fit for this tested structural model [32]. The hypothesized UXIVE Model is then poorly acceptable.

Modified UXIVE Model. To improve the structural model of the hypothesized UXIVE Model, a covariance analysis was conducted. The analysis revealed 32 hypothesized covariances within which 15 statistically significant covariances matched with the tested structural model (i.e., the statistically significant relations from the tested structural model were preserved). According to the covariance analysis, nine hypothesized new relations were added to the conceptual model and six relations were dropped. All the 15 relations of the modified UXIVE Model were statistically significant (*Table 3*).

So, in the modified UXIVE Model (*Figure 4*), the hypothesis 4 is fully validated, and the hypotheses 1, 2, and 3 are partially validated.

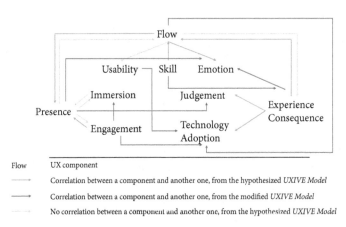

FIGURE 4: The modified UXIVE Model.

4. Discussion

This present research set out to integrate the fragmented theories and research on UX into a unified UX in IVE model named *UXIVE Model*. We analyzed our *UXIVE Model* and questioned the relationships between UX components.

Our first hypothesis stating that a low experience consequence and a high sense of presence greatly enhance the state of flow which influences back the two components is partially validated in the modified model. The results rather show influence of experience consequence on flow and influence of the latter on presence. According to several studies there is indeed a correlation between presence and flow and this relationship is of great interest for game fields (e.g., [9, 10, 33]) due to the immersive experience provided by the two components. However, no known studies focused on the relationship between experience consequence and flow.

Furthermore, the modified model revealed a significant path estimation from flow to technology adoption and from experience consequence to emotion. Studies show interest in the relationship between flow and technology adoption (e.g., [34, 35]) in online games or e-learning fields; studies in this area wish to predict user technology acceptance by measuring the flow. Experience consequences such as motion sickness are known to be affected by emotional factors such as fear, anxiety, and nervousness [36].

Our second hypothesis stating that the sense of presence enhances the degree of engagement and the feeling of immersion, and the same way the two components enhance presence, is partially validated in our modified model. The results rather show influence of engagement on both presence and immersion and no correlation between presence and immersion contrary to other studies (e.g., [5, 10, 37]). In addition, the modified model shows correlation between engagement and technology adoption, presence and emotion, and presence and judgement. The relationship between presence and engagement is indeed well known and studied in several works (i.e., [12, 37–39]), other studies in the game field investigated engagement as being the first state of immersion (i.e., [40, 41]), and more studies in the education field and technology adoption issues investigated engagement through technology adoption (i.e., [42, 43]). Emotional reactions

and presence are related according to studies in virtual environment and game fields (i.e., [44, 45]).

Our third hypothesis stating that the perceived skills influence the state of flow which in turn influences the perceived usability and the emotion is again partially validated in our modified model. The results rather show skill influence on flow which in turn influences emotion. As shown by [46], flow is highly correlated with the user's emotions and just as [47]; he relates flow and skill in their studies.

The modified model revealed a significant correlation between usability and technology adoption, skill and experience consequence, and skill and usability. Perceived usability as enhancing technology adoption is indeed confirmed by other studies (i.e., [10, 48]). Several other studies confirmed that usability perception depends on user skill (i.e., [5, 49]), whereas no studies are known that report on the effects of perceived skill on experience consequence.

Our fourth hypothesis stating that the experience consequence influences the overall judgement and the propensity of adopting the VE technology is validated in the modified model. These findings are in line with Mahlke's model [11] and specify that the judgement is a moderator between the experience consequence and the technology adoption.

Finally, this study revealed new UX components relationships to investigate. Indeed, the modified model states that flow and engagement are the two components influencing presence. Experience consequence and skill are the two components influencing flow. Presence, flow, and experience consequence are the three components influencing emotion. Engagement is the unique component influencing immersion. Skill is the unique component influencing experience consequence and usability. Presence and experience consequence are the two components influencing judgement. Flow, experience consequence, engagement, and usability are the four components influencing technology adoption.

5. Conclusion

This paper examines new relationships among UX components in an IVE framework and confirms others through two steps. First, a review of UX models led us to propose the hypothesized *UXIVE Model*. Second, we assessed the whole theoretical structure with analyses based on SEM and correlations. Results do not allow us to validate hypothesized *UXIVE Model* but allowed us to propose a modified *UXIVE Model* validated in the field of edutainment.

The most significant limitation of this study is the sample size, even if this sample is sufficient according to [30, 31]. To resolve this limitation, the experimental protocol could be pursued in the same conditions to gather a larger participation rate. Another solution to gather a larger participation rate would be to conduct an online experimental protocol. Tools such as "webvr" websites (see, for example, webvr.info) allow the user to experience virtual reality in his browser with any type of virtual reality device. Online experiments usually gather many users (e.g., 1000). Indeed, the SEM analysis recommend that the more variables are included in an SEM analysis; the more participants are needed to guarantee the stability of the results. In addition, more experiments are needed to corroborate the findings in this study as some relationships revealed by the study are relatively new and have not been investigated in previous studies.

The second limitation of this study is the sample profile. 48% of the participants share the same characteristics (e.g., age, sex, studies or work area, and experience with 3D technologies). Although, the target population of virtual edutainment environment is young, it could be interesting to apply these findings to other population because virtual reality devices are more and more reaching every type of profile. This limitation is directly linked to the third limitation which involves the device and content types.

The third limitation of this study is that other types of immersive virtual devices and other types of content are excluded. Indeed, the experiment is conducted with a Head Mounted Display (HMD) with an edutainment application. So, our modified *UXIVE Model* is only valid for *Think and Shoot* on HMD. First, this model should be validated for other immersive edutainment applications such as REARTH [50]). Second, this framework could be extended to different fields such as therapeutic, industrial, or collaborative applications. Third, the UXIVE Model can be experienced through different types of devices such as 6 axes virtual simulators, 6 walls CAVEs, and Z-spaces. Indeed, using our model in other studies from several fields and with different immersive virtual technologies may contribute to generalize our modified *UXIVE Model*.

Acknowledgments

The authors acknowledge Laval Agglomération and the Mayenne Department for their financial support and the participants who took time to engage and provide feedback on this project.

References

[1] D. Hatfield and D. W. Shaffer, "Press play: designing an epistemic game engine for journalism," in *Proceedings of the 7th International Conference of the Learning Sciences (ICLS '06)*, pp. 236–242, July 2006.

[2] N. K. Boots and J. Strobel, "Equipping the designers of the future: Best practices of epistemic video game design," *Games and Culture*, vol. 9, no. 3, pp. 167–181, 2004.

[3] G. Loup, A. Serna, S. Iksal, and S. George, "Immersion and persistence: improving learners engagement in authentic learning situations," in *Adaptive and Adaptable Learning, EC-TEL 2016*, K. Verbert, M. Sharples, and M. Klobučar, Eds., vol. 9891 of *Lecture Notes in Computer Science*, p. 9891, Springer, Cham, 2016.

[4] K. Tcha-Tokey, E. Loup-Escande, O. Christmann, and S. Richir, "Effects on user experience in an edutainment virtual environment: comparison between CAVE and HMD," in *Proceedings of the 35th Annual Conference of the European Association of Cognitive Ergonomics (ECCE '17)*, pp. 1–8, September 2017.

[5] A. E. Blandford, R. Butterworth, and P. Curzon, "PUMA Footprints: linking theory and craft skill in usability evaluation," in *Proceedings of the Human-Computer Interaction (INTERACT '01)*, M. Hirose, Ed., pp. 577–584, 2001.

[6] S. Nichols, C. Haldane, and J. R. Wilson, "Measurement of presence and its consequences in virtual environments," *International Journal of Human-Computer Studies*, vol. 52, no. 3, pp. 471–491, 2000.

[7] T. Schubert, F. Friedmann, and H. Regenbrecht, "The experience of presence: factor analytic insights," *Presence: Teleoperators and Virtual Environments*, vol. 10, no. 3, pp. 266–281, 2001.

[8] C. Dede, "Immersive interfaces for engagement and learning," *Science*, vol. 323, no. 5910, pp. 66–69, 2009.

[9] L.-K. Cheng, M.-H. Chieng, and W.-H. Chieng, "Measuring virtual experience in a three-dimensional virtual reality interactive simulator environment: A structural equation modeling approach," *Virtual Reality*, vol. 18, no. 3, pp. 173–188, 2014.

[10] D.-H. Shin, F. Biocca, and H. Choo, "Exploring the user experience of three-dimensional virtual learning environments," *Behaviour & Information Technology*, vol. 32, no. 2, pp. 203–214, 2013.

[11] S. Mahlke, "User Experience of Interaction with Technical Systems.Theories, Methods, Empirical Results, and Their Application to the Design of Interactive Systems," Tech. Rep., VDM Verlag, Saarbrücken, Germany, 2008.

[12] J. J. W. Lin and D. E. Parker, "User experience modeling and enhancement for virtual environments that employ wide-field displays," in *Digital Human Modeling, ICDHM 2007*, V. G. Duffy, Ed., vol. 4561 of *Lecture Notes in Computer Science*, Springer, Berlin, Heidelberg, 2007.

[13] M. Pereira de Aguiar, B. Winn, M. Cezarotto, A. L. Battaiola, and P. Varella Gomes, "Educational digital games: a theoretical framework about design models, learning theories and user experience," in *Design, User Experience, and Usability: Theory and Practice. DUXU 2018*, A. Marcus and W. Wang, Eds., vol. 10918 of *Lecture Notes in Computer Science*, Springer, 2018.

[14] C. Rico-Olarte, D. M. López, and S. Kepplinger, "Towards a conceptual framework for the objective evaluation of user experience," in *Design, User Experience, and Usability: Theory and Practice. DUXU 2018*, A. Marcus and W. Wang, Eds., vol. 10918 of *Lecture Notes in Computer Science*, Springer, 2018.

[15] M. Csikszentmihalyi, "Beyond boredom and anxiety," Jossey-Bass, 1975.

[16] J. S. Pillai, C. Schmidt, and S. Richir, "Achieving presence through evoked reality, 'Consciousness Research," *Frontiers in Psychology*, vol. 4, no. 86, 2013.

[17] M. Pallot, R. Eynard, B. Poussard, O. Christmann, and S. Richir,

"Augmented sport: exploring collective user experience," in *The ACM Proceedings of Virtual Reality International Conference*, 2013.

[18] R. Eynard, M. Pallot, O. Christmann, and S. Richir, "Impact of Verbal Communication on User Experience in 3D Immersive Virtual Environments," in *Proceedings of the 21st ICE/IEEE International Technology Management Conference*, Belfast, Ireland, 2015.

[19] T. Zhou and Y. Lu, "Examining mobile instant messaging user loyalty from the perspectives of network externalities and flow experience," *Computers in Human Behavior*, vol. 27, no. 2, pp. 883–889, 2011.

[20] D. A. Bowman and R. P. McMahan, "Virtual reality: how much immersion is enough?" *The Computer Journal*, vol. 40, no. 7, pp. 36–43, 2007.

[21] B. G. Witmer and M. J. Singer, "Measuring presence in virtual environments: a presence questionnaire," *Presence: Teleoperators and Virtual Environments*, vol. 7, no. 3, pp. 225–240, 1998.

[22] E. Geslin, S. Bouchard, and S. Richir, "Gamers' versus non-gamers' emotional response in virtual reality," *Journal of CyberTherapy and Rehabilitation*, vol. 4, no. 4, 2011.

[23] J. Heutte, F. Fenouillet, C. Martin-Krumm, I. Boniwell, and M. Csikszentmihalyi, "Proposal for a conceptual evolution of the flow in education (EduFlow) model," in *Proceedings of the 8th European Conference on Positive Psychology (ECPP '16)*, Angers, France, 2016.

[24] C. A. Murphy, D. Coover, and S. V. Owen, "Development and validation of the computer self-efficacy scale," *Educational and Psychological Measurement*, vol. 49, no. 4, pp. 893–899, 1989.

[25] R. Pekrun, T. Goetz, A. C. Frenzel, P. Barchfeld, and R. P. Perry, "Measuring emotions in students' learning and performance: the achievement emotions questionnaire (AEQ)," *Contemporary Educational Psychology*, vol. 36, no. 1, pp. 36–48, 2011.

[26] R. S. Kennedy, N. E. Lane, K. S. Berbaum, and M. G. Lilienthal, "Simulator sickness questionnaire: an enhanced method for quantifying simulator sickness," *The International Journal of Aviation Psychology*, vol. 3, no. 3, pp. 203–220, 1993.

[27] M. Hassenzahl, M. Burmester, and F. Koller, "AttrakDiff: Ein Fragebogen zur Messung wahrgenommener hedonischer und pragmatischer Qualität," in *Mensch & Computer*, G. Szwillus and J. Ziegler, Eds., vol. 57 of *Berichte des German Chapter of the ACM*, 2003.

[28] V. Venkatesh, M. G. Morris, G. B. Davis, and F. D. Davis, "User acceptance of information technology: toward a unified view," *MIS Quarterly: Management Information Systems*, vol. 27, no. 3, pp. 425–478, 2003.

[29] J. C. Nunnally, *Psychometric theory*, McGraw-Hill, New York, NY, USA, 1967.

[30] E. J. Wolf, K. M. Harrington, S. L. Clark, and M. W. Miller, "Sample size requirements for structural equation models: an evaluation of power, bias, and solution propriety," *Educational and Psychological Measurement*, vol. 73, no. 6, pp. 913–934, 2013.

[31] P. M. Bentler and K.-H. Yuan, "Structural equation modeling with small samples: Test statistics," *Multivariate Behavioral Research*, vol. 34, no. 2, pp. 181–197, 1999.

[32] R. B. Kline, *Principles and Practice of Structural Equation Modeling*, Guilford, New York, NY, USA, 1998.

[33] D. Weibel and B. Wissmath, "Immersion in computer games: the role of spatial presence and flow," *International Journal of Computer Games Technology*, vol. 2011, Article ID 282345, 14 pages, 2011.

[34] S.-H. Liu, H.-L. Liao, and J. A. Pratt, "Impact of media richness and flow on e-learning technology acceptance," *Computers & Education*, vol. 52, no. 3, pp. 599–607, 2009.

[35] C.-L. Hsu and H.-P. Lu, "Why do people play on-line games? An extended TAM with social influences and flow experience," *Information and Management*, vol. 41, no. 7, pp. 853–868, 2004.

[36] A. Uno, N. Takeda, A. Horii, Y. Sakata, A. Yamatodani, and T. Kubo, "Effects of amygdala or hippocampus lesion on hypergravity-induced motion sickness in rats," *Acta Oto-Laryngologica*, vol. 120, no. 7, pp. 860–865, 2000.

[37] A. McMahan, "Immersion, engagement and presence," in *The Video Game Theory Reader*, D. M. J. Wolf and B. Perron, Eds., pp. 67–86, 2003.

[38] S. Dow, M. Mehta, E. Harmon, B. MacIntyre, and M. Mateas, "Presence and engagement in an interactive drama," in *Proceedings of the 25th SIGCHI Conference on Human Factors in Computing Systems (CHI '07)*, pp. 1475–1484, May 2007.

[39] L. Jarmon, "Learning in virtual world environments: Social-presence, engagement, and pedagogy," *Encyclopedia of Distance and Online Learning*, pp. 1610–1619, 2009.

[40] E. Brown and P. Cairns, "A grounded investigation of game immersion," in *Proceedings of the ACM CHI'04 Extended Abstracts on Human Factors in Computing Systems*, pp. 1297–1300, 2004.

[41] J. H. Brockmyer, C. M. Fox, K. A. Curtiss, E. McBroom, K. M. Burkhart, and J. N. Pidruzny, "The development of the Game Engagement Questionnaire: a measure of engagement in video game-playing," *Journal of Experimental Social Psychology*, vol. 45, no. 4, pp. 624–634, 2009.

[42] A. Kai-ming and P. Enderwick, "A cognitive model on attitude towards technology adoption," *Journal of Managerial Psychology*, vol. 15, no. 4, pp. 266–282, 2000.

[43] M. Manuguerra and P. Petocz, "Promoting student engagement by integrating new technology into tertiary education: The role of the iPad," *Asian Social Science*, vol. 7, no. 11, pp. 61–65, 2011.

[44] D. Västfjäll, "The subjective sense of presence, emotion recognition, and experienced emotions in auditory virtual environments," *Cyberpsychology, Behavior, and Social Networking*, vol. 6, no. 2, pp. 181–188, 2003.

[45] N. Ravaja, T. Saari, M. Turpeinen, J. Laarni, M. Salminen, and M. Kivikangas, "Spatial presence and emotions during video game playing: does it matter with whom you play?" *Presence: Teleoperators and Virtual Environments*, vol. 15, no. 4, pp. 381–392, 2006.

[46] M. Csikszentmihalyi, *The Psychology of Optimal Experience*, Harper and Row, New York, NY, USA, 1990.

[47] D. L. Hoffman and T. P. Novak, "Flow online: lessons learned and future prospects," *Journal of Interactive Marketing*, vol. 23, no. 1, pp. 23–34, 2009.

[48] H. Holden and R. Rada, "Understanding the influence of perceived usability and technology self-efficacy on teachers' technology acceptance," *Journal of Research on Technology in Education*, vol. 43, no. 4, pp. 343–367, 2011.

[49] L. Faulkner and D. Wick, "Cross-user analysis: Benefits of skill level comparison in usability testing," *Interacting with Computers*, vol. 17, no. 6, pp. 773–786, 2005.

[50] F. Sauret, V. Emin-Martinez, G. Loup et al., "REARTH un exemple de Jeu Épistémique Numérique, de la conception à lexpérimentation," *in CETSIS 2017, Le Mans , France*, 2017.

10

How Influential are Mental Models on Interaction Performance? Exploring the Gap between Users' and Designers' Mental Models through a New Quantitative Method

Bingjun Xie, Jia Zhou, and Huilin Wang

Department of Industrial Engineering, Chongqing University, Chongqing 400044, China

Correspondence should be addressed to Jia Zhou; zhoujia07@gmail.com

Academic Editor: Hideyuki Nakanishi

The objective of this study is to investigate the effect of the gap between two different mental models on interaction performance through a quantitative way. To achieve that, an index called mental model similarity and a new method called path diagram to elicit mental models were introduced. There are two kinds of similarity: directionless similarity calculated from card sorting and directional similarity calculated from path diagram. An experiment was designed to test their influence. A total of 32 college students participated and their performance was recorded. Through mathematical analysis of the results, three findings were derived. Frist, the more complex the information structures, the lower the directional similarity. Second, directional similarity (rather than directionless similarity) had significant influence on user performance, indicating that it is more effective in eliciting mental models using path diagram than card sorting. Third, the relationship between information structures and user performance was partially mediated by directional similarity. Our findings provide practitioners with a new perspective of bridging the gap between users' and designers' mental models.

1. Introduction

Originating from psychology, mental models are applied to Human-Computer Interaction (HCI) to explain people's understanding about how computers work [1]. Information technology (IT) products are developed based on designers' mental models, but what designers believed to be easy to understand is not necessarily true for users. Users interact with IT products in a different perspective from designers. They form their own understanding and predict feedback of IT products [2]. Users whose mental models are different from those of designers encounter interaction difficulties, but certain users with wrong/incomplete mental models can also successfully use IT products [3]. Although actions (e.g., training) have been taken to reduce the gap between users' and designers' mental models, few studies examine whether and to what extent the gap is reduced.

To address the above problem, this study quantified the gap between mental models and investigated its impact on user performance. However, it is challenging to elicit and quantify the gap between mental models, because they are in the users' head and are not directly observable. Many researchers have explored mental models using IT products with a well-defined information structure (e.g., web pages and menus) that clearly reflects designers' mental models. Then, users' mental models of information structures can be elicited. Thus, the extent to which users' mental models differed from those of the designers can be quantified.

Traditional method for eliciting mental models of information structures was card sorting, but mental models elicited by card sorting cannot represent users' understanding of specific directional relationship between elements of information structures. This study proposed a new method, path diagram, to elicit mental models of information structures. The mental models elicited by path diagram can represent users' understanding of directional relationship between elements of information structures. To further quantify the gap between the mental models, this study introduced an index called mental model similarity. Two kinds of mental model similarity are distinguished: directionless similarity, calculated from the card sorting, mainly represents the directionless relationship between elements; directional similarity, calculated from the path diagram, mainly represents the directional relationship between elements. Therefore, two research questions were considered: (i) Which method is more effective in eliciting mental models of information structures? (ii) How influential are directional similarity and directionless similarity on interaction performance?

In this study, websites with three information structures (i.e., net, tree, and linear) were developed to elicit mental models through card sorting and path diagram. Then, a method to quantify the degree of match between users' and designers' mental models was proposed. Based on that, the impact of mental models on performance was analyzed.

2. Literature Review

2.1. Mental Models. The theory of mental models has obscure origins [4, 5], but the notion of mental models first appeared in a book written by the psychologist Craik. Craik [6] believed that a brain could translate an external process into a model of the world, which is "a small-scale model of external reality and of its own possible actions within the head." Since then, it has attracted much attention from researchers, particularly psychologists.

Forty years later, two researchers used the term "mental model." Norman stated that "in interacting with the environment, with others, and with the artifacts of technology, people form internal, mental models of themselves and of the things with which they are interacting. These models provide predictive and explanatory power for understanding the interaction" [3]; Johnson-Laird [7] believed that people could create mental models that were structural analogs of the world, and their ability to construct, manipulate, and evaluate mental models had a hidden strong influence on rational thought.

Subsequent research on mental models can be approximately divided into two branches. The first mainly focused on internal mental processes and cognitive phenomena within the long-standing field of psychology. Typical research interests included the role of mental models in comprehension [8, 9], reasoning [9, 10], and deduction [11]. The second branch stepped out of psychology and applied mental models to support better interaction between people and the external world. Typical research interests include the role of mental models in learning and training [12–15] and using computers and appliances [16–19].

Among the second branch of research, one noticeable trend is a surge in the application of mental models in Human-Computer Interaction (HCI). Norman [20] showed that the root cause of problems in using technology products was the gap between users' and designers' mental models. This highlights a new perspective for HCI, and workers have tried various ways to deliver a design that matches users' mental models [1, 21].

Originally used to explain team effectiveness, Team Mental Models (TMMs) refer to the extent to which team members shared organized understanding and mental representation of knowledge or beliefs relevant to the key content of the team's tasks [22, 23]. Mathieu et al. [24] proposed that team members' mental models consist of four parts: technology; job or task; team interaction; and other teammates' knowledge and attitudes.

Since mental models are within the head, they cannot be directly detected. People's mental models had to be indirectly inferred from observing and analyzing their elements. Many early researchers followed this focus, finding it challenging because mental models had the following five characteristics: (1) incompleteness: mental models are constrained by users' background, expertise, and so forth; (2) vague boundaries: they can be confused with similar/related operations and systems; (3) being unstable over time: they evolve as people forget and learn; (4) they contained aspects of superstitions [20]. (5) Tendency to parsimony: people tend to construct a limited model of the relevant parts of a system [21].

Despite these challenges, researchers have identified various techniques to elicit mental models. General techniques to elicit individuals' mental models and team members' shared mental models were summarized in three comprehensive review papers [25–27]. Specifically, in the field of HCI, techniques to elicit mental models have four major categories: (1) verbalization through interview, thinking aloud, laddering and so forth: verbalization is the most widely used elicitation technique [5]. However, people's verbalization was inconsistent and tended to evolve as they spoke [28, 29]. One solution to this problem is laddering, a modified interview technique, in which people were asked to identify multiple aspects of a problem and explore the relationship between their answers [30]. (2) Rating: people were asked to rate using questionnaires [30, 31], but this technique is not frequently used because relatively few questionnaires are well established. (3) Drawing sketches: people were asked to visually draw how they thought of a concept or the pathways from the start to a specific point in a system [18, 32]. (4) Card sorting: this technique is widely used in eliciting mental models of hierarchical systems [18, 33]. In most cases, the method is effective in eliciting mental models. This is especially true when dealing with information structures without considering the directional relationship. However, card sorting is not adequate for eliciting complete mental models if we consider the directional relationship of information structures.

2.2. Relation between Information Structures and Mental Model Similarity. Mental models are nowadays widely applied to analyze user performance on web pages, which are the best carrier of information structures. Many aspects of human interaction with hierarchical systems involve complex processes; thus, people who interact with hierarchical systems must have some type of mental models. Since mental models represent users' understanding about a system including web pages, we argue that simplicity of information structures has an impact on mental model similarity. Previous studies have indicated that the card sorting is widely used in eliciting mental models of hierarchical systems [18, 33]. Based on this, we proposed Hypothesis (H1a).

(H1a) The more complex the information structures, the lower the directionless similarity.

The directional similarity is calculated from path diagram, which is used to elicit mental models of information structures with directional relationship. We add more details (e.g., directional relationship) to mental models. Based on this, we proposed Hypothesis (H1b).

(H1b) The more complex the information structures, the lower the directional similarity.

2.3. Mental Models and User Performance.

Many previous studies have shown that mental models are correlated with user performance. On the one hand, mental models have a positive effect on user performance. Ziefle and Bay [33] pointed out that the better the mental models of navigations menus, the better the performance using the devices. Young [34] thought that mental models could explain user performance with the systems with which they interact. Dimitroff [35] found that students with more complete mental models made significantly fewer errors when they used the University of Michigan's website. Sasse [36] noted the significant effects of mental models on user performance using Excel. Slone [37] found that users' mental models affected their performance on websites. Brandt and Uden [38] pointed out that novices without strong mental models for information retrieval could not gather information successfully.

Numerous studies have also shown the relationship between TMMs and team performance. For example, Mathieu et al. [24] considered shared mental models as two categories: task and team, finding that both team-based and task-based mental models related positively to subsequent team process and performance. Mathieu et al. [39] demonstrated in a PC-based flight simulator that both task and team models had an impact on performance; the team process was supported by shared mental models and task-work mental model similarity, but not by teamwork mental model similarity, which was significantly related to both team processes and team performance.

On the other hand, workers have found that mental models had either an adverse effect or no significant effect on user performance. Halasz and Moran [40] and Borgman [41] found that, whether users formed a mental model of a system or not, they performed no differently on routine, simple tasks. Norman [3] found that users with wrong/incomplete mental models could use technology products successfully. Payne [42] noted that even wrong mental models did not necessarily result in the bad usage of devices. Schmettow and Sommer [43] found that the degree of match between the mental model and website structure had no effect on users' browsing performance. As for TMMs, Webber et al. [44] found that team members sharing a common mental model with poor quality did not likely perform well.

It is obvious that the research consequences were contradictory. It seems that researchers cannot get the unified cognition of the effects of mental models on user performance. One possible reason is that most researchers do their studies without considering mental model similarity between users and designers. It is necessary for us to investigate mental models' effects on interaction performance involving the mental model similarity. The only study of mental model similarity on interaction performance is seen in Schmettow and Sommer [43]. They found that mental model similarity had no effect on interaction performance. However, the way they elicited mental models was card sorting and they did not consider the directional relationship of information structures. In this paper, we considered more details such as directional relationship to elicit a mental model of information structure and get the directional similarity from path diagram and the directionless similarity from card sorting, which may get different results from what Schmettow and Sommer [43] found. Considering that there are more positive effects than adverse effects in the existing studies, in this paper, we are partial to supporting the positive effects. Therefore, we proposed Hypothesis (H2a) and Hypothesis (H2b).

(H2a) Directional similarity predicts the task completion time; the higher the directional similarity, the less the task completion time.

(H2b) Directional similarity predicts the number of clicks; the higher the directional similarity, the less the click times.

The effects of information structures on user performance have been widely investigated: since mental models are closely related to users' behavior using various devices, a good mental model of information structure will likely enhance user performance. However, there are many other factors influencing user performance besides mental models, for example, users' age and gender. Ziefle and Bay [33] pointed out that younger users were more effective in using a cell phone menu than the older users. Mathieu et al. [24] found that team processes fully mediated the relationship between team mental models and team effectiveness. Mathieu et al. [39] found that team performance was partially mediated by teammates' mental models. Based on these findings, we have assumed that mental model similarity mediated the relationship between information structures and user performance, which is Hypothesis (H3a) and Hypothesis (H3b) (see Figure 1).

(H3a) Directionless similarity will mediate the relationship between information structures and user performance.

(H3b) Directional similarity will mediate the relationship between information structures and user performance.

2.4. Quantitative Methods of Mental Model Similarity.

Elicited mental models are widely used in two ways. First, the difference between elicited mental models can be qualitatively and quantitatively compared. One common quantitative method is to compare the depth and width of the elicited structures. Users use an interface with a well-defined information structure such as phone menus and web pages.

Another quantitative method is to calculate the team mental model (TMM) similarity score, which indicates the percentage of team members' shared, organized understanding and mental representation of knowledge or beliefs relevant to the key content of the team's task [22, 23].

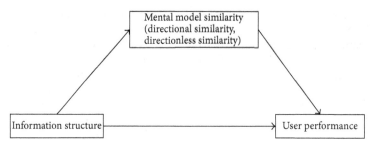

FIGURE 1: The mediation effect of mental model similarity in the relation between information structure and user performance.

Specifically, team members usually rated the relatedness of pairs of statements describing team interaction processes and characteristics of team members on the Likert scale. The response could be analyzed using multidimensional techniques (e.g., the Pathfinder technique) to calculate the similarity score [26, 45, 46].

However, none of these methods can accurately elicit mental models of information structures with directional relationship; also these methods cannot quantitatively calculate the degree of similarity or dissimilarity of the mental models between users and designers of systems. Previous studies [43] have shown that the widely used method of eliciting mental models of hierarchical systems is card sorting, but it is inadequate to elicit mental models without considering the directional relationship of information structures. Also, the previous studies did not introduce a suitable method to quantify the mental model similarity. Wu and Liu [47] proposed a new computational modeling approach, which was composed of a simulation model of a queuing network architecture and a set of mathematical equations implemented in the simulation model to quantify mental workload, to model the mental workload in drive and driving performance. However, the approach proposed was not the quantitative method for calculating the mental model similarity. It was applied to analyze the mental workload in driver information system. Thus, here, we elicit mental models through card sorting and path diagram. Then, we conducted a new method to quantify the degree of mental model similarity.

3. Methodology

3.1. Equipment and Materials. A notebook computer with a touch screen (ThinkPad YogaS1) was used to present web pages, and a whiteboard was used to draw path diagrams. A camera (Sony, HDR-PJ610E) was used to record participants' results of card sorting and drawing the path diagrams. A Morae Recorder was used for counting task completion time and the number of clicks and was also used to present the task specification for the participants. Web pages with different information structures were developed. The web pages were first considered about the navigation structures, which were net, tree, and linear. The depth of tree and net structure was three levels, which was seen common in daily web pages. The width of the bottom level of tree and net structure was nine items, which was also seen in common web pages.

To avoid the effects of familiar knowledge, topics about ancient inventions, ancient books, and ancient historical

TABLE 1: Experience of using technology products of participants.

	Mean	SD
Laptop	0.75	1.14
Tablets	4.95	2.80
Smart phones	4.58	3.42

characters of different Chinese dynasties, which were not widely known, were presented in web pages as the content. There were totally nine different Chinese dynasties and each information structure was made of three different Chinese dynasties. Ancient inventions, ancient books, and ancient historical characters were corresponding to their own dynasties. Two pretests were carried out by two college students, and the interaction forms and content layout were adjusted according to the results. The memory capacity that influences user performance [33] was tested by a KJ-I spatial location memory span tester. Spatial ability was tested through the paper folding test [48]. The original paper folding test was translated into Chinese.

3.2. Participants. A total of 32 students from Chongqing University were recruited. The age of the participants ranged from 21 to 26 years (mean = 23.13, SD = 1.7). The gender was balanced. The experience of using laptops, tablets, and smartphones (see Table 1) was investigated; the results indicated that handheld devices (i.e., smartphones and tablets) were used intensively.

3.3. Task. All participants completed tasks in three different web pages with different information structures: net, tree, and linear. To avoid learning effects and make participants get a full understanding of the information structures of web pages, each participant completed eight tasks in a web page. The order of web pages in which participants completed the tasks is random.

The tasks are searching tasks. Participants found a target and read its content. The target is an item hidden in web pages, which is not widely known for participants. To check whether they read the content carefully, a single-choice test was conducted. Participants wrote down answers on a piece of paper. The test has two questions: one is about what dynasty the target belonged to, and the other one was about which the target is about. Taking "Huang dao you yi" as an example, the task is "Please find "Huang dao you yi" and read its description and then answer the following two questions:

Q1: which dynasty "Huang dao you yi" belongs to? Q2: what "Huang dao you yi" is about?"

3.4. Dependent Variables. The two dependent variables were task completion time and the number of clicks. Task completion time was the average of eight tasks' completion time under each information structure and the number of clicks was the average of the click times to complete all of the eight tasks. They were both measured by the Morae Recorder; only when the participant obtained the correct answers for both questions were the missions completed.

3.5. Independent Variable. The independent variables were the directionless similarity and directional similarity. It is a new quantitative measure proposed here (see Section 3.7), the directionless similarity was calculated from card sorting, and the directional similarity was calculated from path diagram. The mental model similarity was computed for each information structure.

Demographic variables included age, experience of using technology product, spatial ability, and memory capacity. A questionnaire was used to collect basic information about experience of using technology product

The mental model similarity was a between-subject variable, while the information structure was a within-subject variable. That is, each participant used three prototypes. In an effort to avoid learning effects, the order of using prototypes was random.

3.6. Procedure. The experiment took each participant about one hour to complete. It consisted of four tests: a questionnaire test, a memory test, a paper folding test, and a card sorting test.

First, each participant began the experiment by filling out a consent form and a general questionnaire about his/her demographic information and using experience with technology products.

Secondly, a memory test was conducted using the KJ-I spatial position memory span tester. After completing the memory test, the test scores were recorded on paper and were not disclosed to the participants.

Thirdly, a paper folding test was conducted to test the spatial ability of the participants. This test is divided into two parts. The time limit of each part was three minutes to avoid participants losing their patience. The participants needed to find the correct answer independently. The final score of the test is the correct number minus the incorrect number on the test paper. The higher the score, the better the spatial memory ability.

Fourthly, a brief introduction and practice about the experiment were given to each participant. Finally, participants completed tasks on each web page and then went on with the card sorting. The cards were the titles of each node in the information structures. Then, the participants were required to draw a path structure of the experimental web page navigation with a whiteboard stroke. During the whole process, participants were left alone, and questions related to the path were not answered in a relevant way, which aimed at avoiding the subjective impacts of the experimental designer.

At the end, the experimenter conducted a five-minute exploratory interview with the participants to understand their thoughts and feelings about using the three web pages. The questions in the interview included "Q1: Please score the three web pages in this experiment considering information searching, ease of use and user experience. Q2: Please sequence the three web pages according to your experience."

3.7. Quantifying Mental Model Similarity. The method proposed to quantify mental model similarity consists of two parts: one is the method which can be used to elicit mental models of information structures with directional relationship, and the other one is the mathematical equations which can be used to calculate the mental model similarity.

The first part is the method of eliciting mental models. In order to quantify mental model similarity, a method which can be used to elicit mental models with more details such as directional relationship has to be used. Such a method should represent the understanding of elements and directional relationship of a hierarchical system, which are the key factors in eliciting mental model of a hierarchical system. The literature provides several methods to elicit mental models, such as card sorting, which is widely used in eliciting mental models of hierarchical systems [18, 33]. However, card sorting cannot elicit complete mental models of hierarchical systems, particularly the directional aspects of hierarchies.

A new method is needed to reflect the directional information of mental models of hierarchy structures. Web navigation is similar to the real-world navigation. In real-world navigation, people usually take three strategies to find a destination. They remember properties of landmarks such as shape and structure (i.e., landmark knowledge) [49, 50], or the sequential order of landmarks encountered and directional relationship between these landmarks (i.e., route knowledge) [51], or an overview of the environment like a map showing spatial relationships between routes and landmarks (i.e., survey knowledge) [52] to find a destination. This knowledge is also involved in web navigation. Landmark knowledge is mainly represented through card sorting. Inspired by route knowledge, we proposed the path diagram to elicit mental models of hierarchical systems with more details (e.g., directional relationship)

The second part is about quantifying the mental model similarity. The limited research in quantifying mental model similarity was reported by Sinreich et al. [53]. They introduced process chart into eliciting mental models of Emergency Department Management and quantified similarity through four formulae. However, the method was not applied to analyze the mental models of information structures.

The method of quantifying the degree of mental model similarity aims to reflect the extent to users' understanding of the system: it can present causality and logic. In addition, this method should be easy to understand, so that it can be mastered by nonprofessional persons. Thus, in this study, we extended the work of Sinreich et al. [53] as our proposed quantitative method. We calculated mental model similarity in two ways: calculating the directionless similarity from card sorting and calculating the directional similarity from path diagram.

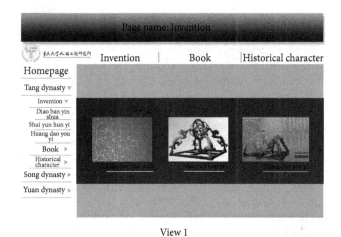

View 1

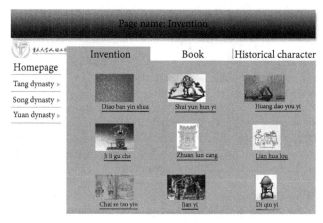

View 2

FIGURE 2: Two views of web page interfaces in this experiment.

The first component represents the elements (nodes) of the different content, for example, "Tang dynasty," "Invention," "Book," and "Historical character" in Figure 2. The directionless similarity measure a^{ij} can be obtained using

$$a^{ij} = \frac{e^{ij}}{e^{ij} + b^{ij} + b^{ji}}, \tag{1}$$

where e^{ij} denotes the number of identical elements in card sortings i and j and b^{ij} denotes the number of elements that exist in i that do not exist in j (see that $b^{ij} = b^{ji}$). It is clear that $0 \ll a^{ij} \ll 1$. In the case that both card sortings are identical in terms of their elements (not necessarily their relationships); then we have $a^{ij} = 1$ while $a^{ij} = 0$ if no common elements exist, and by definition $a^{ij} = a^{ji}$.

The second component represents the relationship between elements (arcs) in the path diagram. A relationship is defined by the elements it connects (there may be more than one connection between elements) and by the direction of the connecting arc, for example, the arcs that connect elements "Tang dynasty-Invention," "Invention-Book," and "Invention-Diao ban yin shua" in path diagram ① in Figure 4. The first step in calculating the directional similarity is to obtain the adjacency matrices. The element of adjacency matrix was the numbers of directed segment between two nodes (e.g., if there were one directed segment from "Tang dynasty" to "Invention," the element is 1).

Based on the adjacency matrix, the sum of all the common arcs c^{ij} and the sum of all exclusive arcs d^{ij} between any two path diagrams i and j can be calculated, as shown in (2) and (3), respectively. Finally, the directional similarity measure r^{ij} can be obtained using (4).

$$c^{ij} = \sum_k \sum_l \min\left\{h_{kl}^i, h_{kl}^j\right\} \tag{2}$$

$$d^{ij} = \sum_k \sum_l \left|h_{kl}^i - h_{kl}^j\right| \tag{3}$$

$$r^{ij} = \frac{c^{ij}}{c^{ij} + d^{ij}}. \tag{4}$$

It is clear that $0 \ll r^{ij} \ll 1$. In the case that both path diagrams are identical in terms of their relationship (arcs), then we have $r^{ij} = 1$ while $r^{ij} = 0$ if no common relationship exists between the two path diagrams. By definition $r^{ij} = r^{ji}$.

These formulae, adapted from Sinreich et al. [53], are validated and used to calculate the similarity between process charts. In this study, we used them to analyze hierarchies and extended their work by adding directions. To analyze directional relationship, an adjacency matrix was used to indicate relationship according to the graph theory. Then, relationship similarity of hierarchical systems was calculated by using formulas (2), (3), and (4).

The process of calculating the mental model similarity can be seen in Figure 3.

In order to illustrate the calculation procedure of the similarity measure, the following example is given (see Figure 4).

From Figure 4, the following values are obtained: $e^{ij} = 13$ and $b^{ij} = b^{ji} = 0$.

Using these values in (1) results in the directionless similarity measure of $a^{ij} = 1$. Using the graph theory, the adjacency matrix h^i can be calculated as follows:

$$H^1 = \begin{bmatrix} 0 & 1 & 1 & 1 & 0 & 0 & 0 & 0 & 0 & 0 & 0 & 0 & 0 \\ 1 & 0 & 1 & 1 & 1 & 1 & 1 & 0 & 0 & 0 & 0 & 0 & 0 \\ 1 & 1 & 0 & 1 & 0 & 0 & 0 & 1 & 1 & 1 & 0 & 0 & 0 \\ 1 & 1 & 1 & 0 & 0 & 0 & 0 & 0 & 0 & 0 & 1 & 1 & 1 \\ 0 & 1 & 1 & 1 & 0 & 1 & 1 & 0 & 0 & 0 & 0 & 0 & 0 \\ 0 & 1 & 1 & 1 & 1 & 0 & 1 & 0 & 0 & 0 & 0 & 0 & 0 \\ 0 & 1 & 1 & 1 & 1 & 1 & 0 & 0 & 0 & 0 & 0 & 0 & 0 \\ 0 & 1 & 1 & 1 & 0 & 0 & 0 & 0 & 1 & 1 & 0 & 0 & 0 \\ 0 & 1 & 1 & 1 & 0 & 0 & 0 & 1 & 0 & 1 & 0 & 0 & 0 \\ 0 & 1 & 1 & 1 & 0 & 0 & 0 & 1 & 1 & 0 & 0 & 0 & 0 \\ 0 & 1 & 1 & 1 & 0 & 0 & 0 & 0 & 0 & 0 & 0 & 1 & 1 \\ 0 & 1 & 1 & 1 & 0 & 0 & 0 & 0 & 0 & 0 & 1 & 0 & 1 \\ 0 & 1 & 1 & 1 & 0 & 0 & 0 & 0 & 0 & 0 & 1 & 1 & 0 \end{bmatrix}$$

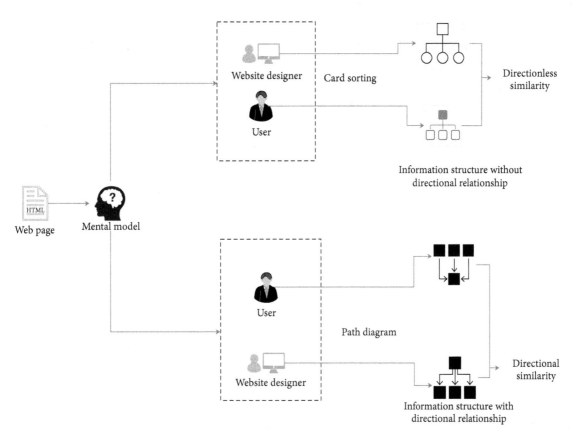

FIGURE 3: The process of calculating mental model similarity.

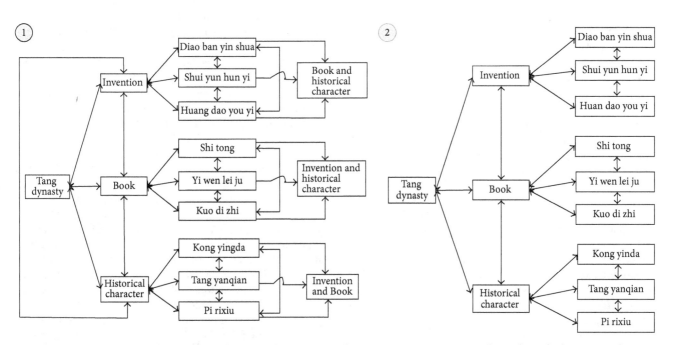

FIGURE 4: An example of two different path diagrams (the segment with one arrow means one-way relationship, which means node A can reach node B while node B cannot reach node A; the segment with two arrows means that node A and node B can reach each other).

$$H^2 = \begin{bmatrix} 0 & 1 & 1 & 1 & 0 & 0 & 0 & 0 & 0 & 0 & 0 & 0 & 0 \\ 1 & 0 & 0 & 0 & 1 & 1 & 1 & 0 & 0 & 0 & 0 & 0 & 0 \\ 1 & 0 & 0 & 0 & 0 & 0 & 0 & 1 & 1 & 1 & 0 & 0 & 0 \\ 1 & 0 & 0 & 0 & 0 & 0 & 0 & 0 & 0 & 0 & 1 & 1 & 1 \\ 0 & 1 & 0 & 0 & 0 & 0 & 0 & 0 & 0 & 0 & 0 & 0 & 0 \\ 0 & 1 & 0 & 0 & 0 & 0 & 0 & 0 & 0 & 0 & 0 & 0 & 0 \\ 0 & 1 & 0 & 0 & 0 & 0 & 0 & 0 & 0 & 0 & 0 & 0 & 0 \\ 0 & 0 & 1 & 0 & 0 & 0 & 0 & 0 & 0 & 0 & 0 & 0 & 0 \\ 0 & 0 & 1 & 0 & 0 & 0 & 0 & 0 & 0 & 0 & 0 & 0 & 0 \\ 0 & 0 & 1 & 0 & 0 & 0 & 0 & 0 & 0 & 0 & 0 & 0 & 0 \\ 0 & 0 & 0 & 1 & 0 & 0 & 0 & 0 & 0 & 0 & 0 & 0 & 0 \\ 0 & 0 & 0 & 1 & 0 & 0 & 0 & 0 & 0 & 0 & 0 & 0 & 0 \\ 0 & 0 & 0 & 1 & 0 & 0 & 0 & 0 & 0 & 0 & 0 & 0 & 0 \end{bmatrix}.$$

$$(5)$$

Using these values with (2) and (3) the common and exclusive path vector can be calculated as follows:

$$c^{12} = 3 + 4 + 4 + 4 + 9 = 24$$

$$d^{12} = 0 + 2 + 2 + 2 + 36 = 42. \tag{6}$$

Based on these values and (4), the directional similarity measure can be calculated as follows:

$$r^{12} = \frac{24}{24 + 42} = \frac{4}{11} \cong 0.36. \tag{7}$$

The directionless similarity is 1 while the directional similarity is 0.36. The calculation results show that the mental model similarity was totally different when we considered the directional relationship of information structures.

4. Results and Discussion

The following sections first examine the effects of the information structures on mental model similarity and then examine the relationship between mental model similarity and user performance. Finally, we examine whether the mediation effect was found.

4.1. The Influence of Information Structures on Mental Model Similarity. Simplicity/complexity generally refers to the level of intricacy or detail in a stimulus [54, 55]. Specifically, the detail could be the number of closed figures, open figures, letters, horizontal lines, vertical lines, and so forth [54].

Complexity of web pages with different information structures consists of two high-level notions: content complexity which is mainly measured through the number and types of objects to load a web page and service complexity which is mainly measured through "the number and contributions of the various servers and administrative origins" [56]. Specifically, if the interaction semantics and UI design are not considered, the structure of website is the focus of complexity. It could be computed through a function which

TABLE 2: Complexity of three information structures.

	Net structure	Tree structure	Linear structure
Nodes	13	13	13
Line segments	33	12	8

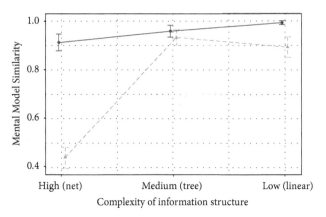

Directional or not
— • — Directionaless similarity
- - ▲ - - Directional similarity

FIGURE 5: The influence of complexity of information structures on mental model similarity.

calculated the number of outgoing links and controls such as buttons and checkboxes [57].

Regarding these studies, objective metrics of complexity of information structures were the number of nodes and links. As shown in Table 2, the numbers of nodes of all three information structures (i.e., net, tree, and linear) are the same, but the net structure has more directional links between any two nodes than the tree structure, which in turn has more links than the linear structure. Therefore, complexity of the information structure has three levels termed low complexity, medium complexity, and high complexity.

Subjective metrics of complexity were consistent with results of objective metrics. Participants rated the simplicity of three websites on a 5-point Likert scale anchored from "easy" to "complex." The average rating for web net, tree, and linear was 4.1 (SD = 0.58), 3.1 (SD = 0.76), and 1.9 (SD = 0.94).

To further examine the influence of complexity of information structures on two different kinds of similarity, one-way repeated ANOVA analysis was conducted. As shown in Figure 5, the results indicated that complexity of the information structures had significant influence on directional similarity ($F_{(2,62)} = 50.51$, $p < 0.001$). Specifically, results of multiple comparison with the Bonferroni corrections indicated that the complex net structure resulted in wider gap between the users' and designers' mental models than the three structure ($Z = 9.081$, $p < 0.001$) and the linear structure ($Z = 8.347$, $p < 0.001$). The complexity of information structures resulted in no differences in directionless similarity ($F_{(2,62)} = 3.056$, $p = 0.0542$). Therefore, (H1a) was rejected, and (H1b) was supported.

TABLE 3: Linear regression results of mental model similarity on user performance.

	The task completion time			The number of clicks		
	B	t	p	B	t	p
Directionless similarity	−3.99	−0.83	0.41	2.99	0.80	0.43
Directional similarity	7.23	3.43	0.00	9.24	6.35	0.00

4.2. The Influence of Mental Model Similarity on User Performance. Linear regression was conducted. The dependent variables were the task completion time and the number of clicks, and there were seven independent variables: directional similarity, directionless similarity, information structures, age, technology product experience, spatial ability, and memory capacity. The results of regression analysis were shown in Table 3.

According to Table 3, the directional similarity was linearly related to the task completion time. Participants take less time to find the target item hidden in the information structures when the directional similarity was lower. This may explain the phenomenon that users who only remember the paths to a special item of web pages take less time to find a target in web pages than those who get a full understanding of elements and relationship of the web pages.

Table 3 also indicates that the directional similarity was linearly related to the number of clicks. Participants clicked less to complete the tasks when the directional similarity was lower and the web pages had more paths to obtain targets such as net structure. Although mental model similarity between the participant and designer was lower in the net structure than in the tree structure and the linear structure, the number of clicks was smaller with the lowest similarity. One possible reason for this is that the net-structure web page has many paths and the elements are connected to each other, while the tree structure and the linear structure are not. This means that users cannot return to the previous page when they need to reach other pages in the net-structure web page, unlike the tree structure and the linear structure.

It can also be inferred that using path diagram to elicit mental models is more effective than using card sorting. It can also verify that the directional relationship of information structures is important, which cannot be ignored in eliciting mental models of information structures.

The mental model similarity was calculated from the information structure. Under each information structure, how does the mental model similarity affect user performance? Correlation analysis and one-way ANOVA analysis were conducted.

The results indicated that only the directional similarity was positively correlated with the task completion time in the net-structure web page. However, either directional similarity or directionless similarity had no significant impact on user performance under each information structure.

In addition, the user performance was not affected by their age, spatial ability, memory capacity, or technology product experience. Moreover, no matter what kind of information structure, the user performance was still not affected by demographic variables. One possible reason is that the participants chosen for this study were all college students: the

differences among them were too small. In other words, the selection of participants has limitations. It may be different when expanding the scope of participants, especially to the elderly, children, and those with lower levels of education.

4.3. Mediation Effects of Mental Model Similarity. According to MacKinnon et al. [58], three modes were used to estimate the basic intervening variable model which were shown in Mod 1, Mod 2, and Mod 3.

$$\text{Mod 1: } Y = cX + e_1 \tag{8}$$

$$\text{Mod 2: } Y = dX + bM + e_2 \tag{9}$$

$$\text{Mod 3: } M = aX + e_3 \tag{10}$$

In these equations, X is the independent variable, Y is the dependent variable, and M is the intervening variable. e_1, e_2, and e_3 are the population regression intercepts in (8), (9), and (10), respectively, c represents the relation between the independent and dependent variables in (8), d represents the relation between the independent and dependent variables adjusted for the effects of the intervening variable in (9), a represents the relation between the independent and intervening variables in (10), and b represents the relation between the intervening and the dependent variables adjusted for the effect of the independent variable in (9) [58]. According to Sobel's [59] test, the mediation effect was investigated. The results of statistical analysis were shown in Tables 4 and 5.

For both the number of clicks and the task completion time, the directional similarity was a significant mediator. However, the effects are only partial mediation because the direct effect is still significant (Tables 4 and 5). The simplicity of information structures had significant effects on the task completion time and the number of clicks. A part of the effect was achieved by directional similarity, which means that user performance was partially influenced by the degree of match between users' mental models and information structures.

Tables 6 and 7 indicate that the directionless similarity was not a mediator; there was no significant mediation effect for directionless similarity on task completion time or the number of clicks. One possible reason is that the directionless similarity was calculated from the card sorting, in which the details about the directional relationship of information structures were not considered, and this would lose the accuracy when using card sorting to elicit mental models.

Both the task completion time and the number of clicks showed partial mediation by the directional similarity. The information structures had a direct effect on user performance. The directionless similarity did not account for the relationship between information structures and user performance, while the directional similarity, as the new index to

TABLE 4: Mediation analysis of the directional similarity as mediator of the relationship between simplicity of information structure and task completion time.

	Point estimate	SE	t	p	Indirect effect	SE	z	N
Mod 1								
Intercept	13.85	1.77	7.82	$9.36e^{-12}$				
Pred	1.77	0.83	2.15	$3.45e^{-02}$				
Mod 2								
Intercept	11.86	1.88	6.31	$1.04e^{-08}$	1.71	0.69	2.47	92
Pred	0.07	1.04	0.07	$9.47e^{-01}$				
Med	7.11	2.74	2.60	$\mathbf{1.10e^{-02}}$				
Mod 3								
Intercept	0.28	0.07	4.00	$5.64e^{-05}$				
Pred	0.24	0.03	8.00	$1.18e^{-11}$				

Note. Med refers to mediator. Pred refers to independent variable.

TABLE 5: Mediation analysis of the directional similarity as mediator of the relationship between simplicity of information structure and the number of clicks.

	Point estimate	SE	t	p	Indirect effect	SE	z	N
Mod 1								
Intercept	1.45	1.15	1.26	$2.10e^{-01}$				
Pred	3.68	0.54	6.81	$8.61e^{-10}$				
Mod 2								
Intercept	0.02	1.21	0.02	0.99	1.23	0.45	2.73	92
Pred	2.45	0.67	3.66	0.00				
Med	5.13	1.76	2.91	**0.00**				
Mod 3								
Intercept	0.28	0.07	4.00	$5.64e^{-05}$				
Pred	0.24	0.03	8.00	$1.18e^{-11}$				

Note. Med refers to mediator. Pred refers to independent variable.

TABLE 6: Mediation analysis of the directionless similarity as mediator of the relationship between simplicity of information structure and the task completion time.

	Point estimate	SE	t	p	Indirect effect	SE	z	N
Mod 1								
Intercept	13.85	1.77	7.82	$9.36e^{-12}$				
Pred	1.77	0.83	2.13	$3.45e^{-02}$				
Mod 2								
Intercept	19.71	4.56	4.32	$4.05e^{-05}$	−0.28	0.23	−1.19	92
Pred	2.05	0.85	2.41	$1.74e^{-02}$				
Med	−6.73	4.83	−1.39	$\mathbf{1.67e^{-01}}$				
Mod 3								
Intercept	0.87	0.04	21.75	$5.39e^{-39}$				
Pred	0.04	0.02	2.00	$2.49e^{-02}$				

Note. Med refers to mediator. Pred refers to independent variable.

TABLE 7: Mediation analysis of the directionless similarity as mediator of the relationship between simplicity of information structure and the number of clicks.

	Point estimate	SE	t	p	Indirect effect	SE	z	N
Mod 1								
Intercept	1.45	1.15	1.26	$2.10e^{-01}$				
Pred	3.68	0.54	6.81	$8.61e^{-10}$				
Mod 2								
Intercept	3.22	2.99	1.08	$2.84e^{-01}$	−0.08	0.13	−0.62	92
Pred	3.76	0.55	6.84	$1.19e^{-09}$				
Med	−2.03	3.17	−0.64	**$5.23e^{-01}$**				
Mod 3								
Intercept	0.87	0.04	21.75	$5.390e^{-39}$				
Pred	0.04	0.02	2.00	$2.49e^{-02}$				

Note. Med refers to mediator. Pred refers to independent variable.

measure the degree of match between mental models, was a significant mediator. Thus, (H3b) was partially supported and (H3a) was rejected.

4.4. Discussion. Users' activities provide objective information of web navigation behaviors and thus could complement users' subjective understanding of web pages. The subjective understanding of web pages is usually elicited through card sorting. However, card sorting is not adequate for eliciting complete mental models if we consider the directional relationship of information structures. To get more objective information from users' activities, we proposed a new method called path diagram to elicit mental models with directional information of hierarchical systems. To further quantify the difference between mental models, mental model similarity was calculated through the mathematical equations. It might be a quick and dirty way to predict user performance. In addition, designers can get more precise information about how users think about the system by applying path diagram into the two phases of interaction process: the designer-to-user communication phase and the user-system interaction phase [60].

The mental model similarity has two major theoretical and practical implications: (1) the mental model similarity provides an index to check if the designers' improvement on their websites is effective, which is quite different from when designer can only check if their improvement is working by means of their feelings; (2) the mental model similarity also provides an index of measuring the usability of websites. People can get a more precise understanding of which kind of website was preferred by comparing mental model similarity of various websites.

Hypothesis (H1a) was rejected and Hypothesis (H1b) was supported. Many studies have shown that information structures are correlated with mental models. For example, Gregor and Dickinson [61] thought that good mental models could design good information structures. Roth et al. [62] pointed out that different information structures had different mental models. However, hardly any studies have investigated the relationship between information structures and mental model similarity between users and designers.

Here, we have explored this relationship; the results showed that information structures had a significant effect on the directional similarity. The more complex the information structures, the lower the directional similarity.

The results also indicated that information structures had no significant effect on directionless similarity. Previous studies also indicated that card sorting lost its validity when dealing with the complex websites such as municipal websites which are complex information structures [43].

Hypothesis (H2a) and Hypothesis (H2b) were rejected. The results indicated that the directional similarity was positively correlated with the task completion time and the number of clicks. When the directional similarity was lower, the participants took less time and smaller number of clicks to find the target. This is different from the findings of Schmettow and Sommer [43]: they discovered that mental model similarity between users and designers had no effect on users' browsing performance of municipal websites. The possible reasons for this may be as follows: (1) path diagram involves specific directional relationship between various elements of an information structure, while card sorting mainly represents a user's understanding of the directionless relationship; (2) culture difference might influence the way users are navigating in websites. Chinese users will benefit from a thematically organized information structure of a GUI system, whereas American users will benefit from a functionally organized structure [63]. Specifically in the card sorting tasks, Chinese subjects were more likely to stress the category by identifying the relationship between different entities, while the Danish subjects preferred to stress the category name by its physical attributes [64]. The participants in the study of Schmettow and Sommer were from Netherland and the web pages used were functionally organized structure, while the participants of this study were Chinese and the websites used were thematically organized structure. Possible influence of cultural difference might be considered in future work. However, the navigation strategy is systematic, focused, and directed when individuals have specific targets or goals [65]. Card sorting cannot describe the users' mental models completely when it relates to information structures with directional relationship. In other words, a better way to elicit mental models was using path diagram rather than card sorting. In addition, the method we proposed to elicit the mental model is predictive.

Demographic variables, such as age, spatial ability, memory capacity and technology product experience had no correlation with user performance. This is quite different to the findings of Arning and Ziefle [66], who indicated that user age and spatial ability were major factors affecting user performance. The possible reasons for this may be as follows: (1) participants in this study were all younger students, while participants in the study of Arning and Ziefle [66] were younger and older adults. (2) This study focused on web navigation on computers, while the study of Arning and Ziefle [66] focused on menu navigation on Personal Digital Assistants, whose small screen makes navigation more challenging and thus set higher requirements for spatial ability.

Hypothesis (H3b) was partially supported and Hypothesis (H3a) was rejected. The mediation effect of directionless similarity on user performance was not found, but a partially mediated effect was found between directional similarity and user performance. The results are different from those of Ziefle and Bay, who thought that the more similar the mental models between the user and designer, the better the performance using the device [33]. One possible reason is that the tasks in the study of Ziefle and Bay [33] were about browsing tasks, while they were searching tasks in this study. It is necessary to distinguish browsing without specific goals and searching specific goals in future studies. Anyway, results implied that designing hierarchical systems according to users' mental models was not the only way to solve problems caused by the gap of mental models between users and designers. Alternatives such as providing navigation aids in complex websites and training may be considered [67].

This study only considered individuals, and the results may not apply to groups where interaction with other people influences constructions of mental models. Mathieu et al. [24] found team processes fully mediating the relationship between team mental models and team effectiveness. However, their subsequent study [39] indicated that team performance was partially mediated by teammates' mental models.

In addition, the results showed that information structures had a direct effect on user performance. They seem to testify that "a meaningful information structure will promote efficient navigation, to ensure that information is organized in a way that is meaningful to its target users is essential when designing websites" [68].

5. Conclusion and Future Research

We have discussed the impact of the mental model similarity between users and designers. A new method, path diagram, was applied to elicit mental models and calculate the similarity and comparably tested to the traditional method.

Path diagram is more effective than card sorting in eliciting mental models of hierarchical systems, particularly considering the directional relationship of hierarchical systems. For general information structures, directionless similarity cannot predict user performance, while directional similarity can predict both task completion time and the number

of clicks. Users will take less time and fewer clicks when the directional similarity is lower. However, for a specific information structure, neither the directionless similarity nor the directional similarity has a significant impact on user performance.

In addition, user performance is not affected by their age, spatial ability, memory capacity, or technology product experience. The results have also shown that it is more generally effective in eliciting the mental model using path diagram compared to card sorting.

Limitations of this study should be noted: (i) participants were sampling from young students, who were not representative. Future studies may consider older adults and those with lower education level; (ii) web pages with mixed information structures and various content were not considered; (iii) multiple tasks (e.g., browsing tasks) were not involved; (iv) possible impact of cultural difference was not examined; (v) changes of mental models were not tracked over time; (vi) similarity calculation required additional human efforts, so future work may explore ways to automatically calculate it.

Acknowledgments

This work was supported by the National Natural Science Foundation of China under Grants nos. 71401018 and 71661167006 and Chongqing Municipal Natural Science Foundation under Grant no. cstc2016jcyjA0406.

References

[1] M. Helander, T. Landauer, and P. Prabhu, "Mental models and user models," in *Handbook of Human-Computer Interaction*, pp. 49–63, Elsevier, 1997.

[2] Y. Zhang, "Undergraduate students' mental models of the Web as an information retrieval system," *Journal of the Association for Information Science and Technology*, vol. 59, no. 13, pp. 2087–2098, 2008.

[3] D. A. Norman, "Design Rules Based on Analyses of Human Error," *Communications of the ACM*, vol. 26, no. 4, pp. 254–258, 1983.

[4] P. N. Johnson-Laird, "Mental models and thought," *The Cambridge Handbook of Thinking and Reasoning*, pp. 185–208, 2005.

[5] M. Volkamer and K. Renaud, "Mental modelsgeneral introduction and review of their application to human-centred security," in *Number Theory and Cryptography*, pp. 255–280, Springer Berlin Heidelberg, 2013.

[6] K. J. W. Craik, "The nature of explanation," *CUP Archive*, vol. 445, 1967.

[7] P. N. Johnson-Laird, *Mental models: Towards a Cognitive Science of Language, Inference, and Consciousness*, Harvard University Press, 6 edition, 1983.

[8] A. Garnham and J. Oakhill, "The mental models theory of language comprehension," *Models of Understanding Text*, pp. 313–339, 1996.

[9] P. N. Johnson-Laird, "Mental models and cognitive change," *Journal of Cognitive Psychology*, vol. 25, no. 2, pp. 131–138, 2013.

[10] J. H. Holland, *Induction: Processes of Inference, Learning, and Discovery*, Mit Press, 1989.

[11] P. N. Johnson-Laird, "Mental models and deduction," *Trends in Cognitive Sciences*, vol. 5, no. 10, pp. 434–442, 2001.

[12] R. A. Schmidt, D. E. Young, S. Swinnen, and D. C. Shapiro, "Summary Knowledge of Results for Skill Acquisition: Support for the Guidance Hypothesis," *Journal of Experimental Psychology: Learning, Memory, and Cognition*, vol. 15, no. 2, pp. 352–359, 1989.

[13] R. A. Schmidt and R. A. Bjork, "New Conceptualizations of Practice: Common Principles in Three Paradigms Suggest New Concepts for Training," *Psychological Science*, vol. 3, no. 4, pp. 207–218, 1992.

[14] J. I. Tollman and A. D. Benson, "Mental models and web-based learning: examining the change in personal learning models of graduate students enrolled in an online library media course," *Journal of education for library and information science*, pp. 207–233, 2000.

[15] I. M. Greca and M. A. Moreira, "Mental models, conceptual models, and modelling," *International Journal of Science Education*, vol. 22, no. 1, pp. 1–11, 2000.

[16] Y.-F. Shih and S. M. Alessi, "Mental models and transfer of learning in computer programming," *Journal of Research on Computing in Education*, vol. 26, no. 2, pp. 154–175, 1993.

[17] P. Fuchs-Frothnhofen, E. A. Hartmann, D. Brandt, and D. Weydandt, "Designing human-machine interfaces to match the user's mental models," *Engineering Practice*, vol. 4, no. 1, pp. 13–18, 1996.

[18] Y.-C. Hsu, "The effects of metaphors on novice and expert learners' performance and mental-model development," *Interacting with Computers*, vol. 18, no. 4, pp. 770–792, 2006.

[19] K. M. A. Revell and N. A. Stanton, "Case studies of mental models in home heat control: Searching for feedback, valve, timer and switch theories," *Applied Ergonomics*, vol. 45, no. 3, pp. 363–378, 2014.

[20] D. A. Norman, The psychology of everyday things. (The design of everyday things), 1988.

[21] M. D. C. P. Melguizo and G. C. van der Veer, "Mental models," *Human-Computer Interaction Handbook*, pp. 52–80, 2002.

[22] R. Klimoski and S. Mohammed, "Team mental model: Construct or metaphor?" *Journal of Management*, vol. 20, no. 2, pp. 403–437, 1994.

[23] S. Mohammed, L. Ferzandi, and K. Hamilton, "Metaphor no more: A 15-year review of the team mental model construct," *Journal of Management*, vol. 36, no. 4, pp. 876–910, 2010.

[24] J. E. Mathieu, G. F. Goodwin, T. S. Heffner, E. Salas, and J. A. Cannon-Bowers, "The influence of shared mental models on team process and performance," *Journal of Applied Psychology*, vol. 85, no. 2, pp. 273–283, 2000.

[25] J. R. Olson and K. J. Biolsi, *10 Techniques for representing expert knowledge. Toward a general theory of expertise: Prospects and limits*, 1991.

[26] S. Mohammed, R. Klimoski, and J. R. Rentsch, "The measurement of team mental models: We have no shared schema," *Organizational Research Methods*, vol. 3, no. 2, pp. 123–165, 2000.

[27] J. Langan-Fox, S. Code, and K. Langfield-Smith, "Team mental models: Techniques, methods, and analytic approaches," *Human Factors: The Journal of the Human Factors and Ergonomics Society*, vol. 42, no. 2, pp. 242–271, 2000.

[28] S. J. Payne, "A descriptive study of mental models," *Behaviour & Information Technology*, vol. 10, no. 1, pp. 3–21, 1991.

[29] Y. Zhang, "The impact of task complexity on people's mental models of MedlinePlus," *Information Processing & Management*, vol. 48, no. 1, pp. 107–119, 2012.

[30] A. L. Rowe and N. J. Cooke, "Measuring mental models: Choosing the right tools for the job," *Human Resource Development Quarterly*, vol. 6, no. 3, pp. 243–255, 1995.

[31] Y. Yamada, K. Ishihara, and T. Yamaoka, "A study on an usability measurement based on the mental model. Access in Human-Computer Interaction," *Design for All and Einclusion*, pp. 168–173, 2011.

[32] S. Y. Rieh, J. Y. Yang, E. Yakel, and K. Markey, "Conceptualizing institutional repositories: Using co-discovery to uncover mental models," in *In Proceedings of the third symposium on Information interaction in context*, pp. 165–174, ACM, 2010.

[33] M. Ziefle and S. Bay, "Mental models of a cellular phone menu. Comparing older and younger novice users," in *Proceedings of the International Conference on Mobile Human-Computer Interaction*, pp. 25–37, International, Berlin, Germany, 2004.

[34] R. Young, Surrogates and mappings: two kinds of conceptual models for interactive, 1983.

[35] A. Dimitroff, *Mental models and error behavior in an interactive bibliographic retrieval system dissertation [Doctoral, thesis]*, 1990.

[36] M. A. Sasse, *Eliciting and describing users' models of computer systems dissertation [Doctoral, thesis]*, University of Birmingham, 1997.

[37] D. J. Slone, "The influence of mental models and goals on search patterns during web interaction," *Journal of the Association for Information Science and Technology*, vol. 53, no. 13, pp. 1152–1169, 2002.

[38] D. S. Brandt and L. Uden, "Insight into mental models of novice internet searchers," *Communications of the ACM*, vol. 46, no. 7, pp. 133–136, 2003.

[39] J. E. Mathieu, T. S. Heffner, G. F. Goodwin, J. A. Cannon-Bowers, and E. Salas, "Scaling the quality of teammates' mental models: Equifinality and normative comparisons," *Journal of Organizational Behavior*, vol. 26, no. 1, pp. 37–56, 2005.

[40] F. G. Halasz and T. P. Moran, "Mental models and problem solving in using a calculator," in *Proceedings of the SIGCHI conference on Human Factors in Computing Systems*, pp. 212–216, ACM, 1983.

[41] C. L. Borgman, "The user's mental model of an information retrieval system," in *Proceedings of the 8th annual international ACM SIGIR conference on Research and development in information retrieval*, pp. 268–273, ACM, Montreal, Canada, June 1985.

[42] S. Payne, "Mental models in human-computer interaction," in *The Human-Computer Interaction Handbook*, vol. 20071544, pp. 63–76, CRC Press, 2007.

[43] M. Schmettow and J. Sommer, "Linking card sorting to browsing performance—are congruent municipal websites more efficient to use?" *Behaviour & Information Technology*, vol. 35, no. 6, pp. 452–470, 2016.

[44] S. S. Webber, G. Chen, S. C. Payne, S. M. Marsh, and S. J. Zaccaro, "Enhancing team mental model measurement with performance appraisal practices," *Organizational Research Methods*, vol. 3, no. 4, pp. 307–322, 2000.

[45] B.-C. Lim and K. J. Klein, "Team mental models and team performance: A field study of the effects of team mental model similarity and accuracy," *Journal of Organizational Behavior*, vol. 27, no. 4, pp. 403–418, 2006.

[46] T. Biemann, T. Ellwart, and O. Rack, "Quantifying similarity of team mental models: An introduction of the rRG index," *Group Processes and Intergroup Relations*, vol. 17, no. 1, pp. 125–140, 2014.

[47] C. Wu and Y. Liu, "Queuing network modeling of driver workload and performance," *IEEE Transactions on Intelligent Transportation Systems*, vol. 8, no. 3, pp. 528–537, 2007.

[48] R. N. Shepard and C. Feng, "A chronometric study of mental paper folding," *Cognitive Psychology*, vol. 3, no. 2, pp. 228–243, 1972.

[49] S. Werner, B. Krieg-Brückner, H. A. Mallot, K. Schweizer, and C. Freksa, "Spatial cognition: The role of landmark, route, and survey knowledge in human and robot navigation," in *Informatik'97 Informatik als Innovationsmotor*, pp. 41–50, Springer, Berlin, Germany, 1997.

[50] R. G. Golledge, T. R. Smith, J. W. Pellegrino, S. Doherty, and S. P. Marshall, "A conceptual model and empirical analysis of children's acquisition of spatial knowledge," *Journal of Environmental Psychology*, vol. 5, no. 2, pp. 125–152, 1985.

[51] E. K. Farran, Y. Courbois, J. Van Herwegen, and M. Blades, "How useful are landmarks when learning a route in a virtual environment? Evidence from typical development and Williams syndrome," *Journal of Experimental Child Psychology*, vol. 111, no. 4, pp. 571–586, 2012.

[52] M. Nys, V. Gyselinck, E. Orriols, and M. Hickmann, "Landmark and route knowledge in children's spatial representation of a virtual environment," *Frontiers in Psychology*, vol. 6, article no. 522, 2015.

[53] D. Sinreich, D. Gopher, S. Ben-Barak, Y. Marmor, and R. Lahat, "Mental models as a practical tool in the engineer's toolbox," *International Journal of Production Research*, vol. 43, no. 14, pp. 2977–2996, 2005.

[54] M. Garc, A. N. Badre, and J. T. Stasko, "Development and validation of icons varying in their abstractness," *Interacting with Computers*, vol. 6, no. 2, pp. 191–211, 1994.

[55] T. J. Lloyd-Jones and L. Luckhurst, "Effects of plane rotation, task, and complexity on recognition of familiar and chimeric objects," *Memory & Cognition*, vol. 30, no. 4, pp. 499–510, 2002.

[56] M. Butkiewicz, H. V. Madhyastha, and V. Sekar, "Understanding website complexity: Measurements, metrics, and implications," in *Proceedings of the 2011 ACM SIGCOMM Internet Measurement Conference, IMC'11*, pp. 313–328, deu, November 2011.

[57] P. Chandra and G. Manjunath, "Navigational complexity in web interactions," in *Proceedings of the 19th international conference on World wide web*, pp. 1075-1076, ACM, 2010.

[58] D. P. MacKinnon, C. M. Lockwood, J. M. Hoffman, S. G. West, and V. Sheets, "A comparison of methods to test mediation and other intervening variable effects," *Psychological Methods*, vol. 7, no. 1, pp. 83–104, 2002.

[59] M. E. Sobel, "Asymptotic confidence intervals for indirect effects in structural equation models," *Sociological Methodology*, vol. 13, pp. 290–312, 1982.

[60] C. S. De Souza and C. F. Leitão, "Semiotic engineering methods for scientific research in HCI," *Lectures on Human-Centered Informatics*, vol. 2, no. 1, p. 122, 2009.

[61] P. Gregor and A. Dickinson, "Cognitive difficulties and access to information systems: An interaction design perspective," *Universal Access in the Information Society*, vol. 5, no. 4, pp. 393–400, 2007.

[62] S. P. Roth, P. Schmutz, S. L. Pauwels, J. A. Bargas-Avila, and K. Opwis, "Mental models for web objects: Where do users expect to find the most frequent objects in online shops, news portals, and company web pages?" *Interacting with Computers*, vol. 22, no. 2, pp. 140–152, 2010.

[63] P. L. P. Rau, T. Plocher, and Y. Y. Choong, *Cross-Cultural Design for IT Products and Services*, CRC Press, 2012.

[64] A. Nawaz, T. Plocher, T. Clemmensen, W. Qu, and X. Sun, "Cultural differences in the structure of categories in Denmark and China," *Department of Informatics, CBS*, vol. article 3, 2007.

[65] G. Marchionini, *Information Seeking in Electronic Environments*, Cambridge University Press, Cambridge, UK, 1995.

[66] K. Arning and M. Ziefle, "Effects of age, cognitive, and personal factors on PDA menu navigation performance," *Behaviour & Information Technology*, vol. 28, no. 3, pp. 251–268, 2009.

[67] J. Park and J. Kim, "Effects of contextual navigation aids on browsing diverse Web systems," in *Proceedings of the SIGCHI conference on Human Factors in Computing Systems*, pp. 257–264, ACM, 2000.

[68] M. L. Bernard and B. S. Chaparro, "Searching within websites: A comparison of three types of sitemap menu structures," in *In Proceedings of the Human Factors and Ergonomics Society Annual Meeting*, vol. 44, pp. 441–444, Los Angeles, Calif, USA, 2000.

11

Incorporating Accessibility Elements to the Software Engineering Process

Wesley Tessaro Andrade, Rodrigo Gonçalves de Branco,
Maria Istela Cagnin, and Débora Maria Barroso Paiva ⓘ

Federal University of Mato Grosso do Sul (UFMS), Av. Costa e Silva, s/n, Cidade Universitária, Campo Grande, MS, Brazil

Correspondence should be addressed to Débora Maria Barroso Paiva; dmbpaiva@gmail.com

Academic Editor: Hideyuki Nakanishi

The expansion of web is a phenomenon that brings several challenges in different segments of the society. Accessibility is one of these challenges and it is related to the digital inclusion and social welfare of the population. Thus, making accessible software available can contribute to solution of problems that currently exist in relation to access to information and services by all citizens. The purpose of this article is to present an approach that integrates accessibility to the Software Engineering process. We also present the Acero tool, which provides computational support to the proposed approach. Results were evaluated and we concluded that the use of the proposal reached the objectives, supporting different stages of the development process and contributing to obtain accessible software products.

1. Introduction

The availability of computers, electronic equipment, and Internet has made a decisive contribution to major changes in modern society. According to the International Telecommunication Union (ITU (www.itu.int)), subordinate organ of the United Nations Organization (UNO (www.un.org)), in the year 2016 approximately 3 billion people worldwide had access to the Internet, accounting for about 40% of the world's population [1]. Digital inclusion implies being concerned with the needs and demands of all people, including those with special access needs, the elderly, low literacy users, among others. Also, it is important to think about how to make the new interactive applications [2] available to everyone, for example, the smart city and the smart home applications including geopositioning, Internet of Things, and other resources [3, 4].

The World Health Organization (WHO (www.who.int)) estimated in 2014 that approximately 1 billion people in the world had some kind of deficiency ranging from visual and auditory deficits to cognitive and motor difficulties. According to WHO, deficiency is the term used to refer to individuals who have limitations or lack of anatomical, physiological, and/or intellectual structure [5].

In general, web accessibility means that people with disabilities, reduced skills, or situationally induced impairments are able to access, navigate, interact, and contribute to information on the web [6].

In spite of the importance to offer resources that enable digital inclusion, web accessibility has not been a priority [7, 8] and there are some justifications to this, such as the lack of technical knowledge of software engineers and developers (little emphasis is given to the subject during the academic training of students), the lack of tools that support the inclusion of accessibility quickly and simply throughout the software lifecycle, and the predominant software development culture that allocates insufficient resources (time, people) to the design and evaluation of graphical interfaces [9, 10]. However, companies and professionals are now noticing that those who neglect the website usability and the development of accessible products may lose an expressive number of users of their software systems [11, 12].

Software Engineering plays a fundamental role in the development of accessible applications, since it can promote the integration between methodologies and specific accessibility techniques and activities at the software development process. According to Sherman [13] and Groves [14] the benefits of incorporating accessibility during the software development process are greater than the costs involved, as there is an increase in the number of users and value added to the final product. Additionally, maintenance activities, generally expensive, can be avoided for inclusion of accessibility.

Software development encompasses many activities, such as requirements specification, design, coding, and testing. It is possible to use computers to aid the entire software development process by using Computer-Aided Software Engineering (CASE) tools that support the execution of repetitive tasks, reduce the complexity of development, and improve productivity.

Therefore, considering the difficulties inherent to the development of accessible web applications and the possibility of extending and improving the existing CASE tools, this article is proposed with a double objective. Firstly, we present the Acero approach, which integrates accessibility into the software development process. Secondly, we present the Acero tool, which provides the computational support to allow the automation of the Acero approach. The inclusion of accessibility is transparent to software engineers and developers, in other words, when using the Acero tool, professionals will be able to generate accessible applications without being experts in the area.

This article is organized as follows: Section 2 presents an overview about accessibility; Section 3 presents related work; Section 4 discusses the background of the approach and tool proposed in this article; Section 5 presents the Acero approach and tool; and Sections 6 and 7 present the empirical study and conclusions, respectively.

2. Web Accessibility Concepts

In many countries, web has become the main source of access to government, educational, news, and leisure information and services. Consequently, its use is replacing or decreasing the use of resources that were once heavily used, such as newspapers and magazines in print versions. Therefore, it is necessary that web be accessible in order to provide equality, opportunity for access and interaction for all people who want to use it [6, 15].

Considering the need to provide accessible content on web, a number of governments have instituted laws that make accessible information available, even if only within the scope of government sites, with the aim of guaranteeing equality of opportunity in access. It is common for these nations to adopt national or international guidelines to standardize the development of products and the availability of content on web.

The W3C international organization launched an initiative whose main mission is to coordinate international, technical, and human efforts to improve web accessibility [6, 15, 16]. It is responsible for the important set of accessibility guidelines, called web Content Accessibility Guidelines (WCAG) [17].

WCAG is a set of documents that explains, through guidelines and recommendations, how to make web content accessible to people with disabilities. WCAG is intended for front-end developers, but it is also useful for assisting developers of assessment tools, developers of audit tools, and developers of quality assurance and validation tools.

WCAG 1.0 was published as the current W3C standard in May 1999 and consists of 12 guidelines, divided into checkpoints and properties associated with each of them. The document presents three main groups:

(i) Level 1: developers must meet a number of success criteria so that one or more groups of people can access the web content. If all success criteria associated with this level are met, the site will have conformity "A".

(ii) Level 2: developers should take an additional set of testable success criteria because; otherwise, one or more groups will have difficulty accessing the information. Compliance with this level is described as "AA".

(iii) Level 3: developers could take a more complex set of testable success criteria to make it easier for some groups to access the web. Compliance with this level is referred to as "AAA".

Due to the evolution and creation of new web technologies, the W3C needed to make improvements to meet these new tools and enable the scalability of the WCAG 1.0 being proposed, therefore, the standard WCAG 2.0 [18].

The definition of WCAG 2.0 standard was based on WCAG 1.0 but new recommendations were also made: one of the main modifications was that instead of the fact that each guideline has checkpoints or checklists, 61 successful criteria were presented, which are declarations that can be automatically or manually tested in order to check whether the web content is accessible or not. It is by means of these success criteria that the conformity levels "A", "AA", or "AAA" are established [19]. WCAG 2.0 is composed of 12 guidelines organized under four fundamental principles [17]:

(1) Perceivable: data and components of the interfaces must be presented to users in a perceptible way.

(2) Operable: user interface components must be operative, regardless of the user's needs.

(3) Understandable: contents and operations on the interfaces should be understandable.

(4) Robust: contents and information should be reliably interpreted by a wide variety of tools, including assistive technologies.

Although WCAG is a nonmandatory technical guidance, some countries use or are inspired by this standard with the aim of providing accessible content in their governmental portals [20]. Some examples are Canada [21], Japan [22], Ireland [23], Italian [24], and Brazil [25].

WCAG 2.1 was published as a W3C Recommendation June 2018 [26]. It extends WCAG 2.0 and content that conforms to WCAG 2.1 also conforms to WCAG 2.0. Following WCAG 2.1 guidelines developers will make content more accessible to a wider range of people with disabilities, including accommodations for blindness and low vision, deafness and hearing loss, limited movement, speech disabilities, photosensitivity, and combinations of these, and some accommodation for learning disabilities and cognitive limitations.

2.1. Assessment Methods and Measurement of Accessibility. The legislations and standards discussed above provide technical guidance on what should be offered in the project and reach only high-level objectives [19].

Evaluation methods contribute to identification of specific failures and coding errors [27]. For greater effectiveness, evaluation methods should be used in conjunction with existing accessibility guidelines and standards. A number of methods for accessibility assessment can be used, such as user-based evaluation [28, 29], conformance evaluation methodology [30], and automated evaluations [31]. It is important to note that evaluation methods can be used together or individually in the desired order [19].

In this research, the use of automated evaluations using existing tools, such as Achecker (http://achecker.ca/checker/index.php) and Access Monitor (http://www.acessibilidade.gov.pt/accessmonitor/), was considered to evaluate the quality of the final application obtained with the utilization of the proposed methodology.

3. Related Work

Recent works have been concerned with accessibility requirements from the early stages of the software development process through tasks and tools that help to elicit and properly implement those requirements. In the latter case, several studies have used model-driven development (MDD) to provide a metamodel of interest domain (e.g., embedded systems, e-commerce, industrial automation systems, etc.) and a metamodel of UI layer, with accessibility requirements incorporated.

Krainz et al. [32–34] propose a MDD approach, in that a metamodel for the domain apps is created in Domain Specific Language (DSL) with accessibility requirements included, and use a set of tools to transform the metamodel into app source code. The outcome from this transformation process is an app prototype with accessibility features (for example, content description for integrated screen reader support or active voice output in selected parts of the app).

Other authors [35] present an approach based on user-centered design (UCD) and on MDD for developing web application and industrial automation systems with accessibility. Models have been elaborated to describe particular UI aspects, as structure or behavior, considering accessibility requirements, as well as domain requirements belonging to industrial automation systems (such as ticket vending machines, washing machines, or automated teller machines (ATM) systems).

In addition, González-García et al. [36] used a MDD approach to create an accessible media player. In a similar way, Zouhaier et al. [37] research adaption of accessible UIs based on models and Miñón et al. [38] show the generation of accessible user interfaces in ubiquitous environments from models.

Other works define software development processes that provide activities and practices in order to produce accessible software, but do not offer support tools.

An agile inclusive process model was defined by Bonacin et al. [39]. This process is based on agile principles and values and it is focused on accessibility and usability of the final product. Its main principles are promote the participation of the users and other stakeholders with the universal access and inclusive design values (i.e., UCD); construct a shared vision of the social context; include more than just technical issues in the development of the system; and promote the digital inclusion through participatory activities. To attend these principles, the process proposed includes many activities related to these issues, including experts analysis, low fidelity prototyping, user acceptance analysis, and workshop with the users.

Rossvoll et al. [40] show an iterative approach with user involvement from the beginning to the end of the software project, containing a set of recommendations based on a UCD process which includes user testing with disabled people and based on experiences from projects for inclusive access developed by the authors. The approach contains both high-level recommendations, such as which overall research methodology to apply, as well as detailed low-level guidelines, such as which activities concerned to accessibility to include in the project workflow and when.

Dias et al. [41] extended a classic model of web application development process to incorporate activities related to users' profile with disabilities and their needs, in order to include accessibility and usability nonfunctional requirements during development. To facilitate the elicitation of these nonfunctional requirements, the authors provide a checklist that contains a list of this type of requirement based on accessibility guidelines and usability heuristics, as well as giving the main needs of users with each type of disability.

Sanchez-Gordon et al. [42] define a software development process, fit to small software enterprises to attend their constraints of staff and budget, which includes accessibility-related tasks in following activities: initiation, analysis, design, construction, integration and test, and delivery. The authors discuss briefly how apply each accessibility-related task when using agile development and they also indicate existing tools, checklists, and standard that can be used during the software development.

Our work becomes a differential in relation to the aforementioned works because it offers a process, supported by tools, that is concerned with accessibility requirements during all the phases of software development. The tools are independent of the application domain and can be used by software engineers according to their needs and skills in order to develop software to attend all users, including users with permanent or temporal disabilities.

4. Background

The approach and tool proposed in this article is the result of some researches that were later integrated. The results of the researches presented in this section can be divided into three parts. In Section 4.1 the methodology for making integration between accessibility elements and software processes feasible is presented. In Section 4.2 the AccTrace tool is presented, a preliminary software tool developed to contemplate the proposed methodology. In Section 4.3, the Homero Framework is presented, which provides support for code generation and webpage creation in accordance with the WCAG 2.0 guidelines.

4.1. A Methodology for Developing Accessible Web Applications. Maia et al. [43] proposed a process for the development of accessible web applications, called MTA, based on ISO/IEC 12207 [44], which suggests the introduction of accessibility tasks in software development subprocesses. The MTA suggests adapting the subprocesses of ISO/IEC 12207 at all stages of development in order to enable the generation of accessible software products. Results of other authors also contributed to the MTA elaboration [45, 46]. The subprocesses and their tasks are as follows:

(1) System requirements elicitation (the software owner and the final users provides information and the accessibility specialist records them)

  (a) Identify the accessibility requirements of the system

    (i) Identify user characteristics: the abilities (and disabilities) of the final users including perceptual, cognitive, motor, etc.
    (ii) Identify domain requirements: the tasks that need to be supported, social and cultural dynamics, environmental factors, and so on
    (iii) Identify technological requirements: the availability of hardware, software, plug-ins and assistive technologies in the context of final users

(2) System requirements analysis (the software owner, the final users, the development team, and the accessibility specialist refine information)

  (a) Specify the accessibility requirements of the system

    (I) Specification is based on answer to the questions

      (i) User characteristics, who is your target audience? What is the level of expertise the target audience have the subject area of the website?
      (ii) Domain requirements, what is the purpose of the website? What sort of tasks do you expect users to be able to perform using the site?
      (iii) Technological requirements, what assumptions can you make about the browsing and assistive technology available to the target audience and

their knowledge of that technology? What other ways already exist to provide access to the information or services provided by the website in question?

  (b) Evaluate the accessibility requirements of the system

    (i) Criteria established by ISO/IEC 12207 are considered: system accessibility requirements are analyzed for relevance, correctness, and testability; consistency and traceability are established between the system accessibility requirements and the customer's requirements baseline

(3) System architectural design (the development team and the accessibility specialist are responsible for producing the design)

  (a) Allocate accessibility requirements to system elements

    (i) The software system is decomposed into a set of hardware and software components together with the assignment of responsibilities for each component. Accessibility requirements are allocated on such components

  (b) Evaluate the architectural design of the system in relation to accessibility requirements

    (i) Criteria established by ISO/IEC 12207 are considered: system design is analyzed for consistency and traceability between the system accessibility requirements and system architecture design

(4) Software requirements analysis (the requirements engineer, the accessibility specialist, and the final users collect accessibility requirements)

  (a) Establish the accessibility requirements of the software

    (i) Use of requirements elicitation techniques (e.g., questionnaires, interviews) to obtain accessibility requirements

  (b) Evaluate software accessibility requirements

    (i) Criteria established by ISO/IEC 12207 are considered: software accessibility requirements are analyzed for correctness and testability, the impact of software requirements on the operating environment is understood, consistency and traceability are established between the software accessibility requirements and the system accessibility requirements, and prioritization for implementing the software accessibility requirements is defined

(5) Software design (the web designer and the accessibility specialist are responsible for producing the design)

    (a) Design the accessible external interfaces

        (i) Provide alternate or multiple views to address trade-offs between different types of user groups and to optimize the user experience of those user groups

        (ii) Establish the layout of the accessible interface elements, such as labels, images, and text editing fields

        (iii) Define other elements considering abilities and disabilities, for example, color and size for low vision final users

        (iv) Define Accessible Navigational Project

    (b) Evaluate the accessibility of the software project

        (i) Criteria established by ISO/IEC 12207 are considered: software accessibility requirements are analyzed for correctness and testability, consistency, and traceability between accessibility requirements and accessible design

(6) Software construction (the development team and the accessibility specialist implement the accessible external interface)

    (a) Specify techniques for accessibility implementation

        (i) Identify programming techniques for accessible interface implementation, such as the Advisory Techniques presented in the WCAG document

    (b) Codify each software unit according to the accessibility techniques

    (c) Plan accessibility tests of each software unit

        (i) Prepare accessibility tests for software, identifying what should be tested, how the accessibility test should be run, what data should be used for the tests, and what results are expected

    (d) Perform accessibility tests of each software unit

        (i) Run the accessibility tests according to the plan and make the necessary corrections

(7) Software integration testing (the testers and the accessibility specialist are responsible for the accessibility testing considering all elements of the software working together)

    (a) Plan accessibility tests of the integrated software

        (i) Define the procedures, accessibility test data of the integrated software and the expected results

    (b) Perform accessibility test of the integrated software

        (i) Run the accessibility tests according to the plan and make the necessary corrections

(8) Acceptance testing (the testers, the final users, and the accessibility specialist are responsible for the acceptance testing)

    (a) Plan accessibility acceptance test of the software with final users

        (i) Define the procedures, accessibility test data for the acceptance test and the expected results considering participation of people with disabilities

    (b) Perform accessibility acceptance test considering participation of people with disabilities

        (i) Run the accessibility acceptance tests according to the plan and make the necessary corrections

(9) System Testing (the testers and the accessibility specialist are responsible for the accessibility testing considering all elements of the system working together)

    (a) Plan accessibility tests in the system

        (i) Define procedures to evaluate whether all elements of the system work correctly in the final user environment

    (b) Perform accessibility test in the system

        (i) Run the accessibility tests according to the plan and make the necessary corrections. Certify compliance with the requirements of the system

MTA was proposed to guide the development process from the initial stages of the project in order to avoid rework in the maintenance phase (in this phase the client usually requests the inclusion of the requirement accessibility, for different reasons, such as the requirement of laws), which can incur high costs. MTA was evaluated by software developers and it was concluded that, considering accessibility tasks integrated to the development process, it was possible to positively influence the final quality of the product in relation to obtain accessible applications.

4.2. Accessibility in the Phases of Requirements Engineering, Design, and Software Coding: A Support Tool. Considering the MTA, Branco et al. [47, 48] developed a plug-in tool for the Eclipse IDE, called AccTrace, which aims to accomplish the following tasks: to associate the accessibility requirements of a software project to the UML models (use case diagram and class diagram) and automatically generate Java classes with the comments of accessibility implementation techniques. It also performed the tracking of the requirements in the different artifacts, generating a traceability matrix.

For the development of tasks proposed by AccTrace, the tool integrates other solutions as follows: the requirements are specified by the Requirement Designer

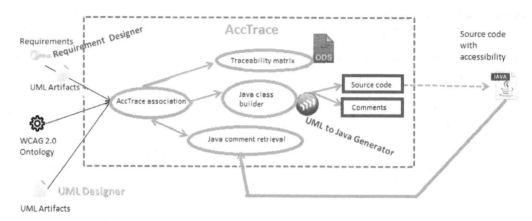

FIGURE 1: AccTrace task flow to generate the code and the traceability matrix of the requirements [47].

(https://www.obeodesigner.com/en/) plug-in, the UML artifacts are elaborated through the UML Designer (http://www.umldesigner.org/) plug-in and classes are automatically generated using the UML to Java Generator (https://marketplace.eclipse.org/content/uml-java-generator) plug-in. Figure 1 shows the AccTrace task flow to generate the code and the traceability matrix of the requirements.

After defining the accessibility requirements and making the connection between them and the UML artifacts, the AccTrace tool is used to perform the association with WCAG 2.0 Ontology [49]. The ontology is a data model, represented in AccTrace tool as a list of implementation techniques, approaches, success criteria, and tests related to the WCAG accessibility guidelines 2.0. In this way, AccTrace tool allows to create a file (extension .acctrace) that relates the ontology to the artifacts and requirements of the software project.

From the .acctrace association file, it is possible to generate a traceability matrix (extension .ods) that presents, in the form of three tables, the relationships: Requirements x UML Models, Requirements x Ontology, and UML Models x Ontology.

AccTrace tool also supports the creation of Java classes with accessibility comments. The UML to Java Generator plug-in was used as the base, which considers as input the .acctrace association file and the UML artifacts file (.uml extension). Classes are then generated with specific comments that allow the user, directly in his/her code, to retrieve the relevant class relationships, aiding the implementation of accessibility.

The tool has three main views, according to Figure 2 . In the editor (AccTrace Editor View-2) it is possible to generate the associations including the UML models, requirements and implementation techniques. In the requirements view (Requirement Associations View-1) it is possible to visualize which requirements associated with the UML model were selected in the editor. In the Specifications View (Accessibility Specifications View-3) it is possible to visualize the implementation techniques already associated, according to the UML model selected in the editor and the accessibility requirement selected in the view of the requirements. In addition, it is possible to remove the associated implementation techniques.

When selecting the UML model and the requirement, it is possible to associate the accessibility implementation technique (mapped on the Ontology) by right-clicking on the UML model, as shown in Figure 3 . These techniques are linked to the requirements and UML models and are stored. Because the artifacts are described in RDF format (requirements, UML models, and ontology), the links are made from the RDF:ID element. Therefore, any UML model that is described in RDF format can be linked and tracked through the traceability matrix and views in Eclipse.

Considering Figures 2 and 3 it is possible to observe the impact of each user need on the system design. The application "Travel Agency" defined the accessibility requirement "provide text alternatives for any nontext content". The Use Case "Offer Catalog Management" was designed and Guideline 1.1 (described in WCAG 2.0) was associated. The reference to the AEGIS Ontology "G134T3: Load each external or internal style sheet into a CSS validator" may also be observed because it includes the accessibility implementation techniques and other pieces of information that may assist in the implementation of the requirement.

A simple application was modeled to exemplify the impact of including accessibility requirements throughout the software process. The application refers to an Internet search engine using keywords. For this application functional requirements and nonfunctional requirements, especially accessibility requirements were defined: "Make all functionality available from a keyboard", "Make text content readable and understandable", etc. Figure 4 shows the association of accessibility guidelines to use cases and UML classes. Also, Figure 5 illustrates the generated code, highlighting the ViewRenderer class, accessibility comments, and implementation details (guidelines and accessibility techniques).

Once the relationship including requirements, UML models, and accessibility implementation techniques are defined, it is possible to automatically generate the traceability matrix by the AccTrace tool in the Open Document Sheet (ODS) format.

4.3. Homero: A Framework for Supporting the Development of Accessible Web Application Interfaces. The Homero Framework [50, 51] was developed using PHP and aims to simplify

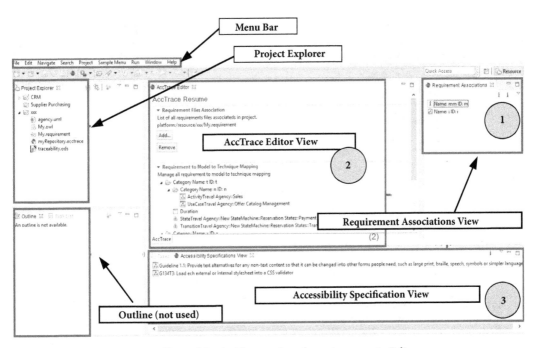

FIGURE 2: View of the AccTrace tool on the main screen in Eclipse.

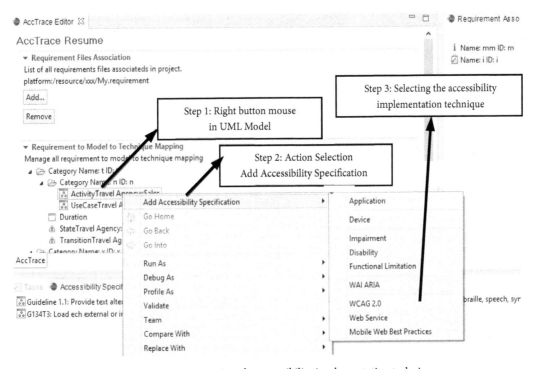

FIGURE 3: Process to associate the accessibility implementation technique.

the implementation of the WCAG 2.0 accessibility guidelines proposed by W3C. It consists of HTML classes that, when instantiated, provide objects that, when executed, provide an accessible HTML code. Homero provides support for the implementation of various types of HTML elements, such as tables, images, lists, texts, and links.

In Figure 6 is possible analyze a code of an application developed using the Homero Framework. When an object

of the image class was created, in line 9, the alternative text was not defined. The second parameter of the constructor was defined with null value, which caused an accessibility error in the final application (Warning-in English: The image assistant text was not specified).

Inclusion of accessibility elements in the phases of the software development process was possible by means of the development of the AccTrace tool and the Homero

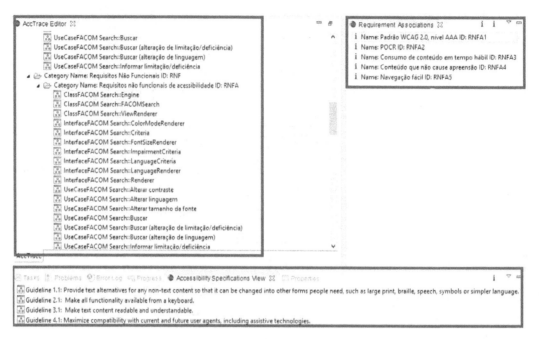

FIGURE 4: Use cases, UML classes, and accessibility requirements association.

FIGURE 5: Source code and accessibility comments.

```
1  <?
2  include ("Homero.php");
3  $header = new Header("Apresentação Homero");
4  $header->setMeta('http-equiv="Content-Type"
5         content="text/html; charset=iso-8859-1"');
6
7  $interface = new Page("pt-br");
8  $interface->setCabecalho($header->generate());
9  $img = new Image("icones/logo.png",null,
10        "Homero", null,null);
11 $interface->setCorpo($img->generate());
12 $interface->generate();
13 ?>
```

Warning: O texto auxiliar da Imagem não foi especificado. in D:\www\Homero\Image.php on line 319

FIGURE 6: Example of an application developed using the Homero Framework [50].

Framework. However, each of the proposals had different focuses; i.e., the AccTrace tool dealt with the requirements engineering and software design phases and the Homero Framework dealt with the implementation phase. In this way, the integration and creation of a tool that could both support the software development cycle in a unified way and be improved was envisaged.

5. Acero: An Approach and a Tool for Development of Web Accessible Applications

5.1. Acero Approach. The high-level architecture proposed in this project is presented in Figure 7. In the upper layer, the main features designed specifically for the Acero approach and the main features of the AccTrace project are represented. The integration layer is responsible for connecting Acero and AccTrace modules to the infrastructure layer. Such infrastructure layer indicates the required servers and systems.

The Acero approach was implemented and the Acero tool was obtained. Next subsection explains details of the approach emphasizing our practical solution.

5.2. Acero Tool. According to the technical report presented by RebelLabs Tools and Technologies Land scape [52], in 2016 Eclipse IDE was used by 41% of Java developers. It was originally designed for Java development; however, it currently supports several other languages such as PHP, C / C ++, and Python. In addition, it has a public license, which allows the developer to create plug-ins to improve their development environment.

Therefore, Acero was proposed as a plug-in for the Eclipse IDE allowing the integration of the AccTrace tool, developed in Java and the Homero Framework, developed in PHP, and other available tools. In addition, the IDE enables communication with web accessibility analysis tools, such as Achecker and AccessMonitor, which are fundamental in the context of the proposal. Finally, it has public license, which allows developers to create new features.

The Acero tool makes it easier to reuse classes from the Homero Framework because it allows the developer to use it at a higher abstraction level. Through the use of a wizard, it is possible to make the semiautomatic filling of the necessary attributes for instantiation of the Homero Framework classes. The Homero module can contribute to productivity and accessibility because the user does not need to search the documentation of the framework to know the methods and their arguments. In addition, the user becomes aware about which fields may affect the accessibility of the content.

By inserting the data in the wizard fields, such as filename, header, coding, and page language, the Acero tool will enable the use of the Homero Framework in the context of the current project, as shown in Figure 8. The result obtained can be observed in Figure 9. On the left side it is possible to observe the file created within the current project and on the right side it is possible to observe the content of the Homero.php file that has the basic template of the Homero Framework.

Using the correct syntax, it is possible to automatically submit a code to the Homero Framework and obtain as output an accessible code (HTML extension). In addition, it is possible to check which errors the user made and how such errors interfere with the accessibility of the content (for example, if the user forgot to fill in some required field).

Figure 10 summarizes the steps considering the execution of a particular source code. When programming and defining the compilation attributes, the developer presses the *Finish* button and it is generated a file in the HTML format that represents the interface. The user will be able to view the interface in the Eclipse IDE's internal browser and obtain additional information in the Acero Output Window, such as errors in the source code.

Another important feature obtained with the integration of the Homero Framework was the possibility of interpreting code written in the PHP language even when the end user does not have a PHP server with the framework installed in their computer (such functionality is useful in limited environments).

The development environment of the Acero tool offers the possibility for the developer to submit the source code to the tools of automatic assessment of accessibility. This module is very important because it allows the user to evaluate in their development environment the compliance of the code with the accessibility guidelines.

As shown in Figure 11, some fields must be completed by developers so that the evaluation can be performed. Basically, the name of the file that will be evaluated, the name of the output file that will contain the results and the accessibility guidelines are required. The guidelines are available according to each evaluation tool selected by the user.

It is possible to assist the developer by alerting them to possible source code errors. For example, if the user inserted an image, the Acero tool can present the main errors that affect the accessibility of the image element so that they can be avoided.

Figure 12 shows an example of using the predictor of Acero over an HTML code. It is possible to notice that the element imagem.png (line 7) exists (indicated by OK in the figure). Differently, for the header element (line 3) there are three errors that can affect the functioning and the accessibility of the final product. Two of the errors, called E_USER_ERROR, prevent the script from functioning (JS and CSS files not found). Otherwise, errors called E_USER_WARNING impair accessibility. In the case of the prediction of the image element (line 7) if the developer does not add auxiliary text to the image, the script will work; however, the image will not be accessible.

The creation of the traceability matrix in PDF format offers the possibility for the developer to quickly identify links between generated artifacts, especially presenting artifacts that can be affected if a change is made. In addition, Acero allows users to check and correct consistency problems in the file that links requirements, UML artifacts, implementation techniques, and source code comments. Therefore, it will be possible to perform reverse tracing, that is, checking the consistency between the .acctrace association file and the

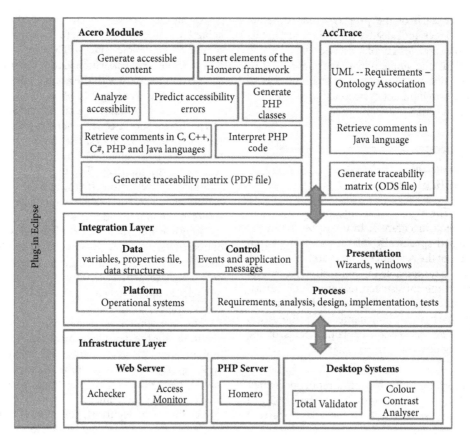

FIGURE 7: Overview of proposed architecture for the Acero approach.

FIGURE 8: Homero Framework and Acero tool integration.

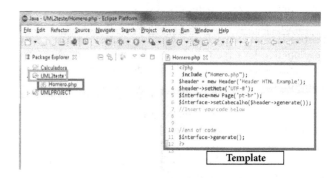

FIGURE 9: Example of file created in the current project containing the basic template for the use of the Homero Framework.

project files. This functionality is useful when modifications occur in the project, for example, creating and deleting requirements and classes.

The Acero tool allows the automatic creation of PHP classes with comments for implementation of accessibility using the UML artifacts and the traceability matrix. In addition, the association between UML artifacts, requirements,

and accessibility ontology may be retrieved. This function is important because the AccTrace tool supports only Java code. With this new feature it is possible to retrieve comments in source code written in PHP, C, C ++, C#, PHP, JavaScript, and Java languages.

It is also important to note that the Acero tool offers the user the possibility of using the Color Contrast Analyzer tool (https://www.paciellogroup.com/resources/ contrastanalyser/). It allows the analysis of contrasts of an interface and simulation from the perspective of users with visual impairment, such as cataract and color blindness. The Total Validator Basic tool allows the validation of guidelines

FIGURE 10: Example of the process to generate an interface accessible from a PHP code and using the Homero Framework.

in the user's source code in offline mode. Both tools are relevant and consolidated in the development of accessible solutions and are indicated by W3C [53]. The integration of these tools in the context of the Acero tool provides the user with a broader development environment as it directly contributes to the automation of accessibility criteria and reduces the possibility of inclusion of errors due to lack of developer knowledge.

6. Evaluation

Two case studies were carried out with the objective of evaluating the effectiveness of the proposed solution, analyzing whether it actually assists in the design and construction of accessible products. Therefore, the evaluation stage took into account Acero approach and tool, including its elements: the MTA process, the AccTrace tool, and the Homero Framework. The main task assigned to the participants was the development of an accessible calculator.

The evaluation of the proposed solution was divided into two stages: initially, as presented in Section 6.1, the MTA process was useful for specifying accessibility elements of the application. Afterwards, the application was developed based on such specification. The second case study, as presented in Section 6.2, used the same specification, however, the focus was to evaluate functionalities of the Acero tool.

6.1. Case Study 1: Focusing on the Acero Approach. The MTA process was used during definition of the main settings for the application, as presented as follows. Accessibility requirements were our main focus.

(1) System requirements elicitation

   (a) The accessible calculator will be developed to users with visual impairment. They will use a screen reader as assistive technology. They will use computer to run the application. It is not intended for use on mobile devices

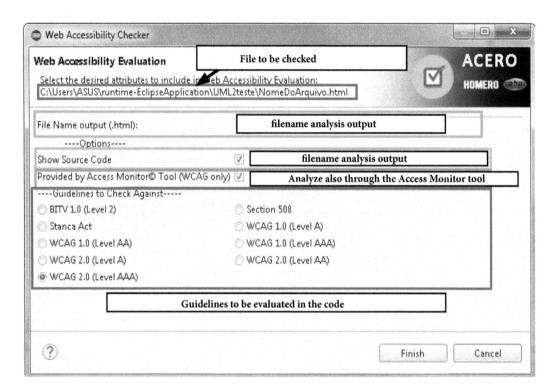

FIGURE 11: Screen shot of the Acero tool used to evaluate accessibility guidelines in a source code.

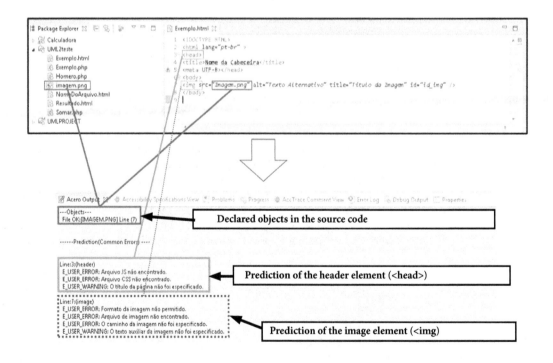

FIGURE 12: Example prediction of resource use in an HTML page using the Acero tool.

(2) System requirements analysis

   (a) The final users use computers frequently and they have completed high school education at least. The application proposal is to allow the execution of the four basic mathematical operations. Final users have previously used similar applications and often use screen readers. Criteria established by ISO/IEC 12207 were considered for accessibility evaluation of system requirements analysis

(3) System architectural design

   (a) The application is very simple and this activity was not relevant

(4) Software requirements analysis

   (a) The end user is a 64 years old man. His deficiency is low vision. He was interviewed and the following accessibility requirements were identified: (a) provide text alternatives for any nontext content; (b) make all functionality available from a keyboard; (c) do not design content in a way that is known to cause seizures; (d) provide ways to help users navigate, find content, and determine where they are; (e) make text content readable and understandable; and (f) help users avoid and correct mistakes. Criteria established by ISO/IEC 12207 were considered for accessibility evaluation of software requirements analysis

(5) Software design

   (a) A prototype of the accessible application was developed prioritizing the use of labels, colors, images, text editing fields and navigational design. Criteria established by ISO/IEC 12207 were considered for accessibility evaluation of the software design

(6) Software construction

   (a) The accessible application was developed using the Acero tool. The HTML language was used to implement accessibility requirements. Accessibility test of each unit was carried out using the Total Validator Basic tool (https://www.totalvalidator.com/tools/). The results allowed to evaluate if the established requirements were implemented

(7) Software integration testing

   (a) The application is very simple and this activity was not relevant

(8) Acceptance testing

   (a) The same user who provided the requirements participated in the acceptance test. In general, the application developed by the students was satisfactory. He suggested changes to the use of labels containing auxiliary texts and navigation design

(9) System testing

   (a) The final user used the NVDA screen reader (https://www.nvaccess.org/) to run the application and he considered that the elements of the system worked correctly when together

The case study was carried out with the participation of eight students enrolled in the Faculty of Computer Science of the Federal University of Mato Grosso do Sul (Facom / UFMS), in modalities of graduation, master's degree, and doctorate. All participants contributed in the context of the MTA process, doing interviews with the end user, specifying, and making design decisions. Additionally, they used the Acero tool to the software codification.

Students received training focusing on a general approach to accessibility (approximately 30 minutes) and information about participant's theoretical knowledge was collected. Seven participants did not have knowledge about accessibility guidelines and about WCAG 2.0.

Students defined the functional and nonfunctional accessibility requirements (interviewing the end user) and designed use case diagrams, class diagrams, and a graphical interface prototype (it was presented to the final user). Finally, the student spent an hour and forty minutes for the application codification and tests.

As a result, participants indicated that they were able to easily understand and perform the proposed activities. The received suggestions were incorporated into the planning of the case study 2 and, basically, aimed to increase training time on accessibility and to include new training on the Eclipse IDE. The final application obtained is presented in the Figure 13.

6.2. Case Study 2: Focusing on the Acero Tool. The second case study was conducted with 14 undergraduate students from the last semester of the Computer Engineering course of the Facom / UFMS. The students developed the application individually: 7 students used the Acero approach and tool and 7 students did not use it. In relation to the profile of the participants, 21% indicated they had excellent knowledge about object-oriented programming and 79% indicated that they had good knowledge; 26% indicated that they had excellent knowledge in PHP, Java, and HTML programming languages and 74% indicated that they had the necessary knowledge to develop applications of medium complexity. In addition, only two students indicated that they had minimal theoretical and practical knowledge about web accessibility. Other participants did not have knowledge about this subject. The following hypotheses were considered:

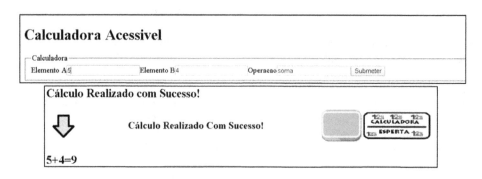

FIGURE 13: Final application for the case study 1 (in Portuguese).

(i) Time:

    (1) H0: the use of the Acero approach and tool does not reduce the time of development of accessible application.

    (2) Ha0: the use of the Acero approach and tool reduces the time of development of accessible application.

(ii) Accessibility of the developed application:

    (1) H1: the use of the Acero approach and tool does not help in the design of accessible application.

    (2) Ha1: the use of the Acero approach and tool assists in the design of accessible application.

In order to mitigate validity threats, training on accessibility (90 minutes) and use of the Eclipse IDE were offered to the participants before the execution of the case study. The same problem of first case study was considered, i.e., development of an accessible calculator. Supporting files and diagrams were provided. The study was divided into five stages:

    (1) Step 1: import the Acero tool files into the Eclipse IDE.

    (2) Step 2: define the application programming logic.

    (3) Step 3: design and implementation of the accessible interface of the application.

    (4) Step 4: interface accessibility analysis.

    (5) Step 5: host the web Application.

Results of the case study indicated that the two groups have relative equivalence in the elapsed mean time for performing steps (1) and (2) (Figure 14). In these steps no group used the Acero approach and tool because it was external adjustments such as file import, definition programming logic and web code hosting. However, in stages 3, 4, and 5 there was a difference in the meantime of execution of the groups, and it can be inferred that in step (3) the Acero approach and tool contributed to the application development, with the mean time less than the group that did not use the tool. In addition, in step (4), participants who used the Acero tool took less time to complete the step. This difference may have occurred due to the inclusion

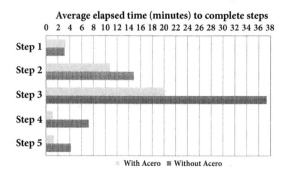

FIGURE 14: Average time for groups to complete the steps proposed in the study.

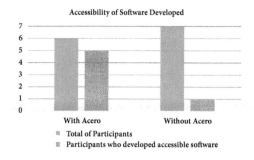

FIGURE 15: Accessibility of the content.

of the evaluation accessibility module in Acero. Therefore, considering the results obtained, it is possible to reject the null hypothesis H0.

Regarding the second hypothesis, as observed in the Figure 15, it is noticed that only one of the students who used the Acero approach and tool did not develop an AAA level application of WCAG 2.0. Without the use of the Acero tool, only one student developed a level AAA application of WCAG (considering the WCAG 2.0 guidelines that are automatically evaluated). Therefore, we can also reject the null hypothesis H1.

It was observed that the use of Acero reached the proposed objectives, supporting different stages of the development process. In addition, it proved to be compatible and promising in supporting integration with other tools, since all participants were able to finalize the proposed script for the study.

7. Conclusions and Contributions

This research was started with the objective of designing a methodology to integrate several tools to provide support to the software engineer and the programmer in relation to the development of accessible web applications. Through the case study, it was verified that this objective was reached because the participants were able to go through the entire development process and generate accessible applications.

As the main results achieved, it is noted that the Acero approach and tool contribute to the following:

(i) Ensuring that accessibility is a constant concern throughout the development phase, supporting each stage of the software process directly in the development environment.

(ii) Promoting the familiarization of software engineers and developers with the accessibility and international guidelines proposed to achieve them.

(iii) Providing mechanisms, such as wizards, that facilitate the use of the tool and the implementation of accessibility guidelines during software design and development.

(iv) Automating processes that were once manual, for example, the traceability matrix generation that maintains the relationships including requirements, UML artifacts, and class accessibility implementation techniques.

(v) Integrating and increasing functionalities in the Acc-Trace and Homero Framework tools. For example, the traceability matrix (previously generated only in the ODS extension) can be generated in the Acero tool in PDF format, a more common format. In addition, the Homero Framework was extended so that it could be used directly within the Eclipse IDE, without the need for the user to be dependent on their documentation or to have knowledge about object-oriented programming.

The choice of the technological tools that could be integrated in order to construct the Acero tool was an important stage of this work. Therefore, a major challenge of this research was to find out which tools were appropriate, the form that each one operated within the application development process, and how to integrate them in a common development environment. The main limitations with respect to the Acero tool are that it supports only Java and PHP programming languages and only considers the WCAG 2.0 guidelines.

The research area that involves the integration between accessibility, development process, and integration of support tools is relatively recent and needs to be improved. Therefore, considering the results obtained in this work, several research proposals can be explored. The following are suggestions for future work:

(1) Include other accessibility standards: designers and developers can choose which standard they would like to consider.

(2) Consider alternatives to the evaluation of guidelines that can not be automated.

(3) Carry out a detailed study of universal design principles and identify possible extension points in the Acero tool that can implement them.

(4) Carry out new case studies considering accessibility specialists and end users.

(5) Provide designers and developers with proposals for architectural models considering different domains (for example, e-gov, e-commerce, etc.). Such architectural models should include accessibility standards and allow the generation of applications in an agile way.

(6) Identify and adopt mechanisms that promote the transfer of knowledge and technology generated for the industry.

In general, it should be noted that this work mainly contributed to the development of an innovative software solution whose focus was to help developers in the design of accessible solutions. The case studies allowed to identify positive points and constraints of the Acero approach and tool and indicated the feasibility of the proposal as an alternative for the development of accessible web applications.

Acknowledgments

The authors thank CAPES and FUNDECT (T.O. 102/2016) for financial support.

References

[1] International Telecommunication Union, ICT Facts and Figures: The World in 2015, Retrieved July, 2018 from: https://www.itu.int/en/ITU-D/Statistics/Documents/facts/ICTFactsFigures2015.pdf.

[2] L. E. Janlert and E. Stolterman, "The meaning of interactivity—some proposals for definitions and measures," *Human-Computer Interaction*, vol. 32, no. 3, pp. 103–138, 2017.

[3] M. C. Rodriguez-Sanchez and J. Martinez-Romo, "GAWA – Manager for accessibility Wayfinding apps," *International Journal of Information Management*, vol. 37, no. 6, pp. 505–519, 2017.

[4] A. Iqbal, F. Ullah, H. Anwar et al., "Interoperable Internet-of-Things platform for smart home system using Web-of-Objects and cloud," *Sustainable Cities and Society*, vol. 38, pp. 636–646, 2018.

[5] World Health Organization, Disability and health, Retrieved January, 2018 from: http://www.who.int/mediacentre/factsheets/fs352/en/.

[6] W3C, Making the Web Accessible, Retrieved December, 2017 from: http://www.w3.org/WAI/.

[7] M. F. Cabrera-Umpiérrez, "3rd Generation accessibility: information and communication technologies towards universal access," *Universal Access in the Information Society*, vol. 15, no. 1, pp. 1–3, 2016.

[8] R. Babu, R. Singh, and J. Ganesh, "AIS transactions on human-computer interaction," *Association for Information Systems*, vol. 2, no. 4, pp. 73–94, 2010.

[9] P. P. Rau, L. Zhou, N. Sun, and R. Zhong, "Evaluation of web accessibility in China: changes from 2009 to 2013," *Universal Access in the Information Society*, vol. 15, no. 2, pp. 297–303, 2016.

[10] H. B. Paulsen, *Finding an Optimal Method for Conducting Accessibility Evaluations of the Norwegian Tax Administration Website, [Master thesis]*, Oslo and Akershus University College of Applied Sciences, 2016, http://hdl.handle.net/10642/3345.

[11] E. Loiacono and S. Djamasbi, "Corporate website accessibility: does legislation matter?" *Universal Access in the Information Society*, vol. 12, no. 1, pp. 115–124, 2013.

[12] S. Giraud, P. Thérouanne, and D. D. Steiner, "Web accessibility: Filtering redundant and irrelevant information improves website usability for blind users," *International Journal of Human-Computer Studies*, vol. 111, pp. 23–35, 2018.

[13] P. Sherman, Cost-Justifying Accessibility, Retrieved October, 2017 from: https://www.ischool.utexas.edu/l385t21/AU_WP_Cost_Justifying_Accessibility.pdf.

[14] K. Groves, "How Expensive is Web Accessibility?" Retrieved September, 2013 from: http://www.karlgroves.com/2011/11/30/how-expensive-is-accessibility/.

[15] I. Management Association, *Assistive Technologies: Concepts, Methodologies, Tools, and Applications: Concepts, Methodologies, Tools, and Applications*, Information Science Reference, 2014, https://books.google.com.br/books?id=LN6WBQAAQBAJ.

[16] M. Ganslandt and M. Sutinen, "Web Standardization," Center for European Law and Economics, 2009, http://www.talkstandards.com/wp-content/uploads/2009/08/web-standards-090828-final.pdf.

[17] Web Content Accessibility Guidelines (WCAG) 2.0, Retrieved October, 2017 from http://www.w3.org/TR/WCAG20/.

[18] How WCAG 2.0 Differs from WCAG 1.0, Retrieved August, 2017 from: http://www.w3.org/WAI/WCAG20/from10/diff.php.

[19] J. Lazar, D. Goldstein, and A. Taylor, *Ensuring Digital Accessibility through Process and Policy*, Elsevier Science, 2015, https://books.google.com.br/books?id=YepDBAAAQBAJ.

[20] L. Moreno, P. Martínez, J. Muguerza, and J. Abascal, "Support resource based on standards for accessible e-government transactional services," *Computer Standards & Interfaces*, vol. 58, pp. 146–157, 2018.

[21] Web Standards for the Government of Canada, Retrieved August, 2015 from: http://www.tbs-sct.gc.ca/ws-nw/index-eng.asp.

[22] Japanese Industrial Standards and Web Accessibility Infrastructure Commission, Retrieved July, 2018 from: http://waic.jp/docs/jis2010/understanding.html.

[23] Disability Act, Retrieved July, 2018 from http://www.oireachtas.ie/documents/bills28/acts/2005/a1405.pdf.

[24] Legge Stanca, Retrieved July, 2018 from: http://www.webaccessibile.org/.

[25] eMAG - Modelo de Acessibilidade em Governo Electrónico, Retrieved June, 2018 from: http://emag.governoeletronico.gov.br/.

[26] Web Content Accessibility Guidelines (WCAG) 2.1, Retrieved July, 2018 from: https://www.w3.org/TR/WCAG21/.

[27] G. Brajnik, Y. Yesilada, and S. Harper, "The expertise effect on web accessibility evaluation methods," *Human–Computer Interaction*, vol. 26, no. 3, pp. 246–283, 2011.

[28] A. P. Freire, *Disabled People and the Web: User-based Measurement of Accessibility [Ph.D. thesis]*, University of York, 2012.

[29] A. Aizpurua, S. Harper, and M. Vigo, "Exploring the relationship between web accessibility and user experience," *International Journal of Human-Computer Studies*, vol. 91, pp. 13–23, 2016, http://dx.doi.org/10.1016/j.ijhcs.2016.03.008.

[30] WCAG-EM Overview: Website Accessibility Conformance Evaluation Methodology, Retrieved October, 2017 from: https://www.w3.org/WAI/eval/conformance.html.

[31] M. Vigo, J. Brown, and V. Conway, "Benchmarking web accessibility evaluation tools: measuring the harm of sole reliance on automated tests," in *Proceedings of the 10th International Cross-Disciplinary Conference on Web Accessibility*, Rio de Janeiro, Brazil, May 2013, http://doi.acm.org/10.1145/2461121.2461124.

[32] E. Krainz, J. Feiner, and M. Fruhmann, *Human-Centered and Error-Resilient Systems Development*, C. Bogdan, J. Gulliksen, S. Sauer et al., Eds., Springer International Publishing, Cham, Switzerland, 2016.

[33] E. Krainz and K. Miesenberger, "Accapto, a generic design and development toolkit for accessible mobile apps," *Studies in Health Technology and Informatics*, vol. 242, pp. 660–664, 2017.

[34] E. Krainz, K. Miesenberger, and J. Feiner, "Can We Improve App Accessibility with Advanced Development Methods?" in *Computers Helping People with Special Needs*, K. Miesenberger and G. Kouroupetroglou, Eds., pp. 64–70, Springer International Publishing, Cham, Switzerland, 2018.

[35] H. Vieritz, F. Yazdi, D. Schilberg, P. Göhner, and S. Jeschke, "User centered design of accessible web and automation systems," in *Information Quality in e-Health*, A. Holzinger and K. M. Simonic, Eds., pp. 367–378, Springer, Heidelberg, Berlin, Germany, 2011.

[36] M. González-García, L. Moreno, and P. Martínez, "A Model-Based Tool to Develop an Accessible Media Player," in *Proceedings of the 17th International ACM SIGACCESS Conference on Computers & Accessibility*, pp. 415-416, New York, NY, USA, 2015.

[37] L. Zouhaier, Y. Hlaoui Bendaly, and L. Jemni Ben, "A MDA-based Approach for Enabling Accessibility Adaptation of User Interface for Disabled People," in *Proceedings of the 16th International Conference on Enterprise Information Systems*, pp. 120–127, SCITEPRESS - Science and Technology Publications, Lda, Portugal, 2014.

[38] R. Miñón, J. Abascal, A. Aizpurua, I. Cearreta, B. Gamecho, and N. Garay, "Model-Based Accessible User Interface Generation in Ubiquitous Environments," in *Proceedings of the Human-Computer Interaction – INTERACT 2011*, P. Campos, N. Graham, J. Jorge, N. Nunes, P. Palanque, and M. Winckler, Eds., pp. 572–575, Springer, Heidelberg, Berlin, Germany, 2011.

[39] R. Bonacin, M. C. C. Baranauskas, and M. A. Rodrigues, *Information Systems*, J. Filipe and J. Cordeiro, Eds., Springer Berlin Heidelberg, Berlin, Germany, 2009.

[40] T. H. Røssvoll and K. S. Fuglerud, *Universal Access in Human-Computer Interaction. Design Methods, Tools, and Interaction Techniques for eInclusion*, C. Stephanidis and M. Antona, Eds., Springer Berlin Heidelberg, Berlin, Germany, 2013.

[41] A. L. Dias, R. P. M. Fortes, and P. C. Masiero, "Increasing the Quality of Web Systems: By Inserting Requirements of Accessibility and Usability," in *Eighth International Conference on the Quality of Information and Communications Technology*, pp. 224–229, IEEE, Lisboa, Portugal, 2012.

[42] S. Sanchez-Gordon, M.-L. Sánchez-Gordón, and S. Luján-Mora, "Towards an engineering process for developing accessible software in small software enterprises," in *Proceedings of the 11th International Conference on Evaluation of Novel Software Approaches to Software Engineering, ENASE 2016*, pp. 241–246, Rome, Italy, April 2016.

[43] L. S. Maia, *Um Processo para o Desenvolvimento de Aplicações Web Acessíveis, [Master thesis]*, Universidade Federal de Mato Grosso do Sul, Brazil, 2010.

[44] ISO/IEC, ISO/IEC 12207 - Standard for Informational Technology - Software Lifecycle Processes (ISO/IEC, 1, ch. de la Voie-Creuse - CP 56 - CH-1211 Geneva 20 - Switzerland), 1998.

[45] D. Sloan, A. Heath, F. Hamilton, B. Kelly, H. Petrie, and L. Phipps, "Contextual web accessibility - maximizing the benefit of accessibility guidelines," in *Proceedings of the 2006 International Cross-Disciplinary Workshop on Web Accessibility (W4A): Building the Mobile Web: Rediscovering Accessibility?* pp. 121–131, ACM, New York, NY, USA, May 2006.

[46] D. Hoffman, E. Grivel, and L. Battle, "Designing software architectures to facilitate accessible Web applications," *IBM Systems Journal*, vol. 44, no. 3, pp. 467–483, 2005.

[47] R. G. de Branco, *Acessibilidade nas Fases de Engenharia de Requisitos, Projeto e Codificação de Software: Uma Ferramenta de Apoio [Master thesis]*, Universidade Federal de Mato Grosso do Sul, Brazil, 2013.

[48] R. G. de Branco, M. I. Cagnin, and D. M. B. Paiva, "AccTrace: considerando acessibilidade no processo de desenvolvimento de software," in *Proceedings of the XXI Sessão de Ferramentas do Congresso Brasileiro de Software: Teoria e Prática*, pp. 117–124, 2014.

[49] AEGIS Ontology, Retrieved July, 2013 from: http://www.aegis-project.eu/index.phpoption=com_content&view=article&id=107&Itemid=65.

[50] R. C. Oliveira, *Homero: Um Framework de Apoio ao Desenvolvimento de Interfaces de Aplicações Web Acessíveis, [Master thesis]*, Universidade Federal de Mato Grosso do Sul, Brazil, 2013.

[51] R. C. de Oliveira, A. P. Freire, D. M. Paiva, M. I. Cagnin, and H. Rubinsztejn, "A Framework to Facilitate the Implementation of Technical Aspects of Web Accessibility," in *Proceedings of the 16th International Conference on Human-Computer Interaction*, pp. 3–13, 2014.

[52] S. Maple, "Java tools and technologies landscape," RebelLabs, 2016, https://zeroturnaround.com/rebellabs/java-tools-and-technologies-landscape-2016/.

[53] W3C - Web Accessibility Initiative – Web Accessibility Evaluation Tools List, Retrieved May, 2016 from: https://www.w3.org/WAI/ER/tools/.

12

A New PC-Based Text Entry System based on EOG Coding

Metin Yildiz ⓘ[1] and Hesna Özbek Ülkütaş[2]

[1]Department of Biomedical Engineering, Baskent University, Ankara, Turkey
[2]Institute of Science and Engineering, Baskent University, Ankara, Turkey

Correspondence should be addressed to Metin Yildiz; myildiz@baskent.edu.tr

Academic Editor: Armando Bennet Barreto

Some disadvantages of optical eye tracking systems have increased the interest to EOG (Electrooculography) based Human Computer Interaction (HCI). However, text entry attempts using EOG have been slower than expected because the eyes should move several times for entering a character. In order to improve the writing speed and accuracy of EOG based text entry, a new method based on the coding of eye movements has been suggested in this study. In addition, a real time EOG based HCI system has developed to implement the method. In our method all characters have been encoded by single saccades in 8 directions and different dwell time. In order to standardize dwell times and facilitate the coding process, computer assisted voice guidance was used. A number of experiments have been conducted to examine the effectiveness of the proposed method and system. At the end of the fifth trials, an experienced user was able to write at average 13.2 wpm (5 letters = 1 word) with 100% accuracy using the developed system. The results of our experiments have shown that text entry with the eye can be done quickly and efficiently with the proposed method and system.

1. Introduction

Various human-computer interaction (HCI) methods have been proposed for the paralyzed or Amyotrophic Lateral Sclerosis (ALS) patients' communication. Some HCI systems are designed to fulfill the most desired patient commands [1–3]. Others have focused on text entry by various virtual keyboards [4–7].

The systems referred to as the Brain Computer Interface (BCI) are, in general, based on choosing the letters of a desired word to be written with a virtual keyboard. The Electroencephalogram (EEG) signals can be used for this purpose. However, only a few words can be written per minute through the conventional EEG based systems [8].

In some studies based on the knowledge that such patients can move their eyes, saccades (30-150 ms), fixations (200-600 ms), and blinks of the eye were used to increase the text entry speed [9]. Often a virtual keyboard is used to write with eyes using optical or electrooculography (EOG) based tracking systems. The performance of optical tracking systems that use simple video cameras may fluctuate in accordance with the ambient light and head movements [9]. It is

possible to determine where the eyes more precisely gaze with pupil-corneal reflection tracking devices. However, its costs are quite high. Moreover, they require precise calibration at every use [9]. In a study using such systems, typing speeds of 20 words per minute (wpm) have been achieved [6]. Kristensson et al. 2012 improved the writing speed to 46 wpm using the automatic word completion software with a similar eye tracking device [10]. These improvements have triggered the studies to develop optical eye tracking devices at low costs for the benefit of larger number of patients [11]. As an alternative to optical tracking, EOG was also used to detect eye movements.

The potential differences between the cornea and the retina during eye movements constitute the EOG signal. Clinically, EOG is used to determine the functional integrity between the retinal pigment epithelium and the photoreceptors [12, 13]. When the eyes are moved to a direction, the EOG signals taken from the electrodes placed around the eyes show changes proportional to the gaze angle. Gaze in different directions one after the other leads to drift in the base line of the EOG signals. Involuntary blinks also make it difficult to predict the gaze direction. So it is quite difficult to determine the gazing point exactly. However, it is relatively easy to determine gaze direction. In this way, control of the electric wheelchair [14, 15], the hospital alarm system [16], and the electrical hospital bed [17] has been done easily by EOG. In order to determine the gaze direction more accurately rule-based [18], neural network [19], hidden markov model [20], clustering and fuzzy logic [21], discriminant analysis [22], nearest neighborhood [7], and support vector machine [23] classification methods have been used. EOG has also been used to determine the intentions, behaviors, and cognitive processes of people and REM stage of sleep [9, 24, 25]. Further details of EOG applications can be found in the studies of Räihä et al. (2011), Istance and Hyrskykari (2012), and Majaranta et al. (2014).

The use of EOG signals to detect eye movements provides some advantages over video-based systems. It does not get affected by environment's light and can process more easily than video images [6, 9]. However, it requires the use of electrodes attached to the patients which may cause some discomfort. Moreover, the EOG measurement system requires electrical safety precautions.

Several methods have been used in EOG based text entry systems. Some of the studies have focused on moving the cursor towards the desired letter of a virtual keyboard by moving the eye in four directions (right, left, up, and down) and the desired letter is selected by the blink of an eye [7, 26–28]. The achieved writing speeds are higher than the BCI systems but it is still insufficient when compared with optical tracking based methods. In another EOG-based approach, it has been tried to draw letters using eye movements [21, 28–31]. This method has been able to improve the writing speed by about 8 wpm, but the recognition rate of written characters is low. As another alternative, coding of letters with several consecutive eye movements has been used. Porta and Turina (2008) encoded the eye movements in different directions for transferring letters and numbers to the computer [32]. In their method, a character was encoded with at least two eye movements. Even experienced people could only write 6.8 words per minute with eyes in this method. The last two methods mentioned have more advantages when compared with others. They do not require a virtual keyboard and can be developed as an embedded system.

Although saccades of the eye are much faster, the writing speed of EOG based methods is limited to 8 wpm. In this study, firstly, various experiments have been conducted to determine moving speed and accuracy of the human eyes in different directions (right, left, up, down, and diagonals) and its combinations. In order to improve the writing speed and accuracy of EOG based text entry systems, a new EOG coding method has been suggested according to the results of these experiments. A real time computer based system was designed to implement our method. The results of the first experiments with the developed method and the system were given below.

2. Materials and Methods

2.1. Determination of the Coding Potential of the Eyes. In EOG-based HCI systems, eye movements at different directions are taken as input. Firstly, various experiments were carried out to determine the subjects' gazing speed to different directions and the implementation accuracy.

At this stage of the study, two channels of a physiologic data acquisition system (BIOPAC MP36) were used to collect EOG data. The EOG signals on the horizontal plane were recorded through the small surface electrodes attached on the two sides of the eyes, while the vertical plane EOG was recorded by the electrodes attached over and under of an eye. Two reference electrodes were attached on the forehead. Sampling rate of the data acquisition system was set to 200 Hz and the cut-off frequency of its filters was set to 0 and 35 Hz. Motion directions were determined offline through a program we had developed in our previous study [18]. Briefly, the baseline of the EOG signals is removed first. The positive and negative thresholds of vertical and horizontal EOGs are calculated by 40% of maximum and minimum EOG amplitudes. The vertical and horizontal EOG signals that exceed these thresholds are coded by specific codes. The gaze direction is determined by a decision tree using these codes. In order to eliminate the effect of involuntary blinks, the encodings in the vertical EOG channel with a duration of less than 100 ms are neglected.

Our study protocol was approved by the ethical committee of Baskent University for clinical experiments. Four female and six male, healthy biomedical engineering senior students (22 ± 2 years old) participated in this part of the study. Their informed consent was obtained before the experiments.

In the first part of the study, the subjects were asked to look straight forward at first. Later, they moved their eyes in one direction and then looked straight again. Each subject repeated this procedure 10 times during 10 sessions (total 100 repeat). Table 1 shows participants' coding durations and recognition rate of the vertical, horizontal, and diagonal eye movement (mean (min-max)) in the first and tenth experiments. The sequential binary permutation of these 8 eye movements can be used to encode all characters in an alphabet. Some results of this trial are also given in Table 1.

According to Table 1, the encoding speed of characters that are coded by single directional eye movements is much higher than others. Diagonal eye movements are relatively slow. As the number of trials was increased, the coding speed of a character was also increased 30-45% for one single direction and 20-30% for the others. However, the accuracy of coding decreased by about 10% with acceleration in the tenth experiment. Another striking aspect revealed in Table 1 is that sequential and/or diagonal eye movements' recognition rate is relatively low. According to these results, we decided that using these eye movements would reduce the speed and accuracy of writing.

Another approach that could allow the encoding of eyes movement was proposed by Barea et al. 2012. They showed that EOG signals produced by eye movements with four different angles (10°, 20°, 30°, and 40°) in one single direction could be separated from each other [33]. In order to determine this methods' efficiency at fast codding, we conducted some trials on several participants. An example EOG signal of these trials is given in Figure 1.

TABLE 1: Speed and recognition accuracy of different directional eye movements.

N=10		First trial		Tenth trial	
Attention directions		Speed (sec.)	Accuracy (%)	Speed (sec.)	Accuracy (%)
Right	→	1,06(0,80-1,21)	92(80-96)	0,69(0,42-0,73)	84(72-88)
Up	↑	1,26(0,88-1,42)	88(76-92)	0,71(0,44-0,84)	80(68-88)
Right diagonal down	↘	1,29(0,82-1,54)	82(72-88)	0,87(0,58-0,93)	76(68-84)
Right-Right	→ →	2,63(2.01-2,89)	84(72-88)	2,14(1,8-2,28)	72(64-76)
Left-Down	← ↓	2,83(2,04-2,96)	80(68-84)	2,23(1,82-2,39)	68(64-72)
Left diagonal down-Up	↙ ↑	3,09(2,06-3,32)	74(62-84)	2,20(1,9-2,64)	64(60-72)

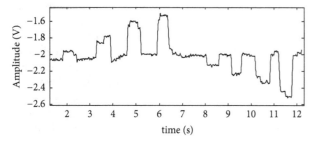

FIGURE 1: Recorded EOG signal when gazing right and left directions with 4 different angles.

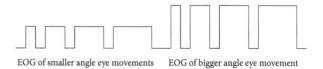

EOG of smaller angle eye movements　　EOG of bigger angle eye movement

FIGURE 2: An illustration of the EOG signals emerging during eye movements into one single direction with two different angles and four dwell times.

The obtained EOG signals can only be recognized if the subjects code the movements accurately. But our experiences have shown that recognition rate can extremely decrease when the subject tries to code these eye movements quickly.

2.2. Proposed Eyes Movement Coding Method. The experiments we have done to see the coding potential of eyes revealed that the diagonal and sequential eye movements decreased coding speed and accuracy. We found out that looking at one single direction with four different angles can shorten the coding time but it is difficult to apply this coding correctly. Consequently, we decided to use eye movements only on four main directions (up, down, right, and left).

In order to increase the number of characters encoded, eye movements in one single direction with two different angles have been used, which can be implemented much more easily than four angles. It is possible to encode only 8 characters with this method. To encode the other characters, subjects need to keep their eyes in one of the directions and angles during specified time periods. Thus, it has been possible to encode 32 and 40 characters for 4 and 5 different dwell times, respectively. An illustration of the EOG signals, which are expected to occur while all characters are encoded in one direction with two different angles for 4 different dwell times, is shown in Figure 2.

In order to standardize dwell times and facilitate the coding process, computer assisted voice guidance was used. When the user looks at one direction with an angle, the character that has the minimum dwell time in this direction and the angle is voiced by the computer. If the user turns their eyes to resting state within the first specified time, the selected character is written on the screen. Other characters in that direction are selected by the extension of dwell time. When

the first dwelling period expires, the second character in that direction is voiced by computer and the user is expected to approve it, and so on. It is known that human can respond to auditory stimuli in about 150 ms [34]. According to this information the minimum waiting time has been determined to be 200 ms. Thus, this has also overcome the problems that can be caused by the involuntary eye blinking.

Finally, in order to enable coding as fast as possible, the most used letters in Turkish alphabet were assigned to the least time-consuming directions and angles. While doing this, three exceptions were applied. In the text entry studies, 5 letters are considered as one word. It can be assumed that the spacing between words is also a frequently used character. Therefore, the shortest and greatest angle eye movement to the right was set as the space between the words. Second, the shortest and greatest angle eye movement to the left was set as the deletion of the last character. Third, the longest and greatest angle eye movement to the left was set as the deletion of the last written word. The position and order of the letters in our coding system are shown in Figure 3. In this sorting, six of the most used characters (about 50% usage rate) have been encoded in the shortest possible time.

2.3. The Developed Two-Channel EOG Acquisition System. The block diagram of the developed two-channel EOG acquisition system is given in Figure 4. An instrumentation amplifier (AD624) with a 130 dB CMRR (Common Mode Rejection Ratio) was used to suppress the electrode half-cell potentials and several hundred millivolts (mV) power line noise (50/60 Hz).

In order to prevent the output offset voltage that can be caused by the difference in electrode half-cell potentials, the differential voltage gain of this amplifier was set to 20. Ground driver circuit is basically used to filter the signals induced by the 50/60 Hz noise. The noise that is received by the electrodes is applied to the patient over a very high resistor

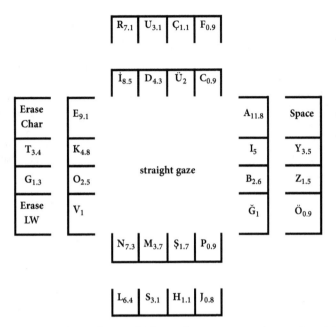

FIGURE 3: Sorting of characters in the proposed encoding method. Dwell times increase from right to left and top to bottom for character choosing. In addition the usage rates of characters in Turkish alphabet in text are indicated as the subindex of letters.

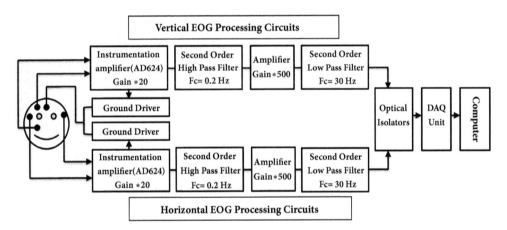

FIGURE 4: Developed EOG acquisition system.

after the phase inversion. This procedure not only increases the CMRR of the amplifier but also limits the current that can pass through the patient's body [35].

Second-order Butterwort filters were designed to filter the EOG signals. According to the ISCEV (International Society for Clinical Electrophysiology of Vision) EOG standards, a 0.5-30 Hz band pass filter is used to prevent base line shift [12]. However, the long dwell times in our coding method have caused us to pull down the low cut-off frequency (0.2 Hz) even further.

An additional amplifier was used to increase the amplitude of the EOG signals to 2-4 Volt level. Consequently, the small differences in the electrodes' half-cell potentials caused a serious offset in the base-line. In order to eliminate this, a potentiometer was connected to the offset adjustment terminals of the amplifier to shift the EOG level to 0 volt at resting state of eyes. To prevent the macroshock hazard, the user contacted circuits were powered with 9-volt batteries. Additionally, optical isolators were used to prevent any leakage current that may be caused by the computer. A Data AcQuisition (DAQ) card (USB-NI6009, by National Instruments) was used for transferring the analog signals to computer in 12 bit resolution.

2.4. Software of the Developed System. The software of the developed system consists of 3 main sections. These are a program enabling DAQ card to receive 2-channel EOG signals, a graphical user interface to control the system, and a program for processing and converting the acquired signal to character by the help of voiced guidance of computers. MATLAB 2007 was used as the development platform for the software. General flowchart of the software is given in Figure 5.

At the beginning of the program, some initial values are assigned and the DAQ card is programed for collecting data

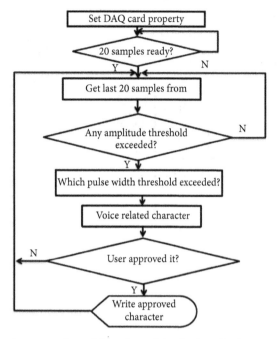

FIGURE 5: General flow chart of the developed software.

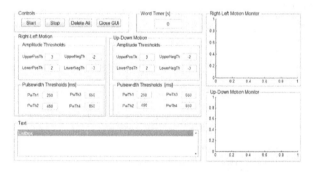

FIGURE 6: Graphic user interface of the developed system.

from 2 channels. The sampling frequency was set to 200 Hz. The collected data were read at every 20 samples (every 100 ms) from the DAQ card and processed as in the flowchart.

The developed graphic user interface is illustrated in Figure 6. The interface was equipped with Start/Stop and Clear/Delete buttons to control the system by the person performing the system tests. The desired character is determined by the EOG signal that exceeded a certain threshold when looking in a certain direction. The amplitudes of the EOG signals that will emerge during the eye movement might be different for different individuals or at different disease levels. For this reason, in order to select the relevant threshold values, the edit boxes have been inserted on the GUI. Before the first use, EOG threshold values should be determined for right-left and up-down eye movement by motion monitor panels in GUI.

When the user moves the eyes in a direction, the program determines which amplitude threshold value is passed and voices the first letter in the relevant direction. As previously

mentioned, most people react to acoustic stimulus in approximately 150 milliseconds [34]. Users can react slowly at the learning stage of the coding method. When they memorize the method, they may react more quickly. Therefore we have added the edit boxes to GUI, which we call pulse width threshold. If the eyes are brought to resting position within a certain time period (pulse width thresholds) after an eye movement, the corresponding character will be written on the text box. Otherwise, the next character at the same direction and angle is voiced and expected to be approved by the user. The GUI is equipped with horizontal and vertical motion monitors that are used to show EOG signals to help with the above adjustments.

3. Results and Discussion

In this section, the performance of the developed EOG based text entry system is presented. Since our ethics committee permission covers the studies with a commercial physiological measurement system, the studies in this section have only been performed on one of the authors. The subject was 23 years old and has a master's degree in biomedical engineering. After a few attempts, the threshold values were set to the values shown in Figure 6. A timer was added to the system to determine the writing speed. The timer that is started when the first character starts to be written is stopped when the desired word is written, which ends with a space character. Elapsed time is shown in a textbox that is added to the system for experimental studies. The coding speed of a text was calculated by considering the space coding as an additional character. The writing speed is calculated in terms of words per minute (wpm) on the assumption that a word consists of 5 characters.

In the first experiments, all of the 29 letters in the Turkish alphabet were coded consecutively. 27 out of the 29 letters were written correctly in the first attempt. Two of them had to be erased and rewritten. So, the accuracy of codification in the first attempt was 93%. The writing speed of this attempt was 12.46 wpm.

In order to test our system, we have chosen words and simple phrases in Turkish (Table 2), which we think can meet the most basic needs of people who are confined to bed. The English equivalents of the words are also given in Table 2. Each word was written 5 times. Coding times, writing speed, and correct coding rate of characters are also given in Table 2.

While the writing speed was 11.84 wpm on average in the first trial, it was 13.2 words per minute in the fifth experiment. The accuracy was 86.2% on average in the first attempt. In the fifth attempt, it reached 100%.

After an adaptation period, it could be written at average 13.2 wpm with 100% accuracy by using the developed system. This performance is much better than conventional BCI systems. A comparison of the EOG-based typing and writing systems is given in Table 3. As can be seen in Table 3, only 8 wpm can be written with the fastest EOG based system developed to date. If it is compared with the other EOG based systems in the literature, our writing speed and recognition performance are the best.

TABLE 2: Test results of proposed method.

Word/Phrase	First Trial			Fifth Trial		
	Writing durations (sec.)	Writing Speed (wpm)	Codding Accuracy (%)	Writing durations (sec.)	Writing Speed (wpm)	Codding Accuracy (%)
Susadım (I am thirsty)	6,80	14,12	86%	6,50	14,77	100%
Acıktım (I am hungry)	9,10	10,55	86%	6,70	14,33	100%
Tuvaletim var (I need to go to the toilet)	14,10	11,06	85%	13,20	11,82	100%
Merhaba (Hello)	8,30	14,46	86%	7,30	16,44	100%
Günaydın (Good morning)	9,00	12,00	88%	8,90	12,13	100%
iyi geceler (Good night)	11,70	12,31	82%	11,00	13,09	100%
Nasılsın (How are you)	8,10	13,33	88%	7,70	14,03	100%
Görüşürüz (See You)	11,10	10,81	89%	10,20	11,76	100%
Işığı aç (Lights On)	9,40	10,21	88%	7,90	12,15	100%
Işığı kapat (Light Off)	12,40	11,61	82%	11,30	12,74	100%
Nerede (Where)	6,70	12,54	84%	4,80	17,50	100%
Üşüyorum (I am cold)	9,80	11,02	88%	9,20	11,74	100%
Çok sıcak (Very hot)	10,40	11,54	89%	9,90	12,12	100%
İlaçlarımı ver (Give me my drugs)	16,50	10,18	86%	15,40	10,91	100%
Mean		11,84	86.2%		13,2	100 %

TABLE 3: Comparison of the EOG-based typing and writing systems.

	Method	Speed	Accuracy
Current study	Coding	13.2 wpm	100%
[7]	Virtual keyboard	A word in 25 sec = 2.4 wpm	81%
[25]	Virtual keyboard-Blink	5 wpm	>98%
[26]	Virtual keyboard	12 sec per character = 1wpm	100%
[27]	Virtual keyboard	11 cpm = 2.2 wpm	-
[21]	Writing	-	50% to 100%
[28]	Writing	Max 8 wpm	87.74%
[30]	Writing	5 sec per character = 2.4 wpm	Average 87.38%
[31]	Writing	34 cpm = 6.8 wpm	95%

cpm: character per minute and wpm: word per minute (5 characters = 1 word).

On the other hand, while text entry can perform more efficiently than most of optical tracking system, it is behind the speed of the Majaranta et al. 2009 and Kristensson et.al.2012 systems. These systems are supported by a professional eye-tracking device. Kristensson et al. 2012 system also benefits from a word completion program to achieve the high speed writing.

The developed system has many advantages over the optical tracking based text entry systems. Since it is EOG based, it is not affected by ambient light. It does not need a virtual keyboard, so it can be produced as an embedded system. It can be used after a simple calibration, such as EOG threshold determination, to be performed during initial use for a user. The system can be adapted to all languages with simple assignments in the program. By adding new dwell times for character encoding, the number of total characters that can be written can be increased.

However, the system has some disadvantages when compared to optical tracking systems. Firstly, electrical safety precautions are required. Since the electrodes used are not stable for a long time, they must be replaced at regular intervals. In addition, cables of these electrodes can cause some discomfort. Furthermore, a certain amount of time is needed to learn the used coding method.

4. Conclusion

In this study, a new method enabling the patients suffering from ALS-like diseases to enter the texts easily, quickly, and accurately to the computer using EOG is proposed. For this purpose, a PC based system has been developed to enable the implementation of the proposed method and various experiments have been carried out.

In the proposed method, eye movements into four main directions with two different angles and four different dwell times were used to encode the characters. A complex pattern recognition procedure is not required to convert the encoded EOG to text. For character recognition, EOG signals exceeding certain threshold values during the respective encodings are enough. The necessary dwell times for the encoding of characters are guided by the computer through voicing the characters.

Consequently, thanks to the proposed encoding method and developed system, text entry can be done easily, quickly, and accurately with EOG. In future studies, applicability of the developed coding method together with the low-cost optical tracking systems can be investigated. Furthermore, the word completion software can be integrated to the system so as to increase the text entry speeds.

References

[1] A. Banerjee, M. Pal, S. Datta, D. N. Tibarewala, and A. Konar, "Voluntary eye movement controlled electrooculogram based multitasking graphical user interface," *International Journal of Biomedical Engineering and Technology*, vol. 18, no. 3, pp. 254–271, 2015.

[2] T. Gandhi, M. Trikha, J. Santhosh, and S. Anand, "Development of an expert multitask gadget controlled by voluntary eye movements," *Expert Systems with Applications*, vol. 37, no. 6, pp. 4204–4211, 2010.

[3] T. E. Hutchinson, K. P. White, W. N. Martin, K. C. Reichert, and L. A. Frey, "Human-computer interaction using eye-gaze input," *IEEE Transactions on Systems, Man, and Cybernetics*, vol. 19, no. 6, pp. 1527–1534, 1989.

[4] D. Miniotas, O. Spakov, and G. Evreinov, "Symbol creator: An alternative eye-based text entry technique with low demand for screen space," in *Proceedings of the INTERACT*, vol. 3, pp. 137–143, 2003.

[5] O. Špakov and P. Majaranta, "Scrollable keyboards for casual eye typing," *PsychNology Journal*, vol. 7, no. 2, pp. 159–173, 2009.

[6] P. Majaranta, U.-K. Ahola, and O. Špakov, "Fast gaze typing with an adjustable dwell time," in *Proceedings of the SIGCHI Conference on Human Factors in Computing Systems*, pp. 357–360, USA, April 2009.

[7] A. B. Usakli, S. Gurkan, F. Aloise, G. Vecchiato, and F. Babiloni, "On the Use of Electrooculogram for Efficient Human Computer Interfaces," *Computational Intelligence and Neuroscience*, vol. 2010, Article ID 135629, 5 pages, 2010.

[8] L. F. Nicolas-Alonso and J. Gomez-Gil, "Brain computer interfaces, a review," *Sensors*, vol. 12, no. 2, pp. 1211–1279, 2012.

[9] P. Majaranta and A. Bulling, "Eye Tracking and Eye-Based Human–Computer Interaction," in *Advances in Physiological Computing*, Human–Computer Interaction Series, pp. 39–65, Springer London, London, 2014.

[10] P. O. Kristensson and K. Vertanen, "The potential of dwell-free eye-typing for fast assistive gaze communication," in *Proceedings of the 7th Eye Tracking Research and Applications Symposium, ETRA 2012*, pp. 241–244, USA, March 2012.

[11] V. Janthanasub and M. Phayung, "Evaluation of a low-cost eye tracking system for computer input," *King Mongkut's University of Technology North Bangkok International Journal of Applied Science and Technology*, pp. 185–196, 2015.

[12] M. F. Marmor, M. G. Brigell, D. L. McCulloch, C. A. Westall, and M. Bach, "ISCEV standard for clinical electro-oculography (2010 update)," *Documenta Ophthalmologica*, vol. 122, no. 1, pp. 1–7, 2011.

[13] P. A. Constable, D. Ngo, S. Quinn, and D. A. Thompson, "A meta-analysis of clinical electro-oculography values," *Documenta Ophthalmologica*, vol. 135, no. 3, pp. 219–232, 2017.

[14] R. Barea, L. Boquete, M. Mazo, and E. López, "System for assisted mobility using eye movements based on electrooculography," *IEEE Transactions on Neural Systems and Rehabilitation Engineering*, vol. 10, no. 4, pp. 209–218, 2002.

[15] G. R. Philips, A. A. Catellier, S. F. Barrett, and C. H. G. Wright, "Electrooculogram wheelchair control," *Biomedical Sciences Instrumentation*, vol. 43, pp. 164–169, 2007.

[16] S. Venkataramanan, P. Prabhat, S. R. Choudhury, H. B. Nemade, and J. S. Sahambi, "Biomedical instrumentation based on electrooculogram (EOG) signal processing and application to a hospital alarm system," in *Proceedings of 2005 International Conference on Intelligent Sensing and Information Processing*, pp. 535–540, IEEE, Chennai, India, January 2005.

[17] N. A. Atasoy, A. Çavuşoğlu, and F. Atasoy, "Real-Time motorized electrical hospital bed control with eye-gaze tracking," *Turkish Journal of Electrical Engineering & Computer Sciences* vol. 24, no. 6, pp. 5162–5172, 2016.

[18] M. Yildiz, "A new coding technique for EOG based writing systems," in *Proceedings of the 19th Signal Processing and Communications Applications Conference, (SIU '11)*, pp. 90–93, Turkey, April 2011.

[19] C. R. Hema, S. Ramkumar, and M. P. Paulraj, "Idendifying Eye Movements using Neural Networks for Human Computer Interaction," *International Journal of Computer Applications*, vol. 105, no. 8, pp. 18–26, 2014.

[20] F. Fang, T. Shinozaki, Y. Horiuchi, S. Kuroiwa, S. Furui, and T. Musha, "HMM based continuous EOG recognition for eye-input speech interface," in *Proceedings of the 13th Annual Conference of the International Speech Communication Association (INTERSPEECH '12)*, pp. 734–737, Portland, Ore, USA, September 2012.

[21] J.-Z. Tsai, C.-K. Lee, C.-M. Wu, J.-J. Wu, and K.-P. Kao, "A feasibility study of an eye-writing system based on electro-oculography," *Journal of Medical and Biological Engineering*, vol. 28, no. 1, pp. 39–46, 2008.

[22] T. Wissel and R. Palaniappan, "Considerations on Strategies to Improve EOG Signal Analysis," *International Journal of Artificial Life Research*, vol. 2, no. 3, pp. 6–21, 2011.

[23] A. Bulling, J. A. Ward, H. Gellersen, and G. Tröster, "Eye movement analysis for activity recognition using electrooculography," *IEEE Transactions on Pattern Analysis and Machine Intelligence*, vol. 33, no. 4, pp. 741–753, 2011.

[24] C. Roda, *Human Attention in Digital Environments*, Cambridge University Press, Cambridge, 2011.

[25] H. Istance and A. Hyrskykari, "Gaze-aware systems and attentive applications," *Gaze Interaction and Applications of Eye Tracking: Advances in Assistive Technologies*, pp. 175–195, 2011.

[26] S.-W. Yang, C.-S. Lin, S.-K. Lin, and C.-H. Lee, "Design of virtual keyboard using blink control method for the severely disabled," *Computer Methods and Programs in Biomedicine*, vol. 111, no. 2, pp. 410–418, 2013.

[27] S. S. S. Teja, S. S. Embrandiri, and N. Chandrachoodan, "EOG based virtual keyboard," in *Proceedings of the 41st Annual Northeast Biomedical Engineering Conference, (NEBEC '15)*, USA, April 2015.

[28] A. López, F. Ferrero, D. Yangüela, C. Álvarez, and O. Postolache, "Development of a computer writing system based on EOG," *Sensors*, vol. 17, no. 7, 2017.

[29] J. O. Wobbrock, J. Rubinstein, M. Sawyer, and A. T. Duchowski, "Not typing but writing: Eye-based text entry using letter-like gestures," in *Proceedings of the Conference on Communications by Gaze Interaction (COGAIN)*, pp. 61–64, 2007.

[30] K.-R. Lee, W.-D. Chang, S. Kim, and C.-H. Im, "Real-time eye-writing recognition using electrooculogram," *IEEE Transactions on Neural Systems and Rehabilitation Engineering*, vol. 25, no. 1, pp. 37–48, 2017.

[31] F. Fang, T. Shinozaki, and S. Federici, "Electrooculography-based continuous eye-writing recognition system for efficient assistive communication systems," *PLoS ONE*, vol. 13, no. 2, p. e0192684, 2018.

[32] M. Porta and M. Turina, "Eye-S: A full-screen input modality for pure eye-based communication," in *Proceedings of the Eye Tracking Research and Applications Symposium, ETRA 2008*, pp. 27–34, USA, March 2008.

[33] R. Barea, L. Boquete, S. Ortega, E. López, and J. M. Rodríguez-Ascariz, "EOG-based eye movements codification for human computer interaction," *Expert Systems with Applications*, vol. 39, no. 3, pp. 2677–2683, 2012.

[34] B. Shneiderman, "Designing the user interface strategies for effective human-computer interaction," *ACM SIGBIO Newsletter*, vol. 9, no. 1, p. 6, 1987.

[35] J. Webster, *Medical Instrumentation: Application and Design*, John Wiley & Sons, 2009.

13

Second Screen Engagement of Event Spectators

Tomas Cerny ⓘ **and Michael Jeff Donahoo**

Computer Science, Baylor University, Hankamer Academic Building, No. 105, Waco, TX 76706, USA

Correspondence should be addressed to Tomas Cerny; tomas_cerny@baylor.edu

Academic Editor: Hideyuki Nakanishi

An effective means of engaging spectators at live events involves providing real-time information from a variety of sources. Consumers demand personalized experience; thus, a single channel perspective fails. Modern entertainment must extend to spectator mobile devices and adapt content to individual interests. Moreover, such systems should take advantage of venue screens to engage in sharing live information, aggregated social media, etc. We propose a second screen application, providing each audience member a personalized perspective, involving mobile devices equipped with Wi-Fi, and spanning to venue screens in hotels, halls, arenas, elevators, etc. Such a system engages both local audience and remote spectators. Our work provides a case study involving experience from the deployment of such an application at the ACM-ICPC World Finals with audiences at the event and around the world. We analyze and categorize its features, consider its impact on the audience, and measure its demands.

1. Introduction

Sporting matches, conferences, cultural events, elections, debates, concerts, and other live events bring opportunities for real-time engagement of the audience. The traditional approach emphases a single stream of information, usually a television broadcast, with a single source of commentary. The sequence of actions in the broadcast program cannot accommodate a multidimensional perspective; thus, the broadcast might not fully engage the audience, thereby degrading the Quality of Experience (QoE). Such an approach is outdated in the era of on-demand service; [1] proposes augmenting the mainstream of information with Second Screens.

Second Screen is a display (e.g., smartphone, tablet, and smartwatch) designed to augment primary viewing by providing additional content. Such devices are typically mobile and interactive, allowing content individualization. Examples include augmenting live sporting events with detailed statistics on selected players, broadcast television with social engagement, etc.

It is important to engage the audience and give an option to participate in the process of information broadcast. Such an extension makes the event more authentic for the audience. Moreover, the audience can express and share its own perspective to others. Furthermore, engaging local audience members in sharing their experience promotes their view to the overall audience, possibly expanding the reach to new followers. There is no single view in Second Screen; users choose the individual perspective to follow, e.g., following the live event, digging into detailed information, seeing updated statistics, etc. An event host should consider Second Screen to provide the audience with wide-angle perspectives full of extensive and easy-to-reach information. Such services power the audience with authentic entertainment impacting the QoE [1].

The personalization and context-awareness [2] might be further extended when considering a cosmopolitan audience with different cultural backgrounds, habits, or pleasure. A single information channel can only partially satisfy such audience. The Second Screen augments the program and extends the individual experience.

Present-day event participants usually possess mobile devices capable of presenting Second Screen services, opening Second Screen interaction to the overall entertainment environment [3]. Furthermore, nowadays event arenas usually provide large screens that can become part of the Second Screen experience by providing a content influenced by the crowd.

Integrating social media further engage users in the new role of mediators that can influence the crowd and crowd experience. This provides a way to share authentic information from a personal perspective, avoiding single (professional) perspective information since all participants comment and judge.

Here we share our experience from analysis, design, and production-level deployment of a Second Screen system, MyICPC, applied to the ACM-ICPC World Finals. As described later, this event involves over 1,000 local and over 10,000 remote participants from 115 countries. A variety of services are provided for the heterogeneous audience, and this article addresses audience demands and reveals which services are the most important, based on our case study. The generalized problem being addressed is the monotony of traditional, passive spectating, and our view on its transformation towards future entertainment systems.

While we do not provide an evaluation of usability or user experience, we show that local audience uses Second Screen to augment the event experience. We explore particular factors that impact audience interest in the service utility [4]. Based on the motivational factors, observations and suggestions researched in this paper, we implement a production-level Second Screen application. The application has been deployed for several years and accessed by a large audience, i.e., tens of thousands of users. We study the audience interest and utilization of our Second Screen application by both local and remote audience involving various device types.

This article is organized as follows. Section 2 provides a survey on related work on Second Screen systems. Section 3 gives background and analysis of information sources or screens available for services in the venue. Section 4 moves the attention towards architectural decisions and system design. A case study sharing practical experience from deployment is in Section 5. The conclusion and future work close the paper.

2. Related Work

Considerable works from a variety of perspectives exist for Second Screen [3–14]. The applicability and research goals can be classified by the target audience, considering both local and remote users. We divide related work into multiple subsections. First, we consider Second Screen services for entertainment such as movies or event reproduction for remote users. Next, discuss the scope of Second Screen applications. The social media subsection discusses the importance for the audience. Next, we elaborate Second Screen engagement in live events. Finally, we address extending spectator experience.

2.1. Passive Entertainment Reproduction Services. When considering passive entertainment, researchers address user's QoE in a home environment using multiple devices augmenting the main TV screen [3, 5, 8, 10]. Research goals pay attention to video broadcasting and network requirements for high-quality streaming of on-demand video [1]. The *passive* home consumer of entertainment can become involved through social networks by sharing the experience

[13]. For instance, [3] considers that consumers would discuss their movie experience over chat. Second Screen augmenting traditional TV programming can bring a novel dimension to sports events with an overlapping program, which is usually at large events such as the Olympic Games. The authors [5] evaluate the use of the Olympic Companion application, collocating viewers to follow multiple simultaneous channels of sports events providing statistics and allowing switching them between different devices or move in time.

The study [3], performed in a home environment, involved 260 tablet users, investigating how users incorporate multiple media into their television viewing experience. The results indicate only a modest interest in using secondary screens to digitally share opinions. Naturally, the engagement of such users is not expected to be significant since they are only receiving and consuming the entertainment experience, specifically movies. One must consider that users paying attention to movie plot on the main TV screen do not necessarily demand interaction. When considering an interactive environment, the outcome is different. The interpretation of such results cannot simply generalize to all environments or to Second Screens. For instance, [4] suggests that environments involving active spectators create an authentic social event atmosphere that motivates spectators to attend the event and share the experience with others over Second Screen. The Second Screen is also often used to complement the information provided on the TV screen [12].

A report on a many-screen prototype application for watching the Olympics, provided by [5], examines users engaging in a parallel view to multiple simultaneous channels and integration with multiple Second Screen devices. Users can watch, share, and control highlight programs. In addition, they can obtain event statistics or replay portions of the broadcast. While users can watch multiple devices at once, the authors noted that users become confused and struggle to maintain comprehension of liveness. The benefit is that users select content based on their interest, even when there is overlap.

The papers [6] and [9] provide a roadmap to the various applications and features of Second Screen. Its applicability to the video content interaction involves replays, playback point selection, or gestures to simplify interaction with the content. It can bring interaction with social media or deliver contextual information for the television content. For sporting events, Second Screen usually gives statistics (e.g., about sports players) to augment the event with related information. Second Screens can mediate these events and provide a better experience to the home audience with combined interpretation and more authentic narrative structure.

2.2. Scope of Second Screens. There is no strict boundary that would distinguish Second Screens from computer-aided assistant-like applications. For instance, consider a situation of a system similar to Second Screen that helps users to accomplish certain tasks, e.g., when a visitor aims to navigate through a large complex hospital. The hospital has its own navigation system, but for a person with health/emotional challenges, the navigation might become difficult. A personal smartphone used for in-house navigation [15] provides a sort of Second Screen. Furthermore, the approach can easily adapt to visitors based on their age or disabilities.

Such systems have a different focus than Second Screen. For Second Screens, the aim is to improve user experience, and the other computer-aided system example aims to assist the user with a particular task. Second Screen is meant as an augmentation system related to a *live* event or a stream of information, while the computer-aided assistant is a more general, on-demand service focused on individual need or specific task instead of a social event. To draw a distinctive example, consider a smartphone hospital navigation system providing social media service. Such an integration is inappropriate. On the other hand, integration to the Second Screen is a good fit.

2.3. Social Media. Previously, we mentioned interaction through social media. In particular, when considering active spectators, we might expect their active involvement in the mediation of the authentic experience through social media [4]. Most importantly the crowd not only generates but also evaluates the authenticity and thus avoids subjective perspective, given by traditional mass media. Naturally, Second Screens should provide the ability to integrate social media interaction. Moreover, social media integration should be an integral part of Second Screens.

The role of social media and networking is elaborated in [3]. Nowadays it competes with the traditional perspective of mass media. Undoubtedly, mass media can bring a subjective perspective that is falsely consumed by the audience. Social media provides a counterpoint for such opinions since all active participants share real-life and instant experience and judge opinions of others. A contemporary audience equipped with mobile devices participates in media crowd sharing through a variety of channels [16]. This changes the traditional perspective of living *with media* into living *in media* [17]. The technological growth creates the basis for multimodal, self-generated, self-directed, and self-selected mass media communication [18]. From such a perspective, the Second Screen seems to have all the prerequisites to become an instrument to share experience and produce media and public opinion. The Second Screen should stimulate the audience interest in publishing personal perspectives [7]. Multiple works consider Second Screens with social media integration as a good instrument to receive public opinion [14]. In [11] the authors analyzed tweets that were published related to TV broadcast and categorize them by their purpose, such as opinions, interpretations, emotions, attention seeking, or sharing information.

2.4. Second Screen at Live Events. When considering live events, the audience divides into active and remote spectators. The active spectators follow the central perspective of the event and may use Second Screen to augment their event experience using personal devices, venue screens, projectors, etc. For remote spectators, Second Screen may act as the central perspective of the event or become the primary source of information. Moreover, both groups may interact through Second Screen; active spectators contribute to the crowds through social media and mediate the authentic experience from the event to others.

Research involving Second Screen at live events aims to bring a new dimension of experience for active spectators or audience. For instance, the Second Screen application can accompany live performances in theatres [6] or impact experience for active spectators in large sporting events [4]. Moreover, Second Screens are applied in museums and galleries [19]; their deployment takes place at concerts [4], allowing the performer to interact with the audience to extend the social impact on the passive audience, while bringing opportunities for public opinion or voting, etc.

Second Screens may find its role at places that would traditionally deny the use of any *distracting* technological device. Live performances can take advantage of Second Screen either from the perspective of media sharing or extra content. When considering video streaming in such events, the multiangle perspectives, zooming, or playback point selection abilities potentially improve audience experience [6]. While previous research shows a certain issue comprehending with liveness [5] or passivity in Second Screen usage [3], the outcome from Second Screen usage in live performance, experienced in [6], shows that the audience is able to keep control over their viewing experiences through the Second Screen video feed while maintaining a presence in the live performance.

Applicability to live sporting events is researched by [4]. Their Active Spectator, as applied to football matches, aims to improve spectator experience. The expected spectator is an active participant (a local audience), creating the atmosphere of the entire event. Their highlighted feature is the ability to access player's biometrical information as well as showing statistics. Note that conventional technology in the arena already employs some Second Screen-like features. For instance, large displays at sporting events augment with local experience, with an overlay resembling and, to some extent, simulating watching the event on television. On the other hand, such features could become available on-demand when involving individual's mobile phone, allowing a replay or selection of available options. Second Screen features might be inspired by such coexisting elements.

2.5. Spectator Experience Model. What convinces individuals to attend such events? The authors [4] suggest that the motivating element for the live event seems to be the social atmosphere at the sporting arena. To spectators, it means a great deal to be part of a large group having a social experience. Their identification and socializing with other spectators are perhaps the crucial factor in their engagement with the event. The personal experience is certainly more than a passive consumption of the sport itself. Specifically, an active attendance impacts the social aspect. There are three main aspects that can be taken into account: the sport itself, the event, and social aspects.

To constitute spectator's experience at sporting events and explore the potential of interactive technologies for active spectating, [4] define spectator's experience model (SPEX). The model opens up a broader perspective on the entire spectator experience and follows the three aspects of *sport, event, and social.* The SPEX model is a good instrument to provide a base for Second Screen services. Consider

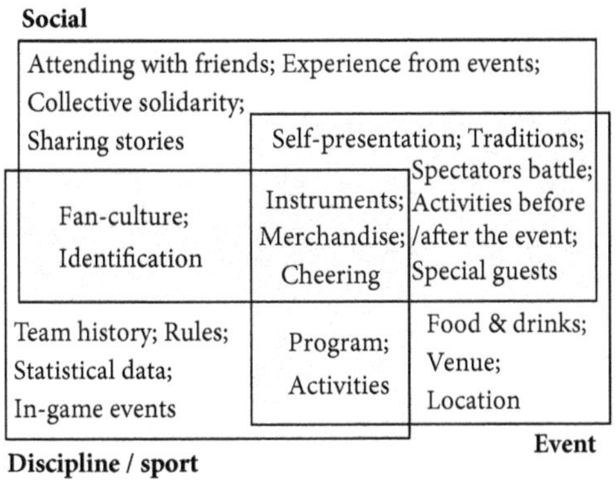

Social

Attending with friends; Experience from events; Collective solidarity; Sharing stories		
	Self-presentation; Traditions; Instruments; Merchandise; Cheering	Spectators battle; Activities before /after the event; Special guests
Fan-culture; Identification		
Team history; Rules; Statistical data; In-game events	Program; Activities	Food & drinks; Venue; Location

Discipline / sport   **Event**

FIGURE 1: The SPEX Model elements constituting the spectator experience.

a generalized SPEX model illustrated on Figure 1. The sport, or a particular discipline, has specific rules, but most likely it also has a history, statistics, and perhaps specific events. Furthermore, there might be related activities, identification with other fans, and overall a culture of fans. This all might involve special forms of cheering teams, support certain merchandise, or suggest some specific instruments supporting identification. The social part may involve stories and interaction with fans, as well as collective solidarity. The event should give spectators a chance to present themselves, follow certain traditions, support event specific activities, or compete with other spectator groups.

2.6. Human Factors: Lurking. Important aspects relevant to effectiveness of Second Screens can be found in research on human factors [20, 21]. It is known that online learning develops through interaction and it is a collaborative process engaging learners actively. However, there is an effect, known as lurking impacting the passive audience, which is relevant to Second Screens. According to [21], up to 90% of online discussion group participants are lurkers. Lurkers are an audience that does not actively contribute to the content and do not produce a post. In [20], the authors consider e-learning and discuss the voluntary participation in virtual interaction to improve learning and consider lurking, evaluating passive participation. In the learning context "lurkers are learners who are bystanders to course discussions". They lack commitment to the community; however, they receive benefits without giving anything back. This is one explanatory factor for the effectiveness of Second Screens. In [20], the authors conclude that a higher degree of visible interactions is not a precondition for higher learning efficiency and lurking must be considered in this activity. The passive lurking is expressed by reading and reflecting on the contribution of all the participants.

3. Background and Analysis of Second Screen Applications

For our analysis, we begin by first considering the physical setup both *before* and *after* Second Screen deploy. Next, we take into account the *local* and *remote* audience or the event information sources. Finally, we evaluate the services and features that improve the experience using the SPEX model, generalizing the sports aspect as a discipline.

The physical setup of events is usually as follows. The event is situated in an arena; it can be a stadium, hotel, conference hall, resort, etc. Such an arena might have restricted zones, such as VIP, secure, and visitors. Each arena has a set of resources such as stages, large announcement screens, projectors and TV screens in hallways, elevators, and possibly hotel rooms. Spectators may (or may not) have a personal device such a phone, tablet, and personal computer. Each arena provides at least access to some mobile network and perhaps even high-density access points with Wi-Fi.

The physical setup for the *remote* audience is often much simpler. The audience follows a website, live stream video broadcast, or social network from a public place such as school, pub, square, or a private place such as a home. The physical setup includes TV screen or access to the Internet with a browsing device.

3.1. An Event without Second Screen. The information sources of a live event correspond to its schedule. The schedule is most likely available on a centralized website, so the main website and the schedule itself are the most critical parts of information sources *before* the event starts. The schedule gives an overview and roadmap to subevents and parallel sessions or stages. There may exist online preevents in which the audience might participate. At this point, audience interaction and their grouping are expected through social networks, so supportive feeds or platforms, such as Facebook, LinkedIn, Twitter, Instagram, YouTube, and VKontakte, are expected to involve the crowd. The website may provide up-to-date statistics, speculations, opinions, and perhaps remarks from the last event.

Once the event starts, we may see the distinction between *local* and *remote* audience. Regarding the *local* audience, the old fashion approach might involve program printouts handed to attendees who themselves follow a static schedule. This may involve arena screens, showing the actual schedule information. In this approach, we do not receive any feedback from the audience nor support their social involvement. Most likely the audience takes pictures of the venue and posts them on their personal social profile. The missing piece is the centralization and online socializing with other attendees. In this approach, each attendee posting media is to be rather isolated. Even if we consider, for instance, posting a Twitter message following a certain hashtag, how do we connect Twitter users with VKontakte users, Facebook users, etc.?

From another perspective, the event has a well-defined schedule, professional mediator, and media team providing pictures and video from the event to the audience through large arena screens or managing a scoreboard. Here the audience is not engaged. What if a random participant takes the best photograph from the world championship? Such a photograph may have limited public exposure. Furthermore, specific participant interests are not highlighted in traditional mechanisms or instruments. Thus, in order to follow specific aspects of the event, each participant must assemble relevant particles himself/herself.

We often see these deficiencies in traditional *local* participation with a static schedule that does not adapt to what the crowds likes. Next, it does not involve the audience in public opinion, self-presentation, feedback to certain subevent, and social network interaction during the event among various participants. The missing piece is a centralized source of information involving professionally made content, event results, audience-generated content, etc., all allowing personalization, real-time event processing, and interaction.

The *remote* audience can follow a TV broadcast, blogger, Twitter feed, or the event website. The deficiency is similar to *local* participation, missing a centralized source of information supporting crowd interaction, and possibly missing an important comment or photograph from the event.

After the event, the media team provides short videos, blogs, photographs, statistics, and perhaps other articles and event mentions, accessible through the website. To some extent, the event website may act as the central place for information, although integration of other third-party information sources is limited. The website plays the main role when publishing information, both before and after the event. During the event, the website does not play a significant role. The audience attention flees in all directions. For instance, the audience follows the event performance, social interaction at third-party providers, the environment, various social media, specific blogs, etc.

Figure 2 draws a simplified interaction between information sources, information destination, its mediators, and consumers. The media team has access to the environment. The team has access to live event information both the public side and internal information that it interprets and mediates to the audience. The team then provides such internal or private information to the website, blogs, or social media. The local audience has access to public live events and, in addition, the social interaction in the environment. When the audience interacts with other sources of information, it might be relevant to custom social media services, blogs, or even the website. Thus, the audience may produce content of broad interest in a distinct space such that it never reaches other members of the audience. The passive audience is the consumer of the outcome produced by the media team and local audience.

3.2. An Event with Second Screen. The Second Screen platform should target a change in the interaction from distributed to a centralized destination. Similar to the situation before and after, the Second Screen platform should act as the website and thus be web accessible. Next, for the live event, the Second Screen platform should centralize contributions from social networks, blogs, and media teams, so that the audience has a single focal point to observe and receive all the information. The transition to the proposal is illustrated in Figure 3.

So far we only analyzed and suggested a centralized view on the interaction among information sources, audience, and their contribution. We did not analyze the features and the possible utility of Second Screen, although centralization is

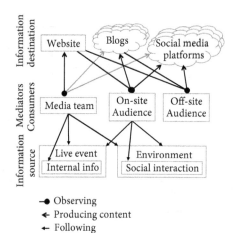

FIGURE 2: Emitting information (traditional env.).

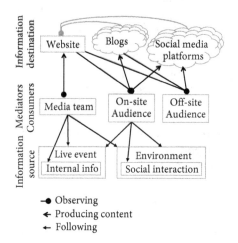

FIGURE 3: Emitting information (Second Screen env.).

an important step as it allows us to provide a custom, context-aware view to an individual. The SPEX model suggests that the Second Screen platform considers various aspects. It should consider the discipline and provide statistics of players' team or actors, or even past events. The schedule is a naturally important element as well as rules all in a structured format so that it is easy to link it to statistics with currently scoring player or performing actor or even location in the venue.

To increase motivation to attend the event, the audience should have the ability to present them. This could be an ability to register their profile, post comments, pictures, and video, or be involved in social media showed on Second Screen. Receiving reaction to their contribution, such as comments, can socialize fans that may normally not meet in person. Furthermore, the public feedback can boost motivation for the audience to contribute with a personal perspective and view. The audience can cheer for their favorite team or actor, and the sponsors or organizers can involve the audience in social quizzes or puzzles to recognize the winner at the event.

The Second Screen should provide the mainstream information on the event. It can involve video broadcast, active scoreboard, and an ability to quickly list details or highlight certain perspectives, angles, or aspects. The crowd in the social network can react to polls from organizers; see statistics on what the crowd likes or how many participants are following a particular team.

To integrate large screens in the arena, venue, hotel, etc., the Second Screen should not only consider a static schedule-like content but also involve live information from the crowd. In particular, the crowd posts a large number of social media and messages reflecting the scenery. The large screens should display the real-time social media content to further engage the audience in involvement since individual's post appears on the screens. Since the crowd contributes to the content and interacts with the large screen content, the content corresponds to the current scene giving an authentic reproduction of the *local* audience scenery to the *remote* audience. At the same time, malicious posts must be filtered on an automated or a manual basis.

Certain events, such as conferences, can even connect the social contributors with their profile and possibly identify their media or professional profile such as LinkedIn. Media content, such as photographs, can be augmented with metainformation to be linked to the schedule and events. In [22], a gallery system recognizes participant faces in pictures. This process can be a semiautomated, involving user profile details with their picture involving automated face recognition in photographs captured at the event. The audience can list their personal gallery during or after the event. Furthermore, a broader media gallery can reconstitute the event with various details. Moreover, metainformation enables integration of media content across various features of Second Screen. For instance, a program event includes photographs from the event, teams are augmented with venue pictures, winning can be tracked with its history, or an awarded actor of the night may be seen the play from various angles when listing actor details.

The Second Screen is an ideal place for announcements for events such as free snacks at intermission or an interview with a famous person. The Second Screen should become the medium for discussion. For instance, consider a large competition with the sudden decision to disqualify a particular team. Judges can provide their rationale or respond to the public.

Next, consider mediators who speculate on who is going to take the lead in a competition or what not to miss in a particular performance. For instance, in a live performance or a concert, the audience is notified that it is about the time that critics have pointed out as the best part of the night, which can serve as a narrator or a guide to the show. The Second Screen should become an instrument to interact with the audience to receive their immediate feedback since; in live events, a two-minute delay might be too late to ask how they like a particular piece or action by the performer.

To summarize, Second Screen features should provide real-time, on-demand services and allow augmentation of the event. Moreover, it is an instrument for announcements as well as a dynamic schedule. It should be possible to access player details, annual statistics, upcoming events, the map of the environment, rules, or static content in a structural form to be able to associate the content with scoring players, etc. The Second Screen should also aggregate real-time statistics for augmenting the event. It should have the ability to present the current scene, for instance, a video broadcasting, scoreboard, interactive map, etc. Particular attention should be given to the simplicity of service integration, such as connecting a schedule and places with media pictures from the crowd, and every entry becomes interactive through social networks. All posts from blogs, social networks, media teams, judges, bloggers, etc. should be integrated into a chronological timeline. All posts, including audience media, should appear in a crowd-gallery involving metainformation to associate it with time, place, person, team, or social media account. These media can highlight related textual content when viewed by the audience.

4. Design and Architecture

The previous sections suggest that Second Screens interact with both remote and local users. What are the options when building Second Screens? Some solutions provide dedicated applications, specific to a given operating system, device, etc. A dedicated application takes advantage of platform-specific features in the user interface to support efficient interaction. There are disadvantages of such native applications. First, the user has to download and install it. Users are understandably resistant to installing new applications since they take up resources and may present security risks. Second, users that do not have a compatible device cannot use such Second Screen apps. While one can implement a version of the application for each platform, the development costs may be considerable. In addition, one must be willing to actively maintain such applications, particularly if they inadvertently introduce a security or system-stability flaw. Thus, for proofs-of-concepts, the dedicated application options seem reasonable, but to interest large heterogeneous audience it might be better to consider a web application. Various device types such as phones, tablets, and personal computers, no matter the platform, can access a web application. Recent technologies available for web provide publish-subscribe mechanism, notifications, and large content streaming, which is sufficient for Second Screens.

Web applications usually involve centralized data, interacting with various sources such as social media and blogs, while having the ability to produce content in real-time. The presentation part of a Second Screen application should adapt to various devices such as mobile phones, tablets, personal computers, large screens, or even smartwatch. The presentation should be responsive, including adjusting to various screen sizes and asynchronously notifying the user in near real-time when new information is available.

At the same time, we must expect scaling ability with respect to the number of users. A large number of media resources can be involved, including images and videos possibly demanding for large storage. This may require balancing and routing to content delivery networks. The Second Screen must have access to the main event information to process them. Such information can involve video broadcasting, direct input from judges or directors, event feed from the internal control system, current scoreboard information, etc.

Second Screens should take advantages of existing frameworks involving enterprise architectures [23]. Such platforms involve multiple tiers, such as client, server, and database tiers. In order to minimize demands placed on the server tier, a significant portion of the computational efforts should be offloaded to client devices. However, we must take into account the fact that the client may be a smartphone with limited resources and abilities.

Our experimentation shows that technologies such as Meteor [24] or Google Web Toolkit [25] are good for interactive pages but do not fit all types of phones or even tablets. In our prototypes, some important pages have a 10+ second load time due to limited hardware. The other extreme is a fully server-side page rendering such as JavaServer Faces [26], but such an approach is not appropriate for real-time applications. In our prototype evaluation, we found that a framework like AngularJS [27] allows incremental page additions to predefined templates and suits to standard nonincremental dynamic content situations.

The server tier is a 3-layer application [23] involving presentation, business, and persistence layer. The server tier requires elastic scalability; therefore, the server application must allow for dynamically expandable computational instances. Given this, the initial design of the application should consider employing Platform as a Service (PaaS) and enable its deployment to the cloud.

Some Second Screen server components must be specialized. For instance, only one instance of the application should send emails, parse input from social media, feeds, etc. and share it with others. One approach is to employ a master-slave architecture, where the master instance parses and broadcasts all new information through messaging system to other instances. Slave instance then through a full duplex communication (e.g., web-socket protocol) announces novel information to clients. Clients interpret the novel information and publish it in the user interface. Recent evolution in application servers, which aim to support PaaS, strips out the need for heterogeneity and introduces a singleton service in a cluster environment. Modern application servers interact in the cluster (e.g., through an Infinispan as suggested by [28]) and exchange information. This allows dynamically installing the singleton service to a single node in the cluster. When such node disappears or fails, the service relocates in the cluster to another node.

The server tier services should provide both HTML outputs and JSON format for dynamic information embedding. The Singleton Services involve parsers of various social media feeds, event feeds with actions from the event, and possibly other inputs. The mechanism to share information for various purposes may benefit from event-driven approaches and messaging systems. For instance, a Twitter message is parsed and announced to observers that check the message for inappropriate content, publish it on the timeline, check whether the content relates to a social competition, and finally, an observer checks the media attachment and adds it to the gallery. Each of these observers is independent to the announcer and

other observers, which allows extensibility of services. An observer may push the received event through a messaging system, such as Redis [29], to other nodes in the cluster that further mediate it to the clients. A new client may request a page that either contains dynamic content that does not further change or that incrementally updates through the full duplex communication. When a client visits a page that incrementally updates, the web browser subscribes to listen for server announcements. Thus, once a message from a messaging system appears, the subscribed client directly announces a novel content. The advantage of coexisting systems involving social media is offloading the hosting of media files and thus delegating the responsibility of content management.

As mentioned previously, Second Screen should consider spanning its services to use indoor venue screens. The simplest solution is to involve a static schedule. An extended option is to update the schedule dynamically based on time. To the engaged audience, the application should consider displaying live announcements and notifications from social media and the crowd. For instance, a screen accommodates up to 16 latest messages and dynamically updates the oldest with new posts. Most likely Second Screen already processes various feeds and channels, such as Twitter, YouTube, Instagram, etc.; thus, when a message gets processed and passes all filters it displays on the screens. This brings motivation to the crowd to get involved and post individual messages via a variety of social channels. The motivation for an individual is to make his or her post visible on the screens and this interacts with the screen and the crowd. Such multisource integration satisfies a variety of contributes since they can use a different application to produce the message content. Moreover, it is a good place for system announcements. In order to control all screens, while having the connection to a web-based Second Screen, the administrator must be given the ability to temporarily change the screen content. Underneath each screen is a web browser using a full duplex communication or polling; thus, it is possible to send control messages directly from the Second Screen and enforce navigation to another page, etc.

Scalability is one of the most important quality attributes. Based on our performance experimentation, we provide suggestions based on our observations. There exists a standard design pattern to deal with transaction management called Open Session in View (OSIV) [30]. In OSIV, each time a request appears from the client tier, a new transaction opens to fetch data from the database by particular services, and the transaction is kept open until the request fully processes. This provides an elegant approach to designing application without manually opening and closing the transaction in the source code of each method, thereby reducing the volume of code while maintaining high readability. Unfortunately, there is a negative side of this pattern. This pattern is used with persistence frameworks to load and lazy-load data and their associated collections when necessary. The advantage is that the responsibility of a manually defined service is offloaded to a framework programmatically, which is convenient; however, we lose control over what data are being loaded and how they are loaded, which potentially introduces significant performance issue. It is a considerable difference from the performance perspective, to load a single object versus thousands of others, while not even being aware of it. Based on our experiments, while OSIV is fine for small audiences, it lacks large scalability so we recommend avoiding it.

Finally, the database tier can involve NoSQL, relational database, or even both. The target domain, features, and complexity of statistics provided by the Second Screen determines the specific decision. In the case of complex data manipulation and table joins, a relational database might suit better. Based on our experimentation, the relational database sustains the large load; furthermore, relational databases can be clustered or use a cache and data virtualization such as Teiid (http://teiid.jboss.org).

5. Case Study

Our case study focuses on the Second Screen for the World Finals of the International Collegiate Programming Contest (ICPC) where the top university students in computing compete. The annual contests are multitier where teams of three contestants from the same university are given a set of algorithmic problems. The team that solves the most problems in shortest time wins. Annually over forty-thousand students attend ICPC contests. The World Finals is the final round, taking place at a single, physical location.

The World Finals event takes five days with a five-hour contest on the last full day and a practice session on the previous day. The contest with 120+ teams takes place at sports arenas or large cultural halls with all teams in one place. The students are selected from 100+ countries worldwide to represent their university.

The venue provides high-speed Wi-Fi and is equipped with screens in the lobby, hotel rooms, and large projectors in the contest room. While students compete in designated area, they are not allowed to use any personal devices or access the Internet during the contest or practice session. On the other hand, spectators are free to use any personal device. Before and after the contest/practice, everybody, including contestants, staff, coaches, and spectators (both on and off-site), can access mobile devices during the entire set of days.

The contest staff has many distinct groups such as judges and system operations producing various information streams such as contest scoreboard, media (video, photo, and blog teams), or analytics to augment the scoreboard and evaluating teams, etc. Some of the staff are responsible for publishing information on social media networks, blogs, picture galleries, video feed, etc.

In 2013 an initial beta version of Second Screen called MyICPC was introduced, integrating information sources such as social media, scoreboard, analytics, and media. The 2014 full version extended the MyICPC with statistics for teams, contestants, or contest attendees and introduced a social challenge called Quest. The rationale behind Quest is to socially engage attendees with activities during the five days. Quest gives multiple tasks (Figures 4 and 5) to the local audience who individually post through social media. Questers are posting pictures and video on Twitter and Instagram. The MyICPC provides polls to solicit public opinion. The major

FIGURE 4: Quest challenges.

FIGURE 5: Quest leaderboard.

element of the MyICPC is the master timeline (Figure 6) that integrates all events in a sequence feed and updates in real-time. Users can follow the schedule with highlighted current time and a map (Figure 7). A gallery (Figure 9) integrates social media, photos, and video both from the professional media team and the crowd. The media team posts pictures with metadata in it as mentioned in [22], link media content with a particular team to the team's statistics (Figure 13), places in the venue, events in the schedule filtered by person, team, or event.

To push MyICPC to the venue screens, a special information kiosk is provided. This kiosk integrates a variety of channels and feeds and shows texts, images, and videos from the audience on the screens. This highlights the current activities on social networks, presents the current schedule, or emphasizes notice. In our setup, the kiosk was presented on screens during registrations, dinners, and other social events. Sample kiosk contents are provided in Figures 17 and 18.

To accommodate all variations of screen size, MyICPC uses responsive user interfaces design. The content adjusts for a range of screen formats. For example, Figure 10 shows the layout on a large computer screen, while Figure 11 demonstrates the tablet layout. AngularJS offloads certain computations to clients, while not demanding enormous resources. Each user can follow preferred content, such as particular team candidates that are highlighted when relevant event occurs (Figure 10). Users can specifically follow the rank in their region by following a regional map (Figure 8). The team perspective (Figure 14) provides live updates on accepted and rejected submissions, rank, passed test cases,

FIGURE 8: Interactive score world map.

FIGURE 6: MyICPC master timeline.

FIGURE 9: Media gallery with metadata.

FIGURE 7: Schedule details page.

FIGURE 10: Scoreboard for desktop.

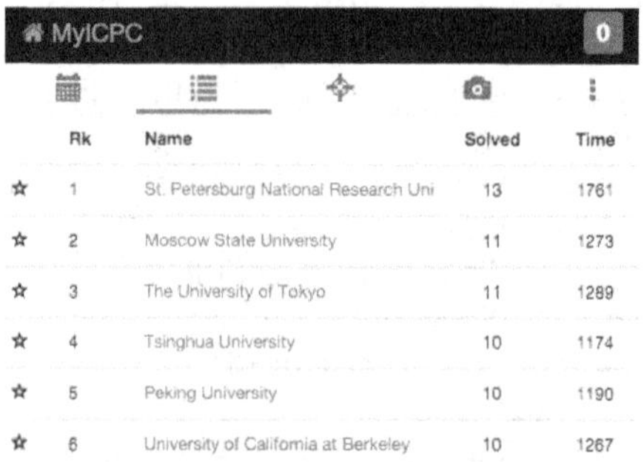

media, or even feedback from code analytics on source code progress (Figure 15). Live updates are displayed in multiple perspectives such as master scoreboard (Figure 12), compressed scorebar (Figure 16), world map (Figure 8), timeline (Figure 6), individual team perspectives, kiosk (Figure 18), etc. Figures 6–18 show selected perspectives of MyICPC.

In our study, we raise these questions to answer regards Second Screens:

 (i) (Specialization) How interested is the local audience?

 (ii) (Applicability) How applicable is the Second Screen to the global audience?

 (iii) (Handle scale) What is the audience size?

 (iv) How does the directed social gaming impact the social media events?

 (v) Which device types are the most dominant and what are the technical characteristics of such devices, e.g., screen resolution and browser.

 (vi) What is the SPEX classified feature popularity in a given time frame for the event?

 (vii) How do feature interests differ between local and remote audience?

 (viii) Are there any differences evaluating features by page views or visit time?

 (ix) How does the device type influence the feature popularity?

At the time of publication, MyICPC was used four times at the World Finals and eight times in regional contests. In

FIGURE 11: Scoreboard for mobile/tablet.

the following sections, we consider access statistics harvested from the World Finals 2014-16. We consider audience access patterns for particular MyICPC perspectives to answer the above questions. The statistics involve MyICPC instances deployed for the 2014 Finals in Yekaterinburg, Russia; the 2015 Finals in Marrakesh, Morocco; and 2016 Finals in Phuket,

FIGURE 12: Scoreboard real-time updates.

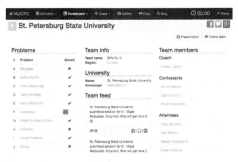

FIGURE 13: Team statistics and history.

FIGURE 16: Scorebar.

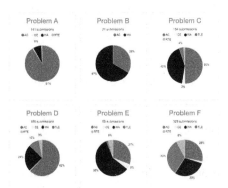

FIGURE 14: Team score statistics.

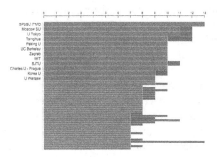

FIGURE 17: Kiosk content I.

FIGURE 15: Code analytics

FIGURE 18: Kiosk content II.

Thailand. For our evaluation, we consider the five days prior to the World Finals competition, the competition day itself and one day after for a total of seven days. For example, at the 2016 World Finals, we collected data starting May 14 and ending May 20. Collection for this period starts and ends at the 00:00 of the current local time zone (UCT+7). The statistics are gathered by Google Analytics [31], and Section 5.7 explains how the statistics are determined with details on the threats to validity.

5.1. Access Statistics. Table 1 gives a summary of the access data in multiple perspectives segments, such as the total audience in the considered period, contest day the audience, peak audience in an hour, average session time, number of sessions, and the total number of processed events.

The first segment *local audience* shows various audience perspectives across the years. The three lines show the registered attendees with the comparison to the audience visiting the organization website and MyICPC. While in the first year the MyICPC audience outnumbered the other monitored entries in the second and third years, it was around two hundred less than the number of registered attendees and 62-73% of the organization website audience.

The *remote audience* comparison between the MyICPC and organization website ranged from 37-48%, which is less than the proportion for the local audience. The local audience is understandably lower than remote, although this is related to the local event attendees each year. Please note that multiple participants traveled throughout the considered period of time and thus they count to both remote and local numbers.

When considering the years, there are significant growths of the *total audience* for both entries. The total audience proportion considering MyICPC and the organization website gives 44%, 38%, and 49% in years 2014-16. This provides a good base estimate to carry out when one considers building a Second Screen for a particular community. Moreover, in our case, there are over four thousand new remote visitors each year and the proportion of local to registered audience remains almost constant, except 2014, which we discuss later in this section.

The *contest day* segment of Table 1 shows the contest day audience details. Considering the total audience number, the contest day itself makes the portion of 67-76% of the entire considered contest period. It is 68-77% portion for the remote audience and 48-54% portion for the local audience. Furthermore, notice that the contest day remote audience doubled over the considered years.

The important entry about scalability is the peak number of users per hour. It is important to know the scale to accommodate resources which will be utilized to serve the demands. From 2014 to 16 the *peak audience in an hour* grew up to 3'318 users per hour in the contest time. While the remote audience peak in an hour grew, the local audience peak reduced to half, although we consider a deviation in the 2014 local audience.

The statistics so far do not say much about the time spent on a page. For this evaluation, Google Analytics provides us with details on an *average user session time* and *the total number of sessions per user*. The local audience has longer, almost twice as long session. Moreover, the local audience has twice as many sessions than the remote audience. This behavior is related to the system features and content that are more focused on the local audience (Quest), e.g., sharing media.

Another considered criterion is the total number of processed *events* by the MyICPC, which considers the contest dates and include messages from Twitter, Instagram, Vine, administrator, etc. Next, we consider the impact of the social game, Quest, on social media, in particular on Twitter messages. Quest is the main motivation to be active on social media, in particular, Twitter, and targets the local audience, which targets the number of sessions per local user. The last segment in Table 1 shows the total number processed Twitter messages (with event hash) and also Quest-related messages (with both event and Quest hash). The statistics do not include Retweets messages or the long-term impact on social media. The number of Quest messages creates around 35-59% of the total Twitter messages. To depict the time effect, as of January 1, 2017, the Marrakesh Twitter with Retweets has grown to 16'329 messages and the Quest messages to 7'034.

From Table 1 we find answers to our questions above. Specifically, it shows the local MyICPC audience in the contrast to the organization website and the registered attendees, from which we can derive the portion of the local audience engage with MyICPC (62-100% of the organization website audience). The remote audience is significantly larger, even though, the local audience spends more time on the MyICPC. In 2016 there was an audience of 1'307 users each with an average of 3.11 sessions lasting on average 15 minutes and 10 sec. This indicates that each local user spent over 47 minutes on the MyICPC. In 2015 it was almost an hour. The audience ratio ranges from 5.6 to 15.8 in favor of the remote audience. This answers Questions (i) and (ii).

The important observation is the peak number of visitors in a particular time frame. The peak number of visitors makes the system administer the critical information on system resource demands. In our case, 3'218 users visited the system during the peak hour. The peak day had the load of sixteen thousand unique visitors. Considering the program across the years in Table 1 we may expect up to twenty thousand visitors in the peak day and around three and half thousand users in the peak hour. This answers our Question (iii).

At this point, we might be interested in the audience daily load. Figure 19 shows the remote and local audience load in a given day, relative to the contest, plotted on a logarithmic scale. Moreover, we see all the considered years 2014-2016 that have similar characteristics. We can note the different progression for the remote audience that peaks around the contest day, while the local audience load spreads across the days.

Considering the *total events* processed; approximately 35-59% of Twitter messages are Quest-related messages, which shows Quest's significant impact on social media, in particular, Twitter. Moreover, Quest is played by the local audience, and thus around 50% of social media produced from the event in 2016 is stimulated by Quest, which is remarkably high percentage and answers Question (iv).

TABLE 1: World Finals 2014-16 statistics.

	Yekaterinburg 2014	Marrakesh 2015	Phuket 2016
Local audience			
Local registered attendees	1'227	1'170	1'544
Local audience at organization website	2'006	1'586	1'780
Local audience MyICPC	2'027	977	1'307
Remote audience			
Remote audience at organization website	28'230	41'447	41'593
Remote audience MyICPC	11'288	15'500	20'095
Total audience			
Total audience at organization website	29'991	42'718	43'043
Total audience MyICPC	13'153	16'333	21'204
Contest day			
Contest day local audience	1'092	472	711
Contest day remote audience	7'748	11'640	15'419
Contest day total audience	8'814	12'099	16'019
Peak in hour			
Max local visitors in one hour	230	140	115
Max remote visitors in one hour	1'576	2'816	3'117
Max total visitors in one hour	1'806	2'929	3'218
Average session			
Average user session - local [mm:ss]	11:25	15:38	15:10
Average user session - remote [mm:ss]	7:02	10:21	7:45
Average user session - total [mm:ss]	8:11	10:59	8:33
Number of session			
Sessions per user – local	3.35	3.72	3.11
Sessions per user – remote	1.69	1.72	1.69
Sessions per user - total	1.96	1.86	1.79
Total events			
Events processed	5'615	4'305	7'057
Twitter messages (excludes Rerweets)	4'290	3'876	6'539
Quest messages (excludes Retweets)	1'491	2'057	3'832

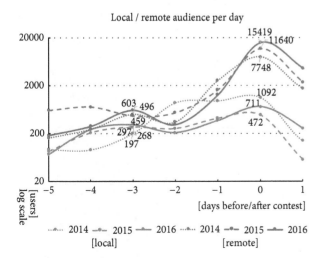

FIGURE 19: Daily remote/local audience load for the 2014-2016 year.

Next, we aim to answer Question (v) and show the characteristics of the particular audience group. Tables 2–4 show details on the *remote* and *local* audience details and proportion of devices, characteristics, operating systems, and browsers. In particular, we can see that the dominant device type is a desktop for the *remote* audience, although they use a rather high percentage of mobile phones and this trend has grown over the years. This trend must be considered in the user interface design of future systems. On the other hand, the *local* the audience tends to limit the tablet use and the percentage of phones and desktops is similar in favor of desktops the last year.

Similarly, Windows is the dominant platform; however, Android almost doubled between 2014 and 2016 for the *remote* audience. For the *locals*, iOS lost dominance, while Windows gained the popularity. The pallet of screen resolutions is dominated by 1366x768 for the *remote*, and 360x640

TABLE 2: World Finals 2014-16 total audience details (TOTAL).

	Yekaterinburg (2014)	Marrakesh (2015)	Phuket (2016)
Desktops	75%	74%	70%
Mobiles	20%	23%	27%
Tablets	5%	3%	3%
1st operating system	Windows 54%	Windows 50%	Windows 48%
2nd operating system	Android 13%	Android 17%	Android 21%
3rd operating system	Mac 11%	Mac 13%	Mac 12%
4th operating system	iOS/Linux 11%	Linux 12%	Linux 11%
1st web browser	Chrome 60%	Chrome 63%	Chrome 67%
2nd web browser	Firefox 16%	Firefox 15%	Firefox 13%
3rd web browser	Safari 13%	Safari 11%	Safari 10%
1st screen resolution	1366x768 32%	1366x768 31%	1366x768 30%
2nd screen resolution	1920x1080 11%	1920x1080 13%	1920x1080 14%
3rd screen resolution	1440x900 7%	1440x900 7%	360x640 12%

TABLE 3: World Finals 2014-16 total audience details (REMOTE).

	Yekaterinburg (2014)	Marrakesh (2015)	Phuket (2016)
Desktops	81%	76%	71%
Mobiles	16%	21%	26%
Tablets	3%	3%	3%
1st operating system	Windows 59%	Windows 51%	Windows 49%
2nd operating system	Linux 12%	Android 16%	Android 21%
3rd operating system	Mac 11%	Mac 12%	Mac 12%
4th operating system	Android 11%	Linux 12%	Linux 11%
1st web browser	Chrome 64%	Chrome 63%	Chrome 68%
2nd web browser	Firefox 17%	Firefox 15%	Firefox 14%
3rd web browser	Safari 9%	Safari 10%	Safari 9%
1st screen resolution	1366x768 35%	1366x768 31%	1366x768 31%
2nd screen resolution	1920x1080 12%	1920x1080 14%	1920x1080 14%
3rd screen resolution	1440x900 7%	1440x900 7%	360x640 12%

TABLE 4: World Finals 2014-16 local audience details (LOCAL).

	Yekaterinburg (2014)		Marrakesh (2015)		Phuket (2016)	
Desktops	763	38%	478	49%	660	50.5%
Mobiles	958	48%	411	42%	567	43.5%
Tablets	275	14%	88	9%	82	6%
1st operating system	iOS	33%	Android	28%	Windows	29%
2nd operating system	Android	27%	iOS	23%	Android	27%
3rd operating system	Windows	20%	Windows	22%	iOS	22%
1st web browser	Chrome	37%	Chrome	56%	Chrome	60%
2nd web browser	Safari	35%	Safari	24%	Safari	25%
3rd web browser	Firefox	10%	Firefox	13%	Firefox	9%
1st screen resolution	320x568	12%	1366x768	17%	360x640	18%
2nd screen resolution	1366x768	12%	360x640	16%	1366x768	15%
3rd screen resolution	320x480	11%	1280x800	7%	1920x1080	9%

for the *locals*. This requires the responsive user interface design considering a broad range of resolutions, with the content visible and attractive.

Specifically, the *local* audience that we measure and summarize in Table 4 tends to be more mobile-oriented, but still, in the last two years, desktops lead usage. There is a significant competition among Windows, Android, and iOS over the year. This shows that building a single operating-system-oriented the application does not address the wide-range of the audience. While the Chrome browser is still the dominant browser, a significant portion of the audience uses Safari and thus web application must be compatible across a wider range of web browsers. In future we expect the screen resolution to get higher with the trends of modern mobile phones.

When we return back to Table 1, we already mentioned the annual growth in the *remote* audience but also note the reduction of the *local* audience in 2015. What could be the reason behind this? Unfortunately, there is no simple answer. Thus, we provide some conjecture points. The 2014 event took place in Russia, and the Russian teams are repeat champions, which may have played a role in increased interest. Next, the Yekaterinburg venue took place in a public stadium in the city center with mass media and local host university support, while Marrakesh was in the private Palmeraie Resort, distant from the center of Marrakesh. In 2016 the physical deployment was similar to 2014. Another possible explanation could be that in 2014 the host provided all attendees with a prepaid data plan SIM-card. This allowed them to use their phone and access Internet in any public location in Russia. The usage of mobile phones almost doubles in 2014 over the other years, and this could play a role in the attendee involvement. Specifically, for the 2014 event, Google Analytics identifies 145 *local* visitors accessing through GPRS service provider, but only 2

in 2015 and 42 in 2016. In 2014, 123 mobile network visitors out of the total 145 used the SIM provider distributed by the host.

5.2. SPEX Model Classification of MyICPC Features. The SPEX model provides a good base for features to support interaction. In this section, we classify the MyICPC features according to the model.

The MyICPC supports social involvement for the local audience with Quest (Figures 4 and 5) and timeline (Figure 6). The audience can direct social messaging to particular events (Figure 10), teams (Figure 13), or schedule (Figure 7) using hash-tags. Their posts are distributed to particular pages based on these hash-tags. The media shared with the posts are aggregate and in a gallery (Figure 9). The MyICPC also provides statistical information on teams (Figure 14) and members. Next, the schedule is provided with its program, locations, or even a bus plan (Figure 7). It also integrates blogs and polls. The competition populates events on the timeline or scoreboard (Figure 12), scorebar (Figure 16), interactive map (Figure 8), code analytics (Figure 15), and live stream video. Detailed views on particular team submissions (Figure 14) or problem solutions are provided as well as code analytics predictions from team submissions. Each team has a profile, where the team problem submissions can be tracked, providing teams pictures, team history, etc.

We select the most popular pages by the access statistics, elaborated in the later section, and classify them by SPEX. For each considered page, we highlight the aspect of the discipline [D], event [E], or social involvement [S] which matches the SPEX model. Moreover, we annotate the page's option to provide a personalized view [P].

Scoreboard $[E \mid D \mid S \mid P]$

   Presents real-time actual score during the contest or practice contest, relates to the main event. Allows highlighting particular teams and following their updates.

Quest $[E \mid S \mid P]$

   Social media game involving solving tasks for the local contest participants.

Team statistics and history $[E \mid D \mid S \mid P]$

   Details on teams, members, integrate social media, photographs, submissions or code analysis.

Timeline $[E \mid D \mid S]$

   Integrates all events and notifications to a time-ordered, self-updating timeline. Highlights events from schedule and supports interaction by prefiled links to each notification.

Live stream $[E \mid D]$

   Live video broadcast.

Code analytics $[E \mid D]$

   Related to the contest/practice providing insight information on teams source code analysis.

Scorebar $[E \mid D \mid S]$

   Graphical compressed version of scoreboard fits to screen.

Interactive map $[E \mid D]$

   Graphical highlight of score on World map or Regional map.

Problem view $[E \mid D \mid S]$

   Highlights global view on code changes in last 5 minutes, submitted problems and their accept/reject ratio with specific submission details.

Schedule $[E \mid S \mid P]$

Event program with links to venue, map allowing personalizing the schedule.

5.3. Audience Temporal Interest Classification. We consider two audience dimensions, the *local* versus *remote* audience and their interaction in a certain time frame. Certain functionality boosts the interests and user involvement *before*, *during*, and *after* the main event, the actual contest.

For instance, Quest (Figures 4 and 5) supports the *local* audience interaction before the contest and so does the timeline (Figure 6). Since audience can direct social messaging to particular events (Figure 10), teams (Figure 13), or schedule (Figure 7), they have a certain control over the content. At the same time, administrators can restrict the posts.

Certain features impact the *local / remote* audience *before* the event, *during* the main event, and *after* it. In order to evaluate the audience interest and classify it by the time frame and location, we select the most popular pages and process them by the access statistics.

In particular, there are two possible statistics to consider. The total page hits or the page visit time. The page hits fit well to static pages. Since the MyICPC pages are interactive, using push technology, they allow the user to follow automated page updates with no page redirects or reloads. For this reason, we focus on the statistics involving page visit time. This considers the time spent on a page until a page redirects or reload happens. The details of the evaluation are provided in the next section.

5.4. Statistics on Feature in Terms of Time at Page. Next, we draw the audience interest, in particular, MyICPC features on given pages. These statistics consider the *local* and *remote* audience during a slightly different period that considered earlier. The 2015 Finals are considered. The period considered in this section divides into 120 hours *before* the contest, 10 hours *during* the contest (3 hours before and 2 hours after it counted to this fragment), and 38 hours *after* the contest. Table 5 presents the main highlights and the following text provides details.

The *local* audience spent almost one thousand hours on MyICPC, 67% *before* the main event, 28% *during* the main event, and only 5% *after*. *Quest* is the dominant feature with 45% of the audience time and even 62% of the time *before* the event. The *scoreboard* is the most dominant *during* the event, but overall it is high as the second most popular feature with 24% of the audience attention. The popularity of the *scoreboard during* the main event is a remarkable 62%. The *team statistics and history*, *timeline*, and *schedule* receive significant *local* audience interest. While the *team statistics and history* keep the popularity throughout the considered time frames, the *timeline* loses the audience *during* the main event. Moreover *schedule* is used mostly *before* the main event. Other pages give only marginal interest to the *local* audience.

In comparison, the *remote* audience shows significant differences. In total, the audience spent 4'601 hours on MyICPC with the division onto 10% *before*, 70% *during*, and 20% *after* the main event. Most importantly 74% of the time,

the audience followed the *scoreboard*. This correlates to the *local* audience interest and the characteristics from Figure 19. The most obvious is the lack of interest in *Quest*, which has the goal and purpose to get local audience attention. Even though *Quest* gets higher attention *before* the event, the overall drops to marginal. A long gap after the *scoreboard* is followed by the *team statistics and history* with rather constant interest 12%. The *timeline* gets the *remote* audience attention mostly before the main event and settles on 4% *during* the main event. Other features, such as *code analytics*, *schedule*, or *live stream* receives only marginal interest. The statistics show rather conservative interests of the *remote* audience.

From the SPEX model perspective, *Quest* relates to the event and mostly to the social aspect of the *local* audience. *Scoreboard* is related to the event and discipline; it supports the social aspect, but much less than *Quest*. The *timeline*, which is similar to *Quest*, is the central location for the social interaction; moreover, the content is related to the event and the discipline. For the *team statistics and history*, the discipline is the dominant aspect; the event and social aspects are rather secondary. *Schedule* is related to the event aspect, and its marginal part is the social involvement. This gives the answer to Question (vi).

Furthermore, we must highlight that the SPEX model does not target the *remote* audience. Additionally, Table 5 shows the differences in the interests in features for the *remote* and *local* audience and answers the Question (vii).

Finally, we answer Question (viii) considering Table 5. From the page visits statistics, *scoreboard* has shown only 13% interest of the *local* audience and 48% for the *remote* audience. The page visit time shows a significantly higher proportion. The reason behind this is that users load it once and follow the page push updates. On the contrary, *team statistics and history* indicate high interest for the *remote* audience by page visits, reaching 24%, but the time on the page is half, similarly to *timeline* with page visits 9% *remote* audience interest in the pages, but with the time one page only a half. Both statistics can give specific perspective, although the time on page fits better to the interactive applications using push communication. For completeness, we show the page visit statistics in Table 6.

5.5. Event Statistics by Time on Page and Device. In this section, we consider the contest statistics and page popularity with respect to time on page by a particular *device* type to answer the Question (ix). These statistics involve the 2015 World Finals. We consider the time of five hours *during* the contest for both *local* and *remote* audience. Next, we also consider the 120 hours *before* the event for the *local* audience. The summary and overview are provided by Table 7.

The main event has similar distribution of *device* types for the *local* audience. The top feature is *scoreboard*. The *desktop* users show higher interest in *timeline* and *teams statistics* and even *live stream*; on the other hand, they had less interest in *scoreboard* than others. Even though the *mobile* phones

TABLE 5: Page visit time statistics [%].

Feature	Local audience				Remote audience			
	Total	Before	During	After	Total	Before	During	After
Hourly distribution [h]	948	632	268	47	4'601	466	3'219	916
Quest	**45**	62	8	34	**1**	23	<0.5	2
Scoreboard[practice]	**24**	7	62	36	**74**	27	75	73
Timeline	**10**	10	2	10	**4**	17	4	5
Team stat. & history	**9**	9	12	13	**12**	16	11	12
Schedule	**6**	7	2	3	**1**	5	1	1
Live stream	**1**	<0.5	2	<0.5	**1**	3	1	<0.5
Scorebar	**1**	<0.5	1	2	**1**	<0.5	1	1
Code analytics	**1**	1	2	<0.5	**2**	2	2	1

TABLE 6: Page view statistics [%].

Feature	Local audience				Remote audience			
	Total	Before	During	After	Total	Before	During	After
Visits distribution	-	79	16	5	-	18	56	26
Quest	**53**	62	13	30	**5**	17	2	4
Scoreboard[practice]	**13**	6	42	25	**48**	21	54	50
Team stat. & history	**11**	10	17	20	**24**	31	22	23
Timeline	**10**	9	12	12	**9**	15	6	9
Schedule	**6**	9	1	1	**2**	2	1	2
Problem view	**<0.5**	<0.5	<0.5	<0.5	**4**	<0.5	4	5

TABLE 7: Time on page by device, time fragment, and audience.

Event frame	5 hours during event						120h before the event		
Audience	Local			Remote			Local		
Device	Mobile	Tablet	Desktop	Mobile	Tablet	Desktop	Mobile	Tablet	Desktop
Total audience[-]	122	35	114	1'219	174	4'775	298	61	381
Page/feature [%]									
Scoreboard	73	70	60	77	81	74	6	10	9
Quest	8	7	4	<0.5	<0.5	<0.5	65	70	57
Timeline	6	8	10	6	7	4	9	4	12
Teams stat.	6	11	12	7	7	12	10	3	8
Schedule	<0.5	2	2	<0.5	<0.5	<0.5	7	8	7
Live stream	<0.5	2	4	2	<0.5	1	<0.5	<0.5	<0.5
Scorebar	2	<0.5	<0.5	2	<0.5	1	<0.5	<0.5	<0.5
Code analytics	2	<0.5	<0.5	<0.5	<0.5	2	<0.5	<0.5	2

have limited *screen resolution;* they followed the *scoreboard* the most. Interestingly enough, the *local* audience had interest in *Quest,* while the *remote* had almost none.

The most dominant *device* type for the *remote* audience is *desktop,* with almost four times as many devices than *mobiles.* *Tablet* usage is marginal. There is the same interest in the main feature *scoreboard.* The *desktop local* audience users more followed the *team statistics and history.* On the other hand, *desktop* users followed much less the *timeline* than the *local* audience. We can see different interest in *Quest during* the main event between both audiences.

For the *local* audience *before* the contest, there is a similar distribution for *mobiles* and *desktops* and few *tablet* users. Naturally, the *screen size* differs as well as the ability to interact. *Mobile* and *tablet* users were more active in *Quest.* This is mostly because of Twitter app integration, which uses the embedded camera for messaging. The *desktop* users followed the *timeline* more than others. *Tablet* users were most active in *Quest* and followed the *timeline* and *team statistics and history* much less than others.

Both statistics *during* the main event show the importance of the *scoreboard;* other features and pages are only

FIGURE 20: Local audience using MyICPC.

FIGURE 21: Real-time scoreboard in action.

secondary when considering the main event. It seems beneficial to provide the *team statistics and history* and the *timeline* and for the local audience additional entertainments such as *Quest*, but other functionalities raise marginal interest to the audience.

To compare the interests for the local audience in different time frames, Table 7 provides both the main event and *before* event perspectives. We may notice the flip from *Quest* and *scoreboard during* the main event as well as increased interest for the *schedule*. Figure 20 shows the *local* audience using MyICPC at the World Finals. Figure 21 shows the real-time progress on *scoreboard* on a *mobile* phone *during* the contest.

5.6. Discussion of Study Results. Our aim in the study was to demonstrate a real production system that reflects our architecture and design suggestions and evaluates the audience interests and characteristics. The system considers many features based on the SPEX model. The evaluation should give the reader practical feedback on audience properties and interest. In the study, we consider both *remote* and *local* audience, since their interest differs. We consider their *devices, screen sizes, operating systems,* and even *web browsers* showing that the Second Screen should expect quite heterogeneous client devices and platforms. Thus, building a native application, e.g., an Android app, would reduce the audience scope only to approximately 20-30%. Next, the design investment should consider various screens ranging from 320x480 to 1920x1080, while future systems may expect to increase the lower bound resolution range. In case of web

applications, they must be optimized for various web browsers.

Specifically, when addressing *local* audience, we expected that the target device is a portable device such as *mobile* phone or *tablet*, but our evaluation shows significant use of *desktops*. This might be influenced by the domain since it is hard to imagine spectator with notebooks in football match. To boost and mediate the participant interaction a social gaming preceding the main event seems like a great instrument. In our case, *Quest* is the source of almost 50% of all processed events. We should point out that these events do not only impact the Second Screen but also all participants social network allowing distant friends to share the individual's experience. The evaluation of the rest of considered system features shows that the audience mostly uses core features, in particular *scoreboard* and *team statistics and history*. The *local* audience shows demands for event-related information such as *schedule* and *timeline*.

Based on the timing, we can expect that remote audience waits for the main scoreboard and in the meantime monitors the *local* audience activity on the Second Screen, but the peak audience arrives for the main event. *Local* audience shows a nice transition from the social gaming interests before the event into the main event interest once the right time comes. Naturally, from the *local* audience perspective there are more demands on the variety of features. Finally, many of provided features consumed a lot of time and investment to develop but receive only a marginal interest from the audience.

There are not really significant interest variations for users with particular devices. Even the *mobile* phone users access mostly the *scoreboard* no matter the screen size. There might be additional support for particular devices from third parties, such as Twitter app integrating phone camera and the Second Screen should take advantage of them. There is perhaps one interesting deviation in the *local* audience with desktops and it is the interest in the *live stream* video. This might be related to users sitting in less convenient locations or hallways following the show privately.

5.7. Threats to Validity. Next, we discuss the threats to validity regarding the study result outcome as well as the possible generalization of results. We divide the text into internal and external validity.

Internal validity: the source of information that we base our evaluation on is a production-level service, Google Analytics, used in industry and research [32]. Unfortunately, this does not guarantee the correctness of the statistical results [31]. We use the free version of the services that has limitations. The paper [31] shows limitations that are related to the total hit limit per month 10 M (page view/event), table aggregation, 500 hits per session, limited event tracking, and revenue strategies, etc. Fortunately, we do not cross the limits.

For Google Analytics, each page loaded by the end user contains a small JavaScript fragment that contacts Google Analytics service indicating the application key accompanied by HTML5 statistics on performance and context. Google Analytics identifies users through the client ID field, a unique, randomly generated string that gets stored in the browser's cookies. This allows Google Analytics to identify users across multiple sessions, even when IP address changes, but not across multiple browsers or devices.

The paper [31] admits Google Analytics inaccuracies. For instance, client-side caching or web accelerators can cache the pages and thus not count repeated visits. Robots and web-crawlers are counted, and over a long sampling interval, this over-counting can be drastic, although our interval was short. Pages with JavaScript errors halt the processing and thus will not show in the statistics, although this is not our case. Certain users with disabled JavaScript (e.g., 2.6% in US based on [31]) will be not counted. Certain firewalls can remove some tags or cookies. In such cases, only the IP address is counted, but [31] states that users can dynamically receive different IP addressed from their Internet service Provider or due to relocation. Users can delete cookies and thus impact the statistics. The paper [31] emphasizes that measuring unique web visitors is fraught with many problems, mostly relevant to longer periods of days and to lost/blocked/removed cookies. Fortunately, our sampling period was not long. Another significant issue is browsing in the incognito mode that skews the statistics, as cookies are not kept across browser sessions. The unique user calculation issue is mostly related to statistics for users with multiple devices or users sharing devices.

A study evaluating accuracy of the Google Analytics performed in (http://www.blastam.com/blog/index.php/2013/02/can-you-trust-your-google-analytics-data) suggests that visits statistics show variation in accuracy 0.89-1.46%. The results are much worse for transactions, revenue, or e-commerce conversion rate, which we did not consider in the study. While not considering full accuracy on the statistics from Google Analytics, it gives us a reasonable approximate feedback on the audience. The classification to Mobile/Table/Desktop users gives us a detailed statistic on user devices, operating systems, or flash versions.

We also need to emphasize the way Google Analytics determines time on page, which is perhaps the biggest threat to validity. It considers page transitions, where the transition to a next page determines time spent on the current page. On the last page, there is no next page so the time on page ends when the user opens the last page, which skews the statistics. In the extreme case user only visits a single page, the page visit count is 1 but the time on page is 0! In our case if the last page was interactive, such as timeline, scoreboard, scorebar, map, and problem view, the time on page is counted 0; thus, our statistics reports a lower bound with respect to time. At the same time, the total number of visitors can be lower.

External validity: our application is representative of a real-world application. The features provided by the application reflect the suggestions given by related work and their base reflects SPEX model. The example is specific to programming contests, although other contexts for the event such as conferences, sports matches, or exhibitions are expected to provide similar features and deal with similar issues or audience distribution. We cannot say that our representation reflects all aspects of future Second Screens. Our example demonstrates practical use and production experience with a Second Screen application. The locations of World Finals represent two particular scenarios providing real-world results. We believe that many noncomputing aspects play a role in the usage by the audience, such as cultural and economic factors or Internet access. The study considered computer-savvy users, as we believe that top programmers and IT staff (participants of the evaluated events) more likely use similar application.

6. Conclusion

In this article, we analyze factors impacting audience involvement and interest in using a Second Screen application. We consider a wide spectrum of audiences, such as home users and active audience using a mobile device as well as regular attendees of the events.

We suggest what to consider when performing an analysis of a Second Screen application that can be accessed by users through conventional web browsers. These users can use their mobile or even desktop devices while receiving real-time services adapting to various contexts, interests, or screens serving both the local and remote audience.

We share a case study involving a Second Screen application called MyICPC. The study involves a large event, the World Finals in Programming. We described particular details on available features and evaluate audience interest considering different time frames, local versus remote audience, or given devices. Out of the statistics provided by Google Analytics, we believe that the majority of the local audience used MyICPC to augment their live experience. We demonstrate audience interest in certain features. In particular, we emphasize interest of the local audience that spent the most time with the social game Quest with peak interest before the event. The scoreboard received the highest remote audience interest during the main event. The remote audience seems to be more conservative than the local. While there are differences in certain interests among the audience such as the schedule page usage, the case study shows that the main design interest should be placed to features such as the scoreboard and social gaming before the event, the timeline, the team statistics, and historical data, and to the schedule. Other features received unimportant audience interest.

Second Screen applications seem to be an evolutionary step to augment large events and venues. Nowadays spectators equipped with ever-improving mobile devices aim to receive the best perspectives, information from the event, or augmenting information. All these services provided through Second Screen increase the quality of their experience. Second Screen applications can impact new audiences and motivate passive users to contribute to their personal experience to the crowd media. Furthermore, this article highlights the benefits, potential, and motivation elements for such applications. While having the production-level experience, we share our design decisions so that reader may avoid prototyping issues. Next, in a particular context, we demonstrate the application of discussed features that support the social/event and discipline aspects of the audience. Finally, we show the real-world audience interest distribution to considered pages with described functionality.

This research contributes to the area of Second Screen applications and their utilization for various events to impact individuals from various angles, providing a personalized form of experience. From the future perspective, there is a high potential for utilization for learning purposes. For instance, it can improve educational settings and be used during conferences or even in the classroom when multiple channels can augment the mainstream of information for the audience.

Acknowledgments

Our research was supported by the ACM-ICPC/Cisco Grant 0374340.

References

[1] N. Staelens, S. Moens, W. Van Den Broeck et al., "Assessing quality of experience of IPTV and video on demand services in real-life environments," *IEEE Transactions on*, vol. 56, no. 4, pp. 458–466, 2010.

[2] K. Hyun-Wook, R. M. Hoque, S. Hyungyu, and S. H. Yang, "Development of middleware architecture to realize context-aware service in smart home environment," *Computer Science and Information Systems*, vol. 13, no. 2, pp. 427–452, 2016.

[3] C. Courtois and E. D'Heer, "Second screen applications and tablet users: Constellation, awareness, experience, and interest," in *Proceedings of the 10th European Conference on Interactive Tv and Video, EuroiTV '12*, pp. 153–156, ACM, NY, USA, 2012.

[4] M. Ludvigsen and R. Veerasawmy, "Designing technology for active spectator experiences at sporting events," in *Proceedings of the 22nd Conference of the Computer-Human Interaction Special Interest Group of Australia on Computer-Human Interaction*, pp. 96–103, ACM, 2010.

[5] E. Anstead, S. Benford, and R. J. Houghton, "Many-screen viewing: Evaluating an olympics companion application," in *Proceedings of the 2014 ACM International Conference on Interactive Experiences for TV and Online Video, TVX '14*, pp. 103–110, ACM, NY, USA, June 2014.

[6] L. Barkhuus, A. Engström, and G. Zoric, "Watching the footwork: Second screen interaction at a dance and music performance," in *Proceedings of the SIGCHI Conference on Human Factors in Computing Systems, CHI '14*, pp. 1305–1314, ACM, NY, USA, 2014.

[7] M. Barnidge, T. Diehl, and H. Rojas, "Second Screening for News and Digital Divides," *Social Science Computer Review*, 2018.

[8] A. Van Cauwenberge, G. Schaap, and R. van Roy, "Tv no longer commands our full attention: Effects of second-screen viewing and task relevance on cognitive load and learning from news," *Computers in Human Behavior*, vol. 38, pp. 100–109, 2014.

[9] R. M. Costa Segundo and C. A. Saibel Santos, "Systematic review of multiple contents synchronization in interactive television scenario," *ISRN Communications and Networking*, vol. 2014, 2014.

[10] L. Cruickshank, E. Tsekleves, R. Whitham, A. Hill, and K. Kondo, "Making interactive TV easier to use: Interface design for a second screen approach," *The Design Journal*, vol. 10, no. 3, pp. 41–53, 2007.

[11] F. Giglietto and D. Selva, "Second Screen and Participation: A Content Analysis on a Full Season Dataset of Tweets," *Journal of Communication*, vol. 64, no. 2, pp. 260–277, 2014.

[12] R. C. Nee and D. M. Dozier, "Second screen effects: Linking multiscreen media use to television engagement and incidental learning," *Convergence*, vol. 23, no. 2, pp. 214–226, 2016.

[13] C. E. Valente and C. T. Souza, "Support architecture for second screen apps dynamic adaptation," in *Proceedings of the 23rd Brazillian Symposium on Multimedia and the Web*, pp. 365–372, NY, USA, 2017.

[14] H. Gil de Ziiga, V. Garcia-Perdomo, and S. C. McGregor, "What is second screening? exploring motivations of second screen use and its effect on online political participation," *Journal of Communication*, vol. 65, no. 5, pp. 793–815, 2015.

[15] M. Macik, E. Lorencova, Z. Mikovec, and O. Rakusan, "Software architecture for a distributed in-hospital navigation system," in *Proceedings of the 2015 Conference on Research in Adaptive and Convergent Systems, RACS*, pp. 369–375, ACM, NY, USA, 2015.

[16] S. Livingstone, "The challenge of changing audiences: or, what is the audience researcher to do in the age of the internet?" *European Journal of Communication*, vol. 19, no. 1, pp. 75–86, 2004.

[17] M. Deuze, "Media life," *Media, Culture & Society*, vol. 33, no. 1, pp. 137–148, 2011.

[18] E. Tsekleves, R. Whitham, K. Kondo, and A. Hill, "Investigating media use and the television user experience in the home," *Entertainment Computing*, vol. 2, no. 3, pp. 151–161, 2011.

[19] P. Dalsgaard, C. Dindler, and E. Eriksson, "Designing for participation in public knowledge institutions," in *Proceedings of the 5th Nordic Conference on Human-computer Interaction: Building Bridges, NordiCHI '08*, pp. 93–102, ACM, NY, USA, 2008.

[20] M. Ebner and A. Holzinger, "Lurking: An underestimated human-computer phenomenon," *IEEE MultiMedia*, vol. 12, no. 4, pp. 70–75, 2005.

[21] B. Nonnecke and J. Preece, "Lurker demographics: Counting the silent," in *Proceedings of the SIGCHI Conference on Human Factors in Computing Systems, CHI '00*, pp. 73–80, ACM, NY, USA, 2000.

[22] T. Cerny and M. J. Donahoo, "MetamorPic: Self-contained photo archival and presentation," in *Information Systems Development*, pp. 149–158, Springer, NY, USA, 2001.

[23] L. DeMichiel and B. Shannon, *JSR 342: Java TM Platform, Enterprise*, 7th edition, 2013, https://jcp.org/en/jsr/detail?id=342.

[24] F. Vogelsteller, *Building Single-page Web Apps with Meteor*, Packt Publishing Ltd, 2015.

[25] R. Hanson and A. Tacy, *GWT in Action: Easy Ajax with the Google Web Toolkit*, Manning Publications Co., Greenwich, England, CT, USA, 2007.

[26] E. Burns and N. Griffin, *JavaServer Faces 2.0, The Complete Reference*, McGraw-Hill, Inc, NY, USA, 1st edition, 2010.

[27] A. Freeman, *Pro AngularJS*, Apress, Berkeley, CA, USA, 1st edition, 2014.

[28] F. Marchioni, *Infinispan data grid platform*, Packt Publishing Ltd, 2012.

[29] J. L. Carlson, *Redis in Action*, Manning Publications Co, Greenwich, CT, USA, 2013.

[30] M. Raible, *Spring Live*, SourceBeat, LLC, 2004.

[31] B. Clifton, *Advanced Web Metrics with Google Analytics*, SYBEX Inc, Alameda, CA, USA, 2008.

[32] D.-G. Tremblay and V. Psyché, "Analysis of processes of cooperation and knowledge sharing in a community of practice with a diversity of actors," *Computer Science and Information Systems*, vol. 9, no. 2, pp. 917–941, 2012.

14

A Rollercoaster to Model Touch Interactions during Turbulence

Alexandre Alapetite ⓘ,[1] **Emilie Møllenbach,**[1] **Anders Stockmarr,**[2] and **Katsumi Minakata**[1]

[1] Technical University of Denmark, Department of Management Engineering, Produktionstorvet 424, 2800 Kongens Lyngby, Denmark
[2] Technical University of Denmark, Department of Applied Mathematics and Computer Science, Asmussens Allé 305, 2800 Kongens Lyngby, Denmark

Correspondence should be addressed to Alexandre Alapetite; alexandre@alapetite.fr

Academic Editor: Pietro Cipresso

We contribute to a project introducing the use of a large single touch-screen as a concept for future airplane cockpits. Human-machine interaction in this new type of cockpit must be optimised to cope with the different types of normal use as well as during moments of turbulence (which can occur during flights varying degrees of severity). We propose an original experimental setup for reproducing turbulence (not limited to aviation) based on a touch-screen mounted on a rollercoaster. Participants had to repeatedly solve three basic touch interactions: a single click, a one-finger drag-and-drop, and a zoom operation involving a 2-finger pinching gesture. The completion times of the different tasks as well as the number of unnecessary interactions with the screen constitute the collected user data. We also propose a data analysis and statistical method to combine user performance with observed turbulence, including acceleration and jerk along the different axes. We then report some of the implications of severe turbulence on touch interaction and make recommendations as to how this can be accommodated in future design solutions.

1. Introduction

The future of aviation and motorized vehicle control will potentially include the integration of touch-sensitive interfaces into the control displays [1]. This would afford a more intuitive, direct, and tangible exchange of information between the user and system, as there is no displacement between control and feedback [2]. This research seeks to explore the effects of turbulence on the user's ability to complete simple touch-sensitive tasks and has been conducted as a part of the ODICIS project (ODICIS European project (2009–2012) http://web.archive.org/web/2013/www.odicis.org/) on "One Display for a Cockpit Interactive Solution"—a European initiative that aims to create a prototype of a future airplane cockpit. The main objective of this project is to develop a large seamless touch-sensitive display to be used in cockpits (Figure 1), and this paper is part of a series of experiments [3, 4]. We argue that the focus of future designs should be on balancing the affordances and constraints of the technology (i.e., multitouch interfaces) and physicality (i.e., vibrations and turbulence) depending on the safety requirements surrounding a given task. Panning a large map of the flight plan during stationary is different from doing checks while taxiing to the runway, which in turn is different from doing engine checks during turbulent conditions. If touch displays are to be implemented successfully into the cockpits of planes or other vehicles, an understanding of how turbulence affects this type of interaction is needed.

We seek to make a contribution to this matter by studying atomic touch interactions such as clicking, dragging, and pinching during various degrees of turbulence along the three axes, using acceleration and also jerk (variation of acceleration) to characterise turbulence. We also provide an original motion simulation approach using a rollercoaster, with appropriate data processing and statistical analysis, which are generic and thus may also be used in domains other than aviation.

2. Background

Touch-screens have been appearing in a multitude of shapes and sizes since the 1960s [5]. The possibility of direct interaction had an immediate appeal owing to its circumvention of the need for unnecessary cognitive mapping between

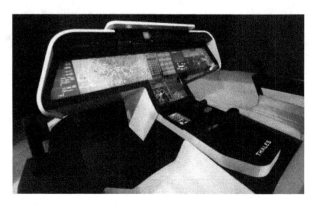

FIGURE 1: A picture of a prototype of future aircraft cockpit as envisioned by the ODICIS project.

an input device and interface [2]. The low cognitive load results in easily learnt interaction behaviour. The fact that there is no need for an independent input device and the relative robustness of the screen itself make this type of interaction relevant in mobile and turbulent situations where simplicity of interaction is of great value [6], e.g., in an airplane cockpit [1, 3, 7] or while controlling other vehicles.

However, touch interaction also has some innate constraints. In the 1980s and early 1990s multiple studies were done that identified touch interaction as a method that was fast and intuitive, but error prone and imprecise compared with other input modalities [8]. The drawbacks of touch interfaces are occlusion (i.e., that the hand covers part of the screen while a selection is being completed), the fact that targets must be larger than the width of the finger (rendering touch a lower resolution selection tool compared to, for instance, the mouse or even touch completed with a stylus) [6], and finally the loss of tactile feedback. Various strategies have been used to create solutions that overcome occlusion and enable high precision selection [4, 6, 8–13].

Safety is one of the main concerns when incorporating touch-sensitive displays into vehicular control, as the consequences of errors are potentially enormous. One way of dealing with safety concerns with tactile interaction is to implement selection sequences of varying complexity, including confirmations [14]. In any case, how turbulence affects touch interaction is of fundamental importance.

The effects of vibrations and turbulence on manual controls have been explored mainly in laboratory environments [15–17] (Lin, 2010), where the amplitude and directions of the vibrations can be controlled [18]. An example of this is a 6-degree-of-freedom (lateral, longitudinal, vertical, pitch, roll, and yaw) Stewart platform [19–21]. This type of reproduction of turbulence is a research field in itself and has been formalised, for instance, in procedures [22] used by NASA (National Aeronautics and Space Administration, USA). One of the main problems with Stewart platforms is forward kinematics—it is very difficult to create a realistic simulation of forward longitudinal motion. Another problem with common Full Flight Simulators (FFS) is that they could not be extreme enough for the purpose, in particular

regarding sustained acceleration higher than 1 g for several seconds.

More recently, however, Hourlier, Guérard, Barou, and Servantie [23] developed and tested scenarios containing simulated turbulence with the help of expert pilots. Their platform was a 6-axis hexapod that could mimic and exceed up to 8 g's of acceleration in a reliable way. This was used to create 6 turbulence profiles that were tested on the expert pilots, who rated the realism and severity of the experienced turbulence, in order to obtain turbulence conditions from mild to severe (according to the FAA (Federal Aviation Administration, USA) turbulence reporting criteria table). Of relevance, a study by Cockburn et al. [24] compared touch and a trackball as input devices during turbulent events simulated with a hexapod (cf. [23]) that delivered vibration along three axes. Results depended on precision requirements of the task such that low precision tasks elicited more accurate and faster performance in the touch input condition, irrespective of vibration level, relative to the trackball input condition. Furthermore, the trackball input condition resulted in more accurate and faster performance in tasks that required high precision, regardless of vibration level, compared to the touch input condition.

Research done on the effects of physical vibrations has for decades focused on tasks such as reading and writing [18, 25–27], though some research has then been done on exploring situational impairments that can occur when using touch on a mobile device while walking and in other contexts [28, 29]. An abundance of research on vibrations is concerned with the effects on manual and visual tasks [15–17, 27, 30]; however, Dodd et al. [31] studied the effect of three levels of turbulence on data entry performance. They used no turbulence as the control condition and light and moderate levels of turbulence (e.g., 35°/s for yaw, pitch and roll and 18°/s for heave, surge and sway for the medium turbulence condition) elicited the highest levels of data entry errors and perceived mental workload and slower completion times. Lancaster, de Mers, Rogers, Smart, and Whitlow [32] had worked on a related project but drove a van to simulate touch interaction during turbulence. They collected completion time, data entry errors, perceived workload, and electromyography in order to obtain an objective measure of touch-interaction performance during moderate turbulence.

Another experiment which was designed to explore interactions that could be applied to various vehicle controls was the study by Lin et al. [33], who compared the performance of a trackball, a touch-screen, and a mouse in a vibrating environment. They initially tested the input devices in a static environment and found that the touch-screen performed the best. However, the error rates of the touch-screen increased severely under conditions of vibration. Taking several performance measures into account, they conclude that the mouse was the best device under conditions of vibration, where the trackball suffered mainly from long completion times and the touch-screen from high error rates [33]. Similarly, Mansfield et al. [17] also found the mouse to be superior to the touch-screen in an experiment simulating the conditions of PC use for train passengers. McDowell et al. [21] found that terrain-induced ride motion of simulated military vehicle degrades reaction time and accuracy of operators (who are not looking outside and thus lack external visual cues). Studying the effect of motion on the use of a touch-screen system for tasks unrelated to driving in a military ground vehicle, Salmon et al. [34] found a positive learning effect, with a degradation of usability due to higher motion, but without characterising their "low" and "high" levels of motion in physical terms (e.g., acceleration along different axes) or the physical abilities of the simulator. As opposed to the elementary touch interactions that we use, Salmon et al.'s experiment tested a number of higher-level tasks such as writing, reading, and a combination of panning and zooming.

Other experiments completed under static conditions show that the touch-screen and mouse excel in different areas, with the mouse being most proficient in dragging tasks and touch for pointing [35]. In the context of a static aircraft cockpit, Stanton et al. [1] found that touch-screens provide a higher usability than trackball, rotary controller, and touch pad, but at the cost of some higher body discomfort.

As it is a younger technology, there is still much room for improvement in the touch technology itself, unlike that of the mouse. For instance, it will be a fundamental improvement when advanced haptic feedback, such as vibrotactile effects, becomes a standard part of touch-screen interfaces. The assumption is that many of the errors that occur for touch under turbulent conditions are due to difficulties in hand and eye coordination [18, 25]. Haptic feedback could aid in eliminating these errors [36].

We believe that a better understanding of touch interactions during turbulence will allow designers to circumvent some of the problems by optimising visualisation and interaction, thereby allowing the advantages of direct manipulation [37] to be realised in a vibrating turbulent environment. This paper seeks to contribute towards that direction, including aspects not addressed in the above-mentioned literature such as the role of jerk (variation of acceleration) and differences among atomic touch interactions that are clicking, dragging, and pinching.

3. Experimental Context

In the ODICIS project, the use of a large single screen with multitouch capabilities without haptic feedback is a fixed choice. Indeed, despite the acknowledged advantages of vibrotactile feedback [36], no technology was available with reasonable efforts at the time of the project that could cope with the needed large screen areas coping with multifinger and multiuser interaction. This large touch-screen must be optimised to suit the needs of pilots both in normal and abnormal contexts. In addition to this, many other lower-level requirements have to be addressed prior to seeking a flight certification, such as redundancy and tolerance to shocks, fire, smoke, extreme temperature, and electrical constraints. The screen and its operators will have to withstand alterations such as sun reflections, dust, fingerprints, and various vibrations and turbulence (which happen at different levels of severity during flights). In this paper, we focus on a single type of perturbation, namely, turbulence. Subsequently, some general rules can be derived on how best to deal with high and low turbulence.

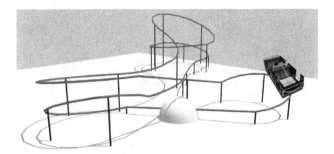

FIGURE 2: An outline of the rollercoaster "Odinexpressen" in Tivoli Gardens, Denmark (not to scale).

In order to create comparable and reproducible results, a certain level of control is required when conducting experiments. The experimental setting had also to be robust enough to run many sessions with different parameters (e.g., different tasks, different test subjects) while maintaining the same sequences and levels of turbulence. These requirements precluded conducting experiments during real flights. A setting was required where turbulence could be produced in a controlled manner.

Due to the cost and difficulty to access a platform simulating motion (such as in some flight simulators) and also due to the already-mentioned physical limitations of Stewart platforms [38], we went in search of an alternative way of exploring the effects of turbulence and vibration on touch interaction. The opportunity arose of using a rollercoaster at the Tivoli Gardens (Tivoli A/S: http://www.tivoli.dk), an amusement park in Copenhagen, Denmark. The chosen rollercoaster was Odinexpressen, a "powered coaster" constructed in 1985. It is about 300 m long and has a speed of about 60 km/h (Figure 2).

An amusement park ride made sense for several reasons not limited to the financial cost. First, realism in regard to the user experience was attained, even if realism in regard to a flight experience was less accurate: some observed turbulence such as strong lateral acceleration is not common for aircraft but may be of interest for other domains and can be filtered out in the data if so desired. The turbulence experienced by the user was severe and, most importantly, occurred in a repeatable sequence, meaning that each test subject experienced the same pattern of turbulence.

Two rounds of experiments were conducted: the "autumn trials" on 29 November 2010 and the "spring trials" on 25 May 2011. History of this article: The experiments occurred during a European research project and, after a long analysis phase, resulted in an extensive internal report. We then attempted a shorter academic publication, which, after a long review process, got some justified critique requiring some changes. We implemented most of the required changes but never finalised them due to each of the authors having changed mission or job after the end of the project. An invitation from the AHCI journal in May 2018 acted as a catalyst to implement the remaining changes, with, in particular, a significant effort to incorporate the most recent references.

FIGURE 3: Experimental setup on a wagon of the rollercoaster.

4. Experimental Design

4.1. Hardware Setup. To simulate the touch-screen that will be used in ODICIS, a state-of-the-art 22″ (56cm) LCD touch-screen was bought. The chosen model was from the 3 M Company (the multitouch display M2256PW) and was about the closest we could get to the high specification characteristics targeted by the OCIDIS screen (that uses a projection system, and infrared cameras for the tactile input) in particular in size and glass surface. The screen uses P-MVA technology, is multitouch and able to track up to 20 fingers with capacitive sensing, and has a resolution of 1680×1050 pixels, a video response time of 8 ms, and a hardware touch point speed of 6 ms.

Significant efforts were devoted to the safe mounting of the screen on a wagon of the rollercoaster. This involved building a metallic structure that would ensure the participants' safety as well as fulfilling the general safety regulations of the amusement park, while simultaneously allowing quick assembly and removal without damaging the wagon. The main safety concern was to ensure that the screen was securely fastened and could not fall off and thus injure either the participants or park visitors. An overview of the setup can be seen in Figure 3.

Each wagon consisted of two pairs of seats. Participants would sit on the rear pair of seats and a large wooden box containing all the necessary equipment was placed in the front seat foot area. The energy was provided by a 12V lead-acid battery of 110Ah.

The box contained a laptop computer with a solid-state drive (a traditional hard-disk drive would not have been able to sustain the vibrations). The laptop PC was mounted in a docking station for more convenient connectivity (e.g., more ports, and screws to secure the video cable). A spatial sensor (compass 3-axis, gyroscope 3-axis, accelerometer 3-axis) was taped to the lid of the box to collect the turbulence data through a USB connection. The model (PhidgetSpatial: http://www.phidgets.com/products.php?product_id=1056) from the Phidgets Company was the "1056 - PhidgetSpatial

3/3/3". The gyroscope worked in the range of $\pm400°$/s with a resolution of $0.02°$/s and a drift of about $4°$/minute. The accelerometer had a resolution of $228\,\mu g$, a range of $\pm5g$ (±49m/s^2), and a noise level at 128 Hz of $\sigma = 300\,\mu g$ on x and y axis, and $\sigma = 300\,\mu g$ on z axis. A GPS device was also embedded for some of the sessions, but the positioning lacked any useful degree of accuracy.

The sensor was queried every 32 ms, that is, 31.25Hz, and the nine parameters of the sensor logged (a sample is provided by Figure 19). Due to the way the motion sensor was mounted, we had the following mapping between the three accelerometer channels and the conventional terminology: A0 = -pitch axis (lateral), A1 = -roll axis (longitudinal), A2 = -yaw axis (vertical). Since the accelerometer reports resistance to acceleration, a positive value was to be understood as the direction of the force (e.g., like gravity directed towards the centre of earth) and the opposite of the movement. Furthermore, for the mapping of the three gyroscope channels we had G0 = -pitch; G1 = -roll; G2 = +yaw.

4.2. Software Setup. The intent of these initial experiments was to gather some general information about the effects of turbulence on the use of a touch-screen. The focus was on fundamental interaction principles (e.g., click, drag, zoom), and not on the use of a full and complex user interface such as what would be found in a plane cockpit. The tools employed to program the software for the experiments had to allow for fast prototyping and robust high-level tactile interaction: the Microsoft Windows Presentation Framework (WPF) was selected on Windows 7, programmed in.NET 4 with C♯ (C Sharp) and XAML (Extensible Application Markup Language). The chosen touch-screen was also directly compatible with the tactile functionalities of Windows 7. The software also logged user activity (e.g., time and location of the clicks, drags) as well as successes and failures in relation to the parameters of the scenarios.

4.3. Participants. During the spring trials, 12 participants (5 female) did a total of 33 turns in the rollercoaster, and 2 of our participants were civil aircraft pilots. All had tried a touch-screen and a rollercoaster before. However, none had tried a touch-screen in a rollercoaster before. Due to various technical difficulties, where the system would occasionally need to be restarted, only 20 of the turns were used for data analysis. Some participants did more than one turn, and this was accounted for in the subsequent data analysis.

4.4. Tasks. Each participant did one or more sessions, consisting of 3 consecutive rounds on the rollercoaster without a stop. The ride itself lasted approximately 3 minutes, which was the normal operational procedure of the chosen rollercoaster.

The software written for the experiments looped through three types of tasks that required a user action to solve them: tap, drag and drop, and zoom. The starting point of the sequence was randomly selected for each session. As soon as a user solved a task, the following task was automatically activated.

FIGURE 4: A yellow circle needed to be clicked by the user (various sizes and locations).

4.4.1. Tap Action. The first type of task to solve was very simple: it required the user to tap (touch with one finger) a yellow circle (cf. Figure 4) displayed at a random location on screen and at a random size ranging from 2 cm to 7.5cm. The minimum size of the yellow circle was chosen so that a fingertip could be placed on it for a click.

4.4.2. Drag and Drop Action. The second type of task still only required one-digit interaction. In order to complete it, the user needed to drag a red disc into a specific location (drop area) on the screen represented by a blue circle (cf. Figure 5(a)). When the red disc was moved over the blue destination circle, the colour changed to a cyan border and yellow background (cf. Figure 5(b)) to indicate that the task could be completed if the red circle was dropped at this precise location.

The location of the drop area was randomly distributed on the screen, and the initial location of the red circle was where it was left at the end of the previous drag and drop task. The software ensured that the random location of the drop area was such that the red circle was not already at the destination.

4.4.3. Zoom Action. The third and last type of task was solved using a two-finger pinching gesture which is translated into zoom, modelled on the zoom gesture used on mainstream touch interfaces such as that of the smartphone or tablet. The objective of this task was to change the size (zoom in or zoom out) of an orange solid square to make it match a preexisting blue square reference frame. This would initially be smaller or larger than the orange solid square that was the target for manipulation. The width of the border of the blue frame expressed a constant tolerance of about 1.4cm.

Two fingertips (not necessarily from the same hand) were placed on the orange solid square (Figure 6(a)). By increasing or decreasing the distance between the fingers, the size of the orange square increased or decreased accordingly (Figure 6(b)). The objective was to match the size of the orange square to that of the reference frame: when the two matched, the frame would change from blue to cyan (Figure 6(c)). At this point, the user could end the manipulation by removing both fingers from the screen. If the user continued the manipulation, the target would be over- or undershot (e.g., from (a) to (b)) and would require further adjustment of the orange square.

The locations of both the orange square and the blue reference frame were always at the centre of the screen, also during manipulations of the orange square. The size of the

orange square was left from the previous task of the same type; the minimum size was 2.8cm, so that two fingertips could be placed on it and manipulate it. The reference frame was of random size, with a minimum size just large enough to include the orange square (2.8cm inside, 5.5cm outside) and a maximum size of 17.5cm.

5. Data Characterisation

Before starting the analyses, some descriptive statistics were made to better understand the sensor data, the variable properties of the three task types, and the global performance of the participants in terms of completion type and number of errors.

5.1. Characterisation of the Physical Turbulence. Figure 7 characterises the three accelerometer axes (A0, A1, A2) as well as the total acceleration (A), which was calculated as an Euclidian distance from the three accelerometer axes. The reported values were aggregated by sessions using a "root mean square" function (RMS). with earth's standard gravity being $1g = \sim 9.8\,m/s^2$, a constant $1g$ was added to A2 (vertical acceleration) to make the comparison with the two other axes A0 (lateral) and A1 (longitudinal) more straightforward. On the rollercoaster used, there was no looping, so this approximation should have been acceptable. One can see from Figure 7 that there was lesser acceleration along the longitudinal axis (A1), with a high density at a low value of around 0.1g. Conversely, lateral acceleration (A0) was dominant.

From the point of view of the participants, when the global speed of the rollercoaster (in m/s) was constant (i.e., for the three axes), no turbulence was experienced at all, even when speed was high but constant. Furthermore, when global acceleration (in m/s^2) was constant, participants adapted to it, as we all do with the constant $1g$ acceleration due to earth's gravity.

Jerk, or the variation of acceleration over time (in m/s^3), should thus be a more straightforward way of characterising the difficulty associated with the experienced turbulence. Figure 8 reports the density distribution of jerk, averaged by RMS over all the sessions. The calculation of jerk was however sensitive to the sampling frequency and smoothing, in particular because the accelerometer data is by nature very noisy.

Finally, as an attempt to better characterise the experienced turbulence, a Fourier analysis was done, but no major frequencies (in Hz) were identified; the signal was closer to white noise than the clean frequencies found, e.g., in flight simulator platforms.

5.2. Characterisation of the Tasks Properties. Some descriptive statistics were also made to characterise the tasks given to the participants. Figure 9 reports the density distributions of the following: the distance from the centre of the screen of the circle to touch for the "tap" task in red; the distance to the target for the "drag" task in green; and the distance to adjust for the "zoom" task in blue.

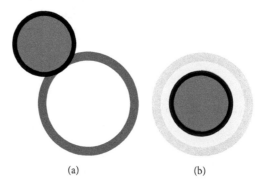

(a)   (b)

FIGURE 5: The red circle needed to be dragged (a) and dropped (b) onto the blue/cyan destination circle.

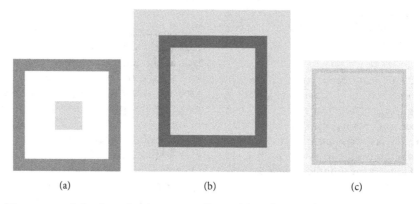

(a)   (b)   (c)

FIGURE 6: The orange solid square needed to be scaled (not too small as in (a), and not too large as in (b)) to match the dimensions of blue empty square (c).

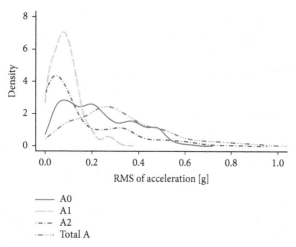

—— A0
--- A1
-·-· A2
···· Total A

FIGURE 7: Density distribution of the RMS of acceleration experienced for all sessions.

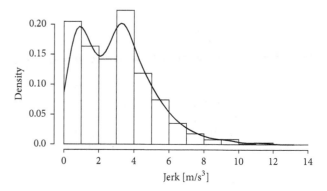

FIGURE 8: Density distribution of the RMS of jerk experienced for all sessions.

5.3. Characterisation of the Participants' Performance.

The two main participants' performance indicators were described by a density distribution of their completion time in Figure 10 and number of errors in Figure 11. Completion time was defined as being from the time when the task was displayed to the participant until the task was solved. One can see in Figure 10 that the "drag" was slower to perform, while "tap" was the fastest.

Errors were defined as actions outside the target areas, e.g., click outside the circle for the "tap" task, drop outside the target for the "drag" task", zoom adjustment outside the range for the "zoom" task, and a number of variations. One can see in Figure 11 that the "drag" task led typically to more errors per session, than the two other types of tasks. A few outliers had a number of errors higher than 15.

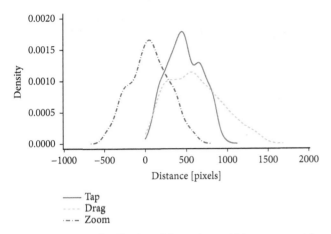

FIGURE 9: Density distribution of the major variable component for each of the three task types.

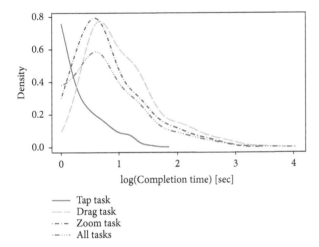

FIGURE 10: Density distribution of the log of completion time for the three task types.

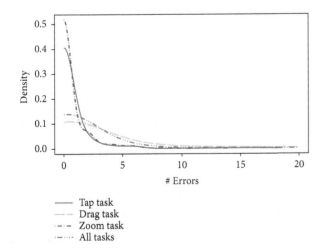

FIGURE 11: Density distribution of the number of errors for the three task types.

6. Data Analysis

This section describes in particular the construction of the statistical analysis of the spring data. The analysis divides each task into two parts: from the time when the task was proposed until the first action was taken (part 1) and from the first action to completion (part 2). Sensor data were smoothed both in each period and in the whole period from initiation to completion with a Gaussian kernel and a bandwidth of 0.6, using the function ksmooth() from the R statistical package. Furthermore, a constant 1g was added to the A2 (vertical acceleration) as a rough compensation for earth's natural gravity and to ease the comparison between the three axes. After this, a root mean square (RMS) was calculated for part 1, part 2, and the total, based on the smoothed sensor data. The Total RMS was used for descriptive purposes, but not for the modelling.

6.1. Analysis of Completion Time. The analysis of the completion time was performed in three steps:

First, the initiation time (part 1) was log-transformed and modelled through a linear model with systematic effects of person ID, task type, distance to screen centre (for "tap"), drag length (for "drag"), zoom type (in/out), numerical zoom-in distance, numerical zoom-out distance, accelerometer RMS values (A0, A1, A2), gyroscope RMS values (G0, G1, G2), and the calculated jerk RMS (J0, J1, J2) for the relevant period, all interactions between sensors, and all interactions between task-related covariates (i.e., possibly predictive variable) and sensors. The end-model served both as input for a model for the whole task completion period and as a result in itself. To justify the inclusion of the many interaction terms, the p-values in the basic model for the interaction terms were plotted in a Q–Q plot (quantile-quantile) against the uniform distribution. If the effect of interaction terms was artificial, and if apparent significance was only a result of mass testing, the p-values should approximately distribute themselves according to a uniform distribution. However, for both this part and similarly part 2, a distinct concave pattern emerged, indicating too many low p-values to conform to a hypothesis of no interaction effects. The model was subsequently reduced through significance testing at a 1% level.

Second, the time from initiation to completion (part 2) was analysed in a similar way.

Third, the significant factors from the first period (person ID, task type related covariates, and sensors related to the first part) were combined with significant factors from the second period (person ID, task type related covariates, and sensors related to the second part), to form the covariates of a model describing the log-transformed full completion time. This model was subsequently reduced through significance testing at a 1% level.

After model reduction, the significant effects were entered into a mixed effects model for each of the three models, where person ID was designated as a random effect, and coefficients were reestimated to provide a model formally independent of the current panel (cf. Table 3).

The results operate with "effects on average". This means that if covariates cov1 and cov2 enter into the model as

β1cov1 + β2cov2 + β3cov1cov2, the "average effect" of covariates cov1 and cov2 is β1 + β3mean(cov2) and β2 + β3mean(cov1), respectively.

6.2. Analysis of the Number of Errors. The number of errors (i.e., the number of erroneous or superfluous user actions), given that the number of errors was positive, was modelled by a Poisson regression model with the natural logarithm as link, with explanatory variables as for completion time. Due to the many interaction terms and limited number of data points, a specific estimation method was chosen. As base model, the model with no interaction terms was chosen, and interaction terms (and any removed main effects) were included successively with subsequent model reduction at a 5% level: first accelerometer data, then gyroscope data, and then jerk for the first period, then the similar variables for the second period. After this, all six sets of interaction terms were included again in the same order, and lastly the model was reduced at a 1% level. After model reduction, the significant effects were entered into a Poisson random effect model with person ID designated as a random effect, and further reduced.

6.3. Relative Importance of the Three Axes. It is also desirable to specify which types of turbulence, and along which physical axis, have most effect on the participants' performance. By selectively removing the covariates of interest (e.g., A0 = lateral acceleration) and estimating the precision of fit of the statistical model by means of an Akaike information criterion (AIC), this approach allows one to estimate the correlation between turbulence along one axis and the participants' performance. Indeed, models with poorer fit are a sign of a higher importance of the variable being removed.

7. Results

The results are divided into four sections: results based on "real" data (i.e., limited to basic operations such as smoothing and averaging), results based on the statistical analysis, further constructions from the model, and results based on a questionnaire.

7.1. Descriptive Statistics. The descriptive statistics are based on real data and not on a statistical model.

In Figures 12 and 13, low jerks are defined as <2.05 m/s^2 and high jerks as >3.75 m/s^2 to form three even-sized groups (low, medium, high). It is remarkable in Figure 12 that between the low and high jerk levels, there is a +55% increase in task completion time for "tap", as much as +178% for "drag", and +81% for "zoom". Though Figure 12 uses jerk to characterise the turbulence, the figure is similar when acceleration is used instead (cf. Figures 20 and 22).

Similarly, one can see in Figure 13 that by far the sharpest increase in errors from the low to high jerk conditions occurred for the "drag" task (+1499%); the error increase was lower for "zoom" (+362%) and lowest for "tap" (+247%). The figure based on acceleration was similar (cf. Figure 21).

While Figures 12 and 13 were well representative, the understanding of the relation between the duration of a task

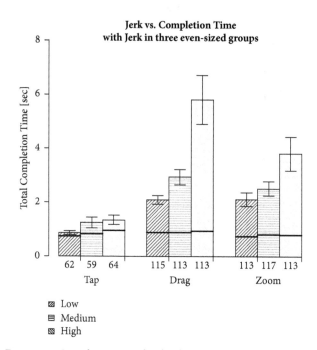

FIGURE 12: Completion time for the three task types depending on RMS of jerk intensity. The number of samples is given below the histograms. Horizontal bars denote the average time to first reaction.

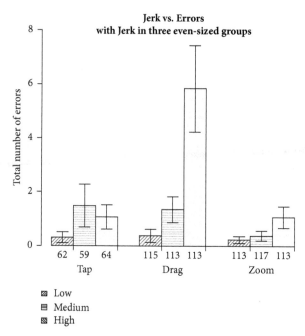

FIGURE 13: Number of errors per trial for the three task types depending on RMS of jerk intensity.

and the level of turbulence was nontrivial. Indeed, it is natural that longer tasks have a level of turbulence closer to average, due to the fact that turbulence is averaged over a longer duration. Therefore, the main possibility of having high levels of turbulence occurs precisely in the case of some short tasks. In order to visualise this effect, a second view of the same data

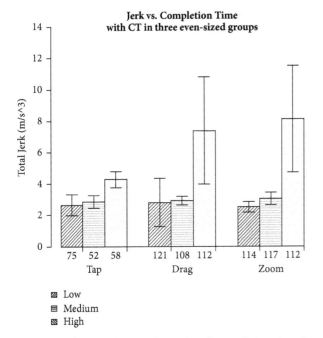

FIGURE 14: Jerk depending on the total task completion time (inversed axes compared to Figure 12).

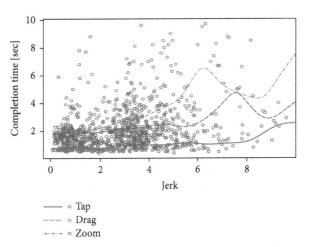

FIGURE 15: Completion time for the three task types depending on RMS of jerk intensity, with standard Gauss kernel and a smoothing window of size 1.

is depicted in Figure 14, which has its axes inversed compared to Figure 12 and has a different aggregation.

It is notable from Figure 14 that the confidence intervals for jerk are wide for the "drag" and "zoom" tasks that have a high completion time. This illustrates that "drag" and "zoom" tasks with a high completion time occur both with high levels of jerk as well as with jerk levels closer to average. However, Figure 14 also shows that tasks with a low (and, to a lesser degree, medium) completion time do not typically occur with high levels of jerk, which dispelled our initial concern.

One can see from Figure 15 that for relatively high jerks, the apparent effect on completion time gets less clear, which can be partially explained by the influence of turbulence other than jerk (e.g., sustained acceleration, rotations) and by a lower amount of data. The "tap" task seemed to be more impacted by high levels of jerk (i.e., above 8 m/s^2) than was the case with "zoom", but this apparent trend would need to be refined by additional data points at those higher levels of jerk.

Concerning the angular speeds (°/s) around the three axes as provided by the gyroscope, Table 1 again shows that, for the task completion time, "drag" was more sensitive to such movements than "zoom", with "tap" being the least sensitive (see also Figures 23, 24, and 25). The increase in completion time was calculated between the lower third and the upper third levels of angular speed. The time to first action was not significantly impacted by the angular speed.

The analysis did not focus much more on the effect of gyroscope data. From the raw angular speed (°/s) provided by the sensor, it would have been necessary to calculate angular acceleration (°/s^2) and then angular jerk (°/s^3) in order to pursue the analysis, as was done to infer jerk from the accelerometer data.

7.2. Statistical Modelling.

The statistical analysis reported in this section allows asking some questions at a higher level than permitted by the raw data collected during the experiments. In particular, it is possible to analyse the influence of some physical parameters more independently, as opposed to the raw data where these parameters are highly intertwined.

During the construction of the model for number of errors, the "drag" task was the only task that interacted with the turbulence measurements, meaning that the level of turbulence had a different impact on the number of errors for the "drag" task than for the two other tasks. It was estimated that for the "drag" task, the average number of errors was 5.25 (confidence interval ci=2.70:9.25), while the number of errors for other tasks was 4.15 (ci=2.23:7.07). Corrected for turbulence, the average errors were 0.12 (ci=0.08:0.17) for the "drag" task and 0.12 (ci=0.05:0.23) for the other tasks.

7.2.1. Turbulence along the Three Axes.

It was possible to estimate along which axis turbulence had the greatest impact on participants' performance, by removing in turn the relevant covariates from the statistical model and calculating the precision of fit with AIC (Akaike information criterion).

For the results reported in Table 2, higher AIC scores indicate poorer goodness of fit and thus higher importance of the covariate being removed. This shows that the combination of acceleration (A) and jerk (J) has the most importance in the model of participants' performance. Acceleration alone is the second most important predictor, followed by gyroscope (G) data and finally jerk alone. The results were consistent for the three axes.

Furthermore, Table 2 shows that the turbulence along the vertical axis was the most important, followed by the lateral axis and then the longitudinal axis.

7.3. Constructions from the Model.

While the statistical analysis yields some significant results on the interaction between various variables, some variables, such as total acceleration, were not in the model (only the three distinct axes were in the

TABLE 1: Effect of angular speed on the task completion time.

	Lower third	Upper third	Increase of completion time		
			"tap"	"drag"	"zoom"
G0 (pitch)	<7.7°/s	>27.3°/s	+39%	+155%	+62%
G1 (roll)	<9.6°/s	>18.4°/s	+25%	+115%	+42%
G2 (yaw)	<14°/s	>36.3°/s	+44%	+153%	+51%

TABLE 2: Akaike information showing the relative importance of the various sensor data on the participants' performance. Higher AIC reflects a higher importance of the corresponding covariate.

Covariate removed	AIC
A2, J2 (vertical)	1084.0
A2 (vertical)	1017.9
A0, J0 (lateral)	970.5
G2 (yaw)	970.2
A1, J1 (longitudinal)	950.3
A0 (lateral)	941.2
A1 (longitudinal)	929.8
G0 (pitch)	927.9
J2 (vertical)	922.9
J0 (lateral)	918.3
G1 (roll)	902.5
J1 (longitudinal)	901.3

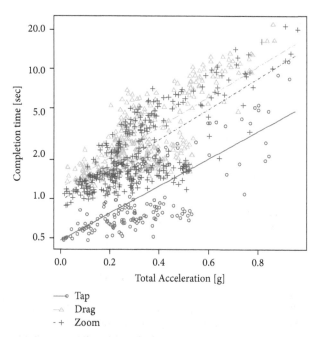

— o Tap
-△ Drag
- + Zoom

FIGURE 16: Evolution of the task completion time when acceleration increased and other parameters were kept at their mean value. Logarithmic scale.

model). Therefore, in this section, we provided some results where one variable was reconstructed and analysed while the other parameters (with which it interacts) were kept at their average value.

7.3.1. Effect of Total Acceleration.
With acceleration on the three axes being the strongest indicator for performance in our statistical analysis, the total acceleration was reconstructed to provide some more tangible comprehensive results. Figure 16 shows that the task completion time increased exponentially with the higher acceleration. The completion time differed significantly ($p<0.001$) for the three different task types (for cut-off, i.e., when acceleration is null). Furthermore, one can see that acceleration had a similar type of exponential effect on the completion time of the three types of tasks, and this was verified by the fact that the gradients of the three curves in Figure 16 did not differ significantly (z-test, $p>0.16$).

7.3.2. Effect of Total Jerk.
Total jerk was reconstructed in an identical manner. Figure 17 shows that the task completion time increases exponentially with the higher jerks. The effect of jerk—as visible from the gradients of the three curves—was less pronounced for "tap" (slope of 1.20) than for the other two task types (z-test, $p<0.03$). While the gradient for "zoom" (1.80) was in turn lower than the gradient for "drag" (1.98), which should have been a sign of "zoom" being less affected by jerk than "drag", the trend is not low enough to be significantly different ($p=0.39$).

7.4. Debriefing.
After the experiments of the autumn session alone, 8 participants were asked some general follow-up questions. One question was about the level of difficulty when using the touch-screen during turbulence, reported on a Likert scale ranging from 1 to 5 (1 being easy and 5 being difficult), as shown in Figure 18.

Finally, the participants were asked which type of interaction they found the hardest. Six participants found "zoom" the most difficult, and the remaining two found "drag" the most difficult.

There was a general consensus that it was quite difficult to use the touch-screen during turbulence. One especially interesting comment made by a civil aircraft pilot was about the experience of the turbulence: *"It is really not the same as the turbulence on board a flight, because those are more up and down, here you were thrown from side to side [...] However, the sense of forward movement is better than in a flight simulator"*—this means that even though the turbulence cannot be truly equated with that of a flight, the sense of propulsion could. Where the level of difficulty was considered high by the participants, the perceived cognitive load of the tasks was considered low (no one gave more than a medium score of difficulty). This matched the intention of the design

TABLE 3: Coefficients for fixed effects in the mixed effects linear regression of log (completion time) on task type and sensor RMS, where participants were included as a random effect. p-values for main effects include removal of any interaction terms. Estimate for participants is the random effect parameter. ∗ indicates that fields marked with an asterisk are for covariates that interact with other variables.

Parameter	Covariate	1.96sd	p
(Intercept)	-0.406466985	0.132506	<0.0001
Drag.type	0.591700803	0.111654	<0.0001
Zoom.in.type	0.790111531	0.090836	<0.0001
Zoom.out.type	0.450479139	0.117261	<0.0001
Drag	0.000433807	0.000139	<0.0001
A2.1part	1.783085961	1.296018	-∗
G0.1part	-0.04793816	0.017872	-∗
G2.1part	0.02191552	0.009063	-∗
J0.1part	0.618026108	0.292735	-∗
J1.1part	-0.325638032	0.496436	-∗
J2.1part	0.609259717	0.445836	-∗
Zoom.out	0.000981373	0.000387	<0.0001
A0.2part	0.321261018	0.497681	-∗
A1.2part	2.632465887	0.848084	-∗
A2.2part	1.850202982	1.280757	-∗
G0.2part	0.074977577	0.02005	-∗
G1.2part	-0.021831022	0.0068	-∗
G2.2part	-0.007884602	0.010191	-∗
J1.2part	0.123748476	0.07522	0.0013
A2.1part:G2.1part	-0.08028268	0.029973	<0.0001
G0.1part:G2.1part	0.000815077	0.000393	<0.0001
G0.1part:J2.1part	0.072423535	0.033729	<0.0001
G2.1part:J2.1part	-0.051373484	0.020583	<0.0001
J0.1part:J2.1part	-0.885565434	0.417899	<0.0001
J1.1part:J2.1part	0.573223371	0.269509	<0.0001
A0.2part:A1.2part	-13.42606928	3.24049	<0.0001
A0.2part:G1.2part	0.073165821	0.027681	<0.0001
A2.2part:G0.2part	-0.071543702	0.0364	0.0001
A2.2part:G2.2part	0.137311499	0.049604	<0.0001
G0.2part:G2.2part	-0.002105894	0.000429	<0.0001

of the experiment, as the focus was on interaction and not on task comprehension.

8. Discussion

Overall "tap" had the fastest task completion time, followed by "zoom" and then "drag", with the last two being close. This was not surprising, as "tap" was the simplest selection strategy consisting of one target and one action. It would be interesting to see what would happen when using tap in a complex interface.

From the descriptive statistics, "drag" was the task type that was by far the most affected by turbulence, both in terms of completion time and number of errors. Furthermore, while "tap" was the least affected by turbulence for the major part of the range of acceleration and jerk experienced during the experiments, there were some subtle indications from the descriptive statistics that this could change for higher levels of turbulence. This would require additional experiments to

form a satisfactory conclusion. This data pattern was similar to the results of Cockburn et al. [24], which showed that their slider/dragging condition had the most errors as vibration increased and that easy tasks such as tapping/clicking were not very affected by vibration/turbulence.

An interesting result of the statistical analysis is that turbulence along the vertical axis was the most important predictor for human performance in our experiments.

The statistical analysis also confirmed the intuitive hypothesis that longer drag and zoom lengths lead to a longer task completion time.

Constructions from the statistical analysis revealed that acceleration had a similar type of effect on the completion time of the three task types and that this effect is exponential. However, Dodd et al. [31] and Lancaster et al. [32] found a monotonic increase in completion time and number of errors as a function of acceleration, which could be due to the differences between turbulence simulator settings and the different stimuli/tasks (i.e., tasks and stimuli were similar but

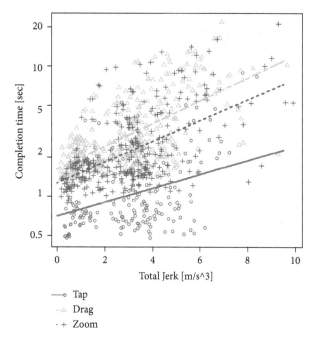

FIGURE 17: Evolution of the task completion time when jerk increased and other parameters were kept at their mean value. Logarithmic scale.

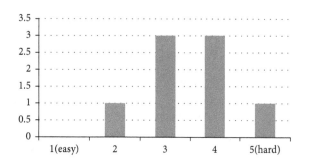

FIGURE 18: Touch-screen reported ease of use while interacting during turbulence.

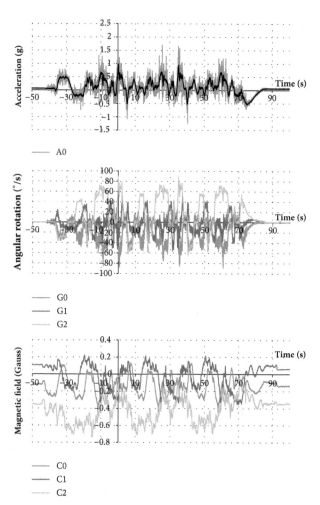

FIGURE 19: Illustration of the variation of the different sensor values during a typical session, grouped by acceleration (accelerometer), angular rotation (gyroscope), and magnetic field (compass). For legibility, only one accelerometer out of three is plotted.

not identical) used between these two experiments and the current study. Additionally, these research groups did not thoroughly analyse their data in terms of jerk, which is a strength of the analyses executed in this current study. One can thus infer that, the longer the tasks take to perform, the more sensitive they are to acceleration. For jerk, "tap" was least affected. The trend reported by the descriptive statistics of "zoom" as less sensitive than "drag" to jerk was still visible in the statistical analysis, but not enough to be significant.

From the above, one can infer that the intrinsic task duration seems to be more important parameter than the type of task as regards how sensitive they are to turbulence.

A great deal of attention was given to the data provided by the accelerometer, but only to a lesser extent to the data from the gyroscope. It might have been interesting to study the effects of the variations of angular acceleration ($°/s^2$) and even angular jerk ($°/s^3$), as these are likely to have a greater

effect than the angular speed alone ($°/s$) used in this article, but this is a task for future research.

In these experiments, the focus was not set on the different types of activation for clicking, as there was neither sufficient time to train the participants nor sufficiently long sessions to test the different variants. However, the strategy chosen for these experiments, namely, of activation on release of the finger (events typically called "Mouse-Up" or "Touch-Up"), should be favoured [38], as it allows adjusting or cancelling a click while the finger is still in contact with the screen.

9. Conclusion

The experiments served their purpose well, namely, to gather some information about the general effect of turbulence on the use of a tactile user interface and to propose a data analysis and statistical method for pursuing more experiments.

The main findings of the paper concern a method for correlating user performance (completion time, number of

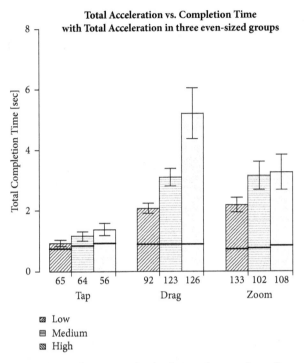

FIGURE 20: Completion time for the three task types depending on RMS of acceleration intensity. The number of samples is provided below the histograms. Horizontal bars denote the average time to first reaction.

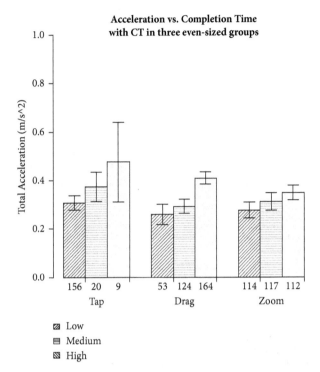

FIGURE 22: Total acceleration depending on the total task completion time (inversed axes compared to Figure 20). The number of samples is provided below the histograms.

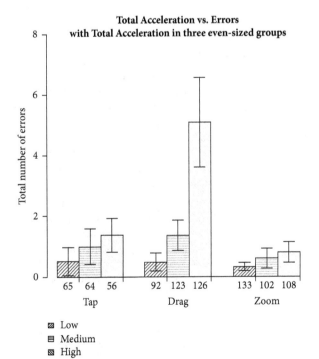

FIGURE 21: Number of errors for the three task types depending on RMS of acceleration intensity. The number of samples is provided below the histograms.

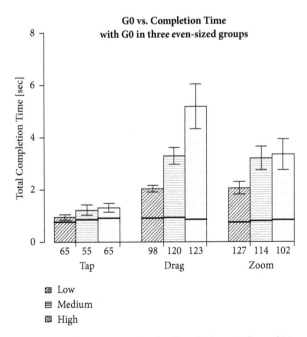

FIGURE 23: Completion time for the three task types depending on RMS of angular speeds (°/s) for G0 (pitch). The number of samples is provided below the histograms. Horizontal bars denote the average time to first reaction.

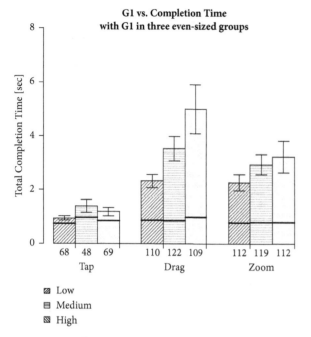

FIGURE 24: Completion time for the three task types depending on RMS of angular speeds (°/s) for G1 (roll). The number of samples is provided below the histograms. Horizontal bars denote the average time to first reaction.

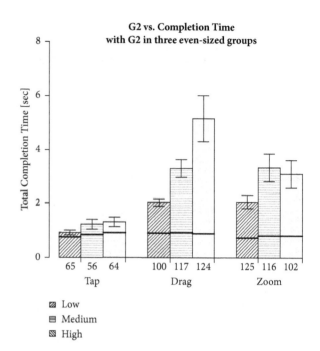

FIGURE 25: Completion time for the three task types depending on RMS of angular speeds (°/s) for G2 (yaw). The number of samples is provided below the histograms. Horizontal bars denote the average time to first reaction.

errors) and sensor data (accelerometer, gyroscope), the effect of turbulence on different touch-interaction tasks, the effect of the drag and drop distance during turbulence, and the effect of the relative zoom distance during turbulence. Furthermore, we could infer a new hypothesis, namely, that the longer tasks take to perform (without turbulence), the more severely turbulence will affect them.

Although we could not confirm one of our initial hypotheses—that jerk alone would be a better predictor for human performance than acceleration alone—we did find that jerk was a significant predictor and that the combination of acceleration with jerk was the best predictor. Additional analyses would be needed to refine the calculation of jerk.

Although conditions were sometimes challenging, no major difficulty was discovered that would prohibit the use of tactile interfaces during the type of turbulence we could produce. Anecdotal evidence confirmed this: one of the aircraft pilots participating in the tests said that, though he was extremely sceptical about the use of tactile interaction prior to the experiments, after having tried it he was much more convinced that tactile approaches could be viable.

Appendix

This section contains some data processing details.

A. Details about Data Preprocessing

In order to be usable for statistical analysis, the raw collected data had to be preprocessed. In particular, it was necessary to perform a temporal alignment to have a common starting point across sessions. Furthermore, although all sessions were very much alike, the speed of the rollercoaster was not exactly identical for a given segment across sessions. Therefore, a temporal normalisation was needed to ensure that each session is progressing at the same speed as the others. This processing, the result of which can be seen on the horizontal axis of Figure 19, has been done in a number of steps:

(1) By plotting the 9 sensor values for a number of sessions, 20 points were visually identified and selected as being particularly easy to find algorithmically in a robust manner across sessions. The criteria for these reference points were to be a local maximum or minimum for one of the 9 sensor values, with at least 5 seconds of data on each side that should not interfere with the detection of the point.

(2) A reference point of particular interest was then selected to become the new time origin (zero). It is located at about one-third of a session and is found by searching for the top 3 global maxima and then selecting the first occurrence in chronological order. A program was written to do that for all sessions, and the result was verified visually.

(3) The program then finds the 20 above-mentioned reference points in each session based on their approximate timestamp (relative to the new time origin).

(8) Finally, both sensor data and user interaction data are divided into segments of 3 seconds based on the new normalised timestamp, so that global statistics can be

performed. In particular, the root mean square (RMS, also called "quadratic mean") is calculated for each of the 9 sensor values on each segment by aggregating the data from all sessions.

Acknowledgments

This project was financed by the EU commission, through a project of the 7th framework: ODICIS, "One Display for a Cockpit Interactive Solution" (2009–2012), involving 9 partners from 7 EU member states, and was led by Thales Avionics (ref. ACP8-GA-2009-233605) (ODICIS European FP7 project funding Web site https://cordis.europa.eu/project/rcn/91181_en.html). We would like to thank the Tivoli Gardens (Copenhagen, Denmark) for granting us access to the rollercoaster and for providing assistance; Julie Eis Eriksen and Ulrik Lundby Hansen in particular deserve mention. Additionally, Philip Anton de Saint-Aubain significantly contributed to this work by conducting the data analysis portion. We would also like to thank Bo Johansen (SAS: Scandinavian Airlines) and Mathias Vitting Hermann (Center Air Pilot Academy) for their participation. Finally, we would like to thank a number of colleagues from the Technical University of Denmark for providing support and inspiration, in particular Doctor Christos Georgakis.

References

[1] N. A. Stanton, C. Harvey, K. L. Plant, and L. Bolton, "To twist, roll, stroke or poke? A study of input devices for menu navigation in the cockpit," *Ergonomics*, vol. 56, no. 4, pp. 590–611, 2013.

[2] Y.-L. Lee, "Comparison of the conventional point-based and a proposed finger probe-based touch screen interaction techniques in a target selection task," *International Journal of Industrial Ergonomics*, vol. 40, no. 6, pp. 655–662, 2010.

[3] A. Alapetite, R. Fogh, D. Zammit-Mangion et al., "Direct tactile manipulation of the flight plan in a modern aircraft cockpit," in *Proceedings of the International Conference on Human-Computer Interaction in Aerospace (Aero '2)*, Brussels, Belgium, 2012.

[4] A. Alapetite, R. Fogh, A. G. Özkil, and H. B. Andersen, "A deported view concept for touch interaction," in *Proceedings of the International Conference on Advances in Computer-Human Interactions (ACHI '13)*, pp. 22–27, Nice, France, March 2013.

[5] E. A. Johnson, "Touch displays: A programmed man-machine interface," *Ergonomics*, vol. 10, no. 2, pp. 271–277, 1967.

[6] P.-A. Albinsson and S. Zhai, "High precision touch screen interaction," in *Proceedings of the SIGCHI Conference on Human Factors in Computing Systems*, pp. 105–112, USA, April 2003.

[7] E. J. Eichinger, "Between laboratory and simulator: a cognitive approach to evaluating cockpit interfaces by manipulating informatory context," *Cognition, Technology & Work*, pp. 417–427, 2014.

[8] A. Sears and B. Shneiderman, "High precision touchscreens: design strategies and comparisons with a mouse," *International Journal of Man-Machine Studies*, vol. 34, no. 4, pp. 593–613, 1991.

[9] D. Wigdor, C. Forlines, P. Baudisch, J. Barnwell, and C. Shen, "Lucid touch: a see-through mobile device," in *Proceedings of the 20th Annual ACM Symposium on User Interface Software and Technology (UIST '07)*, pp. 269–278, Newport Beach, Calif, USA, October 2007.

[10] P. Brandl, J. Leitner, T. Seifried, M. Haller, B. Doray, and P. To, "Occlusion-aware menu design for digital tabletops," in *Proceedings of the 27th International Conference Extended Abstracts on Human Factors in Computing Systems*, pp. 3223–3228, 2009.

[11] F. Echtler, M. Huber, and G. Klinker, "Shadow tracking on multi-touch tables," in *Proceedings of the Working Conference on Advanced Visual Interfaces*, pp. 388–391, Italy, May 2008.

[12] K. Karlson and B. B. Bederson, "Thumbspace: Generalized one-handed input for touchscreen-based mobile devices," in *Proceedings of the 11th IFIP TC 13 International Conference on Human-Computer Interaction*, pp. 324–338, 2007.

[13] B. Shneiderman, "Touch screens now offer compelling uses," *IEEE Software*, vol. 8, no. 2, pp. 93–94, 1991.

[14] D. M. Usher and C. Ilett, "Touch-screen techniques: performance and application in power station control displays," *Displays*, vol. 7, no. 2, pp. 59–66, 1986.

[15] A. M. Wichansky, "Effects of ride environment on intercity train passenger activities," *Transportation Research Record*, vol. 721, 1979.

[16] C. Nakagawa and H. Suzuki, "Effects of train vibrations on passenger PC use," *Quarterly Report of RTRI (Railway Technical Research Institute) (Japan)*, vol. 46, no. 3, pp. 200–205, 2005.

[17] N. Mansfield, Y. Arora, and A. Rimell, "Computer use on moving trains: Which pointing device?" *Contemporary Ergonomics'* p. 255, 2007.

[18] C. H. Lewis and M. J. Griffin, "A review of the effects of vibration on visual acuity and continuous manual control, part II: Continuous manual control," *Journal of Sound and Vibration*, vol. 56, no. 3, pp. 415–457, 1978.

[19] E. Fichter, "A Stewart platform-based manipulator: general theory and practical construction," *The International Journal of Robotics Research*, vol. 5, no. 2, p. 157, 1986.

[20] P. Nanua, K. J. Waldron, and V. Murthy, "Direct kinematic solution of a Stewart platform," *IEEE Transactions on Robotics and Automation*, vol. 6, no. 4, pp. 438–444, 1990.

[21] K. Mcdowell, K. A. Rider, N. Truong, and V. J. Paul, "Effects of ride motion on reaction times for reaching tasks," *SAE Technical Paper 2005-01-1411*, vol. 114, no. 2, pp. 108–115, 2005, ISSN 0096-736X.

[22] S.-T. Wang and W. Frost, "Atmospheric turbulence simulation techniques with application to flight analysis", National Aeronautics and Space Administration, contractor report, NASA CR-3309, 1980.

[23] S. Hourlier, S. Guérard, J. L. Barou, and X. Servantie, "Testing touch screens in realistic aeronautic turbulent conditions (Light to severe)," *SAE International Journal of Aerospace*, pp. 243–247, 2015.

[24] C. Cockburn, P. Gutwin, Y. Palanque et al., "Turbulent touch: Touchscreen input for cockpit displays," in *Proceedings of the 2017 CHI Conference on Human Factors in Computing Systems*, pp. 6742–6753, 2017.

[25] M. J. Griffin and C. H. Lewis, "A review of the effects of vibration on visual acuity and continuous manual control, part I: Visual acuity," *Journal of Sound and Vibration*, vol. 56, no. 3, pp. 383–413, 1978.

[26] M. J. Griffin and R. A. Hayward, "Effects of horizontal whole-

body vibration on reading," *Applied Ergonomics*, vol. 25, no. 3, pp. 165–169, 1994.

[27] J. Sundström and S. Khan, "Influence of stationary lateral vibrations on train passengers' difficulty to read and write," *Applied Ergonomics*, vol. 39, no. 6, pp. 710–718, 2008.

[28] S. K. Kane, J. O. Wobbrock, and I. E. Smith, "Getting off the treadmill: Evaluating walking user interfaces for mobile devices in public spaces," in *Proceedings of the 10th International Conference on Human-Computer Interaction with Mobile Devices and Services, MobileHCI 2008*, pp. 109–118, Netherlands, September 2008.

[29] M. Lin, R. Goldman, K. J. Price, A. Sears, and J. Jacko, "How do people tap when walking? An empirical investigation of nomadic data entry," *International Journal of Human-Computer Studies*, vol. 65, no. 9, pp. 759–769, 2007.

[30] M. E. Lahib, J. Tekli, and Y. B. Issa, "Evaluating Fitts' law on vibrating touch-screen to improve visual data accessibility for blind users," *International Journal of Human-Computer Studies*, vol. 112, pp. 16–27, 2018.

[31] S. R. Dodd, J. Lancaster, S. Grothe, B. de Mers, B. Rogers, and A. Miranda, "Touch on the flight deck: the impact of display location, size, touch technology & turbulence on pilot performance," in *Proceedings of the 2014 IEEE/AIAA 33rd Digital Avionics Systems Conference (DASC)*, p. 2C3-1-2C3-13, 2014.

[32] J. Lancaster, B. De Mers, B. Rogers, A. Smart, and S. Whitlow, "The effect of touch screen hand stability method on performance & subjective preference in turbulence," *SID Symposium Digest of Technical Papers*, vol. 42, pp. 841–844, 2011.

[33] C. J. Lin, C. N. Liu, C. J. Chao, and H. J. Chen, "The performance of computer input devices in a vibration environment," *Ergonomics*, vol. 53, no. 4, pp. 478–490, 2010.

[34] P. M. Salmon, M. G. Lenné, T. Triggs, N. Goode, M. Cornelissen, and V. Demczuk, "The effects of motion on in-vehicle touch screen system operation: A battle management system case study," *Transportation Research Part F: Traffic Psychology and Behaviour*, vol. 14, no. 6, pp. 494–503, 2011.

[35] S. MacKenzie, A. Sellen, and W. A. S. Buxton, "A comparison of input devices in element pointing and dragging tasks," in *Proceedings of the SIGCHI Conference on Human Factors in Computing Systems: Reaching through Technology*, pp. 161–166, 1991.

[36] J. B. F. van Erp and H. A. H. C. van Veen, "Vibrotactile in-vehicle navigation system," *Transportation Research Part F: Traffic Psychology and Behaviour*, vol. 7, no. 4-5, pp. 247–256, 2004.

[37] E. L. Hutchins, J. D. Hollan, and D. A. Norman, "Direct Manipulation Interfaces," *Human–Computer Interaction*, vol. 1, no. 4, pp. 311–338, 1985.

[38] K. G. Bauersfeld, *Effects of Turbulence And Activation Method on Touchscreen Performance in Aviation Environments [M. S. thesis]*, San Jose State University, USA, 1992, http://scholarworks .sjsu.edu/etd_theses/374.

15

Design of a Massage-Inspired Haptic Device for Interpersonal Connection in Long-Distance Communication

Lalita Haritaipan ⓘ,[1] Masahiro Hayashi,[1] and Céline Mougenot[2]

[1]*Tokyo Institute of Technology, Department of Mechanical Engineering, Tokyo 152-8552, Japan*
[2]*Imperial College London, Dyson School of Design Engineering, London, UK*

Correspondence should be addressed to Lalita Haritaipan; haritaipan.l.aa@m.titech.ac.jp

Academic Editor: Thomas Mandl

The use of tactile senses in mediated communication has generated considerable research interest in past decades. Since massage is a common practice in Asian cultures, we propose to introduce massage-based interactions in mediated communication between people in a close relationship. We designed a device for distant interactive massage to be used during online conversation and we assessed its effect on interpersonal connection with eight pairs of Chinese participants in romantic relationships. All pairs were asked to engage in a conversation, either through a video call or through a massage-assisted video call. The findings showed that the use of the massage device significantly increased the perceived emotional and physical connection between the users. The results also showed a significant increase in the engagement in the massage activity, e.g., total massage time and average force per finger, from positive conversation to negative conversation, demonstrating an evidence of the interplay between audio-visual and haptic communication. Post hoc interviews showed the potential of the massage device for long-distance communication in romantic relationships as well as in parents-children relationships.

1. Introduction

In human-computer interaction (HCI) research, affective computing has found applications in online social interaction. Although most existing communication techniques exploit only two of the human senses, visual and auditory, there is a growing interest in bringing the sense of touch to computer-mediated communication, as reported in the review paper by Eid and Osman [1]. Haptic communication refers to communication via the sense of touch. At birth, touch is the most developed sensory modality and it plays fundamental role in communication throughout childhood [2]. However, after humans learn to use languages, haptic communication became mostly neglected. Still, interpersonal touch is still used in intimate relationships, as it is an important form of communication for conveying intimate emotions such as love and sympathy [3]. Indeed recent studies have shown that basic emotions, e.g., anger, fear, and happiness, can be communicated through touch only [4, 5].

In distant communication, human still predominantly rely on visual and auditory senses. New ways of communicating emotions, e.g., emoji or Animoji, are still relying on visual sense. On the other hand, geographically separated family or couples often long for physical presence and interaction [6] and touch-based communication devices are expected to mediate intimate relationships and create a sense of togetherness [7].

In this context, we aim at supporting long-distance communication through haptic interactions created by a massage-inspired device. Our study examines how the use of a vibrotactile device during a video call affects interpersonal connection and sense of togetherness of couples in long-distance communication.

2. Related Studies

2.1. Existing Mediate Haptic Communication Devices. We reviewed existing haptic communication devices and categorized them based on the type of interactions they rely on

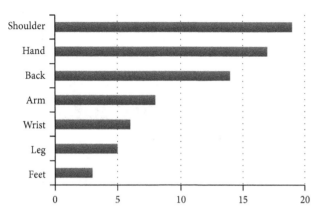

FIGURE 1: Part of body selected for massage in distance communication (N=50, multiple choice responses).

(Table 1). Since mediated physical interaction is not necessary equivalent to mediated social touch [35], we did not include devices that allow remote physical interactions that are not relevant to mediate touch between humans.

2.2. Massage-Based Interactions. Interactions through massage have the potential to be used practically in mediated communication since it is one of the interpersonal interactions that can be done continuously in a period of time without a feeling of awkwardness. Being given a massage by a known person creates a feeling of "being cared for" and "existential well-being" [36]. A hand massage as a "comforting, caring intervention" can "enhance satisfaction with care" [37]. Massage can also be seen as a way of communicating, as it enables mutual interpretation [38]. However, despite the acknowledged importance of massage for emotional well-being, massage-based interactions have never been implemented in mediated communication.

2.3. Cultural Context in Haptic Communication. Human emotion is not only biologically determined but also influenced by environment and culture [39]. While basic emotions are common across cultures, the subordinate categories of emotions are culture specific [40]. Similarly, even if haptic communication is instinct-based, cultures and context still affect the narration to touches. One obvious example is that, in Western cultures, people greet each other with handshaking or even cheek-touching in close friends or families, while, in Eastern cultures, people bows or use gestures without any touching at all. In mediated social touch context, it is important to consider not only the senses generated from the artificial touch, but also the touch etiquette [41]. Guidelines of this culturally aware etiquette have been suggested for the development of social robots [42]. A study about the gestural communication of emotions showed that French participants chose to perform gestures more intensely and faster than Japanese participants [43]. While most previous studies examined mediated touch in Western contexts, our paper focuses an Asian context and we aim at providing culturally grounded insights into the field of tactile mediation for distant communication.

3. Research Question

Through the introduction of a massage-based interactions in long-distance communication, we address the following research question: how does the use of a massage-based device affect interpersonal connection in long-distance communication, e.g., video call?

In the following sections, we report the development of a massage-based device and its experimental assessment with pairs of participants in a romantic relationship, in a distant communication task. We examined how participants perceived the connection with the other person, including sense of togetherness, emotional connection, and physical connection, during a video call, either with or without the massage-based device.

4. Creation of an Interactive Massage Device

4.1. Preliminary Survey. Through an online survey, we collected opinions from the general public about tactile sense distant communication.

4.1.1. Respondents. 50 respondents (25 males, 25 females) aged between 18 and 27 years (M = 21.48, SD = 1.88), from Asian countries (50% from Japan, 50% from nine other Asian countries) participated in the online questionnaire.

4.1.2. Survey Results and Discussions. The questionnaire consisted of nine questions about respondents' general uses of distant communication services and their opinions on tactile senses in distant communication. 65% of the respondents responded that they would like to be able to touch the person on the other side during video call. In the other 35%, 74% of the respondents answered, in another question, that they would like to use a device that provides a feeling of touching each other during a video call, if this device existed. 94% of the respondents thought that enabling tactile sense in distant communication would improve emotional connection. Overall, we observed that most of the respondents liked the perspective of using tactile senses in distant communication, even if they had not thought of it before.

The respondents also had to select a part of the body they would like to be given a massage to, in a distant communication scenario (Figure 1) and "shoulder" was the most popular option (38%).

4.2. Prototyping a Massage Device. We designed and made a prototype that simulates the feeling of massaging through vibrotactile stimulation.

4.2.1. Physical Prototyping of the Massage Device. We designed a device that would consist in two parts, a "sender device" for the person giving the massage and a "receiver device" for the person receiving the massage (Figures 2 and 3) and produce a vibrotactile stimulation on a shoulder. We used force sensitive resistors to collect input through the sender device and vibrotactile motors to create vibrotactile output through the receiver device. Vibration was chosen as the form of pressure output because of the simplicity of

TABLE 1: Existing haptic communication devices categorized by interactions allowed.

Device name	Description	Findings from user tests
Touch only		
ComTouch [8]	A device that converted hand presser into vibrational intensity between users in real time.	Strong relationships between audio and haptic channels were found. Haptic uses were emphasis, mimicry, and turn-taking.
Haptic Instant Messaging [9]	Text messages plus haptic effects, input pad is at a hand, while a vibration output module can be stick to any part of body.	-
Vivitouch [10]	A vibration pad which was paired with visual stimuli.	Haptic sense increases emotions' arousal regardless of how gentle the vibration is, and valence is dominated by visual sense.
CheekTouch [11].	An integrated mobile phone device that vibrates at the cheek if touched during phone call.	The use of the device emphasizes stronger emotions.
UltraHaptics system [12]	Air pressure waves were generated on the user hand from an array of ultrasound transducers.	Participants were relatively good at interpreting arousal than valence using air pressure.
Thermo-message [13]	A wristband with Peltier device that can give hot and cold sensation to the wearer	The perception of thermal expressions is dependent on the context of the situation.
TouchMe [14].	An armband Peltier device for children which parents can send a thermal message to their children anytime.	Multiple uses of thermal interaction could arise by engaging the parents in a new type of interaction with the children.
Touch and Squeeze		
VibroBod [15]	It contains force-sensitive resistors and microphones. Force and location input resulted in different frequencies and vibration patterns in paired device.	At first people were alarmed by the vibrations. Most users found VibroBod generated meaningful experiences.
- [16]	A vibrotactile device sends touch and squeeze as vibrations in the paired device.	Success rate of communicating emotions was 17-75% for valence and 50-83% for arousal.
- [17, 18]	Squeezing resulted in pressure on the wrist, covering with hands resulted in heat, and stroking upward repeatedly resulted in cold feedback.	Pressure emphasizes certain words in the discussion. Warm is used for positive, and cold for negative meaning.
Tap		
Taptap [19]	A wearable haptic scarf that can record, broadcast and playback human touch as vibration.	Male preferred strong vibration while female preferred lighter vibration.
Poke		
Poke [20]	An inflatable surface on smartphone which poke the cheek when the paired user uses a finger to poke their screen.	-
Tickle		
Kusuguri [21]	A smartphone with vibration motors, a user tickles the screen, and the paired user will see finger moving across their screen and feel tickling sensation.	The vibration was not similar to tickle sensation, but the users enjoyed using the device.
Stroking		
Tactile Sleeve for Social Touch [22, 23]	A wearable sleeve consisting of a pressure sensitive input layer and a vibrotactile actuator output layer.	There were some relations between tactile expression and emotions.
Prototype A [24]	A handheld device takes input from stroking thumbs, and outputs in an arm stoking the palm.	Participants liked prototype A more than B, because the stroking is more elegant as input than rotating the knobs, and the output was gentler with only one rotating arm.
Prototype B [24]	A handheld device takes input from rotating a knob, and outputs in four arms stoking the palm.	
Skin-writing		
Skin Drag [25]	A wearable device that has a tractor moving across user's skin.	Users can recognize the shape from skin drag better than from vibrotactile array.
Handshake		
PHANToM [26]	The device represents the force feedback to the users. It was used as a hand shaking device.	Participants were 62% convinced that force from the device represented real-life handshake's feeling.
Immersion Impulse Engine 2000 [27, 28]	Force feedback joystick providing two degree of freedom movements, and maximum force of 8.9 N.	Male participants liked people who mimicked their handshakes more than female participants.

TABLE 1: Continued.

Device name	Description	Findings from user tests
Hand-Holding, Wrist-Holding		
YourGlove [29]	A user holds a robotic hand and the paired hand will contract gently around another user's hand.	Participants liked the HotHands and HotMits more than YourGlove due to the unnaturalness of movement of the robot hand.
HotHands [29]	This device has the shape of human hand and output in heat.	
HotMits [29]	This device is a handprint on a flat surface which produces heat when the other is touched.	
Hug		
HUG [30]	An air inflatable vest that creates presser resembling to a hug when triggered. The input is hugging a doll.	Participants commented that the sound of the pump was too loud but the device itself was interesting.
HugMe [31]	A jacket with arrays of vibrotactile actuators to simulate the sense of touch from a force feedback device.	-
Huggy Pajama [32]	Input is a mobile doll with pressure sensors, sending hug to a haptic jacket with air pumps.	-
HaptiHug [33]	The hug is generated by rotating motors tensing a chest strap worn by users	This method allows the hug sensation without loud noise of pump actuators
Kiss		
Kissenger [34]	An interactive device that transmit force and shape of a kiss between two remote partners.	Most users enjoyed using the device and felt that Kissenger improved their communication.

the creation and its success in communicating emotions [8, 10, 11, 21, 23, 44].

The sender device is an object shaped like a human shoulder to provide the massager with a feeling of similar grip. The receiver device consists of two human-like hands made of LEGO parts. The palm part of each hand is connected to five fingers with spherical pair allowing three degree-of-freedom movements. Each finger also contains a second joint using cylinder cylindrical bore pair allowing the finger to bend, and they are covered by rubber thumb tips. The hands parts were put on the receiver's shoulder and straps were adjusted to keep the device in place and in contact with the shoulder.

4.2.2. Usage Process. A block diagram of the massage device is shown in Figure 4. As for the sender device, in order to detect forces from all ten fingers, ten FSR402 force sensitive resistors are used and placed in positions where ten fingertips would be. Each sensor measures the forces from each fingertip of two sender hands. Sensor value is measured as analog information. There is no force feedback to the sender. As for the receiver device, in order to simulate the touch and massage feeling on the shoulder, ten FM34F vibrotactile actuators (standard speed 13000 rpm with vibration quantity 17.6 m/S^2) are used. Each actuator receives signal from the force sensitive resistor in corresponding position and results in vibration. Here, the analog information from force sensitive resistors is converted to digital information since the limitation of the vibrotactile actuators we used could either be turned off or on only. Hence, the vibrotactile actuators would start vibrating when pressed and continue until the sender stops pressing on the force sensitive resistors. In other words,

the duration of pressing is conveyed by the device, but the strength of the pressing is not.

An Arduino board controls both the sender and receiver devices and Mux Shield allows enhancing the numbers of possible input and output from the board. The devices are connected with wires to prevent any technical delays of signals. For a real-life usage, the devices would be wireless and connected to the Internet.

5. Experimental Evaluation

5.1. Objective. Our objective is to study users' perception of massage-type tactile interaction in mediated intimate communication. We specifically investigate how massage in mediated intimate communication affects the interactions and the perception of the communication, including enjoyment, sense of togetherness, emotional expression, and emotional and physical connection. The experiment examines the impact of massage in conversations, either positive and negative.

5.2. Participants. Eight couples in a romantic relationship, aged 19 to 26 (M=21.56, SD=2.15), participated in the experiment. All participants were from a Chinese cultural background and were recruited through the group of international students at [author's university]. They have a regular practice of video calls with their family members and friends with no experience of using tactile device for communication.

5.3. Experimental Setting. The experiment was conducted in a laboratory with a pair of participants at a time. Each participant was sitting in front of a laptop and was separated from the other participant by a large panel, so they could

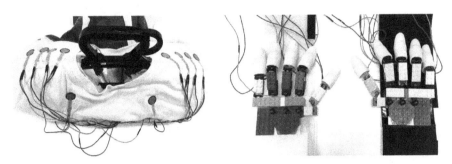

FIGURE 2: Sender device (left) and receiver device (right).

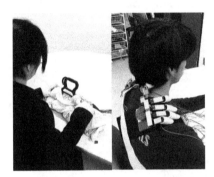

FIGURE 3: View of the sender device (left) and receiver device (right) during operation.

TABLE 2: Existing haptic communication devices categorized by interactions allowed.

	Condition 1: Video call	Condition 2: Video call + Massage
2 pairs	Positive ⟶ Negative	Positive ⟶ Negative
2 pairs	Negative ⟶ Positive	Negative ⟶ Positive
	Condition 2: Video call + Massage	Condition 1: Video call
2 pairs	Positive ⟶ Negative	Positive ⟶ Negative
2 pairs	Negative ⟶ Positive	Negative ⟶ Positive

not see each other. They were required to use sound isolating headphones to prevent hearing any sound or voice directly from each other (Figures 5 and 6).

5.4. Experimental Conditions and Tasks. In the control condition, the communication between the participants was verbal and visual only, i.e., video call through Skype. The second condition was verbal, visual and tactile, i.e., video call through Skype and the massage device. Because the prototype of the receiver device had to be strapped to the chest of the wearer, we asked male participants to act as receivers and female participants to act as senders. In both conditions, the pairs were required to perform two different tasks extracted from Suhonen et al. [17].

Task 1 (have a conversation about a happy topic). It could be something that happened in the past week or month that made you happy or excited, something you achieved that you are proud of, or something you are looking forward to, or anything else that is positive topic.

Task 2 (have a conversation about a sad or angry topic). It could be something that happened in the past week or month that made you sad or angry, something you fail or some troubles you caused, or something coming in the near future that you are afraid of or worrying about, or a complaint, or anything else that is a negative topic.

These tasks were chosen since we believe that the prototype would be used in different ways or different purposes under different types of emotion. The topic could be started

either sender or receiver depending on each pair of participants. In order to counterbalance the order effect, the eight couples were arranged in different conditions and tasks (Table 2).

5.5. Experimental Procedure. In this section, we describe the experimental procedure for the first pair; for the other pairs, only the order of conditions and tasks changed. The overall experiment for each pair of participants lasted around one hour.

The experiment started with a brief explanation about tactile communication and the research objective. The participants were seated on both sides of a big panel and could not see each other. They were asked to imagine that they were sitting in different places apart from each other. Then they were asked to put on headphones and have a conversation through video call about a positive topic (happy) for three minutes. They were then asked to switch to a negative topic (sad or angry) for three minutes. Finally, they were asked to complete a questionnaire about their experience with the device.

Then they were preceded to the second condition, we showed them both parts of the massage device and instructed them how to use the device. They were provided ten minutes to test the device freely and could communicate with each other during the test session. After they were satisfied with the testing, they were asked to put the headphone on and use video call together with the provided massage device. They were asked to talk to each other with positive topic then negative topic for three minutes each. (The order of the tasks was the same as what they did in the first condition.) When both tasks were finished, they were asked to put the headphone off, and filled the same questionnaire.

FIGURE 4: Block diagram of the massage system.

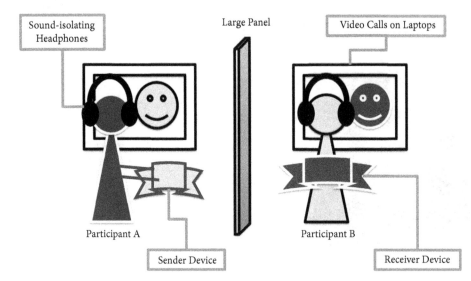

FIGURE 5: Schematic description of the experimental setting.

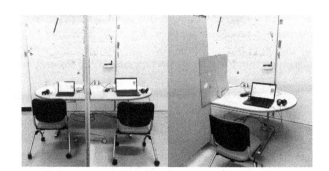

FIGURE 6: Actual experimental setting.

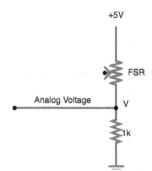

FIGURE 7: Simplified circuit for calculations.

After both tasks were completed, the participants were interviewed together as pair for about 20 minutes. The flow of the interview is free. We asked them to express their opinions towards the tools, their experiences towards tactile communication and their feelings towards the conversation.

5.6. Data Collection and Analysis

5.6.1. Analog Data Collected from Ten Force Sensitive Resistors. The values of ten force sensitive resistors (FSR) were recorded every 200 milliseconds, with the active threshold at 0.17 N. To convert the sensor value to force in Newton unit, the

simplified circuit of one FSR is shown in Figure 7, and nine other FSR are also connecting parallel to this circuit.

First, the value from the sensor (S; range from 0 to 1023) was converted to voltage as follows:

$$V = \frac{5S}{1023} \qquad (1)$$

Then resistance across the sensor (R_{FSR}) is calculated from the following:

$$R_{FSR} = \frac{(5 - V) * 10000}{V} \qquad (2)$$

TABLE 3: Criteria for the assessment of the perceived communication experience.

Criteria	Questions
Enjoyment	Did you enjoy using [1 or 2]∗ communication system?
Sense of Togetherness	With [1 or 2], did you have the feeling that the other person was actually here?
Emotional Expression	With [1 or 2], were you able to express your emotion?
Emotional Connection	With [1 or 2], did you feel emotionally connected with the other person?
Physical Connection	With [1 or 2], did you feel that the person you were talking to was touching you or you were touching the person?

∗ 1: video call. 2: massage-assisted video call

Then R_{FSR} value is compared with the official graph of FSR sensor [45], which can be approximated equation (3) when $\mu C < 1000$.

$$F = \frac{12500}{R_{FSR}} \qquad (3)$$

Four types of data were calculated from timestamp and sensor values:

(1) Average force per finger was the average force (only when over the threshold) from each finger over three minutes.

(2) Total massage times were counted from the number of time that at least one sensor was active. If the inactive duration is less than one second, it will be considered as continuation from previous active time.

(3) Total massage duration was the total duration of each active time that at least one finger is activated.

(4) Average numbers of fingers used were counted from the maximum number of active force sensitive resistors at each time calculated in "total massage times".

There was a technical error on recording the sensors in one pair on positive topic task. Hence their data of both positive and negative topic was excluded from the analysis. There was no error on the vibration feedback; therefore this pair's questionnaire and interview data are included in the analysis. Normality of the data in this section was verified using Kolmogorov-Smirnov test. Hence, paired-sample t-tests were conducted for comparison.

5.6.2. Questionnaire about the Perceived Communication Experience. Participants had to assess their communication experience with video call (condition 1) or video call and massage device (condition 2) in a questionnaire that consisted in five criteria: enjoyment, sense of togetherness, emotional expression, emotional connection, and physical connection (Table 3), on a 7-point Likert scale. Here, we selected to use only self-report measures since the affective responses to haptic stimulation are shown to have significance differences in terms of perceived emotions but not in terms of biometrics measurements (e.g., electromyographic (EMG) measurement and skin conductance (SC) measurement) [46]. Kolmogorov-Smirnov test was used and showed that data was not normally distributed; hence Wilcoxon's signed rank test was conducted for comparison.

5.6.3. Comments and Opinions from the Final Interviews. All the comments were recorded and selections of comments as well as the interpretations of those comments are discussed.

6. Results

6.1. Device Usage Comparison during Positive and Negative Conversations. Paired-sample t-tests were conducted to evaluate the impact of positive and negative conversation on average force per finger, total massage times, total massage duration, and average finger used. There was a marginally significant increase in average force per finger from positive conversation (M = 0.79, SD = 0.33) to negative conversation (M = 0.90, SD = 0.63), t(69) = -1.84, p = .070 (two-tailed). The mean increase in average force per finger was -0.11 with a 95% confidence interval ranging from -0.24 to 0.01. The eta squared statistic (.05) indicated moderate effect size.

For total massage times, there was a statistically significant increase from positive conversation (M = 6.57, SD = 3.05) to negative conversation (M = 12.71, SD = 6.53), t(6) = -3.26, p = .017 (two-tailed). The mean increase in massage times was -6.14 with a 95% confidence interval ranging from 1.88 to -10.75. The eta squared statistic (.64) indicated large effect size. We found no significant difference in total massage duration for positive conversation (M = 54.51, SD = 30.91) to negative conversation (M = 35.07, SD = 12.28), t(6) = 1.68, p = .144 (two-tailed). The magnitude of the difference in the means (mean differences = 19.44, CI: -8.87 to 47.74) was large (eta squared = .32). There was a significant decrease in average numbers of finger used from positive conversation (M = 7.08, SD = 1.50) to negative conversation (M = 4.45, SD = 1.87), t(6) = 2.53, p = .045 (two-tailed). The magnitude of the difference in the means (mean differences = 2.63, CI: -0.08 to 5.18) was large (eta squared = .52).

6.2. Subjective Perception of the Communication with a Massage Device. Participants rated their experiences with the device using 7-Likert scales. A Wilcoxon signed rank test was conducted (Table 4). There was no significant difference in enjoyment, sense of togetherness, and emotional expression. On the other hand, there were statistically significant increase in emotional connection from video call only (Md = 4.50) to video call and massage (Md = 5.00), z = -2.34, p = .019 (two-tailed), with a large effect size (r = .58). For physical connection, there was a statistically significant increase from video call only (Md = 1.50) to video call and massage (Md =

TABLE 4: Median ratings for subjective perception of the communication (N=16).

Mean scores	Video call only	Video call + Massage	p-value (2-tailed)
Enjoyment	5.00	5.50	.527
Sense of Togetherness	4.00	4.00	.094
Emotional Expression	5.00	5.00	.250
Emotional Connection	4.50	5.00	.019*
Physical Connection	1.50	5.50	.001*

*p < 0.05

5.50), z = -3.24, p = .001 (two-tailed), with a large effect size (r = .81).

6.3. Interview Comments. In this section, we report the outcomes of the interview with the participants, with a [#n-XY] code where n indicates their experiment number, X indicates whether they were using sender device (S) or receiver device (R), and Y indicates whether they were male (M) or female (F).

6.3.1. Increase of Emotional Connection. The majority of participants strongly confirmed that the massage device increases emotion sharing in distance communication. A participant commented that the device could help express something facial expressions and words cannot fully express, for example, caring, cheering up, and empathy. And the device makes her feel the presence of the other side [#8-SF]. Another participant stated that the device allowed her to release her anger and that can made her felt happier [#8-SF]. Two participants commented that when they are tired, they would like their girlfriend to send them some touch or massage them [#3-RM, #4-RM]. Another participant commented that he would like to use the device when he is missing his girlfriend [#3-RM].

6.3.2. Effects on Conversation. A participant expressed that the massage device improved the quality of their conversation, making it more meaningful and interactive. She also added that, for her, there used to be no difference between having phone call and video call when they were at a distance, but, with this massage device, video call would be more meaningful, and it would make long-distance relationship less suffering [#4-SF].

In addition, we also observed that some participants would be more likely to have informative conversations when they are communicating without the device. A participant stated that, with the device sometimes they could not focus on their topic, the device itself would become the topic of conversation occasionally. She also commented that actually that was a good thing, because they usually do not have anything important or urgent to talk about anyway, with this device you get another topic to talk about [#2-RM].

6.3.3. Comments on Sender Device. The interviews revealed a major usability issue with the lack of feedback to the sender side after a "massage message" has been sent. A participant stated that she pressed but she doesn't know how strong the other side feel [#2-SF]. Another participant commented that she wanted mutual touch interaction and wanted to feel that she was actually pressing the shoulder of her boyfriend [#9-SF]. However, one participant gave an opposite opinion: she was happy that the massage device did not generate the same kind of feedback as real massage, and she did not need to use a lot of effort to give massage and that it made the device easier to operate since her arm does not get tired easily like real massage [#3-SF].

We believe that the massage device for communication might not necessarily have to provide the same feedback as a real massage, if the couple carries both sender and receiver devices, they can communicate and learn the feedback from each other, we suggest that the differences with a real-life massage might trigger more verbal interactions between the users and thus enrich the communication.

6.3.4. Comments on Receiver Device. One of the major opinions is that vibration is difficult to be felt as a haptic interaction directly coming from the person at the other end. A participant commented that the vibration was too weak [#6-RM]. Another participant expressed that real pressure would be a better option [#4-RM]. Two participants want the touch feeling to be softer, smoother and warmer like human touch [#5-RM, #7-RM]. One participant also stressed how important it is to be able to reflect the strength of the pressure that the other side pressed on the sender device to the receiver device, instead of a digital output [#2-RM]. One participants complained about the weight of the device that it made him tired [#3-RM].

6.3.5. Appearance of the Device. We discussed about the appearance of the device with participants, while there were no specific comments about the sender device, the majority of participants felt that the appearance of the receiver device was a bit scary, because of its human-like thumb tip. They suggested that the device should not look like human hands, but rather be robot hands [#5-RM], animal hands [#9-SF], cartoon characters hands [#9-SF], or even hidden from view [#6-RM].

7. Discussion and Implications

7.1. Massage Behavior in Positive and Negative Conversation. The results revealed that participants interacted with the massage device more actively during positive conversation, e.g., using many fingers at once, with marginally lighter force per finger. On the other hand, the massage behaviors were more focused during negative conversation, e.g., more frequent in massaging, with marginally stronger pressers. However, even if, in negative conversation, the massage was more frequently activated, the total massage duration was not significantly different from positive conversation. This could imply that the duration of each massage was shorter in negative conversation than positive conversation.

Here, due to the nature of receiver device that needs to be strapped to the chest, males are always receivers, and females are always senders in the experiment. This restricts our generalization of this part of the result, since the massage behavior observed in this paper only came from female participants, and this might not be able to represent male population. However, the massage behaviors from both positive and negative conversation showed a good agreement with Huisman [47] which observed that participants mostly used brief and forceful touches for negative emotions, e.g., anger and fear and used prolonged actions to communicate positive emotions, which their experiments consisted of majority male participants (80%). This implies that both genders should have similar trends in behavior regarding emotions.

They also commented that the device enhanced emotion sharing in the way the facial expressions or words cannot express, e.g., caring, cheering up, and empathy, including releasing unwanted emotion on the massage device and feel more relieved.

7.2. Perceived User Experience with the Massage Device. Our findings showed that participants felt significantly more physical and emotional connection when using the device, while there were marginally increases of sense of togetherness and no significant differences in enjoyment and emotional expression. This could be interpreted that the additional of haptic senses in terms of massaging made participants felt more connected physically and also emotionally. It could help them feel a little more together than without the device; however it is still far from really being together, hence only marginally significance difference. Here, it is possible that if we increase participant numbers, the result could be significantly similar to a study by Basdogan et al. that used the PHANToM, a one-point haptic device in the market, in collaborative environment context and showed significant increases in sense of togetherness [48].

On the other hand, the massage device only allows one action to perform with (massage) even if with freedom of forces or fingers, participants did not use the device directly for trying to send emotion to the other, but rather let the interaction be natural and emotions could result in subtle differences in massage behaviors. Finally, enjoyment seems to be independent from use of the massage device, but dependent on the conversation with their partner.

7.3. Design Implications. There are two types of haptic feedback: tactile feedback (temperature, pain, physical displacement of the skin) and kinesthetic feedback (force, weight) [35]. Real-life massage would normally make the massage receiver feel both types of feedback at the same time; tactile feedback: physical displacement of skin and warmth from hands, kinesthetic feedback: force and weight from hands. We created the receiver device to imitate the weight of having people's hands on the shoulder and by using fabric together with rubber fingers; this would cause warmth from the receiver body temperature naturally after the device is worn for a short period. In real-life massage, these are considered as almost fixed values, since it depends only on the characteristic of the hands of the massage giver. Here, we simulated physical displacement of the skin using vibrotactile feedback, similar to many studies that successfully use vibrotactile arrays to represent touch, e.g., [8, 10, 11, 21, 23, 44]. We acknowledged that the force feedback is not successfully conveyed by our device, but our objective is not to make real-life massage possible in distance, but rather to complement video call with haptic feedback and interaction that are inspired by massage.

Although our sample size (N=16) was somewhat limited, we could find statistically significant differences in the results. Our sample consisted in young couples of university students because estimates suggest that up to half of university students might be in long-distance relationships at some time in their life [49]. Finer results would be found with a larger sample of participants, especially by including a wider range of age. Also, the experiment was conducted in Japan and the participants were Chinese students residing in Japan. Therefore, we believe that all participants had experienced long-distant communication with their family and might have already formed specific needs and impressions towards long-distance mediated communication. At the same time, they might not be fully representative of the general population and other potential users.

As for the scenarios of use, all participants answered that the primary targets would be couples in long-distance relationship. One in four female participants said that they would like to use the massage device with their close friends, while no male participant seemed interested in this scenario. Most participants (87.5%) suggested that they would like to use the device in long-distance communication with their parents, probably influenced by their actual current situation of being apart from their parents. To their opinion, more than the function, the fact of doing a massage for their parents would be important, as it could precede a symbolic message that they are caring for them and showing love to them. In fact, the mediated massage device has a potential to be used for elderly people, since there are numerous studies aiming to support communication for elderly people, but massage device has not been studied [50]. If a massage chair for elderly people is created, it could be a practical way to allow their family members to massage them even when they live far away to reduce their loneliness and increase their social interactions with their family. Target users for this scenario of use could be Chinese students overseas and their parents living in China, as the Chinese population of students is one of the most mobile in the world, with more than 500,000 people studying outside their home country [51]. The massage device could play an important role in supporting long-distance mediated family relationships in Chinese and other Asian cultural contexts where massage is a common practice among family members and filial piety a key virtue.

8. Conclusions

Our study investigated the use of a massage device in distance communication between people in a romantic relationship. The results demonstrated statistically significant increases in terms of emotional and physical connection, when using the massage device together with video call, as compared to using video call only. In addition, the interactions with the massage device were significantly more active during positive conversation and significantly more frequent and marginally stronger during negative conversation. We also discussed about rooms for improvement in the next potential future massage device that would allow conveying emotions between couples and family, thus to support mediated communication especially in Asian cultural context.

Acknowledgments

This work was supported by the Department of Mechanical Engineering, Tokyo Institute of Technology.

References

[1] M. A. Eid and H. Al Osman, "Affective haptics: current research and future directions," *IEEE Access*, vol. 4, pp. 26–40, 2016.

[2] T. Field, *Touch*, MIT Press, 2003.

[3] B. App, D. N. McIntosh, C. L. Reed, and M. J. Hertenstein, "Nonverbal channel use in communication of emotion: how may depend on why," *Emotion*, vol. 11, no. 3, pp. 603–617, 2011.

[4] M. J. Hertenstein, D. Keltner, B. App, B. A. Bulleit, and A. R. Jaskolka, "Touch communicates distinct emotions," *Emotion*, vol. 6, no. 3, pp. 528–533, 2006.

[5] M. J. Hertenstein, R. Holmes, M. McCullough, and D. Keltner, "The communication of emotion via touch," *Emotion*, vol. 9, no. 4, pp. 566–573, 2009.

[6] A. J. Merolla, "Relational maintenance and noncopresence reconsidered: Conceptualizing geographic separation in close relationships," *Communication Theory*, vol. 20, no. 2, pp. 169–193, 2010.

[7] M. Hassenzahl, S. Heidecker, K. Eckoldt, S. Diefenbach, and U. Hillmann, "All you need is love: Current strategies of mediating intimate relationships through technology," *ACM Transactions on Computer-Human Interactions (TOCHI)*, vol. 19, no. 4, 2012.

[8] A. Chang, S. O'Modhrain, R. Jacob, E. Gunther, and H. Ishii, "ComTouch: design of a vibrotactile communication device," in *Proceedings of the 4th ACM Conference on Designing Interactive Systems: Processes, Practices, Methods, and Techniques (DIS '02)*, pp. 312–320, London, UK, June 2002.

[9] A. Rovers and H. van Essen, "HIM: a framework for haptic instant messaging," in *Proceedings of the Extended Abstracts of The 2004 Conference*, Vienna, Austria, April 2004.

[10] Akshita, H. Sampath, B. Indurkhya, E. Lee, and Y. Bae, "Towards multimodal affective feedback : Interaction between visual and haptic modalities," in *Proceedings of the 33rd Annual CHI Conference on Human Factors in Computing Systems, CHI 2015*, pp. 2043–2052, Republic of Korea, April 2015.

[11] Y. Park, S. Bae, and T. Nam, "How do couples use CheekTouch over phone calls?" in *Proceedings of the 2012 ACM Annual Conference*, Austin, Tex, USA, May 2012.

[12] M. Obrist, S. Subramanian, E. Gatti, B. Long, and T. Carter, "Emotions mediated through mid-air haptics," in *Proceedings of the the 33rd Annual ACM Conference*, pp. 2053–2062, Seoul, Republic of Korea, April 2015.

[13] W. Lee and Y. Lim, "Thermo-message," in *Proceedings of the 28th of the International Conference Extended Abstracts*, Atlanta, Ga, USA, April 2010.

[14] S. Lee and T. Schiphorst, "Warmth and affection: exploring thermal sensation in the design of parent-child distant interaction," in *Human-Computer Interaction. Novel User Experiences*, M. Kurosu, Ed., vol. 9733 of *Lecture Notes in Computer Science*, pp. 3–14, Springer International Publishing, 2016.

[15] K. Dobson, D. Boyd, W. Ju, J. Donath, and H. Ishii, "Creating visceral personal and social interactions in mediated spaces," in *Proceedings of the Conference on Human Factors in Computing Systems, CHI EA 2001*, pp. 151-152, Seattle, Wash, USA, April 2001.

[16] J. Rantala, K. Salminen, R. Raisamo, and V. Surakka, "Touch gestures in communicating emotional intention via vibrotactile stimulation," *International Journal of Human-Computer Studies*, vol. 71, no. 6, pp. 679–690, 2013.

[17] K. Suhonen, S. Müller, J. Rantala, K. Väänänen-Vainio-mattila, R. Raisamo, and V. Lantz, "Haptically augmented remote speech communication: A study of user practices and experiences," in *Proceedings of the 7th Nordic Conference on Human-Computer Interaction: Making Sense Through Design, NordiCHI 2012*, pp. 361–369, Copenhagen, Denmark, October 2012.

[18] K. Suhonen, K. VΣΣnΣnen-Vainio-Mattila, K. MΣkelΣ, K. Väänänen-Vainio-Mattila, and K. Mäkelä, "In User experiences and expectations of vibrotactile, thermal and squeeze feedback in interpersonal communication," in *Proceedings of the Proceedings of the 26th Annual BCS Interaction Specialist Group Conference on People and Computers*, 2012.

[19] L. Bonanni, C. Vaucelle, J. Lieberman, and O. Zuckerman, "TapTap: A haptic wearable for asynchronous distributed touch therapy," in *Proceedings of the Conference on Human Factors in Computing Systems, CHI EA 2006*, pp. 580–585, Montréal, Québec, Canada, April 2006.

[20] Y.-W. Park, S. Hwang, and T.-J. Nam, "Poke: Emotional touch delivery through an inflatable surface over interpersonal mobile communications," in *Proceedings of the 24th Annual ACM Symposium on User Interface Software and Technology, UIST 2011*, pp. 61-62, Santa Barbara, Calif, USA, October 2011.

[21] M. Furukawa, H. Kajimoto, and S. Tachi, "KUSUGURI: A shared Tactile Interface for bidirectional tickling," in *Proceedings of the 3rd Augmented Human International Conference, AH'12*, Megève, France, March 2012.

[22] G. Huisman, A. Darriba Frederiks, B. Van Dijk, D. Hevlen, and B. Krose, "The TaSSt: Tactile sleeve for social touch," in *Proceedings of the 2013 World Haptics Conference (WHC 2013)*, pp. 211–216, Daejeon, South Korea, April 2013.

[23] G. Huisman and A. Darriba Frederiks, "Towards tactile expressions of emotion through mediated touch," in *Proceedings of the CHI '13 Extended Abstracts on Human Factors in Computing Systems*, p. 1575, Paris, France, April 2013.

[24] E. Eichhorn, R. Wettach, and E. Hornecker, "A stroking device for spatially separated couples," in *Proceedings of the the 10th international conference*, Amsterdam, The Netherlands, September 2008.

[25] A. Ion, E. Wang, and P. Baudisch, "Skin drag displays: Dragging a physical tactor across the user's skin produces a stronger tactile stimulus than vibrotactile," in *Proceedings of the 33rd Annual*

CHI Conference on Human Factors in Computing Systems, CHI 2015, pp. 2501–2504, Seoul, Republic of Korea, April 2015.

[26] M. O. Alhalabi and S. Horiguchi, Tele-Handshake: A Cooperative Shared Haptic Virtual, Press, 2001.

[27] J. N. Bailenson, N. Yee, S. Brave, D. Merget, and D. Koslow, "Virtual interpersonal touch: Expressing and recognizing emotions through haptic devices," Human–Computer Interaction, vol. 22, no. 3, pp. 325–353, 2007.

[28] J. N. Bailenson and N. Yee, "Virtual interpersonal touch and digital chameleons," Journal of Nonverbal Behavior, vol. 31, no. 4, pp. 225–242, 2007.

[29] D. Gooch and L. Watts, "YourGloves, HotHands and HotMits: Devices to hold hands at a distance," in Proceedings of the 25th Annual ACM Symposium on User Interface Software and Technology, UIST 2012, pp. 157–166, Cambridge, Mass, USA, October 2012.

[30] F. F. Mueller, F. Vetere, M. R. Gibbs, J. Kjeldskov, S. Pedell, and S. Howard, "Hug over a distance," in Proceedings of the Conference on Human Factors in Computing Systems, CHI EA 2005, pp. 1673–1676, Portland, Ore, USA, April 2005.

[31] J. Cha, M. Eid, L. Rahal, and A. El Saddik, "HugMe: An interpersonal haptic communication system," in Proceedings of the 7th Edition IEEE International Workshop on Haptic Audio Visual Environments and Games, HAVE 2008, pp. 99–102, Ottawa, Canada, October 2008.

[32] J. K. S. Teh, A. D. Cheok, Y. Choi, C. L. Fernando, R. L. Peiris, and O. N. N. Fernando, "Huggy pajama: A parent and child hugging communication system," in Proceedings of the 8th International Conference on Interaction Design and Children, IDC 2009, pp. 290-291, Milano, Italy, June 2009.

[33] D. Tsetserukou, "HaptiHug: a novel haptic display for communication of hug over a distance," in Haptics: Generating and Perceiving Tangible Sensations, vol. 6191 of Lecture Notes in Computer Science, pp. 340–347, Springer, Berlin, Germany, 2010.

[34] E. Saadatian, H. Samani, R. Parsani et al., "Mediating intimacy in long-distance relationships using kiss messaging," International Journal of Human-Computer Studies, vol. 72, no. 10-11, pp. 736–746, 2014.

[35] A. Haans and W. IJsselsteijn, "Mediated social touch: A review of current research and future directions," Virtual Reality, vol. 9, no. 2-3, pp. 149–159, 2006.

[36] B. S. Cronfalk, P. Strang, and B.-M. Ternestedt, "Inner power, physical strength and existential well-being in daily life: Relatives' experiences of receiving soft tissue massage in palliative home care," Journal of Clinical Nursing, vol. 18, no. 15, pp. 2225–2233, 2009.

[37] K. Kolcaba, V. Schirm, and R. Steiner, "Effects of hand massage on comfort of nursing home residents," Geriatric Nursing, vol. 27, no. 2, pp. 85–91, 2006.

[38] K. Ekerholt and A. Bergland, "Massage as interaction and a source of information," Advances in Physiotherapy, vol. 8, no. 3, pp. 137–144, 2006.

[39] C. Lutz, Unnatural Emotions: Everyday Sentiments on a Micronesian Atoll and Their Challenge to Western Theory, University of Chicago Press, 1988.

[40] J. A. Russell, "Culture and the categorization of emotions," Psychological Bulletin, vol. 110, no. 3, pp. 426–450, 1991.

[41] J. B. F. Erp and A. vanToet, "Social touch in humancomputer interaction," Human-Media Interaction, vol. 2, 2015.

[42] J. B. F. Van Erp and A. Toet, "How to touch humans: Guidelines for social agents and robots that can touch," in Proceedings of the 2013 5th Humaine Association Conference on Affective Computing and Intelligent Interaction, ACII 2013, pp. 780–785, Geneva, Switzerland, September 2013.

[43] L. Haritaipan and C. Mougenot, "Cross-cultural study of tactile interactions in technologically mediated communication," in Cross-Cultural Design, vol. 9741 of Lecture Notes in Computer Science, pp. 63–69, Springer International Publishing, 2016.

[44] Y. Wang, B. Millet, and J. L. Smith, "Designing wearable vibrotactile notifications for information communication," International Journal of Human-Computer Studies, vol. 89, pp. 24–34, 2016.

[45] Using an FSR — Force Sensitive Resistor (FSR) — Adafruit Learning System. https://learn.adafruit.com/force-sensitive-resistor-fsr/using-an-fsr.

[46] C. Swindells, K. E. MacLean, K. S. Booth, and M. Meitner, A Case-study of Affect Measurement Tools for Physical User Interface Design, Canadian Information Processing Society, Toronto, Canada, 2006.

[47] G. Huisman, "A touch of affect: Mediated social touch and affect," in Proceedings of the 14th ACM International Conference on Multimodal Interaction, ICMI 2012, pp. 317–320, Santa Monica, Calif, USA, October 2012.

[48] C. Basdogan, C. H. Ho, and M. A. Srinivasan, "An experimental study on the role of touch in shared virtual environments," ACM Transactions on Computer-Human Interactions (TOCHI), vol. 7, no. 4, pp. 443–460, 2000.

[49] D. J. Canary and M. Dainton, Maintaining Relationships Through Communication: Relational, Contextual, and Cultural Variations, Routledge, 2003.

[50] W. K. Bong, W. Chen, and A. Bergland, "Tangible user interface for social interactions for the elderly: a review of literature," Advances in Human Computer Interaction, vol. 2018, Article ID 7249378, pp. 1–15, 2018.

[51] ICEF Monitor, A Record Number of Chinese Students abroad in 2015 but Growth Is Slowing, ICEF Monitor - Market intelligence for international student recruitment, 2016.

16

Evaluating the Authenticity of Virtual Environments: Comparison of Three Devices

Aila Kronqvist,[1] Jussi Jokinen,[2] and Rebekah Rousi[1]

[1]*University of Jyväskylä, P.O. Box 35, 40014 University of Jyväskylä, Finland*
[2]*Aalto University, 02150 Espoo, Finland*

Correspondence should be addressed to Aila Kronqvist; aila.j.kronqvist@student.jyu.fi

Academic Editor: Mariano Alcañiz

Immersive virtual environments (VEs) have the potential to provide novel cost effective ways for evaluating not only new environments and usability scenarios, but also potential user experiences. To achieve this, VEs must be adequately realistic. The level of perceived authenticity can be ascertained by measuring the levels of immersion people experience in their VE interactions. In this paper the degree of authenticity is measured via an *authenticity index* in relation to three different immersive virtual environment devices. These devices include (1) a headband, (2) 3D glasses, and (3) a head-mounted display (HMD). A quick scale for measuring immersion, feeling of control, and simulator sickness was developed and tested. The HMD proved to be the most immersive device, although the headband was demonstrated as being a more stable environment causing the least simulator sickness. The results have design implication as they provide insight into specific factors which make experience in a VE seem more authentic to users. The paper emphasizes that, in addition to the quality of the VE, focus needs to be placed on ergonomic factors such as the weight of the devices, as these may compromise the quality of results obtained when examining studying human-technology interaction in a VE.

1. Introduction

Advancements in virtual environment (VE) technology have enabled new ways to design, prototype, and evaluate other technologies [1–4]. The latest VE laboratories seem promising in their ability to create environments rich in detail and fidelity, while allowing the researcher to retain experimental control [5, 6]. This is encouraging for topics in human-technology interaction (HTI) research, such as user experience. Furthermore, the particular benefit of this in HTI research can be seen in cases which more or less demand the observation of interactions in realistic use contexts [7]. Timeliness and situatedness (context and environment) are two key facets of user experience [7]. For this reason, VEs offer researchers and designers the opportunity to create (simulate) the conditions of life-like human-technology interactions, for the purposes of observing and scientifically analyzing the affects and emotions involved in these interactions, via a variety of user experience methods applicable to their own research and design goals and intentions. However, in order to study life-like experiences in VEs in an

ecologically valid way [8, 9], the simulated environments and interactions need to be experienced as authentic [1, 6, 7, 10].

While in experience research, studies using VEs have acknowledged the need to consider validity [1, 6, 11, 12], common frameworks for assessing the validity of VEs in user experience studies are still lacking. This paper presents the development and piloting of a "quick and dirty" methodological assessment framework for measuring the authenticity of experience during a VE experiment. The framework requires common metrics for measuring the fidelity and naturalness of the VE experience. The framework introduced here, with its standardized measures for assessing the authenticity of the VE experiment, can be used as a benchmark to assess the strength of the experimental results and inferences made from the VE in relation to real-life human-technology interactions.

When considering the utilization of VEs for the purposes of studying usability, or user experience, the experience of presence is paramount. Through achieving a high sense of presence, there are possibilities to simulate interactions in a number of environments and contexts, without having to physically leave the laboratory. The process of studying usability, for instance, requires that a user, or participant, is able to naturally interact and utilize a device or system in order to ascertain whether or not the design in question is learnable, efficient, memorable, error-free (or that the user has the ability to recover from errors quickly), and satisfying Nielsen [13]. These interactions necessitate that both actors—device/system and user—are present in a natural way. Moreover, research delving into more detail regarding user experience as a broader paradigm in HTI requires that interactions are examined in as natural settings as possible [14]. This research includes studies which focus on going beyond the instrumental and physical, social, and psychological analysis and previous as well as anticipated user experiences [7]. Thus, users, designers, and even researchers need to experience the sense of *being there*.

2. Presence, Affordance, and Control in Virtual Environments

A VE is a technologically generated environment, which allows the user to experience presence in a place other than where she or he is physically located [15]. In order to have an authentic experience in a VE, the user needs to be able to *feel presence*, that is, experience "being there," or being immersed in the environment [5, 16]. The feeling of presence is fundamental to our sense of what is real. Thus, presence is closely related to how people tangibly interact with objects in an environment [15]. Differences can subsequently be drawn between reality and images in contrast to reality (or virtual reality) in which the potential to interact with the environment and its contents is paramount; images only reflect and represent a version of reality. Consequently, another main difference between the two is the perceiver's inability to locate actual objects in space in a way which allows for this tangible or concrete interaction [17]. One cannot grab and smoke a pipe in a painting, and one cannot climb the mountains in a landscape photograph, even if techniques such as induced perspective and an implied third dimension allude to the character of *affordance*, an understanding of the ways in which objects (even pictorial) afford use and thus benefit the user through action and function [18].

Presence has been referred to as a "normal awareness phenomenon" [19] that demands focused attention and comprises sensory stimulation; factors in the environment which allude to and entice involvement to facilitate immersion; and internal tendencies within the person to become involved [19]. In his chapter "Immersion in Virtual Worlds" Calleja [20] describes the tendency and problematics of employing the terms "presence" and "immersion" to characterise the involved nature of people within virtual environments. Calleja [20] argues that the concept of "immersion" has been too widely used in relation to vastly different domains from artistic experience, to literature, cinema, and gaming, and due to this diversity in application has caused a lack of consensus regarding its specific definition. "Presence," originating in Minsky's [21] and "telepresence" utilized in

reference to telerobotics were already applied to the character of *authenticity* in VEs. Previous application of the term occurred in reference to Sutherland's [22] prototype of "The Ultimate Display" to describe the experience of *being there in the environment.*

Similarly to immersion, discussions on presence are highly interdisciplinary, which in turn causes debate and discrepancy in definition [23]. The presence debate has attracted scholars from the fields of psychology, philosophy, design, and communication to name some, who have adopted the concept in various forms to suit alternative theories such as simulation theory [24]; involvement [25]; the theory of play in psychology [26]; and affective disposition theory [27]. While debate continues, an overarching understanding of presence has been characterised not only as the sensation of *being there*, but also as that of *interacting there*, in the spaces of both the virtual and the physical worlds [28]. Thus, the feeling of presence is action-related and relates to a person's propensity to act, their ability to situate themselves in a social or physical space [29]. Presence is the experience of being able to transfer one's own knowledge about the world into interaction with the world [30]. Riva et al. [31] have gone even further to describe presence as "a selective and adaptive mechanism" allowing one to establish action-related boundaries through distinguishing between the "internal" and "external" facets of sensory flow [32].

Presence in the realm of human-computer interaction can be categorized into several different types: media presence, "the perceptual illusion of nonmediated presence" [33]; social presence, the feeling of existing and interacting with other intelligent beings [34]; copresence, the sensation of being in a mediated room with a mediated person [35]; physical, spatial presence and telepresence, the feeling of being there in the distal environment, and spatial awareness through the interaction of spatial representations [36]. Nonetheless, in cognitive science presence is seen as an embodied intuitive metacognitive process which bestows agency, enabling people to control their own actions through the process of comparison between perception and intention [32]. Presence consists of dynamic and continuous interaction between human sensory perception and cognitive and affective processes [33, 34]. The key to producing a sense of presence in technologically mediated environments is to develop the design to a standard to which a person loses the ability to detect the technological medium through which the environment (virtual) is communicated or represented [33].

In the case of the present study, technology on the one hand aids interactions and facilitates the sensation of presence within the virtual environments, as *invisible technology* (this is one perspective towards viewing what Streitz and Nixon [37] term as the "disappearing computer") or the "illusion of nonmediation" [33], while on the other hand, here the VEs themselves provide environments in which people (study participants) can come into contact with other technologies, the artefacts, and services under scrutiny—the *visible technology*—in order to experience these in simulated use situations. Thus, from the perspective of *affordance*, technology helps with this interaction: it is in our way of considering technological artefacts as a means to an end that makes these artefacts appear to us as technological in character. Therefore, technological artefacts in VEs need to be able to satisfy the expected affordance, which refers to the actions for which the object allows [11, 18, 38, 39]. Coined by Gibson [18] the term affordance refers to the way in which people do not see things (or in this case environments) in and of themselves. Rather, people see and understand objects and systems in terms of what they afford them to do, and how this will potentially result in reward or detriment. In terms of design, experienced affordance may include easy to life (how well the design suits a person's life situation), reachability and tactile qualities, status symbol, feeding excitement, and reliability.

In other words, affordance refers to how people understand environments and associated phenomena as not objects, or isolated pieces of information, but rather, in terms of what they do, and their expected repercussions. Thus, perceived phenomena are understood in terms of how they will influence and support people's actions. In fact, regarding Gibson's "ecological approach to visual perception," it may be observed that people possess two ways of *seeing* or perceiving VEs [18]. On the one hand, people perceive the affordances of what is inside the VE (or picture), and on the other hand they can perceive the VE itself in terms of what *it* affords as a design. The idea behind increasing presence is to reduce the gap between these two modes of seeing, by heightening a person's sense of affordance in virtual properties. Thus, VEs which seek to induce *authentic* experiences of presence need to suggest affordances to technologies represented in the environment. For example, in the physical world the design of a chair alludes to the affordance of supporting someone who sits on it. Likewise, in the VE, the observer should also experience the chair as having the same affordance as in the physical world, even though in the VE the chair does not necessarily possess this functional property.

For this reason, control or the sense of control is important when experiencing presence if a person feels as though they can control and influence their environment or utilize/manipulate what is afforded to them through the representations of, for example, technological devices and interfaces ready for testing; they are more likely to experience what is inside the VE as *real* [30]. Some of the mechanisms for inducing a sense of control and affordance include feedback, space, distance, form, size, and movement [5, 40]. Thus, the definition of presence as action-related immersion has two clear implications for the design of an authentically experienced VE. The user of a VE should, in order to feel presence, be able to locate objects of the VE relative to her or himself and to experience a degree of control over the objects. Both implications involve technical requirements, which the VE needs to pass in order to be useful in studying how people experience technologies. This entails sufficient resolution and depth of the simulation [41, 42], the ability of the user to move in the environment and study it from multiple perspectives [11], and the means of letting the actor interact fluently with the environment [6].

Achieving sufficient simulation resolution has been shown to be one of the main requirements of an authentically experienced VE. Yet only recently the level of technology has been adequate enough for the reliable projection of high resolution VEs [42–44]. High resolution in itself is not enough to create the experience of a rich and realistic environment. In order to better facilitate the user's ability to pinpoint the locations of the objects in the VE, the depth of the simulation can be increased by creating three-dimensional (3D) stereoscopic projections [41, 45]. Increased depth can be added by utilizing different modalities [43], such as surround sound, which has been shown to increase the level of immersion in the environment [46, 47].

Sufficient resolution and depth of the VE are required for authentic environments, but they do not necessarily provide sufficient action-orientation, which is essential for the feeling of presence. In order to fully experience presence in an environment, the user needs to be able to move in it. Otherwise, there would be no difference between looking at a picture and truly being in an environment [17, 48]. To facilitate naturalistic movement in a VE, the simulation needs to react to the movements of the user, and the visual presentation needs to be shifted accordingly in order to simulate movement in the VE [11]. This coupling of the user and the simulation increases the feeling of presence by connecting the act of moving to the visual presentation of the environment. Further, the actor should be able to interact with the simulated environment in order to truly experience it [6, 11]. One way to do this is to have the user wear special gloves or hold a pointer, which can be tracked and visually represented to the user in the simulation [49, 50]. By visualizing these handheld pointers as objects of the VE, the user is given the means to interact with the simulated environment and gain visual feedback from this interaction [6]. Other mechanisms such as haptic feedback can boost the experience of interacting with the VE; however, this experiment focused on the effects of visual constructions of VE authenticity. This meant that the gloves and pointers were apt for this type of investigation as they enabled interaction, without influencing the evaluation of the primarily visual experience.

The ecological validity of HTI studies conducted in VEs depends, therefore, largely on the amount of the feeling of presence, and lack of simulator sickness, a side effect of the visual perception of movement, of which the vestibular understanding of the body is being stationary. Although the need to assess the validity of the experience in a VE has been noted before [11, 49], a common framework for evaluating the authenticity of VE experience is still lacking. This framework needs to incorporate the factors described above in clearly operationalized metrics that are quick and easy to use, producing data, which are useful for comparing different VE implementations. In the current experiment, subjective measurement scales for the authenticity of the experience are developed and tested in comparison of different VE devices. This is an emerging field, and although theories such as presence [19] and immersion [20] have proven influential, there is still a lack of efficient and practical tools for measuring experienced authenticity in VEs, while reporting the level of simulator sickness induced.

2.1. Simulator Sickness. VEs have been promising in their ability to simulate situations and environments in which people experience the sensations of *being there* and *interacting there.* One major side effect however has been the onset of simulator sickness, or cybersickness. Awareness of simulator sickness has existed since the mid-1950s from the time of the first helicopter flight simulators [51]. A widely used explanation for simulator sickness is Sensory Conflict Theory [52–54]. Sensory Conflict Theory posits that simulator, or cybersickness, results from conflict in the two primary sensory systems involved in perceiving the VE: the vestibular system, providing information regarding movement as well as the head's orientation in space [55], and the perceived visual sense of self-motion, vection which is the deceptive feeling of self-motion although a person is stationary (e.g., such as when one is sitting on a train and the adjacent train begins to move) [56]. Thus, simulator sickness is seen to be caused by discrepancy in what is perceived and consciously experienced (i.e., self-movement), and the actual physical state of the body (stationary position). Thus, the visual system informs the individual about specific details and movement in the visual environment, but the vestibular system, used to regulate the head's orientation, does not correlate with the visual information, as the person is *not actually moving* [53].

The physical symptoms resulting from this conflict of sensory information include headache, vertigo, eye strain, cold sweats, fullness of stomach, nausea and vomiting, disorientation, dryness of mouth and ataxia, numbness, tingling in the hands and feet, and difficulty in coordinating muscle movements [57]. Correlations have been observed between an individual's age and the likelihood; they are to experience simulator sickness [58]. Thus, the older an individual is, the more likely they are to experience simulator sickness [51]. The effects of simulator sickness rarely last longer than 12 hours [51]. Various techniques have been proposed and tested to alleviate the likelihood of simulator sickness, such as the introduction of independent visual backgrounds to decrease balance disturbance [59]; ensuring that VE interaction sessions do not exceed two hours [51]; and adaptation [58] or habituation [60], a brief or trial acclimation session in the VE several days before actual testing or experimentation. Thus, the ideal result of employing VEs in the systematic measurement of user experience and other human-technology interaction observations is the optimal sensation of presence, combined with the least possible (or *no*) reporting of simulator sickness.

3. Authenticity Index and Framework

Through their operationalization of the *presence question-naire* (PQ) and *immersive tendencies questionnaire* (ITQ), Witmer and Singer's study on presence [19], shows that there is a slight correlation between task performance and presence in VEs. This aspect can be seen as one of the explanatory factors for research concentrating on VE authenticity in a variety of contexts ranging from learning [30, 61–63]; work and collaboration tools [64]; tools for experimental psychology and neuroscience [65, 66]; the arts [67]; and gaming and entertainment [68]. Thus, a unifying factor is the act of interacting through doing and achieving action goals in these environments. While PQ [19] is widely used in the study of presence in immersive technologies, it has the

drawback of being extremely long and arduous to complete. This not only induces fatigue in participants responding to the questionnaire but also takes away from the immediacy of the experience being reported in the evaluation form. Thus, the aim of developing the *authenticity index* was to create a tool for measuring the degree to which people (participants) experience reality in VEs, which was both succinct and accurate. The authenticity index consists of a questionnaire designed to measure immersion, control, and the side effect of simulator sickness. The questionnaire needed to be short enough for subjects to answer easily and efficiently, but detailed enough to provide rich data to measure authenticity. Lightness, in terms of easy comprehension and efficiency to answer, is desirable since the feeling of presence needs to be assessed relatively quickly. The required components contributing to the characteristics of immersion and control can be interpreted from themes presented by Witmer and Singer [19], which are seen in Table 1.

The authenticity index was generated from two different categories: (1) describing how well the subject was immersed in the environment and (2) the level of control she or he experienced when working in the environment. The factors measured in order to create the authenticity index are seen in Table 2. The number of experienced technical problems was added to indicate the degree to which these technical disturbances decreased the feeling of control.

4. Method and Materials

4.1. The Virtual Environment. The experiment was conducted in a VE laboratory, which was a large room with one wall-sized video screen (size 358 × 221 cm, resolution 1280 × 720) and eight cameras. The VE used in the experiment was modelled using the Unity game engine (Unity3D, version 3). Three different devices were used to project the simulated environment to the participants (Figure 1). The first device, a headband, had markers attached to it to track the movements of the user, allowing the coupling of the user and the visual projection. OptiTrack VR trackers with a MiddleVR software platform were used to accomplish the coupling. The VE was projected onto the video screen as a normal two-dimensional projection. For a 3D effect, stereoscopic *3D glasses* (XPAND 3D; size: large) were used as the second device. The glasses included markers to track the participant. It was hypothesized that the glasses would receive a higher score for the feeling of presence in comparison to the headband due to the added third-dimensional depth. However, it was also noted that stereoscopy might induce additional simulator sickness [69, 70]. Hence, it was hypothesized that the score for simulator sickness would be higher for the 3D glasses as compared to the headband.

The third device used in the VE projection was a *head-mounted display* (HMD). The participants wore a Sony HMD (Sony HMZ-T2; HD oled panel, FOV 45 degree), completely covering their vision. The HMD also used stereoscopy and thus allowed for a three-dimensional representation of the environment [71, 72]. The wall screen was not seen by the participants while wearing the HMD but was left on for the experimenters' observations. Tracking and coupling of

TABLE 1: Factors hypothesized to contribute a sense of presence [19].

Control factors	Sensory factors	Distraction factors	Realism factors
Degree of control	Sensory modality	Isolation	Scene realism
Immediacy of control	Environmental richness	Selective attention	Information consistent with objective world
Anticipation of events	Multimodal presentation	Interface awareness	Meaningfulness of experience
Mode of control	Consistency of multimodal information		Separation anxiety/disorientation
Physical environment modifiability	Degree of movement perception		
	Active search		

TABLE 2: Factors used to create authenticity index.

Category	Factor
Immersion	Feeling of presence
	Anticipated affordances compared to fulfilled affordances
Control	Feeling of control
	Discovery ratio
	Amount of technical problems experienced

the user movements were implemented as with the other devices. Of the three devices, the HMD was hypothesized to have the best score for the feeling of presence, because it completely occluded the participant's vision and obscured any visibility of the laboratory itself [71]. However, because of the stereoscopy and immersiveness, the HMD was also hypothesized to result in the highest level of reported simulator sickness [71].

In all of the task conditions, the participants used a handheld controller (FragFX Shark PS3 Classic with self-added trackers) to interact with the VE [49, 50]. The controller had markers attached, which enabled a projection of the controller in the simulation fashioned as a hand-sized cylinder with a white line protruding from it. The line helped the participant to point at objects, and its color changed to green when the object which was being pointed at possessed interactive features (e.g., an interactive button, or the ability to pick up an object). The physical controller had a button for triggering these actions.

The VE environment used in the experiment consisted of a garage with a car inside. The physical skeletal structure of the interior of the car was constructed in the middle of the room and consisted of a chair, a steering wheel, and a gearstick (see Figure 1). Figure 2 shows the projection of the car dashboard onto the laboratory wall. Most of the tasks required the participant to sit in the car. However, there were additional tasks in which the participant was asked to walk around the vehicle's exterior.

4.2. Participants and Tasks. $N = 15$ participants (8 women and 7 men) were recruited for the experiment. Their mean age was 31.9 years, SD was 12.5, and age range was 20–63. This is a highly varied age sample and as mentioned above in relation to simulator sickness, increased age can have an impact on the degree of symptoms experienced. However, during this pilot study, the objective was to test the effectiveness of the *authenticity index* as a reliable instrument for measuring the level of authenticity experienced in the simulated environments, in accordance with the tested devices. Thus, in a study focusing specifically on the VEs and devices, a higher degree of control would be implemented in relation to the selection criteria of participants (such as age). All of the participants had a driver's license and most drove daily or weekly (two reported that they drove less than monthly). The experimental design was a counter-balanced within-subjects design. Each participant conducted tasks in three blocks, using all three devices in a counter-balanced order. In each task block, the participants conducted nine tasks, which were similar but not identical (except the first task, see below) between the blocks.

The experiment started with the participant sitting in the chair (inside the virtual car model), and the experimenter asking the participant to name all visible instruments on the virtual dashboard of the car. This task, called the *discovery task*, was used to test the ability of participants to recognize objects in the simulated environment, as well as give them the chance to familiarize themselves with the VE. The discovery task was conducted at the beginning of all three task blocks, with all three devices. For the purposes of the analysis, only the first task block of each participant will be referred to as in the succeeding blocks the dashboard was already familiar.

After the participant had completed the discovery task, the experimenter verbally presented the rest of the tasks one by one. The tasks were as follows: checking the odometer reading; checking the fuel tank reading; reporting the gear-stick configuration; putting the gear into reverse; testing the loudspeakers of the car by using the radio; adjusting the lights, checking, or changing the current radio frequency; naming the buttons on the steering wheel; selecting the highest gear; locating the seat warmer controls; and opening the window. In addition to the tasks which the participants conducted while sitting inside the car, there were tasks requiring the participants to step outside the car model, and into the garage. These tasks were checking for dents or rust in the exterior of the car; visually inspecting the tire pressures or wheel rims; and visually inspecting the windows.

From the above listed tasks, in addition to the discovery task, this paper reports the analysis and results of the *loudspeaker task* and the task of inspecting the exterior of the car (*inspection task*). The loudspeaker task was chosen because it highlights interaction with the environment.

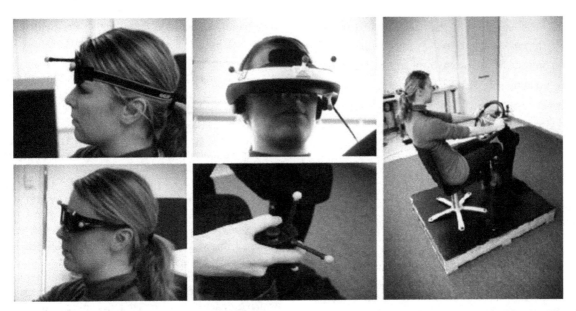

FIGURE 1: The devices used in the experiment: upper left: headband; lower left: 3D glasses; upper centre: head-mounted display (HMD); lower centre: the controller; right: car skeleton.

FIGURE 2: The VRE wall screen behind a participant.

The inspection task was chosen as it required participants to step out of the car, which hence entailed movement inside the VE. As with the discovery task, only the results of the first task block of each participant are discussed here.

4.3. Data and Analysis. Two main sources of data were used in this study. Firstly, participants were asked to complete questionnaires, which allowed for the statistical examination of the hypotheses. Secondly, the participants were asked to verbally think aloud during the tasks. Additionally, they were interviewed at the end of the experiment. This resulted in textual data about the participants' experiences, complementing the numerical, more standardized data. This paper focuses on reporting the results of the questionnaires, utilizing some of the findings resulting from the thinking aloud data and interviews to explain the results. However, due to the length and detailed nature of the results, the thinking aloud data scrutinized via protocol analysis are not included in this current paper.

4.4. Questionnaires. Presence questionnaire (PQ) [19] is a widely used method for measuring the feeling of presence in VEs. For the purposes of the experiment reported here, PQ was considered too long and detailed to be truly effective in capturing the dynamic and ephemeral impressions of authenticity in VEs. The measures presented in this paper are intended to be used to give validity to user experience studies conducted in VEs. It is probable that in these kinds of studies other questionnaires, closer to the focus of the study, such as specifically targeted user experience measurements, are also utilized. This makes a "quick and dirty" alternative to the tradition PQ even more appealing, as it frees space (and time) for researchers and designers to focus on the issues specifically at hand. Hence, the feeling of presence needs to be assessed relatively quickly, which was the goal of the scales presented here. PQ was used as a basis for the creation of the faster, easier to fill questionnaire.

Based on the discussion in the introduction, the feeling of presence was operationalized in two subjective scales: feeling of control and immersion. To measure the participant's sense of being in the VE, and ability to locate objects, a scale of *immersion* was created. This contained the following four items, adapted from the PQ [19]:

(i) I was immersed in the environment.

(ii) The visual elements of the environment felt natural.

(iii) The experience in the virtual environment was congruent with a real world experience.

(iv) I could inspect the objects of the environment.

To measure the participant's ability to interact with the simulated environment, a scale of *control* was created. This contained the five following items, adapted from the PQ:

(i) I could control what happened in the environment.

(ii) I felt the environment reacts to my actions.

(iii) I felt my actions in the environment were natural.

(iv) I could anticipate the results of my actions.

(v) My actions to control the environment were natural.

The questionnaire was completed by the participants after each task block in order to enable within-subjects comparison of the devices. The scale of the items for immersion and control was from one ("very much disagree") to five ("very much agree"). The scale was presented to the participants as numbers (1–5), as well as text. Cronbach's alphas, indicating the reliability of the scales, were calculated separately for immersion and control between the three devices. The immersion alphas were for the headband $\alpha = 0.77$, the 3D glasses $\alpha = 0.78$, and the HMD $\alpha = 0.90$. The control alphas were for the headband $\alpha = 0.81$, the 3D glasses $\alpha = 0.70$, and the HMD $\alpha = 0.82$. The reliability of the scales was considered sufficient ($\alpha > 0.70$), and the items were calculated into summated scales by averaging the sum of the items. This procedure retained the original scale of the variables (from one to five), which made comparing the three conditions easier.

In order to test the hypothesis that the different devices had different scores for the feeling of presence, nonparametric repeated measures Friedman tests were conducted for the two summated scales. Dunn-Bonferroni tests were conducted for pairwise comparisons between the conditions. Nonparametric testing instead of the analysis of variance was conducted, because the number of the participants was small.

For measuring simulator sickness, a modified simulator sickness questionnaire was constructed by choosing eleven items from the standardized simulator sickness questionnaire [70]. The items were general discomfort, fatigue, headache, eyestrain, difficulty focusing, increased salivation, nausea, difficulty concentrating, blurred vision, dizziness (eyes open), and dizziness (eyes closed). The scale of the items was from one ("not at all") to five ("very much"). The simulator sickness questionnaire was presented to the participants after each task block, and at the very beginning of the experiment for a baseline measure.

In order to analyze the experiences of simulator sickness, the nine questionnaire items were summed together and averaged to create a summated scale. The sum variable, simulator sickness, retained the original scale of the modified questionnaire (1 = "no sickness at all," 5 = "extreme sickness"). The comparison of simulator sickness between the conditions was analyzed using the Friedman test. Further, exploratory item-level analysis was used to reveal the most prominent items of simulator sickness by individually comparing the means of the conditioned responses to the baseline responses. In order to compare the conditions using one measurement, a principal components analysis (PCA) including the three sum variables (immersion, control, and simulator Sickness) was conducted. The component scores of the three sum variables were used to calculate a standardized index value for each of the three devices. The constructed authenticity index was then compared between the conditions using Friedman test. Based on the hypotheses above we predicted that the HMD would receive the best index score.

4.5. Think Aloud Protocols and Interviews. In addition to the questionnaires, the think aloud method was used to collect data about the behaviour of the participants during the tasks. The participants were asked to verbalize their thinking at all times while conducting the tasks. At the beginning of the experiment, the participants practiced thinking aloud by performing simple calculations in their head while verbalizing the contents of their thought. The participants were also constantly reminded to think aloud by asking them to verbally repeat each task instruction.

The verbal reports of the participants were analyzed using protocol analysis [73]. The methodological assumption is that the participants verbalized the contents of their working memory, and these data are useful in understanding the participants' mental representations of the environment in which they acted [74]. The sequences of actions were gathered from verbalizations in order to see how the tasks were solved and if any problems were encountered during the tasks. The sequences were used to identify problematic tasks which were then analyzed in more detailed level (the radio task and the inspection task). At the end of the experiment, the participants were also shortly interviewed about their experience and asked to give feedback from all three VE techniques. The interview answers were compared to the results of the statistical analyses of the questionnaire answers.

4.5.1. The Discovery Task. The first task of the participants was to freely name all visible controls in the dashboard of the car. Out of the 28 possible objects, the lowest number named by a participant was five and the highest 22. On average, the participants named 11.1 instruments (mdn 10.5). The average number of instruments detected with the headband, when it was the first condition, was 7.8 (mdn 7.5), the 3D glasses 13.0 (mdn 13.0), and the HMD 13.0 (mdn 15). A post hoc Wilcoxon test revealed the difference between the detected instruments in the headband condition and the 3D glasses condition to be statistically significant, $p = 0.011$. The difference between the headband and the HMD was not statistically significant, $p = 0.056$. These results partly support the hypothesis that adding the third dimension increases the feeling of presence of the participants, as they are able to locate more objects in the environment.

As an interesting notion concerning the action-relatedness of the sense of presence, the verbalizations revealed that, in addition to the visual search, the participants also tried to interact with the discovered instruments (e.g., activating the windscreen wipers after discovering the wiper lever). The participants were eager to try the instruments while discovering them, but unfortunately most of the instruments had no functionality in the VE model. Although the discovery task was only to name the visible instruments of the dashboard, the lack of interaction with the instruments was judged as a hindrance for completing the task. This lack of interaction most likely caused decreased experienced authenticity in all conditions.

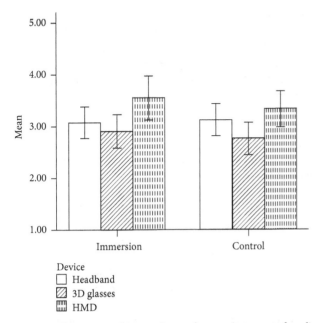

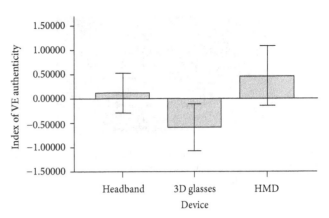

FIGURE 4: The mean of the standardized VE authenticity index between the devices. The lines represent 95% confidence interval.

FIGURE 3: The means of immersion and control summated scales between the three devices. The lines represent 95% confidence interval.

5. Results

5.1. Immersion, Control, and Simulator Sickness. The means of the summated scales between the three devices are shown in Figure 3. The distributions of immersion between the devices were different, $\chi^2(2) = 8.8$, $p = 0.012$. Pairwise comparisons revealed that the differences between the HMD and the 3D glasses and the HMD and the headband were statistically significant, $p = 0.008$ and $p = 0.022$. The difference between the 3D glasses and the headband was not statistically nonsignificant, $p = 0.715$.

The difference in the distribution of control between the conditions was also statistically significant, $\chi^2(2) = 12.3$, $p = 0.002$. Pairwise comparisons revealed that the difference between the HMD and the 3D glasses was statistically significant, $p = 0.001$. The other pairwise comparisons were statistically nonsignificant (3D glasses and headband $p = 0.121$, and HDM and headband, $p = 0.068$). The results partly support the hypothesis that the HMD has the best score for feeling of presence. However, contrary to the hypotheses, the 3D glasses did not perform well in immersion and control scales, although the differences between the conditions were not very large.

The simulator sickness scale scores were low for all devices. The mean of the baseline simulator sickness was 1.14, for the headband 1.12, the 3D glasses 1.25, and the HMD 1.14. The distribution was nevertheless different between the devices, $\chi^2(2) = 12.0$, $p = 0.002$. In pairwise comparisons, the difference between the headband and the 3D glasses was statistically significant, $p = 0.003$, but the others were not. The result suggests that none of the devices caused notable amounts of simulator sickness, but the 3D glasses seemed to introduce slight sickness. At the item-level analysis,

the main items contributing to the mildly higher simulator sickness score of the 3D glasses were eyestrain, concentration difficulties, general discomfort, and blurred vision.

The three sum variables were then combined into an index of authenticity by using single-component PCA. The component explained 61.9% of the total variance. The component loadings of the sum variables were control 0.90, immersion 0.86, and simulator sickness −0.55, indicating strong positive correlation between the two scales of feeling of presence, and a negative correlation between feeling of presence and simulator sickness. Due to standardization, the mean of authenticity was 1.00, and hence less than average values were negative. This is visible in Figure 4, which shows the comparison between the devices. The distribution of authenticity which was different between the devices was statistically significant, $\chi^2(2) = 9.7$, $p = 0.008$. Pairwise comparisons revealed that only the difference between the 3D glasses and the HMD was statistically significant, $p = 0.002$. While effect-sizes for nonparametric tests are not commonly reported, it is possible to visually inspect Cohen's d from Figure 4. Because the VE authenticity index is scaled, a difference of 1.0 in the means of two conditions equals the effect of $d = 1.0$. Thus, the difference between 3D glasses and HMD is large ($d > 0.8$) and clear to detect.

5.2. Think Aloud Protocols and Interviews

5.2.1. The Discovery Task. The first task of the participants was to freely name all visible controls in the dashboard of the car. Out of the 28 possible objects, the lowest number named by a participant was five and the highest 22. On average, the participants named 11.1 instruments (mdn 10.5). The average number of instruments detected with headband, when it was the first condition, was 7.8 (mdn 7.5), the 3D glasses 13.0 (mdn 13.0), and the HMD 13.0 (mdn 15). A post hoc Wilcoxon test revealed the difference between the detected instruments in the headband condition and the 3D glasses condition to be statistically significant, $p = 0.011$. The difference between the headband and the HMD was not statistically significant, $p = 0.056$. These results partly support the hypothesis that adding the third dimension increases feeling of presence of

FIGURE 5: The radio used in the radio task. Red arrow points to the correct button for turning the radio on. Blue arrow shows where the participants tried first to start the radio.

the participants, as they are able to locate more objects in the environment.

As an interesting notion concerning the action-relatedness of sense of presence, the verbalizations revealed that, in addition to the visual search, the participants also tried to interact with the discovered instruments (e.g., activating the windscreen wipers after discovering the wiper lever). The participants were eager to try the instruments while discovering them, but unfortunately most of the instruments had no functionality in the VE model. Although the discovery task was only to name the visible instruments of the dashboard, the lack of interaction with the instruments was judged as a hindrance for completing the task. This lack of interaction most likely caused decreased authenticity in all conditions.

5.2.2. The Radio Task. The radio task served as a demonstration for interaction with the VE. As such, it revealed problems associated with the feeling of presence in simulated environments. Resolution details, problems with tracking, and the lack of feedback from physical interaction were all observed to hinder participants' immersion in the environment. In addition, the verbalizations revealed that the controller was not perceived as a natural replacement for hands, but as an artificial and relatively unstable interface between the subject and the VE. This caused utterances of distrust towards the controller.

The first subtask of the participants in the radio task was to start the radio. Finding the correct button to turn on the radio was not easy: the participants first tried to press the large round button in the middle, highlighted with a blue arrow in Figure 5. However, the correct button was the smaller button to the left, highlighted with a red arrow. The confusion was partly caused by the insufficient resolution of the simulation: the correct button was labelled as "Radio," but the participants were not able to read the label clearly. Therefore, they had to hunch and move their head closer to the radio in order to inspect it and read the small text. Moving, especially with the 3D glasses, was considered unnatural, and such an easy task as leaning forward to inspect a radio proved to be difficult.

The second problem in the radio task was in the lack of feedback from incorrect button pressing. Bringing the controller close to the correct button changed the coloring of the controller pointer from white to green, but with

noncorrect buttons, the color stayed white. This leads to confusion, as the participants were uncertain if the button they were trying to press was incorrect, or if they just failed to position the controller properly. The participants became frustrated, as they felt that the controller did not adequately let them to interact with the radio.

5.2.3. The Inspection Task. At the beginning of the inspection task, participants were told that they now needed to see if the car had dents, if it was rusty, or if the tires or windows were broken. Many of the participants did not realize that they could step outside of the car model. Some participants tried to put their head through the door of the car while seated. After trying to solve the problem from inside the car model, some asked if they could step outside the car, but others had to be prompted to do so. The novelty of the idea of stepping outside the model was also evident in the immediate verbalizations of the participants when they stepped out of the car.

Technical problems concerning tearing and freezing of the simulation were observed when the participants walked next to the car. Because the tracking area was limited, any movement outside the specified area, or crouching to see under the car model, was prone to cause tracking problems and subsequent simulation errors. After the initial astonishment at being able to roam the VE, the technological constraints of the laboratory served as a disillusioning and disappointing element.

6. Discussion

The authenticity of a virtual environment (VE) was evaluated between three devices by asking participants ($N = 15$) to conduct tasks in a virtual car model. The devices were a headband, 3D glasses, and a head-mounted display (HMD). The participants were asked to detect objects in the environment, interact with the environment, and move around in the environment. Their actions during the tasks were investigated, and responses to posttask questionnaires were analyzed. Comparisons between the devices resulted in a proposal for a VE authenticity index.

VE authenticity was measured by subjective questionnaire scales for the feeling of presence (operationalized into the feelings of immersion and control). The first hypothesis was that introducing 3D-stereoscopy by having the participants wear 3D glasses or an HMD, instead of a tracker headband, would increase the feeling of presence [73]. Using 3D glasses or the HMD resulted in more detected instruments in the detection task when compared to using only the headband, which partly supported the hypothesis. One possible explanation for this is that the participants experienced the depth of the 3D-environment as more interesting and thus focused more on its exploration [41]. However, although the 3D glasses resulted in more detailed detection, the device received the lowest score for the immersion and control scales. The HMD on the other hand received the highest score on both scales, although when compared to the headband, the difference was not statistically significant.

Although lengthy, widely used questionnaires for assessing the feeling of presence exist [19], our goal was to construct a short but still reliable scale for constant validation of VE experiments. The scales for measuring the feeling of presence worked well with only a few items (four or five), as supported by proven reliability. The scales also highlighted understandable differences between the devices, giving support for the construct validity of the scales. The benefit of a small "authentication questionnaire" is that it leaves room for longer questionnaires concerning the experiences of the system being evaluated in the VE, while still providing input for the evaluation of the authenticity of the measured experience.

The metrics for VE authenticity were combined in an authenticity index, which allowed an easy comparison between the devices. Principal component analysis provided support for the claim that the feeling of presence is dependent on the ability to both locate objects (immersion) and interact with them (control). Comparison of the authenticity index between the devices suggests that experiences with the HMD were most authentic. However, the authenticity score for the HMD was not as stable across participants as with the headband, as was evident in the larger confidence intervals for the HMD. This encourages future studies exploring the individual differences in how authentic a VE is experienced.

In postexperiment interviews, participants reported that while the HMD provided a novel, immersive experience, the headband was less cumbersome and still capable of providing sufficient immersive experience. 3D glasses were reported to have problems with resolution and clarity. The HMD and the headband were both favoured: the HMD gave the best support for the feeling of presence, but longer tasks were more pleasant to conduct while wearing the less invasive headband. We suggest that even at the risk of reduced immersion, a noninvasive combination of headband and wall screen may work better for VE studies in HTI, at least until HMD technology has better matured in terms of both virtual fidelity and physical ergonomics.

The authenticity index variable proved to be capable of revealing differences between the devices. As such, it provides a promising start to creating a valid and reliable measure for VE authenticity. The next steps are to combine it with the observations made from the talk aloud verbalizations. For example, regarding the handheld controller as a tool rather than an actual bodily extension can be used as a questionnaire item. It should also be possible to combine the result of the discovery task with the subjective scales. From the definition of presence it should follow that the subjective feeling of presence is positively correlated to the number of detected items. In the experiment reported here, the number of discovered items was not included in the authenticity index, as the number of participants was relatively small: for each device, there were only five participants using the device in the first task block; thus the discovery task resulted in the clearest differences between the device. In the subsequent task blocks, the car interior was familiar, and the discovery task was relatively trivial. However, below it is suggested that a discovery task should be operationalized as a standard measure for the VE authenticity index.

The results from the discovery task serve as a reminder of the action-relatedness of the feeling of presence [17, 48]. Participants were eager to interact with the items they discovered. Finding out that a windscreen wiper lever, for example, does not actually activate the wipers is detrimental to the feeling of presence in the VE. Thus, while locating the lever in space increases immersion, not being able to interact with it decreases the feeling of control and nullifies perceived affordance. In other words, participants found that the expected affordances in the environment were not in fact present. The problems with the lack of interaction were observed also with the radio task. Participants were not able to interactively explore the radio interface and started to doubt if the handheld controller was still functional, or if they were using it properly. The notion of expectations regarding the affordances of the VE should be operationalized in a measure, such as questionnaires before and after use. This measure could then be incorporated in the VE authenticity index.

Lack of physical feedback from interaction may, however, also be beneficial for HTI research in VEs. One important finding arose in the qualitative data which is not much reported in this paper. This referred to the relationship between motor functions and conscious experience and how this in turn supports the weighting of affordance and control on experience of presence. Motor functions are often implicit and an interruption in the implicitly expected tactile feedback causes explicit awareness of these motor functions [75]. This was visible in the verbalizations of the participants during the radio task. While the lack of tactile feedback decreases immersion, it also makes the interaction more explicit to the user. The increased awareness may cause the participant to notice problems, which she/he would have passed over in a real-life experiment. This notion may be useful for VE usability studies, focusing on certain interactions, since high fidelity prototypes are not necessarily a requirement for identifying usability problems [10].

In addition to the radio task, the inspection task, requiring the participants to step outside the car model, indicated problems with the validity of the VE experience. Navigating the space was only possible, if the participants' mental maps of the environment afforded this action-relation [76]. The participants had trouble understanding that they should have exited the car, which indicates that they were not completely —on the level of mental representation—immersed in the environment. Their representations of the VE did not afford the possibility of stepping outside the vehicle, or the impossibility of moving one's head through a solid door.

Problems associated with the technical limitations of the VE used in the study serve as a reminder for designers of VE experiments. Devising tasks, which involve the risk of technical problems, should be discouraged. Not only do technical problems during the interaction confound the results relating to the problematic task itself, but also the resulting distrust towards the environment may make all subsequent tasks confounded. Not only is it therefore the function of the environment in itself which allows for its authentic experience, but also authenticity is dependent on how well the tasks have been designed to conform to the limitations of the environment.

Category	Factor
Immersion	Feeling of presence
	Anticipated affordances compared to fulfilled affordances
Control	Feeling of control
	Discovery ratio
	Amount of technical problems experienced

7. Conclusion

The goal of the study was to propose and develop a framework for evaluating the authenticity of a VE laboratory experiment, especially in the context of HTI. Analysis of questionnaire responses for the feeling of presence and feeling of control revealed several underlying authenticity subfactors. The suggested subfactors for the VE authenticity index are listed in Table 3.

In future studies, these subfactors should be included in the authenticity index as means of more accurately ascertaining the experience of presence in VEs. Furthermore, due to the indications of high reliability and construct validity indicated in the measures, the operationalization of the *feeling of presence* and *feeling of control* in this study can be viewed as sufficient. The factors should together capture the subjective experience of actually "being in" the VE and being able to interact with it naturally. *Discovery ratio* should be operationalized as the number of functions or features discovered either at the start of the experiment or throughout the experiment, divided by the number of discoverable functions or features. This ratio would hence indicate how well the participants were able to find the intended functions or features of the environment.

Anticipated affordances compared to fulfilled affordances should be operationalized as either a questionnaire, presented to the participants before and after the use, or a number of expected but not fulfilled affordances during the experiment. While a questionnaire scale would be easier to be reliably operationalized, the actual number of expected but not fulfilled affordances would be a more objective measure of how well the VE realized the interactive expectations of the participants. Of course, the latter method requires thinking aloud, and this might not always be a viable choice in an experiment. *Technical problems* should also be operationalized either as subjective assessment after use or in terms of the number of encountered problems, with the same caveats as in the affordances measure.

Although the above subfactors of authentic VE experience are considered as existing on an equal level, when computing the final factor using either principal component analysis or factor analysis, it should be noted that it is possible to construct more internally complex representations of authentic VE experience. For example, one could hypothesize that the discovery rate is the causal antecedent of the feeling of presence, while fulfilled affordances are the causal antecedent of the feeling of control. Using structural equation modelling

for such hypotheses would be, while an interesting study, very demanding on resources, as such a study would necessitate a large number of participants in order to be valid. However, understanding the causalities of VE experience is necessary for designing authentic environments, and hence these kinds of studies should be pursued.

The reason for using a VE laboratory in HTI research is that it simultaneously provides the flexibility of a simulated environment and the control of a laboratory experiment. A VE can be used to evaluate design prototypes in early stages of development. Changing the context of the evaluation, such as varying the scenarios, is relatively easy. Thus, VEs enable the study of user experience in diverse use contexts and situations already in the early stages of development. This is highly valuable from both the industrial and scientific perspectives as (a) substantial savings can be made from user experience findings and subsequent glitches before too much investment has been made in development and production and (b) contextual factors can be isolated and experimented in terms of gaining more precise data relating to influential elements in user experience and other interaction dynamics.

One aspect to remember however is that when using a VE laboratory to evaluate prototypes and interaction scenarios, it is important to indicate the extent to which the participant experiences reality in the simulated environment. While technological improvements and clever task design, which takes the technological limitations into consideration, potentially improve the authenticity of a VE study, the validity of the experiment should always be evaluated with a standardized framework. There are design implications for the authenticity index in relation to its capacity to provide data regarding the level of authenticity experienced in the VE contingent to specific purposes. Different validity measures for VE authenticity have been proposed, such as participant performance [49] and long questionnaires [19], but what is lacking is a common, easy, and fast framework for assessing the authenticity of the VE experience. The experiment reported here serves as a pilot study in constructing a metric for this purpose.

Acknowledgments

The authors would like to thank Harri Hytönen from Elomatic Oy for his cooperation in this study. We would also like to thank the University of Jyväskylä for supporting this study as well as funders of this project, Tekes.

References

[1] I. D. Bishop and C. Stock, "Using collaborative virtual environments to plan wind energy installations," *Renewable Energy*, vol. 35, no. 10, pp. 2348–2355, 2010.

[2] A. Covaci, C. C. Postelnicu, A. N. Panfir, and D. Talaba, "A virtual reality simulator for basketball free-throw skills development," in *Technological Innovation for Value Creation*, pp. 105–112, Springer, Berlin, Germany, 2012.

[3] M. J. Tarr and W. H. Warren, "Virtual reality in behavioral neuroscience and beyond," *Nature Neuroscience*, vol. 5, pp. 1089–1092, 2002.

[4] H. Wu, Z. He, and J. Gong, "A virtual globe-based 3D visualization and interactive framework for public participation in urban planning processes," *Computers, Environment and Urban Systems*, vol. 34, no. 4, pp. 291–298, 2010.

[5] J. M. Loomis, J. J. Blascovich, and A. C. Beall, "Immersive virtual environment technology as a basic research tool in psychology," *Behavior Research Methods, Instruments, & Computers*, vol. 31, no. 4, pp. 557–564, 1999.

[6] K. M. Stanney, M. Mollaghasemi, L. Reeves, R. Breaux, and D. A. Graeber, "Usability engineering of virtual environments (VEs): identifying multiple criteria that drive effective VE system design," *International Journal of Human Computer Studies*, vol. 58, no. 4, pp. 447–481, 2003.

[7] M. Hassenzahl and N. Tractinsky, "User experience—a research agenda," *Behaviour and Information Technology*, vol. 25, no. 2, pp. 91–97, 2006.

[8] L. Berkowitz and E. Donnerstein, "External validity is more than skin deep," *American Psychologist*, vol. 37, no. 3, pp. 245–257, 1982.

[9] U. Neisser, *Cognition and Reality*, W. H. Freeman and Company, San Francisco, Calif, USA, 1976.

[10] J. Sauer, K. Seibel, and B. Rüttinger, "The influence of user expertise and prototype fidelity in usability tests," *Applied Ergonomics*, vol. 41, no. 1, pp. 130–140, 2010.

[11] B. Dalgarno and M. J. W. Lee, "What are the learning affordances of 3-D virtual environments?" *British Journal of Educational Technology*, vol. 41, no. 1, pp. 10–32, 2010.

[12] F. Rebelo, P. Noriega, E. Duarte, and M. Soares, "Using virtual reality to assess user experience," *Human Factors*, vol. 54, no. 6, pp. 964–982, 2012.

[13] J. Nielsen, *Usability Engineering*, Elsevier, Amsterdam, The Netherlands, 1994.

[14] V. Roto, E. Law, A. P. O. S. Vermeeren, and J. Hoonhout, *User Experience White Paper. Bringing Clarity to the Concept of User Experience*, 2011, http://www.allaboutux.org/files/UX-White-Paper.pdf.

[15] R. Schroeder, "Defining virtual worlds and virtual environments," *Journal of Virtual Worlds Research*, vol. 1, no. 1, pp. 1–3, 2008.

[16] K. M. Stanney, G. Salvendy, J. Deisinger et al., "Aftereffects and sense of presence in virtual environments: formulation of a research and development agenda," *International Journal of Human-Computer Interaction*, vol. 10, no. 2, pp. 135–187, 1998.

[17] M. Matthen, "Two visual systems and the feeling of presence," in *Perception, Action, and Consciousness*, N. Gangopadhyay, M. Madary, and F. Spicer, Eds., pp. 107–124, Oxford University Press, Oxford, UK, 2010.

[18] J. J. Gibson, *An Ecological Approach to Visual Perception*, Houghton Mifflin, Boston, Mass, USA, 1978.

[19] B. G. Witmer and M. J. Singer, "Measuring presence in virtual environments: a presence questionnaire," *Presence*, vol. 7, no. 3, pp. 225–240, 1998.

[20] G. Calleja, "Immersion in virtual worlds," in *The Oxford Handbook of Virtuality*, pp. 222–236, Oxford University Press, Oxford, UK, 2014.

[21] M. Minsky, "Telepresence," OMNI Magazine, 1980, http://web.media.mit.edu/~minsky/papers/Telepresence.html.

[22] I. Sutherland, "The ultimate display. Information processing techniques," in *Proceedings of the IFIP Congress*, pp. 506–508, New York, NY, USA, 1965, http://worrydream.com/refs/Sutherland%20-%20The%20Ultimate%20Display.pdf.

[23] C. Klimmt and P. Vorderer, "Media Psychology 'is not yet there': introducing theories on media entertainment to the presence debate," *Presence: Teleoperators and Virtual Environments*, vol. 12, no. 4, pp. 346–359, 2003.

[24] K. Oatley, "A taxonomy of the emotions of literary response and a theory of identification in fictional narrative," *Poetics*, vol. 23, no. 1-2, pp. 53–74, 1995.

[25] P. Vorderer and U. Ritterfeld, "Children's future programming and media," in *The Faces of Televisual Media: Teaching, Violence, Selling to Children*, E. L. Palmer and B. Young, Eds., pp. 241–262, Lawrence Erlbaum Associates, Mahwah, NJ, USA, 2003.

[26] R. Oerter, *The Psychology of Play: An Activity Oriented Approach*, Quintessenz, Munich, Germany, 1993.

[27] D. Zillmann, "The psychology of suspense in dramatic exposition," in *Suspense: Conceptualizations, Theoretical Analyses, and Empirical Explorations*, P. Vorderer, H. J. Wulff, and M. Friedrichsen, Eds., pp. 199–231, Lawrence Erlbaum Associates, Mahwah, NJ, USA, 1996.

[28] G. Riva, "The psychology of ambient intelligence: activity, situation and presence," in *Ambient Intelligence*, G. Riva, F. Vatalaro, F. Davide, and M. Alcañiz, Eds., chapter 2, pp. 17–33, IOS Press, Amsterdam, Netherlands, 2005.

[29] A. Spagnolli and L. Gamberini, "A place for presence. Understanding the human involvement in mediated interactive environments," *PsychNology Journal*, vol. 3, no. 1, pp. 6–15, 2005.

[30] T. Reiners, H. Teras, V. Chang et al., "Authentic, immersive, and emotional experience in virtual learning environments: the fear of dying as an important learning experience in a simulation," in *Proceedings of the Teaching and Learning Forum*, Perth, Australia, January 2014, https://ctl.curtin.edu.au/events/conferences/tlf/tlf2014/refereed/reiners.html.

[31] G. Riva, J. A. Waterworth, E. L. Waterworth, and F. Mantovani, "From intention to action: the role of presence," *New Ideas in Psychology*, vol. 29, no. 1, pp. 24–37, 2011.

[32] G. Riva and F. Mantovani, "Extending the self through the tools and the others: a general framework for presence and social presence in mediated interactions," in *Interacting with Presence: HCI and the Sense of Presence in Computer-Mediated Environments*, G. Riva, J. Waterworth, and D. Murray, Eds., pp. 9–31, DeGruyter, Berlin, Germany, 2014.

[33] M. Lombard and T. Ditton, "At the heart of it all: the concept of presence," *Journal of Computer-Mediated Communication*, vol. 3, no. 2, 1997.

[34] K. Lee and C. Nass, "Designing social presence of social actors in human computer interaction," in *Proceedings of the ACM SIGCHI Conference on Human Factors in Computing Systems (CHI '03)*, pp. 289–296, Fort Lauderdale, Fla, USA, April 2003.

[35] W. A. Ijsselsteijn, J. Freeman, and H. de Ridder, "Presence: where are we?" *Cyberpsychology and Behavior*, vol. 4, no. 2, pp. 179–182, 2001.

[36] M. Matelli and G. Luppino, "Parietofrontal circuits for action and space perception in the macaque monkey," *NeuroImage*, vol. 14, no. 1, pp. S27–S32, 2001.

[37] N. Streitz and P. Nixon, "The dissappearing computer," *Communications of the ACM*, vol. 48, no. 3, pp. 32–35, 2005.

[38] D. A. Norman, *The Psychology of Everyday Things*, Basic Books, New York, NY, USA, 1988.

[39] D. A. Norman, "Affordance, conventions, and design," *Interactions*, vol. 6, no. 3, pp. 38–43, 1999.

[40] W. Barfield, D. Zeltzer, T. Sheridan, and M. Slater, "Presence and performance within virtual environments," in *Virtual Environments and Advanced Interface Design*, W. Barfield and T. Furness, Eds., pp. 473–513, Oxford University Press, New York, NY, USA, 1995.

[41] J. Häkkinen, T. Kawai, J. Takatalo, R. Mitsuya, and G. Nyman, "What do people look at when they watch stereoscopic movies?" in *Stereoscopic Displays and Applications XXI*, vol. 7524 of *Proceedings of SPIE*, San Jose, Calif, USA, February 2010.

[42] T. Ni, D. A. Bowman, and J. Chen, "Increased display size and resolution improve task performance in information-rich virtual environments," in *Proceedings of the Graphics Interface (GI '06)*, pp. 139–146, Canadian Information Processing Society, Quebec, Canada, June 2006.

[43] H. Q. Dinh, N. Walker, L. F. Hodges, C. Song, and A. Kobayashi, "Evaluating the importance of multi-sensory input on memory and the sense of presence in virtual environments," in *Proceedings of the IEEE Virtual Reality (VR '99)*, pp. 222–228, March 1999.

[44] C. H. Lewis and M. J. Griffin, "Human factors consideration in clinical applications of virtual reality," in *Virtual Reality in Neuro-Psycho-Physiology*, G. Riva, Ed., pp. 35–56, IOS Press, Amsterdam, The Netherlands, 1997.

[45] W. Ijsselsteijn, H. de Ridder, J. Freeman, S. E. Avons, and D. Bouwhuis, "Effects of stereoscopic presentation, image motion, and screen size on subjective and objective corroborative measures of presence," *Presence: Teleoperators and Virtual Environments*, vol. 10, no. 3, pp. 298–311, 2001.

[46] D. Murphy and F. Neff, "Spatial sound for computer games and virtual reality," in *Game Sound Technology and Player Interaction: Concepts and Developments*, M. Grimshaw, Ed., pp. 287–312, Information Science Reference, Hershey, Pa, USA, 2011.

[47] R. Nordahl, S. Serafin, and L. Turchet, "Sound synthesis and evaluation of interactive footsteps for virtual reality applications," in *Proceedings of the IEEE Virtual Reality Conference (VR '10)*, pp. 147–153, IEEE, Waltham, Mass, USA, March 2010.

[48] G. Riva, "Is presence a technology issue? Some insights from cognitive sciences," *Virtual Reality*, vol. 13, no. 3, pp. 159–169, 2009.

[49] E. Dubois, L. P. Nedel, C. M. D. S. Freitas, and L. Jacon, "Beyond user experimentation: notational-based systematic evaluation of interaction techniques in virtual reality environments," *Virtual Reality*, vol. 8, no. 2, pp. 118–128, 2005.

[50] I. Poupyrev, T. Ichikawa, S. Weghorst, and M. Billinghurst, "Egocentric object manipulation in virtual environments: empirical evaluation of interaction techniques," *Computer Graphics Forum*, vol. 17, no. 3, pp. 41–52, 1998.

[51] D. M. Johnson, *Introduction to and Review of Simulator Sickness Research*, Army Research Institute, Field Unit, Fort Rucker, Ala, USA, 2005.

[52] G. E. Riccio and T. A. Stoffregen, "An ecological theory of motion sickness and postural instability," *Ecological Psychology*, vol. 3, no. 3, pp. 195–240, 1991.

[53] J. LaViola Jr., "A discussion of cybersickness in virtual environments," *ACM SIGCHI Bulletin*, vol. 32, no. 1, pp. 47–56, 2000.

[54] J. Reason and J. Brand, *Motion Sickness*, Academic Press, London, UK, 1975.

[55] H. Gleitman, *Basic Psychology*, Norton and Company, New York, NY, USA, 1992.

[56] J. Dichgans and T. Brandt, "Visual-vestibular interaction: effects on self-motion perception and postural control," in *Perception*,

R. Held, H. Leibowitz, and H. Teuber, Eds., vol. 8 of *Handbook of Sensory Physiology*, pp. 755–804, Springer, Berlin, Germany, 1978.

[57] J. Casali, "Vehicular stimulation-induced sickness, vol. 1: an overview," IEBOR Technical Report 8501, Naval Training Systems Center, Orlando, Fla, USA, 1986.

[58] J. E. Domeyer, N. D. Cassavaugh, and R. W. Backs, "The use of adaptation to reduce simulator sickness in driving assessment and research," *Accident Analysis & Prevention*, vol. 53, pp. 127–132, 2013.

[59] H. B.-L. Duh, D. E. Parker, and T. A. Furness, "An 'independent visual background' reduced balance disturbance envoked by visual scene motion: implication for alleviating simulator sickness," in *Proceedings of the SIGCHI Conference on Human Factors in Computing Systems (CHI '01)*, pp. 85–89, ACM, Seattle, Wash, USA, March-April 2001.

[60] P. A. Howarth and S. G. Hodder, "Characteristics of habituation to motion in a virtual environment," *Displays*, vol. 29, no. 2, pp. 117–123, 2008.

[61] C. Dede, "The evolution of constructivist learning environments: immersion in distributed, virtual worlds," *Educational Technology*, vol. 35, no. 5, pp. 46–52, 1995.

[62] C. Guetl, T. Reiners, S. Gregory et al., "Operationalising gamification in an educational authentic environment," in *Proceedings of the IADIS International Conference on Internet Technologies & Society (ITS '12)*, Perth, Australia, September 2012.

[63] M. Roussou, "Learning by doing and learning through play: an exploration of interactivity in virtual environments for children," *Computers in Entertainment*, vol. 2, no. 1, p. 10, 2004.

[64] S. Y. Hu and G. M. Liao, "Scalable peer-to-peer networked virtual environment," in *Proceedings of 3rd ACM SIGCOMM Workshop on Network and System Support for Games (NetGames '04)*, pp. 129–133, Portland, Ore, USA, August 2004.

[65] J. Blascovich, J. Loomis, A. C. Beall, K. R. Swinth, C. L. Hoyt, and J. N. Bailenson, "Immersive virtual environment technology as a methodological tool for social psychology," *Psychological Inquiry*, vol. 13, no. 2, pp. 103–124, 2002.

[66] G. Riva, "Virtual reality in neuroscience: a survey," in *Virtual Environments in Clinical Psychology and Neuroscience*, vol. 58 of *Studies in Health Technology and Informatics*, pp. 191–199, IOS Press, Amsterdam, The Netherlands, 1998.

[67] M. A. Moser and D. MacLeod, *Immersed in Technology: Art and Virtual Environments*, MIT Press, Cambridge, Mass, USA, 1996.

[68] D. A. Bowman and R. P. McMahan, "Virtual reality: how much immersion is enough?" *Computer*, vol. 40, no. 7, pp. 36–43, 2007.

[69] J. Häkkinen, M. Pölönen, J. Takatalo, and G. Nyman, "Simulator sickness in virtual display gaming: a comparison of stereoscopic and non-stereoscopic situations," in *Proceedings of the 8th Conference on Human-Computer Interaction with Mobile Devices and Services (MobileHCI '06)*, pp. 227–230, ACM, Espoo, Finland, September 2006.

[70] R. S. Kennedy, N. E. Lane, K. S. Berbaum, and M. G. Lilienthal, "Simulator sickness questionnaire: an enhanced method for quantifying simulator sickness," *The International Journal of Aviation Psychology*, vol. 3, no. 3, pp. 203–220, 1993.

[71] R. Patterson, M. D. Winterbottom, and B. J. Pierce, "Perceptual issues in the use of head-mounted visual displays," *Human Factors*, vol. 48, no. 3, pp. 555–573, 2006.

[72] T. Shibata, "Head mounted display," *Displays*, vol. 23, no. 1-2, pp. 57–64, 2002.

[73] K. A. Ericsson and H. A. Simon, *Protocol Analysis*, MIT Press, Cambridge, Mass, USA, 1993.

[74] D. Murphy and F. Neff, "Spatial sound for computer games and virtual reality," in *Game Sound Technology and Player Interaction: Concepts and Developments*, M. Grimshaw, Ed., pp. 287–312, Information Science Reference, Hershey, 2011.

[75] A. Baddeley, *Working Memory, Thought, and Action*, Oxford University Press, Oxford, UK, 2007.

[76] B. S. Santos, P. Dias, A. Pimentel et al., "Head-mounted display versus desktop for 3D navigation in virtual reality: a user study," *Multimedia Tools and Applications*, vol. 41, no. 1, pp. 161–181, 2009.

Permissions

List of Contributors

Hasan Mahmud, Md. Kamrul Hasan and Abdullah-Al-Tariq
Systems and Software Lab (SSL), Department of Computer Science and Engineering, Islamic University of Technology (IUT), Dhaka, Bangladesh

Md. Hasanul Kabir
Department of Computer Science and Engineering, Islamic University of Technology (IUT), Dhaka, Bangladesh

M. A. Mottalib
Department of Computer Science and Engineering, BRAC University, Dhaka, Bangladesh

Lumpapun Punchoojit and Nuttanont Hongwarittorrn
Department of Computer Science, Faculty of Science and Technology, Thammasat University, Pathum Thani, Thailand

Robson P. Bonidia and Danilo S. Sanches
Bioinformatics Graduate Program, Federal University of Technology-CP (UTFPR), Paraná, Brazil

Luiz A. L. Rodrigues and Jacques D. Brancher
Computer Science Department, State University of Londrina (UEL), Londrina, Paraná, Brazil

Anderson P. Avila-Santos
Technology College, National Service Industrial Learning of Paraná (SENAI), Londrina, Paraná, Brazil

Gabriel Alves Mendes Vasiljevic, Leonardo Cunha de Miranda and Erica Esteves Cunha de Miranda
Department of Informatics and Applied Mathematics, Federal University of Rio Grande do Norte (UFRN), 59078-970 Natal, RN, Brazil

Mohammad Zohaib
Department of Computer Science, BMS College of Engineering, Bangalore 560 019, Karnataka, India

Carolin Straßmann and Nicole C. Krämer
Social Psychology Media and Communication, University Duisburg-Essen, 47057 Duisburg, Germany

Astrid M. Rosenthal-von der Pütten
Individual and Technology, RWTH Aachen University, 52062 Aachen, Germany

Shiroq Al-Megren, Joharah Khabti and Hend S. Al-Khalifa
King Saud University, Information Technology Department, Riyadh 12371, Saudi Arabia

Pei-Luen Patrick Rau, Yu Chien Tseng, Xiao Dong, Caihong Jiang and Cuiling Chen
Institute of Human Factors & Ergonomics, Department of Industrial Engineering, Tsinghua University, Beijing 100084, China

Katy Tcha-Tokey, Olivier Christmann and Simon Richir
Arts et Métiers ParisTech, LAMPA EA 1427, 2 bd du Ronceray, 49000 Angers, France

Emilie Loup-Escande
Université de Picardie Jules Verne, CRP-CPO EA 7273, chemin duThil, 80025 Amiens, France

Guillaume Loup
Université Bretagne Loire, LIUM EA 4023, avenue Olivier Messiaen, 72085 Le Mans, France

Bingjun Xie, Jia Zhou and Huilin Wang
Department of Industrial Engineering, Chongqing University, Chongqing 400044, China

Wesley Tessaro Andrade, Rodrigo Gonçalves de Branco, Maria Istela Cagnin and Débora Maria Barroso Paiva
Federal University of Mato Grosso do Sul (UFMS), Av. Costa e Silva, s/n, Cidade Universitária, Campo Grande, MS, Brazil

Metin Yildiz
Department of Biomedical Engineering, Baskent University, Ankara, Turkey

Hesna Özbek Ülkütaş
Institute of Science and Engineering, Baskent University, Ankara, Turkey

Tomas Cerny and Michael Jeff Donahoo
Computer Science, Baylor University, Hankamer Academic Building, No. 105, Waco, TX 76706, USA

Alexandre Alapetite, Emilie Møllenbach and Katsumi Minakata
Technical University of Denmark, Department of Management Engineering, Produktionstorvet 424, 2800 Kongens Lyngby, Denmark

Anders Stockmarr
Technical University of Denmark, Department of Applied Mathematics and Computer Science, Asmussens Allé 305, 2800 Kongens Lyngby, Denmark

Lalita Haritaipan and Masahiro Hayashi
Tokyo Institute of Technology, Department of Mechanical Engineering, Tokyo 152-8552, Japan

Céline Mougenot
Imperial College London, Dyson School of Design Engineering, London, UK

Aila Kronqvist and Rebekah Rousi
University of Jyväskylä, 40014 University of Jyväskylä, Finland

Jussi Jokinen
Aalto University, 02150 Espoo, Finland

Index